In the 1930s, Red Army Command maintained what was often an offensive doctrine. The plan was to fight a bloodless victory on foreign ground. An offensive by the Worker's and Peasant's Red Army was to unfold as per the classic Blitzkrieg – it was with good reason that some of the higher-ranking commanders had studied at the German General Headquarters Academy. Furthermore, all the technical achievements of the period were taken into account. The assault would begin with air strikes from strategic aviation: armadas of huge bombers would attack key targets deep inside enemy territory. At the same time enormous numbers of airborne troops would be dropped behind enemy lines, armed with a range of equipment. These airborne troops would capture bridges, and roads, and take communications, and transport links out of action. Heralded by a powerful artillery attack, supported by tactical aviation the tanks, armoured vehicles, and trucks carrying motorised infantry would advance.

There was a basis for such optimistic forecasts. Since the Soviets were in possession of such a quantitative, and qualitative advantage (and this was certainly the case) they were definitely able to advance. In the USSR aviation was undergoing development ahead of schedule, as were armoured tank technology, airborne assault troops, and chemical weapons. If the Soviets had tanks, aircraft, and chemical weapons, albeit in small quantities, any potential enemies would possess them too. The airborne assault troops however were a distinctly Soviet innovation. In this respect it was the Soviets that held an unquestionable advantage. It was here that the first groups of airborne paratroopers were dropped, and the first tanks and guns were dropped from the skies. The Red Army was conducting mass airborne assault operations during the course of exercises when no other nation on Earth had airborne assault troops.

In other fields Soviet military science and technology in many cases copied existing Western achievements. Licenses were obtained, or examples of foreign materiel were simply copied. As far as the airborne troops were concerned the Soviet military, and the designers were in unchartered territory, having come up with a number of innovative solutions, which were later adopted by the armed forces of other nations.

In this book the armament, equipment, and military hardware developed for airborne troops is described, both in terms of the actual technology, and the clearly fantastical, which only reflected the unrestrained imagination of the designers. A significant amount of attention is devoted to the aircraft, from which it was planned airborne troops would be dropped. The exercises that saw airborne troop drops are described, as well as the role airborne troops played in actual operations in the period up to 1941.

This book has been written on the basis of a number of documents that the author has discovered in the archives, and in museum collections. This work draws upon the memoirs of the pioneer military paratroopers in the USSR, some of which have never been published before.

Vladimir Kotelnikov was born in Moscow on 9 December 1951. He graduated from the Moscow Aviation Institute (University) in 1975 and was engaged in research and development in the area of high-temperature strength. Vladimir obtained the academic degree of Candidate of Science in 1981 and read lectures on aircraft piston engine design at the Moscow Aviation Institute.

Since the 1980s, Vladimir has conducted archive researches on the history of Russian aviation of the interwar and Second World War period. In addition, he paid specific attention to the history of foreign aircraft testing and operations in Russia. As a result of his work, he has had several hundred articles and dozens of books published across Russia, the Ukraine, Poland, the UK, France, Germany, Spain and the US – among them *Americans in Russia*, *Russian Piston Aero Engines*, *Early Russian Jet Engines*, *Air War Over Khalkhin Gol* and *Le Petlyakov Pe-2*.

Being an aviation historian, he received a diploma of a professor of the Academy of Aviation and Aeronautics Science, and currently acts as a consultant on piston aero engines design to Russian aviation museums, as well as to different aircraft restoration groups.

Since 2003, Vladimir has held the post of editor of the *Aviakollektsiya* aviation history magazine, which is published in Moscow.

Red Assault

Soviet Airborne Forces 1930-41

Vladimir Kotelnikov

Translated by Kevin Bridge

Helion & Company

Helion & Company Limited
Unit 8 Amherst Business Centre
Budbrooke Road
Warwick
CV34 5WE
England
Tel. 01926 499 619
Fax 0121 711 4075
Email: info@helion.co.uk
Website: www.helion.co.uk
Twitter: @helionbooks
Visit our blog http://blog.helion.co.uk/

Published by Helion & Company 2019
Designed and typeset by Farr out Publications, Wokingham, Berkshire
Cover designed by Paul Hewitt, Battlefield Design (www.battlefield-design.co.uk)
Printed by Henry Ling Limited, Dorchester, Dorset

ISBN 978-1-912390-79-3

British Library Cataloguing-in-Publication Data.
A catalogue record for this book is available from the British Library.

For details of other military history titles published by Helion & Company Limited contact the above address, or visit our website: http://www.helion.co.uk.

We always welcome receiving book proposals from prospective authors.

Contents

Abbreviations

AGOS	Aviation, Hydro-aviation and Prototype Aircraft Production
DRP	Dynamo-Reactive (Recoilless) Gun
GUAP	Principal Directorate of the Aviation Industry
GVF	Civil Air Fleet
KhAZOS	Kharkov Aviation Plant of Prototype Manufacturing
NII GVF	Scientific Research Institute of Civil Air Fleet
NII VVS	Air Force Scientific Testing Institute
NKAP	People's Commissariat for the Aviation Industry
NKTP	People's Commissariat for Heavy Industry
OGPU	United Principal Political Directorate
OKDVA	Special Red-Banner Far East Army
OKPB	Special Design and Manufacturing Bureau
OTB	Special Technical Bureau
RKKA	Worker's and Peasant's Red Army;
RVS	Revolutionary Military Council;
STO	Council for Labour and Defence;
TsAGI	Central Aero- and Hydrodynamics Institute.
UVVS	Air Force Directorate;
VAMM	Military Academy of Mechanisation and Motorisation
VOIZ	All Union Society of Inventors
VVS	Air Force

Acknowledgements

The author would like to extend his sincere thanks for the help in preparation of this book to the following individuals (in Russian alphabetical order): A. Arkhipov, M. Baryatinskiy, G. Gagin, M. Khairulin, A. Kirindas, M. Kolomiets, O. Leonov, M. Maslov, M. Muratov, G. Petrov, V. Rigmant, G. Sloutskiy, S. Chmelyuk, A. Yugenson and N. Yakubovich.

Introduction

At the beginning of the 1930s the Workers' and Peasants' Red Army (RKKA) was going through a period of rapid modernisation. The re-equipping of the RKKA was considered a task of paramount importance in the world's only socialist state, surrounded as she was on all sides by capitalist enemies. The country would make do with many things, but not when it came to weaponry. The enormous sums of money, which were spent on re-equipping the Armed Forces, would steadily begin to bear fruit. In terms of the numbers of tanks, guns, and aircraft the country was initially on a par with the leading nations, and then overtook them. The Red Army was actively preparing for a 'battle of materiel'. Although the horse still held sway on the parade ground, the clip-clop of hooves was steadily replaced by the clank of tank tracks. Not one of her neighbours was in a position to compete with the USSR in terms of military might. Several types of weapons, which the Red Army acquired, did not have any analogues in the West. Soon the Soviet military began to think of themselves as invincible.

In the 1930s Red Army command maintained a purely offensive doctrine. The plan was to fight a bloodless victory on foreign soil. Similarly, two fundamental combat scenarios were examined. In the first of these scenarios the enemy would invade the territory of the USSR and would be dealt a crushing blow and withdraw back behind the lines, with the Red Army hot on their heels, and 'not a shred' would be left of the aggressor. In the second scenario everything would stem from uprisings among the proletariat in neighbouring countries and the Soviet Union would rush to the aid of their proletarian brothers, scrambling over state borders as they went, one after another.

In both these cases the Red Army would mount a decisive attack. This attack would unfold in the same way as the classic *blitzkrieg*. It was with good reason that some of the commanders (they were not yet marshals) had studied at the General Headquarters' Academy in Germany. Furthermore, all the technical achievements of the period were taken into account. The assault would begin with air strikes from strategic aviation: armadas of huge bombers, escorted by fighters, would unleash all manner of bombs on the enemy, unguided, and radio-controlled cruise type missiles would cover the ground with poison gas mixtures. They would strike key targets deep inside enemy territory: destroying ports, airfields, military garrisons, large factories, and railway junctions.

Other aircraft meanwhile would deploy huge numbers of airborne troops, equipped with a range of armament, behind enemy lines. They would then capture bridges, and roads, taking communications, and transport infrastructure out of action as they did so. Tactical aviation would then join the battle. Soviet fighters, using their numerical advantage, would gain air superiority. Following a powerful artillery barrage tanks, and tankettes would move forward. These would be supported by light bombers, and ground attack aircraft. The advance would progress with armoured cars, motorcyclists, and trucks conveying mechanised infantrymen at the forefront. In keeping with tradition, space was found in this echelon for horses pulling machine-gun carriages ...

Subsequently the plan envisaged the joyful shouts, and bouquets of flowers, thrown onto the tanks that had liberated the people of another nation from the grip of those blasted, greedy capitalists.

There was however a basis for such optimistic forecasts. Since the Soviets held a considerable qualitative, and quantitative advantage (and this was definitely the case) they were certainly able to advance.

Red Army command would assiduously follow the latest developments in the art of war, incorporating them into their plans. Aviation was developing ahead of schedule, as was the development of armoured tanks, airborne forces, and chemical weapons. If potential enemies possessed tanks, aircraft, and chemical weapons, albeit on a lesser scale, then the airborne forces were an innovation that was developed within the Soviet Union itself. In this respect it was the airborne forces that took an undeniable priority. It was in the Soviet Union that the first groups of airborne troops were deployed by parachute, and where guns, and tanks were first dropped from the skies. The Red Army was conducting large-scale airborne troop operations when no other country anywhere in the world had any airborne forces at all.

This book is dedicated to the creation, and development of Soviet airborne forces in the period leading up to the Great Patriotic War. In other fields Soviet military science and technology in many cases copied existing Western achievements. Licences were acquired, or German and American aircraft were simply copied, along with German aircraft engines and chemical weapons equipment, English tanks, and Czechoslovak guns. Thus in doing so both the Soviet military, and the designers broke new ground, and they are justifiably proud of it.

1

First Steps

The first airborne assaults in the USSR were not training assaults, they were performed in as realistic a combat environment as possible. These assaults however were landing deliveries: the aircraft landed and deployed rank and file infantrymen who were not equipped with any kind of special equipment. The conflict moreover was an internal one, and there was no front line, nor was there any logistics area behind the lines in the usual sense of the word.

Almost immediately after the establishment of Soviet power in Central Asia rebel forces appeared in these areas, and their enemies dubbed them *Basmachi.* They were led by the former *khan*'s, and *bai*'s, while the key personnel was composed of people who were not happy with the changes that were taking place: the land reforms, under which land and cattle were confiscated from the rich, and the undermining of the role of the Muslim religion, which in this part of the world was highly influential, as well as the introduction of Soviet education, which was also extended to women, and so on. The numbers of those unhappy with these changes grew as a result of a multitude of mistakes made by the ruling powers: there were very few people among the representatives of the local populations who were educated to any degree, while the supervisors who had been sent from Russia did not know the language, nor the customs of this part of the world. Everyday bandits joined the ranks of the *Basmachi*, and there was always a ready supply of bandits on the fringes of a huge country.

The forces of the Turkestan front were drafted in to fight the *Basmachi*, the forces from this front were subsequently reformed into the Turkestan (Central Asian) military district. Units from the Unified State Political Directorate (OGPU) were also drafted in, as well as border guards, militia, and volunteer detachments made up of local people. These forces had cars, artillery, armoured vehicles, and aircraft.

The theatres of combat were sparsely populated, and the transport network was basic. It was therefore a very sensible decision on the part of Soviet command to draft in aircraft for air transport. Furthermore, Soviet command had been actively studying the activities of the English in their colonial operations in Mesopotamia, and Palestine. The British would deliver food, armament, ammunition, medicine, and small numbers of reinforcements by air. The action against the *Basmachi* in essence was also a small colonial war, so the experience gained from the British was always going to come in useful.

The military in Central Asia only had the two-seat Ju-21 reconnaissance aircraft at their disposal. When necessary another person could be squeezed into the rear cockpit of this aircraft, or a corresponding cargo, but that was all. In order to support combat operations against the *Basmachi* a decision was taken to use civil aviation aircraft. At the end of 1923 the Central Asian division of the Russian Volunteer Air Fleet Society (joint-stock company) *Dobrolyot* was founded. The bread and butter of this organisation were flights that were undertaken on contract to the military. The division received five, single-engine all-metal aircraft that had been manufactured in Germany. These were Junkers F.13s, which in the USSR had been designated Ju-13s. By July 1925 their number had grown to ten. From the beginning of 1924 the Air Force (VVS) of this district had received three of these same aircraft.

The capabilities of the Ju-13 were very limited. The aircraft was designed for a crew of two (a pilot, and a flight mechanic), and four passengers. The aircraft was able to carry a 350kg load in place of the latter. If the flight mechanic did not fly with the aircraft, and the rear seats in the cabin were removed, the pilot was able to raise

The whole history of this Ju-13 that was photographed on the Central Airfield in Moscow can be traced by its markings. The number on the side shows that it was first registered in Germany. Then it was acquired for the *Dobrolyot* company, aircraft that served in this organisation had red transverse lines on the wing. Lastly the Junkers was transferred to the RKKA VVS and a red star appeared on the fin.

the load capacity up to 450kg. When necessary the wounded could be accommodated in the Ju-13, with two casualties lying down, or four in a sitting position.

From 1927 aside from the routine flights, the transport aircraft that had been delivering small groups of reinforcements, as well as armament, and ammunition, began to take on an emergency medical evacuation role. Three aircraft landed 15 Red Army troops, along with their armament, and ammunition, at a village that was under threat of being attacked by the *Basmachi*.

In 1928 a reconnaissance detachment was deployed using a landed assault into a remote district. Aerial reconnaissance revealed a group of bandits that had departed westwards. They were attacked from the air twice, after which the enemy dispersed, losing themselves in the bush among the saxaul. It was decided to search for tracks on the ground that may lead to where the *Basmachi* had gone. The intention in this operation was to use four Ju-13 passenger aircraft, but in reality only three were used. Sat in each of these aircraft was a pilot, a flight mechanic, and three assault troops. The latter had been drafted in from the ranks of the senior commanders of military units, and the detachment was led by a cavalry commander. The group received two light machine guns, and one Maxim heavy machine gun.

The terrain where this search was to take place, was characterised by several huge sandy hollows, which were interspersed with similar sandy hillocks, overgrown with saxaul. The reconnaissance aircraft found a solid area of *takir soil* (a salt marsh) about 2–3km distant, but only one aircraft could land on this surface. It was decided to land on a salt lake, an open, level area of sand located some 6–7km away.

The aircraft carrying the assault troops flew in a group, they were escorted by three reconnaissance aircraft, which were ready to provide covering fire. On landing the wheel of one of the Junkers aircraft sank into the sand, and it was then dragged with some difficulty onto more solid ground. The reconnaissance aircraft made sure the detachment had landed safely, and returned back to base.

One pilot was left behind to guard the Ju-13s along with three flight mechanics, and a machine-gunner armed with a Maxim. The rest, having dispersed into two groups of five (each group was armed with a light machine gun, while the rest were armed with carbines) would investigate the area in different directions, but nothing of any significance was found. The commander gave the order to return.

In order that the Junkers aircraft were able to take-off from the soft ground, some of the water was drained out of them. Two of the aircraft took off safely, but the magneto on the third aircraft had failed and repair work began.

An accident involving a military Ju-13, that was used in the operation in Central Asia, that took place in Tashkent on 17 May 1930. This aircraft belonged to the 35th Aviation Detachment and was flown by its pilot S. Simonenko.

Sometime later one of the Ju-13s that had taken off earlier arrived to assist, delivering spare parts. After the repairs had been completed both aircraft returned to base.

It is often stated in the literature that a larger airborne operation was carried out the following year. During the operation to push back the *Maksum* bandits to the small town of Gharm some 45 soldiers were delivered to this location using aircraft. A Ju-13 was only able to carry six combatants, even counting the pilot, and that would bring this number up to more than seven. Neither the civil, nor the military air fleets had any aircraft that were capable of carrying any more people. The author has not been able to find any details, or confirmation in the documents belonging to the military district, or the air brigade, or *Dobrolyot* itself (this detachment would certainly have been activated if more than three aircraft were involved). Thus in the memoirs of O.I. Gorodovikov, who had commanded the cavalry soldiers in this region at the time, there is a description of an episode involving landing delivery of troops, but this episode is described in a very different way.

In April 1929 in Gharm there was an incident in which one (!) aircraft landed in this location, which had been attacked by the *Basmachi*, and which deployed five people: three machine-gunners, a divisional commander, and his adjutant. They were all armed with light machine guns. This small team joined those who had already been fighting, significantly enhancing their fire power. The deciding factor however in the conclusion to this battle was not the machine guns, but the diamonds on the Divisional Commander's tabs. A former White Guard officer who had been serving the bandits leader as a military advisor, allegedly saw them in his binoculars and thought that the Divisional Commander had not just arrived on spec, but that there was a large regular unit of the Red Army nearby, which the *Basmachi* would not be able to fight. He managed to convince *Qurboshi* (commander of *Basmachi* group) of this, and his people retreated from Gharm.

This story written by O.I. Gorodovikov is much more realistic, than the one written by the journalists, but one has to also consider the facts!

In September 1931 during the liquidation of the so-called 'Koymat's alignment', two aircraft from the 95th Transport Detachment delivered a machine-gun section armed with Maxim and ammunition to a small settlement that had been surrounded by *Basmachi*. Moreover, a single Ju-13 was used, along with a large, three-engine ANT-9. This latter aircraft type, which was designed to carry nine passengers, had only just begun to enter service with the RKKA VVS at the time. The town was successfully defended with the help of the machine-gunners.

Thus the Red Army's first airborne assaults had taken place in Central Asia, and they were landing deliveries.

2

Grokhovskiy and Company

Actual paratroopers, as well as fully fledged airborne forces appeared in the USSR a little later. The equipping of these forces with everything they needed to turn them into a new branch of the armed forces is indelibly linked to the name of Pavel Ignatievich Grokhovskiy (1899–1946). He was a unique individual. He was considered an enthusiast, a fanatic, a genius, and an adventurer, and even something of a trickster. In my opinion, he was all of those things at the same time. One of the first Soviet parachutists, and one of the participants in the world's first airborne assault, and the first head of the Central Aeroclub in Moscow, D.I. Moshkovskiy provided an excellent characterisation, he said that Grokhovskiy was 'deadly crazy'.

This man's life was illuminating, and extremely varied. Many authors write that his education was limited to all but a parochial school. This however is not true. The reason behind this error possibly lies in a form that Grokhovskiy once completed in his own hand. There in the section entitled "Education" he had written "secondary education – four years". This is how the conclusion was arrived at that he had undertaken four years of education. Grokhovskiy though had completed elementary school in his native Tver, and he had then entered a non-classical secondary school (an ordinary secondary school). It is true that he did not complete his schooling there, having fled when he was 15 to the front to fight in the First World War. As a result of this Grokhovskiy had completed four years of elementary school, and four years of secondary school; that's eight in total. Thus he was a little more educated than a couple of the people's commissars were. For an operational pilot though in those days, when flight was considered an art form, and not a science, and when any additional education for a pilot was considered harmful, Grokhovskiy was really able to brag about his knowledge. Naturally he did not have an engineering degree, and nobody had taught him about aerodynamics, and the strength of materials, and this would manifest itself on a number of occasions in his designs.

His restless nature took this 'deadly crazy' man to one place, and then another. He returned to Tver from the front line a year later, having fallen ill again with Typhus. In October 1917 Grokhovskiy became a chemist's apprentice in Petrograd. He however did not stay long at the chemist, having joined a detachment of revolutionary sailors. He then took part in the revolution itself, serving as a sailor on the battleship *Petropavlovsk* and fighting the whites. He fought well, earning a trophy Mauser from Detachment Commander P.E. Dybenko. After arriving back in his native Tver on leave he found himself in the thick of the counter-revolutionary revolt. Grokhovskiy was arrested, and was sentenced to death by firing squad, but he escaped! At the beginning of 1921 the young *bolshevik* was appointed to the lofty position of Commissar of the Black Sea, and Azov Sea coastlines. He was however not destined to reach his posting: the train was halted by a group of bandits. Any communists that were found on the train were dragged out, and shot. Grokhovskiy himself was shot, with the mandate that he had been given pinned to his chest, but Grokhovskiy survived, even after being hit with two bullets!

Meanwhile in 1922 Grokhovskiy suddenly decided he wanted to learn to fly; he got his way and the following year he graduated from pilot school No. 2 in Borisoglebsk. His subsequent career path was a very traditional one: junior pilot, senior pilot, and then flight commander. In the second half of the 1920s Grokhovskiy served in the 29th Squadron in Evpatoria. This squadron operated old Fokker D.VII biplane fighters, which had been acquired in Holland. This squadron belonged to the Black Sea Fleet Air Force. For the reader's information: at that time no separate naval aviation branch existed in the USSR, and the naval air forces came under the RKKA VVS, within

P.I. Grokhovskiy at the peak of his career: as a Division Commander, Head of the Experimental Institute under the NKTP, and Cavalier of the Order of Lenin.

M.N. Tukhachevskiy, Head of RKKA Armament and Deputy People's Commissar for Military and Naval Affairs.

the auspices of the Air Forces of the military districts. In the spring of 1928 Grokhovskiy was transferred to the 44th Squadron in Novocherkassk.

It was while he was serving in this location that Grokhovskiy first demonstrated his capacity for ingenuity. The pilot proposed replacing the standard practice bombs (which were designed for training targets) with metal casings, and cement inside, with some very cheap clay bombs. These bombs were manufactured in the form of vessels that were filled with chalk. The chalk was coloured, so it was very easy to tell who had hit the target. Then Grokhovskiy perfected the sleeve cone, which the pilots would use in aerial gunnery training. The Air Force Directorate (UVVS) was informed of the pilot's new innovations, and the inventor was sent to Moscow. Sometime later he was offered the chance to get involved professionally in creating different types of innovations.

A new stage in Grokhovskiy's life began in the spring of 1929 at the Air Force Scientific Testing Institute (NII VVS), which at that time was located on the Central airfield at Khodynka, which had not been in existence up to this point. It was at Khodynka that he first became involved in all manner of things, such as building a 'flying test range' for example. This was an R-1 aircraft, from the aft cockpit of which the operator would trail various aerial gunnery targets. It was in the summer however that Grokhovskiy first completed a parachute jump. He was taken up in a Fokker C.IV reconnaissance aircraft. He jumped from the wing and the parachutist pulled the rip cord far too early, and the cord became caught in the aircraft tail wheel. The material however was torn, and the parachute inflated. His troubles though did not stop there. A strong wind nearly pushed him onto the roof of a two storey building. The pilot fell into an allotment next to a gypsy camp. The enterprising gypsies readily stole the silk canopy, and cut it up into strips. This imported American Irvin parachute cost approximately two years' wages for a senior pilot. It is possible that this is what forced Grokhovskiy to consider replacing the silk with something cheaper.

In any case this 'deadly crazy' man became completely obsessed with parachuting. He would jump at any given opportunity. His fourth jump almost ended in tragedy. As a result of an unfortunate landing Grokhovskiy became caught up in the airfield's barbed wire fence, he damaged his spine, and for some time he was partially paralysed. This though did nothing to dampen the enthusiast's spirit. Not only did he carry on jumping, but he started to create his own parachute designs. He was for the most part engaged in conducting experiments

An inspection of the achievements of the OKPB VVS, 2 August 1934, on the Central airfield in Moscow.

using models. His wife sewed small canopies together, and her husband would drop them with different cargoes attached, from the roof of a three storey building, studying the specifics of the way they fell to the ground. Then Grokhovskiy moved on to full size parachutes, for both people and cargo.

Evidently it was at this stage that the idea that would become the future paratrooper first formed in his mind. He however did not restrict himself to this. Ideas flowed out of this young inventor like a fountain. You name it, he proposed it … equipment for transporting people, and cargo by air, propaganda bombs for dropping leaflets, parachute cable barrages, and cluster bombs. His main task though remained airborne troops equipment. His enthusiasm was noted and in April 1930 a design department was created from the 5th Department of the NII VVS, and P.I. Grokhovskiy was named as its head. The task that he had been assigned was dubbed 'Airborne infantry'. The department initially was a small one; aside from the head there were eight people working in this department: Titov, Malynich, Zuyev, Modin, Ognev, Preobrazhenskiy, Sakharov, and Sosnin. The first deputy head, I.V. Titov, like Grokhovskiy, did not have any education to any significant level, prior to this he had been an aircraft technician.

This small collective busied itself with everything that a paratrooper could possibly need: parachutes, a special flying suit, and equipment, as well as packages for delivering a variety of cargoes. Subsequently the collective also moved into working on alternative airdropping equipment.

In what was a relatively poor and technically backward country, Grokhovskiy imagined enormous numbers of paratroopers with an abundance of different equipment, and it was not only the collective that became carried away with his ideas, but also the leadership of the VVS. He promised to deliver everything behind enemy lines that a paratrooper might need. He actively engaged in self education, but did not have any firm basis for this. A multitude of ideas formed in the inventor's mind, but he was not able to decipher which of these ideas were feasible at that time, and which were not. It is no coincidence that it is not so much blueprints that are found in his documents, as sketches. Anything that is not capable of flight is made to take flight in these sketches: vehicles, that would otherwise be destroyed by the landing, go into battle in terrifying numbers. This man did not have any idea of the actual capabilities of indigenous industry at that time, and thus many of his inventions turned out to

P.I. Grokhovskiy (in a peaked cap, seating with his back to the photographer) on the fuselage of a TB-3 briefs paratroopers ahead of demonstration jumps.

be fruitless. At the same time however some of Grokhovskiy's ideas clearly foreshadowed the future of airborne troops, and were realised many years later.

Since he did not have any real understanding of computational methods, or of modelling methods, the designer adopted an 'organoleptic' methodology. This meant the collective would make something, and it would break, so they would strengthen it, and it would break again, until they ended up with something useful.

Grokhovskiy's saving grace was partly that many of the country's leadership, together with the high ranking military officers had not distinguished themselves in terms of the depth of their education in that period either. It is very evident from the plans they put together they were writing 'from a wish list' without any serious assessment of the situation. It was just they wanted things to be that way. The prevailing atmosphere at that time was just that: "There is nothing a Soviet citizen cannot do" ... Grokhovskiy charmed the leadership with his ideas, promising a completely new type of war, not like the First World War, or the Civil War had been at all.

He was however very adept at 'selling' his ideas. It is probable that this unorthodox person remained a showman at heart. With each new invention he would organise demonstrations of his designs, as though he was arranging presentations for 'clients' – the leadership of the VVS, and the RKKA VVS, as well as the country's top leadership. Maybe the fact that he was still engaged in amateur activities, writing plays, and poetry, had some effect on him.

So what are his albums worth in themselves? Each year Grokhovskiy would report on his work in a picturesque album (which of course was classified). This was done to a high standard: a thick paper, beautiful photographs, and sketches, interleaved with a tissue paper, and leather bound with brass edges. In a specific order: on the first page there would be a portrait of Stalin and the customary eulogy, and on the second page a portrait of the People's Commissar for Military and Naval Affairs, Voroshilov, while on the third would be a portrait of Grokhovskiy himself, in full parade uniform.

The First Deputy Head of the OKPB VVS, I.V. Titov.

N.P. Blagin, who was actively involved in work on airborne equipment in the first half of the 1930s at the NII VVS.

Similar albums were produced for every visit of a high level delegation, or for an official demonstration of a piece of equipment. Moreover, individuals of a higher rank produced their own albums. These included without fail a photograph of the leader in question on the cover, both a group, and an individual photograph, along with new equipment, and of course with Grokhovskiy, and finally one taken at the subsequent banquet.

Grokhovskiy's principal rival at that time was N.P. Blagin (1896–1935), who was also a pilot. Although he was the son of a lieutenant-colonel in the Tsarist army, and a hereditary landowner, he nevertheless joined the Red Army in 1918, subsequently becoming a member of the Bolshevik party. He, like Grokhovskiy, did not have any further technical education, but it goes without saying that he had a higher level of general knowledge. Blagin studied at a vocational secondary school, and then in the cadet corps. In 1920 he graduated from flying school, and in 1930 he was invited to work at the NII VVS.

Blagin's small group worked alongside Grokhovskiy on the very same projects. The ideas of both designers were discussed at a meeting in the office of the Assistant Head of the NII VVS V.S. Konnert held on 25 May 1931 and for the most part they were accepted. The designs put forward by Blagin's collective were more considered, and were notable for a certain conservatism, which produced positive results. During the course of testing his designs were often acknowledged as being more reliable than similar designs put forward by Grokhovskiy.

At that time however an individual's background was of no small significance. In 1922 Blagin was excluded from the party for this reason, and was blamed on more than one occasion since he was considered a class enemy. In January 1932 the pilot was transferred to the Central Aero and Hydrodynamics Institute (TsAGI) where he undertook experimental work. After that Grokhovskiy did not have any real competitors left in the NII VVS.

Blagin died in 1935, after he flew into the wing of the giant *Maksim Gorkiy* aircraft, which led to a terrible tragedy. Then he was dubbed an 'aerial hooligan', but now the majority of historians think that he tried to perform his dangerous trick under orders. It was just that this order was given verbally and nobody wanted to take responsibility for it later.

V.I. Bekauri, Head of the OTB.

For a short time the Special Technical Bureau of Military Designs was working on the question of transporting heavy loads (the name of this bureau was abbreviated to Ostekhbyuro, or the OTB), which was led by V.I. Bekauri (1882–1938). This organisation was located in Leningrad. It was there that the first attachments were manufactured to transport motorcycles, and cars by air. After 1931 however the factory was reconfigured in a different direction, manufacturing specifically air launched mines, and torpedoes, as well as radio-controlled military equipment.

Parachutes from 1930 were designed in a parachute design workshop, which later became Factory No.1 in Tushino. To begin with this factory was led by M.A. Savitskiy. It was there that parachutes were designed, and manufactured, and it was also at this same collective that parachutes of all kinds were developed, which were subsequently manufactured *en masse* in the USSR.

Grokhovskiy trod on everyone's toes in turn with an enormous amount of energy. He achieved his big idea by stepping across any boundaries, and specifications, and would always complain 'up the chain' about anyone who was slowing the pace of the work. The designer ignored the traditional blueprint for creating a new item of military equipment: a technical proposal, a preliminary design, a set of diverse calculations, a technical specification, and then a prototype. A series of examples were rapidly manufactured based on primitive drawings, which were often all but devoid of any calculations. As the work progressed the examples were refined, but this too was often done 'by sight'. Serious violations of the accepted safety measures became the norm in the design department. As a result of these he made a number of visible, and invisible enemies. Grokhovskiy was considered a jumped up adventurer, he was dubbed a 'tinkerer' and a 'self-taught specialist'. The Chairman of the Air Force Scientific-Technical Committee P.S. Dubenskiy treated him very cautiously, and considered the inventor's ideas 'technically suspect'. The finance department of the Air Force Directorate (UVVS) would write reports again and again concerning unauthorised expenses. For their constant violations of financial discipline Grokhovskiy, and Titov were given a personal reprimand in December 1930 from the Head of the UVVS P.I. Baranov.

The Head of RKKA Armament M.N. Tukhachevskiy, who was appointed in June 1931 proved to be a reliable defender of Grokhovskiy. He himself was an enthusiastic person, having made a daring leap from the ranks of the sub-lieutenants to the commander's ranks, missing out almost all of the intermediate steps. Tukhachevskiy was in many ways as much of a fantasist as Grokhovskiy. To give the army commander his due however: he showed an active interest in new military equipment, he tried to study new military hardware, and supported the designers (although it was true he was not always objective in this). When the new Head of the Directorate, Ya.I. Alksnis, who by nature was a complete perfectionist, replaced P.I. Baranov he made a point of complaining to Tukhachevskiy about the serious breaches of safety rules, and he received a response to the effect that he either reject Grokhovskiy's ideas, or overlook fact that Grokhovskiy was always ignoring instructions. That is to say demonstrate a personal preference. Moreover, Grokhovskiy either did not know many of the norms, and rules, or

V.S. Vakhmistrov, Head of KB-29.

just chose to ignore them. He was never taught the rules of design, and in this case he was completely self-taught. He made up his own rules as and when he needed to.

On 15 July 1931 Grokhovskiy demonstrated his achievements to the party, Soviet, and military leadership. I.V. Stalin himself was present. An 'aviabus', which was a system that allowed both troops, and equipment to be lowered to the ground without using parachutes (this will be described in detail later) was dropped from a TB-1 aircraft. Dogs and chickens were offloaded from the 'aviabus'. Overall however this was not a triumph. Some of the cargo bags, bicycles, and ammunition, as well as a car that were dropped from the aircraft were destroyed. The designer blamed the leadership of the NII VVS for all this, saying they had slowed down the testing, as well as the final adjustments to the parachute equipment. The actual loss of the 'Ford' he claimed was as a result of direct sabotage. The Deputy Head of the NII VVS ordered everything, whether it was broken or not, to be taken into one of the hangars, stamped, and that a guard be appointed to protect it. Sentries were ordered not to let anyone inside until the equipment was inspected by a special commission. When the commission was formed, and they entered the hangar they actually did find the central aperture on the canopy sewn up with twine and secured to the side of the canopy. They even found a needle!

Overall it all ended quite favourably for Grokhovskiy. He was awarded an engraved Korovin pistol, and a Certificate of Merit, while his Deputy I.V. Titov was given a Harley-Davidson motorcycle. Furthermore, Tukhachevskiy did not forget about the designer's constant squabbles with the leadership of the NII VVS. In April 1932 he withdrew this department from the structure of the institute, after forming the Special Design, and Manufacturing Bureau (known as the Oskonprobyuro, or the Special Design and Manufacturing Bureau, OKPB). P.I. Grokhovskiy became the head of this bureau. At that time the bureau came under the direct responsibility of the UVVS.

The OKPB transformed fairly rapidly from a small group of enthusiasts into a proper design organisation, with its own workshops, and a flight detachment. At the end of 1932 new premises were designated for this organisation and an experimental factory was constructed on the edge of the Central airfield. Apart from that the bureau fed Aircraft Manufacturing Plant No. 47 in Leningrad with orders for parachute equipment.

At the OKPB the working methodology remained as before: the bureau designed its own equipment, manufactured it, and carried out its own testing. Moreover, Grokhovskiy would often check his own equipment personally. This group was dubbed 'Grokhovskiy's circus' in recognition of the unusual nature of their experiments. Famous pilots such as A.F. Anisimov, V.P. Chkalov, and M.S. Kaminskiy formed part of the 'circus' at various times.

Grokhovskiy, in view of his post, arranged a higher position for himself – wearing a Brigade Commander's rhombs instead of a Lieutenant's cubes, and he got away with it! The designer's response was a simple one: "Who is going to engage with me on a serious level in any other way?" He used his own logic in this case. In the Red Army at that time there were no titles, just positions and categories. If you commanded a squadron you were a squadron commander, if you commanded a division you were a divisional commander. The heads (who led the non-combatant institutions, and organisations) could be compared to commanders of various ranks, with the addition of a specific category. Grokhovskiy was not punished, but he was later to officially attain the rank of Divisional Commander.

From 19 September to 5 October 1932, state testing of parachute equipment took place outside Leningrad. Different cargo solutions were tested, which were dropped by parachute, as well as the parachutes themselves that were tested for use by people, and also for cargoes. In addition, a variety of delivery, and landing methods were tested. Over the course of this time motorcycles, and sidecars were dropped by parachute, a cargo cage was dropped twice, a 76mm mountain gun was dropped three times, as well as a 'Ford A' car, a T-27 tankette was dropped once, along with a medicine cabinet that was also dropped once. The majority of this was accepted and was ordered in prototype batches for combat testing.

The fly in the ointment was a message stating that Grokhovskiy, as he left, had taken five parachutes with him that were listed at one of the VVS stores. In response to an order to return the equipment he had stolen, he replied: "I am not going to return the parachutes, I need them myself for parachute jumps". He pretended to the upper leadership that he needed them. Evidently equipment tended to go missing somehow or was transferred from one balance sheet to another.

On 1 January 1933 a number of the latest technical developments produced by the OKPB were demonstrated in a hangar on the Central airfield. Specifically, attachments for Harley-Davidson motorcycles were presented for the R-5 aircraft, which would allow the motorcycles to be dropped by parachute, as well as packages for delivering weaponry, dynamo-reactive (recoilless) guns, and fuel, together with an aviabus designed to hold 200kg of cargo. All this was inspected by the military, and by industry representatives. At the end of the year the designer was awarded the Order of Lenin.

For many though in the UVVS Grokhovskiy was a 'thorn in their side'. He was again reproached for the reliability of his primitive designs, and for his reckless spending, and his striving to cover every eventuality. This is what E.I. Tatarchenko, the Head of the Air Force Airborne Service said about him in April 1933 " ... the technical oversimplification, and opportunism cultivated by Grokhovskiy represents the greatest threat". This figure really did leap from one thing to another. It is possible that only Leonardo da Vinci, and Lomonosov could be compared to him in terms of the breadth of their interests. The steady stream of reports that were passed upwards through the ranks played their role. In summer 1933 the People's Commissar Voroshilov ordered that the OKPB be terminated as an independent organisation, and that it be brought under the NII VVS as a Airborne Department. On 16 August 1933 the OKPB ceased to exist, and the airborne department emerged a little later, on 1 September.

The designer's plans to create an Experimental Air Force Airborne Institute using his own experience fell through. Grokhovskiy however did find an acceptable exit out of this situation with the help of Tukhachevskiy. The People's Commissar for Heavy Industry G.K. Ordzhonikidze accepted him into his leadership. In March 1934 an Experimental Institute was set up as part of the People's Commissariat for Heavy industry, and Grokhovskiy was named as the Chief Designer, and the Head of this institute. A significant proportion of the employees who had worked at the OKPB followed him. Furthermore, the Head, and his deputies retained their status as soldiers, as well as their uniform, and their various privileges. That was the system in place at the time, under which specialists were transferred from the RKKA to the military industrial complex.

It was at this institute that Grokhovskiy was in his element. He managed to secure enormous amounts of funding, on a level comparable to experimental aircraft development. Whatever the institute was engaged in. Naturally a great deal of attention was still focussed on airborne equipment, but the institute also undertook aircraft manufacturing, as well as the production of incendiary, and guided ammunitions, jet propelled, winged, and non-winged missiles, chemical, and bacteriological weaponry, and special transportation systems, including radio-controlled devices (so-called 'telemechanically controlled' systems). There was no room for showing any kind of a peaceful disposition, or sentimentality in this case. Special bombs were developed for example to poison the populations of large cities by infecting the water intakes at water treatment plants. Indeed, who but Grokhovskiy would think of the idea of spraying Maltese fever bacteria into clouds that were heading towards the territories of neighbouring countries? In the end a whole complex was developed to grow these bacteria *en masse* ...

The institute was trying to train pilots from a very young age, or as teenagers to be more precise. Medical experiments were carried out: Specifically, jumping from high altitudes without oxygen equipment. For some reason these tests were carried out on women. There were kennels where dogs were trained in sabotage. A torpedo was designed, which would be controlled by a dog. This however was never actually manufactured, but an attack was simulated using a small motor boat. This device operated in the same way as a helmet-mounted sight, wherever the dog looked, the boat would steer. The device was designed to explode on contact with a target vessel. A trainer would tempt the dog from on board this vessel with some sausage. The transmission to the controls was purely mechanical, so a large, strong dog was used, a German Shepherd.

The Experimental Institute was even engaged in manufacturing amusement rides for municipal parks. It was true however that these rides were actually primitive training simulators. It was at the Experimental Institute that the USSR's first parachute tower was developed. In the pre-war years towers such as these could be found standing in towns across the country. It was on these towers that recruits were taught how to put on, and engage the harness system, and how to group together correctly on landing. These skills could then be developed much more cheaply than jumping from an aircraft, or from a tethered balloon.

Today historians are of the opinion that Grokhovskiy did not like engineers. He really did not like old school specialists, who possessed a thorough knowledge, and a great deal of experience. These people would very often demonstrate to the inventor why his invention could not be realised. Grokhovskiy was not able to argue with them in their language, a dialogue of formulae, and figures, so all he was able to do in response was to dash off reports, accusing them of being a 'retrograde', or even of 'sabotage'. The latter was more or less the norm when resolving technical arguments. To make an accusation to a competitor under Article 58 ("Counter-revolutionary activity"), which was interpreted in a completely arbitrary fashion, was considered to be a very effective way of putting down an argument. If one is to consider that just a few years prior to this the legal process for the *Prompartiya* trial had taken place, which saw many of the old engineers put behind bars, the opinion of Grokhovskiy, as an active Bolshevik, and a former Commissar could outweigh any formulae, or calculations.

So the inventor was able to work very well with the new, Soviet engineers, and gain their approval. It was no bad thing that they had a much lesser degree of knowledge than their older colleagues, and that they did not have any experience. Then again these individuals did not know that they could not do such and such in a certain way, and looked for their own ways to solve the tasks that had been put before them, which nobody anywhere in the world had attempted to solve up until this time. Sometimes they were successful!

On 2 August 1934 Grokhovskiy organised a mass demonstration of the institute's achievements. This was an amazing demonstration. Some 40 parachutists jumped out of a single TB-3, and dogs, pigs, chickens, cars, guns, and a tankette were dropped from other aircraft. A special airborne assault aircraft, a G-37, flew over the airfield. This aircraft then dropped a variety of cargoes in cargo boxes, and bags. To demonstrate the safety of the packaging, electric light bulbs, and even large, fresh eggs were packed inside. The jewel in the crown however was the dropping of a cargo cage containing thermos containers. A woman parachutist landed alongside, quickly changing her flying helmet for a snow-white headdress, which at that time had become the indispensible attribute of waiters, and dinner ladies, and began to serve guests. They were offered baguettes, cutlets, and *borshch*. She was assisted by a male colleague, who had also parachuted in, dressed as a chef. Anyone who so wished could enjoy a hearty, three course meal.

On 18 August that same year at an aviation event cats, dogs, and pigs were parachuted from an ANT-9. The programme also included a drop of 12 women from an ANT-9, and 100 parachutists were dropped from a TB-3 in a single jump.

The year 1935 was successful for Grokhovskiy. The culmination of large-scale exercises just outside Kiev was a large, combined assault, using both parachute, and land assault troops. A series of new developments that had been produced by the Experimental Institute were used. The following year exercises on an even larger scale were carried out in Belorussia.

A host of accusations however continued to be heaped on Division Commander Grokhovskiy. He was blamed for the institute's enormous expenses. The accusations alleged that money was being spent irrationally. The Experimental Institute suffered from the same maladies that the whole of Soviet industry suffered from. A lack of qualified specialists led to positions being occupied by so-called 'practising engineers', who lacked education. If in Germany in an organisation of a similar level the head of department needed to have a doctoral academic degree, then in the USSR by no means all of them had even graduated from secondary school. What is more party officials who had been promoted could be found at an even higher level, who did not have any idea of the nature of what they were actually meant to be leading. A number of students who had not finished their studies worked at the Experimental Institute. Moreover, in comparison with other countries, the state was overloaded with bosses, inspectors, and clerical workers as well as by those who were serving the leadership apparatus.

Grokhovskiy was continuously violating the accepted system for development that had proved itself in practice. The full set of design documentation for many of his designs was missing, and calculations were either not carried out at all, or were highly simplified. In its place, in order to manufacture a single prototype example, test it and systematically improve it, a small batch of a given invention was manufactured, which subsequently would turn out to be not fit for purpose. Redesigns were required, for which provision had not been made on the balance sheet. Enormous sums of money were needed for this to happen.

Funds were spread around a multitude of projects. In order to cover the breakdowns in certain areas, they were again incorporated into the plans but under different names.

Many of the vitally important materials in the USSR were either completely lacking, or the quality left much to be desired. The currency was always divided very sparsely and required a number of documents to be drawn up, as well as a long drawn out correspondence with various levels of authority. Soviet production was always bedecked with plans before it was actually realised. If something was required that had not previously been envisaged a requisition would need to be filled in, which would then be reviewed, and maybe it would be incorporated ... into the plan for the subsequent year! Grokhovskiy would often succeed in obtaining something as an exception, but not always.

It is also worth acknowledging that the operational effectiveness of the institute, even though it was so expensive, was actually very low. The overwhelming majority of the developments were not even projects, but beautifully laid out sketches, along with a narrative description. Some of Grokhovskiy's ideas, such as the airborne descent pods, as well as the parachutes made from nainsook were taken out of operation quickly because of the significant defects that came to light. In reality up until the start of the Great Patriotic War only a few types of cargo packages had been used, along with the parachutes to go with them, and the PG-12 attachment used for transporting military equipment underneath a TB-3.

The messages concerning Grokhovskiy's violations of financial discipline for his own ends were quite another matter. He considered all the institute's designs to be his own invention and registered them in his own name and would award himself what were for that time huge bonuses. The inventor would not deny this either, claiming that his employees merely realised his own ideas.

Gradually Grokhovskiy was stripped of his patronage from the powers that be. This was linked to the machinery of repression that was being turned even tighter. On 18 February 1937 the People's Commissar for

Heavy Industry G.K. Ordzhonikidze shot himself in anticipation of his trail. On 11 May that same year Marshal M.N. Tukhachevskiy was stripped of his position as First Deputy to the People's Commissar for Defence and was sent to command troops in the secondary Volga Military District. On 22 May he was arrested, and in June his trail was set, after which he was shot along with a number of other high-ranking military representatives.

Having lost his support Grokhovskiy did not remain in his position for long. He was removed from his post as the Head of the Experimental Institute and was made the Head of the Economic Directorate of the Central Council at Society for Cooperation in Aviation and Chemical Production (*Osoaviakhim*). Why this irrepressible person was to be broken so that he ended up doing five years of clerical work is not clear. With the introduction of new titles, the inventor was reconfirmed in his post not as a Divisional Commander but as a Colonel. In 1942 Grokhovskiy was again accused of financial violations and was arrested. He died in a camp from consumption in 1946.

The Experimental Institute did not survive for long without Grokhovskiy and in 1938 it was disbanded. This was linked to a discussion by the VVS Military Council, in March 1938, concerning: "The state of experimental airborne equipment from 1934–37". The state that this work was in came under severe criticism. By way of a decision that was taken by the Military Council the supply of airborne equipment was entrusted to the VVS Technical, and Material Supply Directorate, while development, as well as state, and combat testing was entrusted to the NII VVS.

Issues surrounding airborne equipment back in the spring of 1937 had been transferred to KB-29, which was led by V.S. Vakhmistrov. This design bureau was engaged in producing a range of designs connected to aviation. Vakhmistrov himself was developing his idea for the *Zveno* for an aircraft that was able to act as a carrier of smaller aircraft. Other subdivisions were working on pressurised cockpits, and high-altitude equipment for pilots. Brigade 'D' that was working on airborne equipment was led by A.I. Privalov (1906–95); he had previously worked at the TsAGI, and at the Experimental Institute. This brigade modified a series of designs that had been produced back in Grokhovskiy's time, as well as creating several new designs including a very successful DPT-2 attachment for transporting military equipment. On 4 March 1940 KB-29 design bureau was transferred and came under P.O. Sukhoi, becoming an aircraft manufacturing design bureau, and Factory No.289 was designated as the development facility. In return on 30 November the new Factory No.468 was developed, and a design bureau was created under it. Privalov was made Director, and Chief Engineer of his factory. The factory in actual fact did not yet exist, and the People's Commissariat for the Aviation Industry (NKAP) accepted what was an unfinished factory named after Vorovskiy in Beskudnikovo (at that time this location was a suburb of Moscow). Therefore, the designers were temporarily housed in Factory No.84 in Khimki; they were transferred to Beskudnikovo in May 1941.

Under the leadership of Privalov, cargo carrying beams were developed for DB-3, PS-84, and TB-3 aircraft, as well as new attachments for carrying motorcycles, and sidecars, as well as 45mm anti-tank, and 76mm field guns by air, and dropping them by parachute. These successfully passed state testing at the NII VVS in April 1941, not long before the start of the Great Patriotic War.

3

Assault at Klochkovo Farmstead

The world's first airborne assault was carried out in the Soviet Union in 1930. It was led by Leonid Grigoryevich Minov (1898–1978). This interesting person was one of the pioneers of parachute activity in the country. During the First World War and the Civil War he served in the infantry, but in 1920 he decided to transfer to aviation. In May of that year Minov graduated from the pilot's and observer's school in Moscow and immediately went to fight in Poland. On his return he continued to study at the flying school in Zaraysk, where in 1921 he received his pilot's diploma, and he then went on to study at the 1st Moscow Higher Military Pilot's School. It was there that Minov became an instructor, and he went on to become Head of the flying school.

From April 1925 Minov worked at the embassy in France as an aviation procurement consultant. Specifically, he supervised the realisation of the Soviet order for Farman *Goliath* heavy bombers. On his return from Paris in 1927 a new position was found for Minov in the Commission for the Study of Flight. This organisation oversaw issues surrounding flight crew training, and flight safety, as well as monitoring the accident rate. At one of the meetings in 1928 Minov spoke in favour of providing all VVS pilots with parachutes. This was a relatively new thing at that time, and in the USSR was practically unheard of: in Russian, and subsequently in Soviet aviation pilots flew without parachutes. Minov was entrusted with studying this question and was sent to the USA to visit the Irvin Company that produced parachutes, and trained crews in how to use them. The introduction of this means of saving a pilot's life in aircraft accidents was entrusted to the Commission for the Study of Flight.

On his arrival in America in the spring of 1929 the Soviet pilot spent several months getting himself acquainted with the Irvin factory in Buffalo, as well as with parachute design, and with the technique for making safe parachute jumps. The latter however is not possible without a practical element. Minov himself donned a parachute and jumped on 13 June. This fateful date caused some significant confusion for the Americans, but they got around the superstition easily enough by just writing "the eve of the 14". Minov sent a telegram to Moscow: "The first jump was successful". A further two jumps took place, including one on 7 July as part of a contest to judge the accuracy of landings in a specified location in the small town of Pomona. It was there that Minov incidentally achieved a respectable result. The company issued the Soviet pilot with a certificate: "This is to certify that citizen of the USSR L.G. Minov has undergone a course in the inspection, care, maintenance, and use of parachutes manufactured by the Irvin Company".

On his return from the USA, Minov led a small group of instructors and riggers that travelled around different aviation units and trained pilots in the use of parachutes. In July 1930 this group arrived in Voronezh to train the crews of the 11th Air Brigade that had been deployed there in the art of making parachute jumps.

With this goal in mind the FG-62 aircraft was selected from the 3rd Detachment, 59th Squadron. The French twin-engine wooden biplane bomber the Farman F.62 *Goliath* operated under this designation. Of the four aircraft that were purchased of this type only three remained in service by the time these events were taking place. They were all based in Voronezh and were used there as training aircraft during the course of crew training for the indigenous TB-1 bombers that were just entering service. The FG-62s were also used for other, auxiliary roles. Thus the *Goliath* was also drafted in for parachute training: L.V. Kondratyev who served at the time in Voronezh later recalled: "The Farman *Goliath* was very predisposed to parachute training. It was not a particularly fast aircraft and the door on the starboard side of the fuselage allowed for an easy exit".

L.G. Minov, the organiser of the world's first parachute airdrop.

Parachute training for flight crews was afforded some significance since the parachute was to be the principal object of a pilot's equipment. For pilots, navigators, flight mechanics, and gunners the programme was mandatory, but volunteers from the ground-based services were also allowed to jump. In total 59 servicemen graduated as parachutists.

Then from Moscow an order came through: "The senior pilot of the Commission for the Study of Flight comrade Minov is hereby ordered ... to prepare for an 'airborne assault' using parachutes". The author has not been able to establish who it was who actually came up with the idea of the parachute assault. In the literature it is mentioned that the term 'airborne assault' first appeared in the text of a paper that was prepared at the Headquarters of the Leningrad Military District on the orders of the then commander M.N. Tukhachevskiy. The identity of the author, or authors of this section of the paper however has gone unrecorded. In 1928 Tukhachevskiy conducted a war game scenario in his district that featured an assault; but this only exists on paper.

Minov was required to select between 10–15 servicemen who were suitable for carrying out this mission, and to conduct additional training with them. It was decided that since this new innovation in the art of war had been proposed by such dedicated enthusiasts it would be tested during the course of manoeuvres organised by the Moscow Military District that were to take place not far from Voronezh.

In the scenario for the exercises the 'reds' had just attacked the forces of the 'blues' that were advancing on Voronezh. The supply of reinforcements to the 'blues' needed to be cut off. It was alleged that saboteurs were operating behind their lines. In order to enhance their combat capability, armament, ammunition, as well as "organisers, and leaders of a guerrilla movement" had to be brought in. It was proposed that in accordance with an order issued by the Commander of the 1st Army of the 'reds' a group of four TB-1 bombers would drop two detachments of parachutists (in total between 12–15 people) on a single drop site, as well as guns, including machine guns, in parachute bags. A 76mm mountain gun also needed to be dropped by parachute. After that the 'partisans' and the parachutists were to attack the guards protecting a bridge across the river Don south of the station at Liski. According to the scenario some 60–70 enemy soldiers were guarding the bridge on the Voronezh–Zadonsk railway line, and were armed with three 75mm guns, and four machine guns. After eliminating the guard, it was planned to 'blow' the bridge.

Minov in the United States prior to his first parachute jump, 13 June 1929.

The intention was to obtain the parachutes for the airborne troops from those that had been issued to the 11th Air Brigade. Assault parachutes were still yet to appear at that time, so Irvins were used, which were intended for aircrew. Special parachutes, and packaging however were required for various cargoes. These were still not yet in series production, although there were prototype variants. For the purposes of these exercises a small batch of Blagin's cargo parachutes were manufactured with specially designed bags. According to another document they were to use parachutes with cargo bags that Grokhovskiy had designed. The mountain gun was never supplied, and the parachute harness was not supplied for it either. As a result, the "pipe got smaller, and the smoke thinner". They had to make use of what they had.

The paratroopers were drawn from the ranks of the 11th Air Brigade, in accordance with the instructions "they were to be drawn first and foremost from willing participants". Eleven individuals were selected: Moshkovskiy, Mukhin, Filippov, Yegorov, Cherkashin, Freyman, Zakharov, Kukharenko, Peydus, Kovalenkov, and Povalyayev. The twelfth member of the team was the Commander of the improvised detachment, L.G. Minov. The parachutes were assembled by the rigger Baranov, who had arrived in Voronezh along with Minov.

Only four TB-1 bombers participated in these exercises, and one of those quickly developed a technical problem. The bombers were marked up as being on the 'red' or the 'blue' side. The commanders prevented these aircraft from being used to drop parachutes. They had to draft in a *Goliath* aircraft from the 59th Squadron, which was piloted by Gromov (the same surname as the famous test-pilot). Interestingly it was the crewmembers who were first given parachutes, but they felt very uncomfortable since their seats were not designed for them. The *Goliath* was only able to carry no more than six passengers at a time, so the assault was split into two stages. The aircraft had to make two round trips there and back.

A rehearsal was preliminarily held on Voronezh airfield: the first group jumped from an altitude of 250m, and the second from an altitude of 500m.

On 12 August 1930 (many authors mistakenly specify this date as 2 August) 12 paratroopers carried out a descent near Klochkovo farmstead over the course of two flights, jumping from an FG-62 aircraft. Each of them was given a Nagant revolver and two grenades, while the rest of the equipment was delivered in cargo bags.

3.3 The twin-engine Farman *Goliath* bomber (the FG-62) of the 11th Air Brigade on Voronezh airfield.

Minov briefs paratroopers ahead of a jump.

The first six parachutists led by Minov landed at approximately 0800hrs. They jumped at intervals of approximately one second. The troops were divided according to their weight. The first to leave the aircraft were those who weighed the most. A fierce wind blew on the ground, but the paratroops landed without any injuries, or incurring any losses. The spread between the members of the different groups was around 180–200m. After they had landed it emerged that the paratroopers were located approximately a kilometre away from the landing site. They were supplied by three R-1 biplanes from the 35th Squadron, which dropped armament (in the shape of rifles, and DP light machine guns) and ammunition. It was proposed that the parachutes would be destroyed, after burying them in the ground. In actual fact nobody was allowed to damage these expensive imported Irvins, and so it was decided that the 'destruction' would be nominal.

Minov shows how to jump out of an aircraft correctly.

Paratroopers, who have been trained in the 11th Air Brigade, photographed next to an inflated parachute canopy.

Participants in the world's first parachute airdrop standing next to a *Goliath* bomber.

The second group of paratroopers ahead of their embarkation on the aircraft, first on the left is the group's Commander Ya.D. Moshkovskiy, while in the center is parachute rigger Baranov.

Launching the first group of parachutists, 12 August 1930.

L.G. Minov, who had commanded the world's first parachute airdrop (on the left) and the Commander of the second group of paratroopers Ya.D. Moshkovskiy.

Since Voronezh was only a short distance away the *Goliath* would return quickly. The second group, which was led by D.Ya. Moshkovskiy was in place just 25 minutes after the first. This second group was landed some 750m further on. Three I-3 fighters from the 15th Squadron provided air cover for the descent from a nominal enemy.

The paratroops did not see any further nominal action. They were taken back to the airfield by truck. This was merely a proof of concept – dropping combatants onto an unprepared site behind enemy lines. It turned out that this was possible even on limited funds. The descent near Klochkovo farmstead was the first of its kind in the world. The parachute had gone from being a lifesaving invention, to a means of conducting a military manoeuvre that had never been seen before, delivering forces behind enemy lines to carry out a surprise attack. This opened up a whole series of new possibilities for the Red Army, which they wanted to realise as soon as possible.

In other countries the first airborne assaults were carried out approximately a year later. In 1931 the French dropped a reconnaissance sub-division behind nominal enemy lines during the course of exercises. In northern Italy later that same year, some 30 mountain riflemen were dropped by parachute along with their weapons (including machine guns), ammunition, and demolition supplies.

L.G. Minov, the organiser of the world's first airborne assault, continued his 'tours' around aviation units, training all the new paratroopers. In 1933 he went to work at *Osoaviakhim*, where he was engaged in the development of gliding, and of parachuting as a sport. In 1934 he became the first person in the Soviet Union to be awarded the title of Master of the sport of parachuting. In 1940 Minov was arrested on a false allegation and spent the next seven years in a camp, and another seven in exile. On his return to Moscow he was rehabilitated, and quickly became the Chairman of the Federation for Aerial Sports in the USSR.

4

What does a Paratrooper Require?

In order to achieve real combat capability in an airborne assault, a series of issues needed to be resolved in the first instance. The troops themselves had to be transported to the required location by air, for which aircraft were needed that had a large carrying capacity, and which were able to accommodate a large number of passengers. They then needed to be able to descend from the air down to the ground, on parachutes, or by some other means. Furthermore, the paratroopers needed a special flying suit, which was warm, windproof, and comfortable both in flight, and in the course of a jump (aircraft at that time were not heated, and it was by no means warm at altitude). Aviation at that time was not capable of transporting large numbers of people, so quality had to compensate for quantity: in terms of excellent training for crews, and fire power. The combatants and their commanders had to be selected carefully (based on medical parameters – not everyone was able to fly, based on the stage of development they found themselves in, and their level of training) and they had to pass a special training course. The firepower was provided by equipping the troops with automatic weapons, and subsequently by a variety of innovations in the art of war. Paratroops were able to carry a light weapon (right up to a light machine gun) with them, while it was planned to drop the rest in special bags fitted with cargo parachutes. Detachments would be supplied behind enemy lines with ammunition, medical supplies, and provisions in the very same way.

The effectiveness of military action by airborne troops was enhanced through mobility. That is to say the troops needed different forms of transport that would be dropped by air (the optimum variant would be to drop these without having to land the aircraft first). If vehicles were armed, and were fitted with armour to boot, then the strike capabilities of the airborne troops would increase by orders of magnitude. The vehicles however required fuel, and oil, which also had to be transported by air and dropped.

It was planned to supply the detachments that had already landed with a variety of communications systems, which would allow them to communicate with each other, and with aircraft that were ensuring that everything the paratroops needed was dropped by air. The communications systems would also allow paratroops to communicate with the upper leadership beyond the front line.

In the end the military theorists had to solve the question of how to use the new possibilities that had been laid before them rationally. They had to work out the tactics for an airborne assault, write new statutes, and prepare plans for future operations with the 'airborne infantry', which would subsequently be supported by armoured vehicles.

Let us now look at how the designers, and the military solved these challenges.

5

Concepts of Deployment

The first thing to do was to define clearly how the paratroopers were to act in a theatre of war. When all is said and done the development of special outfit, armament, and equipment would stem from the challenges that arose from missions put before the paratroops themselves.

By the spring of 1932 military theorists had already developed these scenarios and drawn up the 'airborne infantry's' tactics. The airborne assaults were divided into strategic (with a drop range of approximately 200km from the front line), operational (with a drop range of up to 100km) and tactical (with a drop range of less than 80km) troops. The latter were considered a secondary, and would rarely be carried out, and only as an exception rather than a rule. The airborne forces deployments were classed as paradropping, landing, and mixed in accordance with their method of landing. After the aviabuses appeared, another distinction was made for low-altitude airdrops from altitudes close to the ground without parachutes. The paradropping were considered the safest for the aviation units used, but there were limits on the numbers of troops and equipment, as well as on the equipment types used. The same aircraft would be capable of carrying approximately a quarter more soldiers without parachutes, and no special training was required for personnel in this case either. As a whole the UVVS envisaged that losses from airborne drops would be greater than those resulting from bombing operations.

Another division of airborne forces was in place, which saw them divided according to the missions they would undertake. First and foremost, they were entrusted with sabotage operations behind enemy lines. Paratroopers were to blow up bridges, tunnels, stores, oil storage depots, power stations, dams, artillery, and aircraft factories, and to disrupt railway operations, set up ambushes along roads, and put aircraft on airfields out of action. It was also envisaged that paratroops would damage communications lines (telephone and telegraph systems) and intercept communications. With this in mind they would carry special tools. The telegraph however could be used in a different way, to spread disinformation, for which it was proposed paratroops would carry telegraph set with them.

Evidently the intention was that they would disrupt any mobilisation on the part of hostile forces around enemy territory, whilst attacking the assembly points. One of the documents produced by the UVVS categorised this as "wreaking havoc behind enemy lines". Elsewhere it makes reference to "spreading panic among the enemy populace".

A great deal of attention was paid to military action by airborne troops against airfields. Different variants of these operations were developed. For example, taking over airfields with the intention of hijacking the aircraft on them. Naturally this would require pilots, who moreover were familiar with the specifics of enemy aircraft to form part of the detachment. A different scenario envisaged creating panic on an airfield, so that enemy aircrew would take to the skies in their own aircraft, where Soviet fighters would wait for them. This was known as 'forcing an air battle'. If a raid is well organised in this given scenario however there would never be an air battle at all, Soviet aircraft would just open fire at 'sitting ducks', since aircraft on take-off are very vulnerable.

The number of paratroopers would depend on the mission. A sabotage group could be deployed using a single aircraft. It was proposed that the group would be dropped by parachute in a 'recess' some 20–30km from the target. Some two to three days ahead of the main group three to five reconnaissance personnel would be deployed. They could either act independently or liaise with Soviet intelligence agents active in the area.

Information concerning targets and missions for a specific operation would be relayed to the commanders. It was forbidden for them to carry any of the documents they had been given with them, except for maps: they had to memorise the principal information. The paratroopers were only to be relayed this information once they had reached the airfields, and only then in general terms. They were to select only those targets for these operations, which they could destroy quickly.

After the detachment's main group had landed, they would proceed to the sabotage location at the double. In order to confuse any enemy forces following them it was recommended to the paratroopers that they liaise with the local population, asking directions ... to another location.

They had to proceed in a dogleg pattern, sending forward diversion groups to simulate the advance of the main detachment. When camping by night in a settlement the commander had to take some of the local population hostage advising that their hostages would be shot if attacked, or if runners were sent to the pursuing enemy forces. It was forbidden for them to spend the night in domestic houses. The justification for this rule stated that the fear of the local houses being robbed by Red Army soldiers (was "unacceptable").

After their march to the target the paratroopers were to wait, in order to attack under cover of darkness, or at dawn.

Aside from explosives, the saboteurs were able to use incendiary devices and chemical weapons. The list of potential missions for these troops included "creating chemical trails in the path of an enemy advance, or retreat". Sabotage could also be achieved using special tools for dismantling railway tracks, taking out gun emplacements, cutting down telegraph poles, and cutting cables.

After the mission had been completed (and it was normally quick) the airborne troops that had been engaged in sabotage could be evacuated by sea, or by air, or remain behind enemy lines, after forming part of a new sabotage detachment. In the majority of cases it was envisaged that personnel would be evacuated on several large aircraft deployed specially for this purpose. With this in mind it was necessary first of all to find a suitable landing site. Evacuation was considered the most dangerous part of the entire plan.

The second group would include objectives that would be fulfilled jointly with the Army and the Navy. For example, supporting raids using horses, and mechanised units. In 1933, the Revolutionary Military Council (RVS) of the USSR issued an order to develop plans for paratroopers, motorised and mechanised units, and cavalry to work together. Paratroopers could capture and hold bridges and river crossings, as well as road junctions until the Red Army's main detachment reached them. The capture or destruction of coastal batteries and the capture of beachheads for an amphibious assault was envisaged in this plan. In such situations the paratroopers would join forces with Red Army units and would then pull back behind the lines to prepare to carry out the mission they had been set.

The paratroopers however were also entrusted with organising an uprising behind enemy lines. This came under the category of "special political objectives". It was thought that it would be worthwhile for the Red Army to engage in a war with a nation state, so that the local workers and peasants would be caught up with the fight. Partisan detachments would appear, as well an underground resistance movement and it is possible that some of the military units would side with the protesters. The Head of the RKKA VVS Ya.I. Alksnis wrote in May 1933: "Only the Red Army, and the USSR alone are able to seize the opportunity that has presented itself with the advent of airborne paratroopers, with both hands. The USSR has likely enemies within, but in countries that are being torn apart by a bitter class war, how many more devoted allies do our enemies have?"

These enormous number of soldiers however had to be supplied with armament, and ammunition, and they also had to be augmented with qualified specialists – explosives experts, machine-gunners, snipers, as well as trained commanders, that are able to deploy them "wherever they are needed". Combatants from the airborne troop detachments needed to play a part in these functions. The documents state: "The paratroopers once they have landed should act as a yoke for the consolidation of revolutionary forces in a given region".

The concept of a raiding airborne force – one that is mobile – also appeared. This force would be larger in number and would use various means of deployment. This being the case the method of deployment, whether it was using parachutes or by landed deployment was made possible by various forms of transport: bicycles, motorcycles, cars, and even light armoured vehicles. Up to 50–60 vehicles could be used (which included cars, pickups, and one and a half tonne trucks). It would also be possible to capture different forms of transport (including railway one) in the local area. The possibility that the combatants would capture large numbers of trophy horses was also taken into consideration. Fuel and oil would be delivered for the vehicles partly by air and would partly be obtained locally. The same was true of provisions. The paratroopers would be issued with sufficient rations for three days and no more. They could then be dropped by air, with their hot food in thermos flasks, but this was considered an unnecessary luxury. The paratroopers were allowed to obtain food from the local population, but this would be in exchange for money. This money would be issued specially to the commanders. It was true though that no indication was given as to whether the commanders were to be given Soviet roubles, or foreign currency (or gold): they were at the end of the day about to operate within the territory of a foreign country.

The raiding paratroopers differed from sabotage troops in terms of their impressive fire power. They had to traverse a distance of up to 50–100km behind enemy lines, inflicting damage in various forms on the enemy. Specifically, this could take the form of a chain of sabotage activity, and moreover small groups could break away from the main column, leading them away from the route taken by the main group of raiding paratroopers. The motorcyclists would also carry out reconnaissance, as well as guarding the column whilst it was on the move, carrying out flanking manoeuvres, attacking the enemy from the flanks, or from behind the lines, and they would also act as a rear guard during the course of a withdrawal.

During an operation the paratroopers would be augmented by Red Army soldiers, who had been liberated from their captivity as prisoners of war. Subsequently when the element of surprise has died down, the equipment would either have been destroyed, or taken out of action, and the troops remaining in the formation (it was envisaged that losses would be significant) would have pulled back one way or another, either that or the combatants would attempt to break through the front line. Wherever possible the airborne troops, as in the previous example, would be transformed into a partisan detachment.

For some reason it was thought that airborne operations would be very short – no more than one and a half to two days, of which three to four hours would be taken up by the deployment, and occupying a given area.

The idea of a 'counter assault force' seemed very original. The enemy would land airborne troops in a location, where Soviet forces were either absent, or were thin on the ground. In response the Red Army would push their airborne troops closer to eliminate the enemy forces. It was true that these interesting ideas were first described at a time when only the USSR had airborne forces, and the forces that were to hand were in the early stages of development.

To begin with all these concepts were drawn up with small detachments in mind, consisting of up to 100–200 men. It was from this line up that the first airborne detachments were formed. For the most part this was considered a realistic assessment of the possibilities of deploying people and equipment by air. The twin-engine TB-1 was able to carry ten people, and the four-engine TB-3 could carry up to 30. That is to say 20 TB-1s, or seven TB-3s would be needed to carry 200 paratroopers. These paratroopers however required additional cargo, and additional aircraft would be needed to deliver this equipment.

It would take no more than 30 minutes to deploy a group of this size, and a paratrooper would need to be ready to fight 5–10 minutes after landing.

Heavy aircraft were steadily becoming more common in Soviet aviation, and some of them were specially equipped for carrying paratroopers and their equipment. As the VVS capabilities grew the scope of the operations that airborne forces were able to undertake also increased.

At the beginning of 1933 an order came through from the Head of the VVS Ya.I. Alksnis, which stated: "The RVS of the USSR attaches a great deal of importance to the widespread development of the airborne forces. Paratroopers would play a huge part in a future revolutionary and class war, in which the RKKA would participate".

In the various headquarters work got underway on developing large-scale airborne operations with large numbers of aircraft being drafted in, as well as whole divisions of paratroopers, and air mobile units – in other words an army transported by air.

Before a large-scale assault could happen however reconnaissance paratroopers would be dropped, who were responsible for destroying communications, as well as the enemy's command and control capabilities. This would be followed by a large-scale airborne assault. Paratroopers could be armed not only with rifles, and hand grenades, but also heavy machine guns, cannons, and light tanks.

An airborne assault however (known as a 'support echelon') was envisaged only as the first phase of an operation. A landed assault should follow an airborne one. The first wave of parachutists would need to secure a suitable site. The aircraft for the landed assault would use this site, which would be guarded by the parachutists, to land. These landed assault troops would carry infantry, heavy armament, and armoured vehicles. Attachment systems, and cargo platforms were designed and manufactured to transport the military hardware. They would be carried between the undercarriage legs on the TB-1, and TB-3 bombers.

It would also be possible to develop a variant for the first wave using aviabuses or assault gliders, as well as an alternative operation consisting of three stages. In the latter case the first wave would also consist of airborne troops. The aim of this was to occupy a defensive position around the chosen site, and receive the second wave as it came in, which would arrive in the aviabuses. This wave would deliver heavier armament, as well as sapper detachments with saws, axes, and spades. The sappers would build an airfield on which the third wave would land.

The plan developed by the military theorists in the RKKA VVS following the rejection of the use of aviabuses became a two-stage one: a parachute assault, then a landed assault. This tactic would remain the principal one right up until the beginning of the 1940s.

Interestingly, Anglo-American forces acted in almost the same way in the assault in the jungles of Burma at the end of the Second World War. It was just that they replaced the aviabuses with gliders. The paratroopers prepared a site for the assault gliders to land, and in turn, these delivered an air-mobile airfield construction company. Bulldozers the size of a writing desk, as well as other compact equipment were extracted from the gliders, which would immediately set to work. Four days later an airfield was ready that was able to accept twin-engine C-47 aircraft. They would deploy the overwhelming majority of forces, artillery, mortars, jeeps, and mules, which were able to access areas where a car would be vulnerable in off-road conditions.

6

Parachutes

As the reader would have already realised, the parachute was considered the principal means of delivering the assault from the very beginning. What though was the situation regarding parachutes in the Soviet Union at the time?

A Balloon factory in Moscow had been manufacturing parachutes in small numbers since 1915 for balloonists, who had been taking to the skies in tethered balloons. Indigenous parachutes were manufactured in this factory that were designed by G.E. Kotelnikov. The canopy on this parachute could be packed away into a pannier made from tin that could be worn as a knapsack, and which had a spring-loaded lid; another spring located under a plate underneath helped to launch the parachute material into the air. The circular canopy was sewn from silk. This design, which was later designated the RK-1, was the world's first knapsack style parachute. In the application for a patent dated 27 October 1911 the inventor named it "An emergency knapsack for aviators, with a parachute that deploys automatically".

Kotelnikov was not an engineer, he served as a clerk, and subsequently worked as an actor in the theatre. He manufactured the first two prototype examples of the parachute using money from the V.A. Lomach company. On 6 June 1912 he dropped a mannequin successfully using one of these parachutes near the village of Salyuzi (now Kotelnikovo) just outside Gatchina. The parachute design was put forward to the Russian War Department but was rejected. In December of that same year a similar attempt was made in France, but again without success although a student V. Ossovskiy there did complete a demonstration jump using this parachute. Only in the course of the First World War did the Russian War Department order RK-1 parachutes and following this around 70 pieces were manufactured.

In 1917 French *Jucmes* parachutes began to be imported into Russia. The cotton and silk canopy folded into bags, which would be attached to the side of the cradle slung under a balloon. From July French parachutes began to be manufactured in workshops belonging to an aeronautical battalion of the South-Western Front, at the *Treugolnik* factory, and in the balloon workshop. Up until November 1917 when production stopped during the October Revolution, some 400 had been manufactured.

Both types of parachutes were considered reasonably uncomfortable to use and were not sufficiently reliable. Balloonists would only use them rarely, and pilots would never use them. This position remained the same even after the establishment of Soviet power. From September 1921 following the death in August of a student of the Higher School of Aeronautics Molchanov in a training jump using a *Jucmes* parachute when his straps broke, the use of parachutes in Russia was no longer practised. It was discovered that the silk and cotton canopy and the straps would decompose; the silk parachutes designed by Kotelnikov were in better condition, but there was still a fear of using them.

In 1923 a small batch of *Heinecke* knapsack parachutes were acquired in Germany. Officers in the *Reichswehr* were trained in using these parachutes. In Moscow the instructor was *Oberleutnant* W. Tribner, who had trained some 40 men. They carried out training jumps from a balloon, and form an old Sopwith aircraft. At an air show Tribner himself jumped out of a Ju-13 aircraft. In a newspaper report he was, rightly, named as "German pilot Trepler". The *Heinecke* parachute was tested at a Scientific-Test Airfield. It was there that a conclusion was reached that the landing speed of this parachute was very high. No more German parachutes were purchased.

The designer of the world's first knapsack parachute, G.E. Kotelnikov.

In this period G.E. Kotelnikov continued his innovative work. His RK-2 model only distinguishable by virtue of its semi rigid knapsack: the back plate and the soft vents. In summer 1923 six examples of the RK-2 were manufactured. On three of these parachutes the canopies were manufactured from silk, two were manufactured from *madapolam*, and one was manufactured from *calico*. Thus the designer wanted to see whether it would be possible to replace expensive silk with a cheaper material. The best results though were obtained from the silk parachutes.

In 1924 the RK-3 appeared with a completely soft knapsack. In the first variant, which was known as the *Prozlyot* the knapsack was sewn into the back of the flying suit. The second had a standard knapsack. Kotelnikov complained about the lack of money, the lack of quality in the finish, and the fact that testing was protracted. Neither the RK-2, or the RK-3 however were of interest to Red Army Command and did not enter series production.

Only in 1926 did parachutes come back into favour in the USSR. Examples of parachutes were purchased in Great Britain, Germany, Italy, France, and the USA, as well as in Japan, and were tested at the NII VVS, where a special parachute section was created, which would later become a division. Japanese parachutes were considered to be of the best quality for their silk and the accuracy with which they were sewn together. The most interesting example was the parachute produced by the Irvin company, which was actually accepted as a sample. The founder of this company, the American pilot L. Irvin designed several very successful parachutes such as these, which could be packed into a soft knapsack. These parachutes used a small rip cord to deploy the main canopy. The Irvin was not cheap, around 1,000 roubles and something, or around twice as expensive as the German example.

The Irvin parachutes began to be issued to test pilots at the Scientific-test airfield. On 23 June 1927 the famous pilot M.M Gromov took off in the new I-1 monoplane fighter designed by N.N. Polikarpov. The aircraft entered a spin, and the pilot was not able to pull the aircraft out of the spin and had to bail out. Gromov landed back on the airfield safely using his Irvin canopy. The Irvin company later sent him a badge in the shape of a golden caterpillar, this was later issued to all pilots who had used these parachutes successfully. Interestingly the pilot did not want to take the parachute with him, but he was ordered to. It was unusual it was true, and uncomfortable

G.E. Kotelnikov and a mannequin, which was used to test the knapsack parachute.

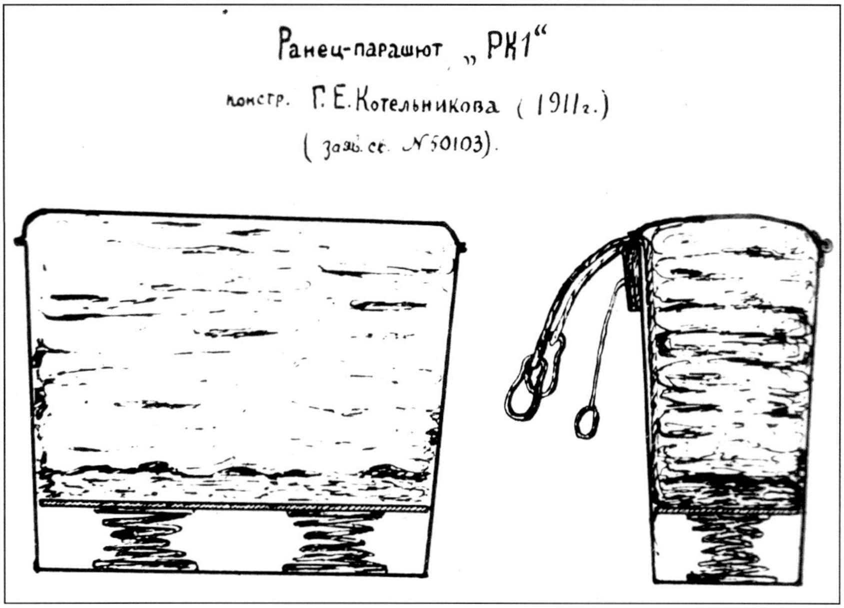

The RK-1 knapsack parachute designed by G.E. Kotelnikov.

to sit on since the cockpit of a fighter was not designed to accommodate a knapsack. Nevertheless. this overseas innovation had proved its worth.

In October 1927 the Scientific and Technical Committee under the UVVS agreed with the State Rubber Association *Rezinotrest* to copy the American parachute for Soviet pilots. The *Kauchuk* factory (which was the former Balloon plant) was to manufacture two prototype examples. This work was led by engineer Fomin. He was given an Irvin parachute that had been purchased with foreign currency, which was unstitched completely. In order to define the required strength samples were cut from the canopy, and from the straps, which were strength tested for tearing. It was envisaged that everything would be developed from analogous Soviet materials.

The work at the *Kauchuk* factory muddled along. The factory management was under pressure to complete a production plan related to the factory's core products (balloons) and parachutes were as useful for the factory plan as a hole in the head. Fomin subsequently refused to undertake any further work on the Irvin. The leadership handed this project over to the NII VVS; and VVS Academy graduate M.A. Savitskiy, who at the time held the position of Head of the Parachute division was assigned to it. In accordance with the order that had come through from the Scientific-Technical Committee of the UVVS dated 2 November 1928 the finished parachute was to be handed over by March 1929, but March was subsequently amended to June.

By December 1928 some of the details had been changed. It emerged however that the Irvin that had previously been received had been dismantled to such a degree that nobody remembered how to put it all together. Another

Leslie Irvin with one of the parachutes he designed.

Parachute designer M.A. Savitskiy.

American parachute was sent from the NII VVS. Delays however followed delays. The original deadline of 8 June 1929 was missed. The canopies that had been sewn together were unpicked and sewn back together again. On 27 June the factory handed over two parachutes, designated NII-1s. Representatives from the NII VVS condemned them as defective; the knapsacks had been cut wrongly, the webbing around the edges it turned out was not sufficiently dense, and traces were discovered that indicated where the panels had been adjusted. By the end of June however the first jump had been completed in an NII-1. This parachute was far from an Irvin in terms of quality. After having only fulfilled the requirements of the agreement with great difficulty the *Rezinotrest* refused to carry out any further work on parachutes.

In accordance with the Scientific-Technical Commission's five-year plan in July 1929 it was proposed that two types of pilot's parachutes would be manufactured in the USSR, one parachute for the flight observer, as well as two 'rocket-powered chutes for night reconnaissance' (evidently this would be something akin to a parafoil with a rocket engine). There was no mention of airborne assaults. In practice, however, everything turned out slightly differently.

On 13 January 1930 in New York a license agreement was signed with Irvin. The Soviet side was represented by *Amtorg,* which at that time performed the functions of a trade representation. The point being that diplomatic relations did not exist back then between the USSR and the USA, but equipment was purchased. For this purpose, the *Amtorg* organisation was set up in America, which was treated as a local company, but which was owned by the Soviet government. The real customer however was *Aviatrest,* which was not hidden from the Americans. The agreement envisaged a license for five different types of parachute, including one cargo parachute, as well as support to set up production for up to 1,000 parachutes per annum. In order to train Soviet workers, the Americans were to deliver 50 parachutes in kit form so that they could be manufactured in the USSR. The agreement allowed the

R-5 biplane crews preparing for a sortie. On the left is the pilot, his PL-1 parachute is hanging behind him on its straps, on the right is the flight observer wearing a pack with PN-1 parachute on his chest. Both parachutes are Soviet copies of an Irvin.

Soviet Union to sell copies of the Irvin to Iran, Afghanistan, and Mongolia. The acquisition of 1,650 parachutes, the majority of which would be for VVS personnel, was also envisaged in the agreement. Shipping was due to begin on 1 January 1931 and conclude on 1 April 1932.

Kotelnikov spoke out strongly against the assimilation of Irvin production, as he considered that production of his RK-3 had more to offer. He was especially displeased with the deployment of the auxiliary chute, which in his view appeared unsafe. In an article published in 1936 Kotelnikov, capturing the *zeitgeist,* even wrote that "Saboteurs who had already been identified" had selected the American parachute. His opinion however was ignored higher up the chain.

Whilst he was spending the summer of 1930 on a work placement in the USA, Savitskiy arranged a small workshop on the Arsentyev Pereulok in Moscow. To begin with only eight people worked here. Since the documentation from Irvin's had still not arrived, the workshop began by manufacturing some further examples of the NII-1. Some sources indicate that in 1930 three of these parachutes were manufactured. Later the workshop manufactured Irvins from the imported parachutes delivered in kit form, the first batch consisted of three pieces.

In order to manufacture the American parachutes a special enterprise – Factory No. 1 of the Moscow Textile and Sewing Union under the People's Commissariat for Light industry was set up on the basis of the old workshop. This was led by the same individual M.A. Savitskiy. Introduction of the Irvin into production did not go smoothly. There was a shortage of silk, from which the canopies were sewn at that time, and indigenous thread was not as dense, or as strong as the imported material. Large silk panels and the cords for the straps were manufactured by *Sholkotrest*. Experiments were carried out with cords made from linen. The cutting and sewing technique was largely assimilated on the job through trial and error, although engineers were sent on work placements abroad. The rip cords, and the metal tubes that they went in were imported, and 250 kits were purchased of these. The rest

A paratrooper in full kit for a training jump: he is wearing a PT-1 parachute.

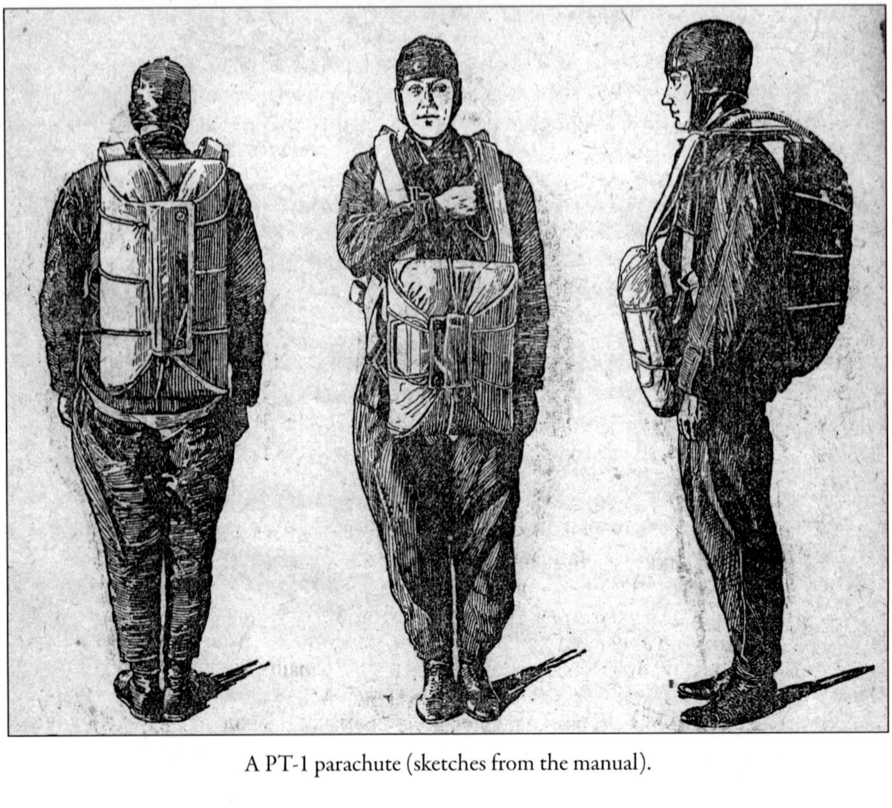

A PT-1 parachute (sketches from the manual).

Test parachutist G.M. Ivanov pictured with a PD-1 parachute.

P.I. Grokhovskiy with one of the parachutes he designed. The original caption states that this is a G-1, but it is more likely to be a G-4 parachute.

A group of employees of the OPKB VVS after a group jump using cotton parachutes, in the front seat of the pickup is P.I. Grokhovskiy.

of the metal components were manufactured by Factory No.33. Production steadily got underway of parachutes for pilots, both combat and training chutes.

The Irvin company model was taken as the basis of these parachutes. They had identical circular canopies, but differed in terms of shape, and where the actual knapsack was positioned. The PL-1 was intended for the pilot and was packed inside a recess in the pilot's seat. The PN-1 was worn on the chest, and they were intended for use by flight-observers. The third type that was put into production was a training (PT-1) parachute. This was worn

Parachutes were first tested using mannequins and sandbags. In this photograph a mannequin is being dropped from an R-Z aircraft, September 1937.

on the back, and had a reserve canopy, which would deploy in the event that the first one became entangled with a strap for example. In this instance the main chute would not detach.

In accordance with an order issued by the Council of People's Commissars dated 15 June 1931 it was envisaged that 10,000 of these nominal parachutes would be produced in 1932, and that production would be increased up to 2,000 parachutes per month by the end of the year. The term 'nominal' is used because the amount of work differed for each parachute. The parachutes for pilots and flight observers were accepted one at a time, the small cargo parachutes were handed over when half of the number had been manufactured, and in the case of the larger parachutes for dropping military hardware the coefficient would increase to five. In 1933 the production was to double, and to triple in 1934. Moreover, there was clearly no regard for the conditions of the licensing agreement.

Thus the task that had been assigned to supply the VVS with parachutes was solved. The *Air Fleet Herald* magazine wrote in 1933: "The USSR's Air Fleet has been fully supplied with indigenously manufactured parachutes". Moving forward foreign parachutes were only purchased as one off examples in order to study them.

The paratroopers however needed a completely different kind of parachute than those used by pilots. A paratrooper had to be ready to go into battle whilst still in the air, that is to say he had to jump with all his armament, and ammunition. A group of parachutists may operate independently for several days, and paratroopers needed provisions, medicines, and entrenchment tools for field fortifications. From this it is possible to conclude that a parachute designed for an airborne assault would need to be designed to carry more weight, taking into account all the equipment. One of the requirements was the accuracy of the landing. A paratrooper not only needs to control the parachute but also to ensure a good degree of grouping for the company of paratroopers on landing. At the same time the parachute needs to be as cheap as possible, since it is most likely to be dropped behind enemy lines. In 1932 an order was issued to reduce the cost of an assault parachute by up to 200 roubles.

This was possible by replacing the expensive silk with some other material. In 1930 on the initiative of P.I. Grokhovskiy examples of parachutes were manufactured from a cotton and silk material, and from percale, and nainsook. He though was not a pioneer in this respect. Up until the revolution in the Balloon factory experiments had been carried out with percale, which was a canvass used for aircraft skins. The reader may recall that the *Jucmes*

A parachutist with a PD-6 parachute.

A parachutist with a PD-10 parachute.

parachutes were manufactured from a cotton and silk material. G.E. Kotelnikov also trod a similar path with his RK-2.

The canopy for Grokhovskiy's parachute, which was worn on the back was deployed manually, using a rip cord that was attached to the launch aircraft. The new parachutes were not so strong as silk parachutes, they would be packed away in storage and tended to rot. The straps for these parachutes were actually manufactured from washing lines. Therefore, the materials were very cheap.

The experiments began by dropping two sandbags (weighing 100kg each) on parachutes made from percale in the presence of the Head of the NII VVS V.S. Gorshkov.

On 11 January 1930 Grokhovskiy's parachutes were examined by the People's Commissariat for Military and Naval Affairs K.E. Voroshilov. In summer of that same year mannequins were dropped using these parachutes from a TB-1 bomber on the Central Airfield in Moscow: they all landed successfully. In comparative tests six mannequins landed successfully using Grokhovskiy's parachutes (three of these were manufactured from percale, and another three from nainsook), and one of the Irvins actually failed to deploy. Grokhovskiy himself jumped on more than one occasion using his own parachute.

State testing however, which took place in July and August 1930, ended with an assessment of 'unsatisfactory'. The parachutes made from the replacement materials had few problems. Due to their more porous structure however materials such as these were more permeable to air. The canopy had to be made much bigger than a silk canopy. It would deploy more slowly and was heavier. Given an equal diameter the speed of descent for a parachute made from percale or nainsook was higher, than for a silk parachute. Correspondingly the parachute hit the ground harder. Parachutes manufactured from cotton and silk material could not be package stored, even if they were inlaid with talcum powder. The strength of these parachutes fell far short of expectations. In August 1931 all the parachutes that Grokhovskiy had brought were torn in the course of two days of testing. The only

Paratrooper and instructor K.F. Kaytanov speaks at a meeting in Moscow on 12 August 1935. A few months previous to this photograph he had been awarded the Order of Lenin for his achievements.

comfort was that when parachutes manufactured using substitute materials were used, the impact became more forgiving, and the stability improved somewhat.

A prototype G-40 assault parachute was manufactured in 1931 (the parachute received the same designation as a later cargo chute, and this was commonplace for Grokhovskiy's designs), which was sewn from nainsook, and had a diameter of 8.2m, and weighed 10kg. This parachute did not have a normal strap system and could only be used in conjunction with a G-55 flying suit with shoulder straps sewn into the suit. Factory No. 1 manufactured a batch of these parachutes. The canopy it turned out was heavy and cumbersome. In order to save weight Grokhovskiy cut back on the canopy area, and in doing so consciously increased the rate of descent.

Testing of another variant the G-5 in November–December 1931 also ended with an assessment of 'unsatisfactory'. It was designed to be packed into underwing cradles, which will be described later on. Nevertheless M.N. Tukhachevskiy's G-5 was put into production in December 1931 but was later withdrawn.

Even in series production the parachutes that were manufactured from other materials were not cheap to produce. The material itself was cheap, but more of it was needed than for silk parachutes. The deployment became more complicated because of the larger area and the total length of the rip cords, and the straps became longer. A parachute made from nainsook and with cotton and silk straps cost 731 roubles, and with silk straps the price went up to 1,109 roubles. A Soviet silk copy of an Irvin was light, strong, and reliable, and cost 934 roubles (an original would cost approximately the same, but in gold). Moreover, an Irvin allowed for the harness system, while Grokhovskiy's did not need to take it into account, since Grokhovskiy's parachutes had the harness sewn into a paratrooper's flying suit (in the case of the G-55), which was considered separately.

In the end a compromise was reached. From 1931 work began on production of the PD-1 assault parachute, and by the end of the year some 70 of these had been manufactured. In terms of the design this was an Irvin parachute that was worn on the back and which was made from silk (in terms of the peripheral wedges), and

Commander paratrooper folding down a parachute (a sketch of 1937).

partly from percale (from which all the rest was made); the straps were made from a silk and cotton material. The parachute had a PZ reserve chute. The PD-1 was officially accepted into production in 1932.

This type of parachute soon became the main product manufactured at Factory No.1, far more of these parachutes were manufactured than any others. By that time the enterprise had moved to Tushino, occupying the site of a former cotton printing mill.

Grokhovskiy though continued to experiment, not only changing traditional materials but also the established designs. The PTP (G-44) Accurate Landing Parachute had twin canopies. A smaller canopy 2m in diameter would open first, followed by a second that was larger (with a diameter of 7.6m). Grokhovskiy called this a 'stepped' system. The time taken for a paratrooper to make a descent was reduced, but the grouping of a detachment on landing was enhanced. The parachute passed state testing in July 1935 and was recommended for combat testing but did not enter series production.

The G-58 'gyroscopic' parachute appeared very original, it was cut from wedges of material and was spun as it fell in a similar way to an auto-rotating helicopter main rotor. The deployment of the parachute and the untwisting was achieved using a small propeller, which first had to be opened out. This device was proposed in 1931 but was never realised. Elliptical canopies were also tested. In 1935 a triangular parachute was tested, which would have enabled a paratrooper to glide for a long period of time.

Parachutes were not only created for people, but also for dogs, and even for horses. The 'canine' parachutes were actually manufactured, and tested, but as far as the parachutes that were designed for horses were concerned, this work was limited merely to estimates.

In 1932 an idea appeared of having two parachute types in military units: with dark canopies for the summer, and white canopies for winter. The motivation behind this was based on camouflage. This suggestion however was ignored, evidently, for economic reasons. An attempt to attach detachable insignia to the commander's canopies, which would have been visible from above never caught on either.

In 1933 the PD-1 was withdrawn from production and was replaced by the more modern PD-2. The latter was produced in 1936 when the PD-6 with an area of 60.3m^2 first appeared. In that same year a batch of several dozen PD-6s were sent to France for export. In October an instructor, Captain K.F. Kaytanov followed in their footsteps. He trained the first French military parachutists. Therefore the 'paras' have Russian roots ...

By this time parachute Factory No.1 had been transformed into a powerful manufacturing plant, for which new workshops were constructed. The enterprise had its own design bureau where F. Churikov, I. Mukhin, N. Lobanov, I. Glushkov, and F. Tkachev. The new examples were tested by professional test pilots, who had a whole aviation detachment at their disposal, consisting of U-2, UTI-4 (which is a two-seat I-16 aircraft), and later SB, and R-Z aircraft. The parachutes also suffered "teething troubles". Problems arose with canopies not inflating properly, parachutes becoming entangled with straps, and tears in the material.

In 1939 the PPD-1 'Doronin's parachute device' successfully underwent testing in the air and the parachute opened within the set time. The three Doronin brothers, Nikolai, Vladimir, and Anatoliy, who were students of the Moscow institutes made this device to enter an *Osoaviakhim* competition that was announced in October 1936. They used components in their design that were taken from a standard alarm clock. The device turned out to be splendidly reliable. In front of the commission after switching the device on, they hit it against a wall, twisted it for a while on a rope above their heads, and as a finale they drove a nail into it. Even after all that the PPD-1 deployed successfully. The outcome was the first prize of 10,000 roubles and the order of the Badge of Honour for the older brother, For Distinguished Labour medals for the other two. The device was put into production and began to be issued to parachutists.

In 1940 a new assault parachute, the PD-10 appeared (with an area of 72m^2), which was designed to carry a heavier load, and then a year later the PD-41 emerged (with an area of 69.5m^2). The latter did not have a standard round shape, but a square shape. In order to ensure the rate of descent was the same as for a round canopy, the area of this parachute would be reduced by ten percent. A square parachute was also more technologically advanced, easier to manufacture, and more economical to deploy. The first square canopy was designed by N.A. Lobanov and was tested in 1937 by N. Ostryakov.

The PD-10 and PD-41s parachutes were issued to airborne units at a period of time just prior to the start of the Great Patriotic War.

7

Clothing and Equipment

The designers also thought about clothing for the paratroopers. To begin with paratroopers would jump wearing ordinary flying suits, and helmets. A special suit later appeared, which was easier to produce, and cheaper.

Grokhovskiy proposed special boots with a sprung, or pneumatic sole. Similar footwear was tested successfully and N. Ostryakov who has already been mentioned above jumped in these boots. The military however refused to accept them into service. A soldier has to walk or run a great deal after landing and in the rather cumbersome boots that Grokhovskiy designed it is not as easy to do this as in more ordinary footwear. The special G-55 suit mentioned above, with the parachute harness system already sewn into the suit (the so-called 'combined suit and parachute bag') system was not introduced into service either.

In the spring of 1932 a special uniform was proposed for paratroopers, which could easily be transformed into civilian attire. Combatants could blend in with the local population wearing this suit. This idea however never got off the drawing board.

As the airborne troops remained part of the VVS the paratroopers were issued with a standard uniform worn by land-based forces, with the exception that instead of shoes they would often wear boots with leggings. In winter as with all Red Army soldiers/paratroopers would walk around in warm felt boots. They would carry out their jumps dressed either in their summer or winter suits as the season dictated (the winter ones were insulated with fur) and helmets. Paratroopers were also given a pair of protective goggles.

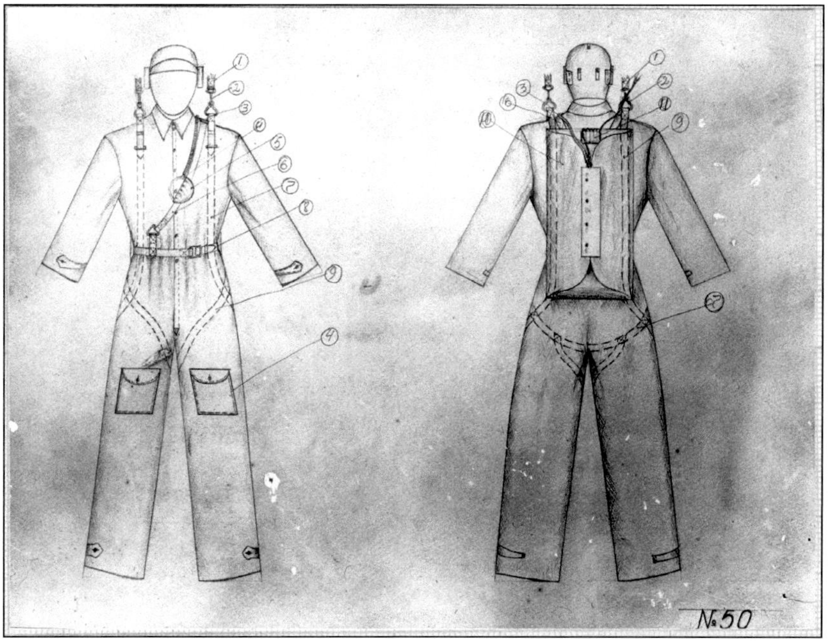

The G-55 suit designed for a G-40 parachute. The dotted lines show the straps for harness, which had been sewn into the suit.

In 1934 T.V. Dolbinin conducted research that was aimed at determining the suitability of boots, and shoes. He collected statistics on injuries among airborne troops and organised test parachute jumps in different footwear to provide a comparison. As a result, boots were given the lowest rating, with high boots coming in a close second. Dolbinin himself proposed special high boots sewn from strong canvass, and with a leather sole, toe cap, and heel. This footwear however did not catch on.

After the transfer of airborne brigades to the land forces the uniform remained almost the same, with blue tabs. The cut of these suits changed slightly (to simplify them), and apart from that almost nothing changed in terms of clothing right up until the outbreak of the Great Patriotic War. In place of boots paratroopers were issued with high boots: the commanders received leather ones, while the troops were given shoes with boot tops made from *kirsa* (a cheap leather substitute). In the second half of the 1930s both combatants and commanders began to wear forage caps (as per the entire RKKA) in place of their original woollen *Budyonovka* helmets.

P.I. Grokhovskiy proposed that several of the airborne troop detachments wear 'bulletproof cuirasses' – a prototype of the modern-day bulletproof vest. Examples of these were manufactured and tested in 1935 but the Red Army only began to use a similar protection in the course of the war with Germany.

8

A Paratrooper's Weapons

As the reader will recall, the comparatively low numbers of paratroopers it was proposed were to be partially compensated for in terms of fire power and excellent training for the personnel. A light, but sufficiently powerful weapon was required. Therefore, a decision was taken to significantly increase the numbers of light machine guns in the available armament. To begin with the parachutists were jumping very lightly armed: during the first assault near Klochkovo farmstead they were given a Nagant revolver each, and two grenades. The remainder was dropped in cargo bags, which were loaded with carbines, and light machine guns.

Later, a gamble was taken on the Mauser C96 German automatic pistol. This really was an excellent weapon, which would sometimes double up as a pistol-carabile. It was designed for precise fire at a distance of up to 200m and the butt of the gun, attached to the handle also served as a holster. In Russia in the First World War and the Civil War pistols were in circulation which were 1912-models with a barrel length of 140mm, and subsequently the 7.63mm *Bolo* model began to be imported from Germany for the RKKA VVS with a shortened barrel (99mm) and a magazine designed to hold ten rounds. A paratrooper was supposed to jump, armed with a Mauser and two grenades.

The Mauser however was only suitable for close range fire and for engaging the enemy immediately after the parachutist had landed. For subsequent operations a decision was taken to use a tried and tested combination of rifles, and light machine guns. The commanders retained the 1895 Nagant revolvers purely as an auxiliary weapon. This was a reliable weapon but required a great deal of effort to pull on the trigger and was slow to reload. From 1931 onwards, the commanders received 7.62mm TT 1930-model pistols in place of their revolvers, these weapons were designed for Mauser type rounds. The magazine was capable of holding eight rounds. In 1933 the pistol was modernised, and the result was the 1933-model TT.

The paratroopers would drop rifles in cargo bags. At the beginning of the 1930s the 7.62mm 1891 *Mosin* magazine rifle, which soldiers nicknamed the 'three-line rifle' was in service with the RKKA. This nickname came about due to the fact that the calibre of the barrel corresponded exactly to three lines (to tenths of an inch). This powerful weapon ensured a firing range of up to 2,000m. The customary Russian steel-cut bayonet would be attached to this rifle. The magazine could hold five rounds with the help of a casing. Of the three examples produced in Russia during the Tsarist period (the infantry, Cossack, and Dragoon variants) only one remained in the Soviet period, the Dragoon variant (the cavalry rifle). In 1930 a series of modifications were introduced into the design of the 'three-line rifle', after which it began to be manufactured as an 1891/30-model rifle. In the 1930s heavy bullets were added to the old bullets (which at that time were known as light bullets), these were long range bullets, which ensured a much greater degree of accuracy over a distance of more than 500m), and tracer bullets, as well as armour piercing, and armour piercing incendiary bullets. Some of these rifles were manufactured to a higher quality with a PT and VP optical sights, and from 1939 – with PU sight, as 1931 model sniper's rifles.

The 'three-line rifle' however was cumbersome and heavy. Parachutists therefore were often issued with 1907-model carbines, a shortened version of the rifle, which weighed half a kilogram less. A bayonet was not attached to a carbine rifle. A modified version of this weapon was the 1938-model carbine (which also did not have a bayonet).

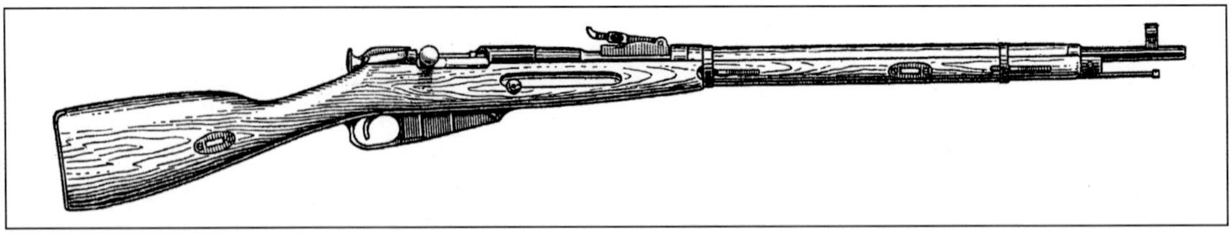

'Three-line rifle' – 7.62-mm 1891/30-model rifle. The nickname was linked to the fact that the calibre of the rifle was equal to three lines (tenth of an inch). This powerful weapon was distinguishable by its large sight range, but was also heavy and cumbersome. A variant of this gun was produced with an optical sight.

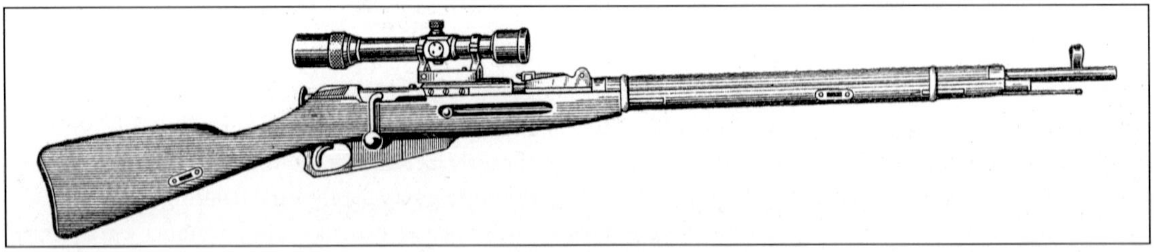

An 1931-model sniper's rifle with an optical sight.

The small numbers of paratroopers were to be balanced by an increase in the proportion of light machine guns. The 1927-model DP machine gun was also in service with the RKKA. This gun used the same rounds as the 'three-line rifle'. The feed was achieved from a large, flat disc that held 47 rounds; the disc rotated as the weapon was fired. The auxiliary discs were not only carried by machine-gunners, but also by other soldiers. The DP machine gun was characterised by its light weight, reliability, and technological simplicity. It was easy to dismantle and assemble, and was not afraid of dust, dirt, water, or snow. It was however not possible to fire long bursts from the DP, since the barrel would overheat. In accordance for the standards for 1936 an airborne brigade would be issued on 90 light machine guns. There was one in each section, and machine-gun platoons were to be included in the battalions. The proportion of DP was much less than in the rank and file rifle regiments: a light machine gun was issued to approximately every fifth, or if not every fourth soldier.

The 1910/30-model Maxim heavy machine guns of 7.62mm calibre were used in the first airborne units and were mounted on the standard Sokolov wheel carriages. These were water-cooled and were fed with rifle rounds using a web belt (that held 250 rounds) packed in boxes, but the water jacket made them very vulnerable. Their cumbersome nature, together with their weight made them very uncomfortable for parachutists (they weighed 66kg including the stand). The heavy machine guns were tranported ready assembled using a landing delivery, they were also delivered partly dismantled in parachute bags. Subsequently the Maxim became the sole preserve of paratroopers. Only one machine gun remained in the special purpose battalions – in the anti-aircraft section. This was either mounted on the universal wheeled/tripod carriage or on a special tripod and was fitted with an anti-aircraft sight. At the end of the decade, paired and quadruple anti-aircraft assemblies were introduced, including the ones mounted on GAZ-AA trucks.

Four grenade launchers are listed in the inventory of the weapons that an airborne detachment formed in 1931 had at its disposal. Evidently this referred to the so-called Dyakonov small mortar. These actually represented rifle grenade launchers that were based on the 'three-line rifle'. This weapon entered service with rifle regiments and was used effectively in operations against the *Basmachi* in Central Asia. The crew for the grenade launcher consisted of two men: one would aim and fire the weapon, the other would set the delay timer for the grenade to explode and would arm it.

In 1932 it was decided that the fire power for airborne detachments would be enhanced, and the pistols, and automatic rifles (submachine guns) in the various units were replaced. In 1931 some 500 examples of the Tokarev submachine gun was manufactured that used a 7.62mm round from a TT pistol. The Tokarev, which weighed approximately 3kg was capable of automatic fire with a rate of fire of up to 1,200 rounds per minute, or of firing

The People's Commissar for Heavy Industry G.K. Ordzhonikidze inspects a rifle that had been dropped using a parachute bag.

A 1927-model 7.62-mm DP light machine gun.

A 7.63-mm Mauser *Bolo* pistol.

A weapon set that a Soviet paratrooper would bring with him in the mid 1930s: a 1907-model carbine (shortened version of the 'three-line rifle') with two cartridge pouches, and two RGD-33 hand grenades with a tarpaulin bag that was designed for them.

An 1895-model 7.62-mm Nagant revolver, this was a personal weapon for the commanders.

individual shots. It was possible to fire accurately over a distance of up to 200m. The capacity of the magazine was 21 rounds. This weapon was issued to units for combat testing. In 1932 soldiers of the Separate Detachment No.3 also received this weapon, and this will be examined in more detail later. It would appear that a suitable weapon had been found for the paratroopers. It emerged relatively quickly however that this sort of gun was only good for close combat. The round from a TT was not considered powerful enough, and the rate of consumption of the ammunition, which was not easy to obtain behind the lines, was excessive. Therefore, the Tokarev submachine guns were not in service for very long. The airborne forces had to revert to their previous combination of 'three-line rifles' and DP light machine guns.

In 1933 a conclusion was reached that guns, right up to a light machine gun, had to be carried by the paratroopers themselves right from the start. They no longer simply jumped with rifles, and machine guns but began to fire them whilst in the air, as well as throwing hand grenades.

In 1936 it was decided that the majority of the combatants instead of their rifles, and carbines would be issued with "automatic guns" (this is how they are described in the document). In another document dated that same year there is a mention of automatic carbines. A similar weapon was developed in the USSR in the middle of the 1920s. It is possible that this referred to the Simonov AVS-36 automatic rifle that was introduced into service that year in the RKKA. The magazine could hold 15 rounds from a 'three-line rifle'. The AVS-36 could fire single shots accurately and was also capable of firing short bursts a distance of up to 1,500m. For hand to hand fighting a folding bayonet was proposed. Several airborne brigades were armed with these rifles up until the autumn of 1939. Their fire power was significantly enhanced with these weapons. However, in the course of the war with Finland in 1939/40 it emerged that in contrast to the 'three-line rifle', which was a traditionally hardy Russian weapon, the AVS-36 required constant careful maintenance, and adjustment. In severe frosts it would sometimes cease to fire completely.

In 1938 the self-loading Tokarev SVT-38 appeared, which was designed around this same standard round. This was more complicated and more expensive to produce but was more reliable in operation. This became the

A 1930-model TT pistol, which replaced the Nagant.

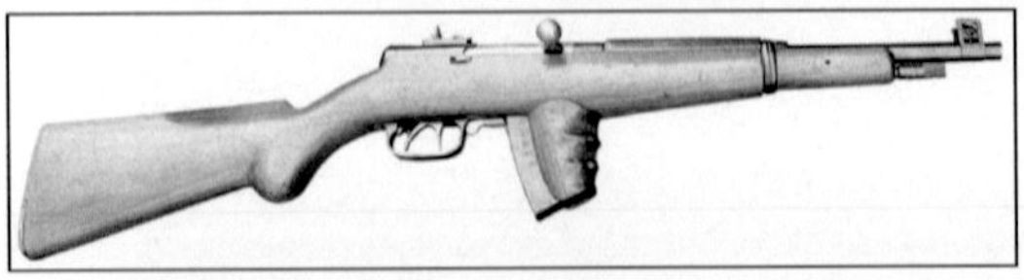

A 1932-model Tokarev submachine gun, this was issued in 1932 to some of the combatants serving in Special Purpose Detachment No. 3.

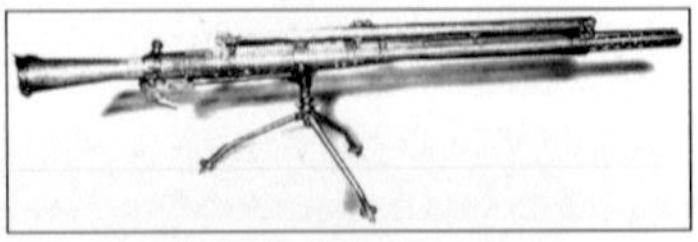

A 37-mm Kurchevskiy PTRK anti-tank gun designed in 1932.

A 1910/30-model Maxim heavy machine gun mounted on a Sokolov wheeled mount together with a box containing the fabric ammunition belt that was designed for it. In case of a landing delivery it would be transported in fully assembled form, and if it were dropped by parachute it would be semi-dismantled.

Maxim heavy machine gun mounted on a universal wheeled tripod mount in a position for firing at enemy aircraft. If installed on a special gun mount, it could be used as singular, paired, or quadruple units which were also in service with the airborne forces.

A crew in position with a mortar (rifle grenade launcher) designed by Dyakonov: the first crewman aims and fires, the second sets the charge in the grenade to the correct position and charges the mortar.

principal weapon for parachutists. Some of the SVT-38s were produced to a higher specification and were fitted with a PU optical sight for snipers. In 1940 production work began on the lighter SVT-40 rifles.

The 7.62mm PPD-40 submachine guns were introduced as standard weapons for paratroopers, which were designed around a pistol round, approximately a third of combatants would be issued with these weapons. The sighting range for the PPD-40s was exactly 500m, and 73 rounds were accommodated inside the disc magazine.

Chemical, and incendiary weapons were also envisaged for paratroopers – in terms of spraying equipment and even flame throwers worn in backpacks. The spraying equipment could be used in two ways: to spray poison agents, or for decontaminating equipment from toxic mixtures. In 1935 K.F. Kaytanov, and N.A. Yevdokimov jumped from two R-5 aircraft in gas masks, and a chemical protection suit, and two sets of spraying equipment were dropped from a third aircraft. The aim was to test the possibility of landing on a contaminated area and treat it. The flamethrowers were introduced into service with the paratroopers much later. In 1940 the ROK-2 appeared that weighed 23kg and could carry 10 liters of fuel mixture.

Grokhovskiy had proposed that paratroopers be issued with small recoilless guns, which could be fired from the shoulder. He called this weapon a "portable, hand-held recoilless assembly". An example of this weapon was manufactured and tested in 1935. In fact, this was a grenade launcher, which was produced much earlier than the German *Faustpatron* and *Panzerfaust*, and the American *Bazooka*. It was just that for Grokhovskiy's gun

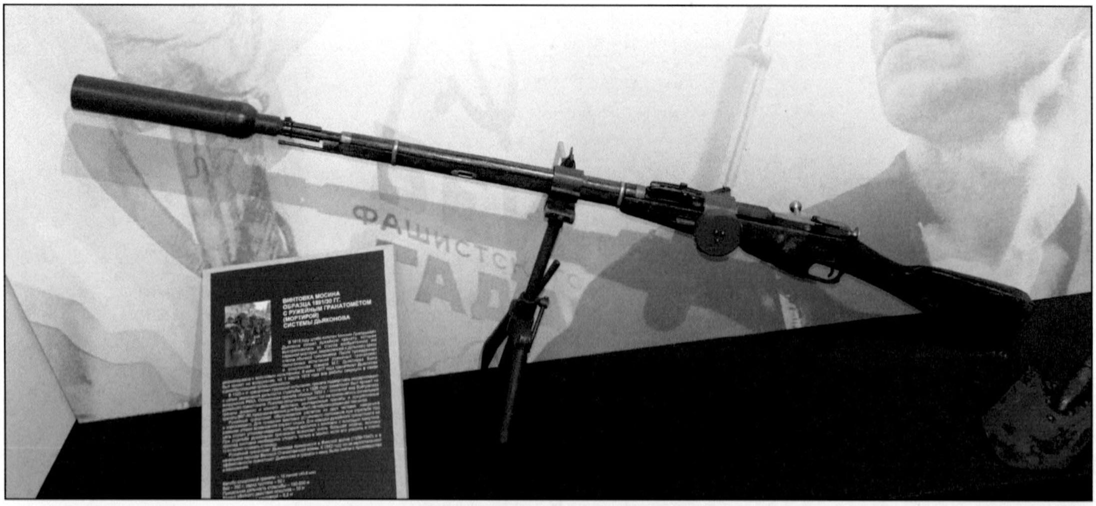

An 1891-30 'three-line rifle' with Dyakonov-system mortar.

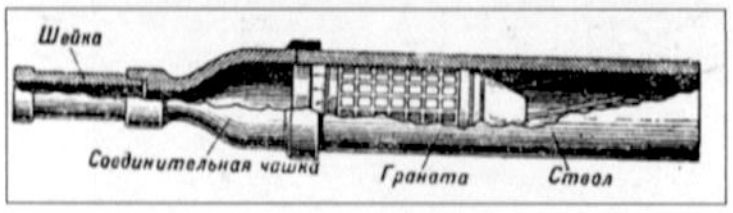

A cross-section of the mortar with a grenade inside.

Captain N.A. Yevdokimov (in the photograph) along with K.F. Kaytanov were the first to test how the paratroopers conducted themselves in chemical warfare conditions. In May 1935 Yevdokimov along with five other paratroopers were awarded the Order of Lenin.

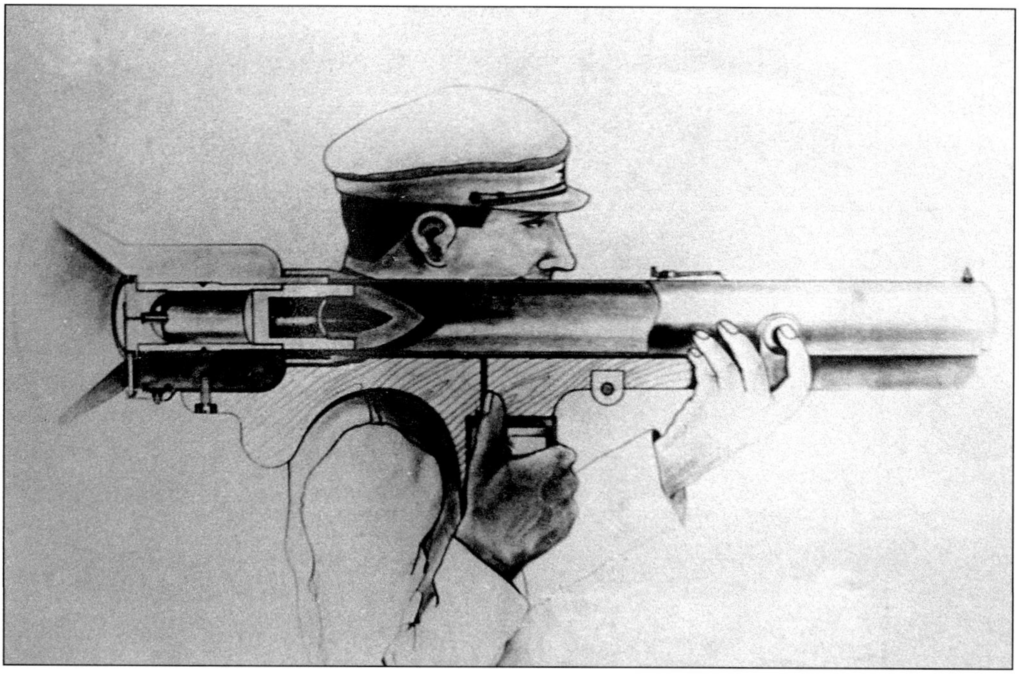

A portable recoilless hand gun designed by Grokhovskiy.

the cartridge was not a rocket, but a high-explosive fragmentation weapon (cumulative cartridges had yet to be invented at that time).

In that same year of 1936 anti-tank weapons were envisaged for paratroop regiments that had been formed in the Far East. In the Red Army at that time 1932-model Kurchevskiy 37mm PTRK single-shot, anti-tank guns, which were in fact small recoilless guns, which were fired from a collapsible tripod were in service. They entered series production in 1933. Evidently, they were issued to paratroopers. The classic anti-tank guns of various calibres at that time still only existed as prototypes. The PTRK distinguished itself in terms of its accuracy and its poor armour piercing ability, in 1938 they were withdrawn from paratroop units.

The armament for paratroopers was augmented by different types of grenades, some of the paratroopers would carry these with them, and some would be dropped in cargo bags, and crates. For example, in the Separate Detachment No.3 that is described above the combatants were issued with five grenades. To begin with these were 1914-model Rdultovskiy grenades, which were well-known by their nickname of *Butylka* (Bottle, in Soviet times they were often known as RG-14s). This was an offensive type grenade, that is to say the strike radius (of around 5m) was significantly less than the distance it could be thrown (some 30–40m). The RG-14 was suspended from the belt using a special ring. A shortcoming of this weapon was the fact that it was complicated to use, and it took a long time to prepare and throw. In 1930 a standardisation of these types of grenades was carried out and a detachable splinter casing was added, after which the designation '1914/30 grenade' was introduced.

In 1933 the defensive and offensive RGD-33 Dyakonov grenade was introduced into service, and this too had a detachable splinter casing. This was more compact, and lighter than the RG-14. It was worn in a special bag with a strap that passed over the shoulder, and which could hold two grenades. The RG-14 was supplied as a kit, with a separate explosive casing, detonating fuse and a lever. A soldier, once he had received the grenade would assemble it ahead of a battle, and after that it was impossible to disengage the lever. Use of clusters of three to five RGD-33 grenades was also envisaged. Moreover, the grenades were linked together in such a way that one of their levers would be facing one side, while the remaining levers – to the other side. It was planned to use these clusters against tanks, armoured cars, and fortifications. With this in mind a special RPG-40A anti-tank grenade was subsequently introduced, which was capable of piercing armour up to 20mm thick.

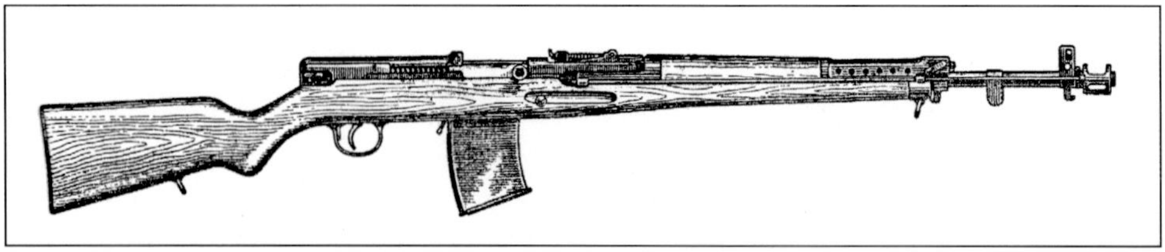

A 7.62-mm Simonov AVS-36 automatic rifle.

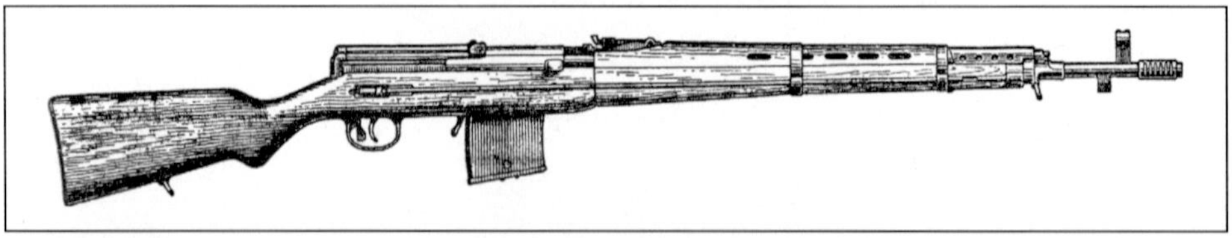

A 7.62-mm Tokarev SVT-38 semi-automatic rifle.

Degtyarev's 1934-model (upper) and 1940-model (lower) 7.62-mm PPD submachine guns.

An anti-tank RPG-40 hand grenade.

An F-1 defensive hand grenade known by the nickname *Limonka*.

At the end of the 1930s the assortment was augmented by F-1 offensive grenades (put simply these were known as *Limonka*'s), which had a large radius over which the splinters would be cast when it had exploded. It was envisaged that this would only be thrown from under cover. In the future it was planned that paratroopers would be issued with, in addition to cluster, and incendiary grenades, chemical (poison) ammunition.

In the interest of sabotage activities kits containing demolition equipment were developed. Aside from the usual anti-personnel, and anti-tank mines the secret BEMI high explosives entered service with the paratroop forces, these weapons would explode on receipt of a radio signal. They were characterised by their high yields, and were designed first and foremost to destroy buildings, and bridges. The radio set, which sent the signal also entered service with airborne forces. There was also a proposal that the paratroopers would drop a large quantity of demolition charges in cartridges or in blocks, explosives of various kinds, and a Bickford fuse. The paratroopers were expected to fashion explosive devices of some kind out of all this whilst in the field.

9

'Grokhovskiy's Coffins'

Over the course of the initial development of airborne forces there were no dedicated transport aircraft in service with the RKKA VVS. Military aviation possessed two-dozen German Ju-13s, which have been described above, and individual examples of English manufactured passenger aircraft. All the latter belonged to the 1st Heavy Squadron in Leningrad and were used for training purposes.

Reconnaissance aircraft, and light bombers were capable of carrying two or three paratroopers each or a corresponding amount of cargo. How many aircraft would actually be needed though to transport an entire platoon? Heavy bombers were also in service. The category of heavy bomber, by the standards of that time, included any aircraft with more than one engine. The most numerous of these being the twin-engine indigenous bomber, the TB-1. However, the fuselage of this aircraft was too cramped to carry a significant number of soldiers, since it was designed to carry bombs, and bombs are heavy, but also compact.

A start was made on finding a solution in the use of external attachments. Experiments began into using small cradles mounted under the wings of single-engine aircraft. The first such design was created under the leadership of P.I Grokhovskiy for an R-2 (R-1SP) biplane at the beginning of August 1930. More than anything else this thing was reminiscent of an iron-sided coffin without a lid. From the inside it had been lined with dermatine, a cheap leather substitute, and there was a soft cushion that would be used to support a person's head. The parachute was housed above the head. A paratrooper would lie down inside this cradle and remain there until he was dropped. Once over the required location the aircraft flight observer would pull the bomb release lever and a cable would release a safety pin and a rubber mounting would rotate the cradle. The paratrooper would fall out and the rip cord attached to the cradle would deploy a G-5 parachute. From a paratrooper's perspective everything happened automatically so officially this device was designated the "automatic red army soldier deployment device". The "deployment device" held two advantages: it enabled the aircraft lifting capability to be used more fully and ensured that a whole group of paratroopers could be dropped at any one time.

The lifting capacity of the R-1SP, a variant of the R-1 fitted with a 'Puma' engine was not very high. It was more than likely that the aircraft carried a single cradle under the fuselage. A standard R-1 with a *Liberty* engine (an M-5) was capable of carrying two cradles under the lower wing, the R-5 could also carry two or four, and the twin-engine TB-1 bomber could carry twelve, and subsequently sixteen, under the fuselage and the wings. The unit for the TB-1 was designated the G-39, and the one for the ANT-9 (in reality this was never fitted, although it was planned to fit this to five aircraft) was designated G-60. The cradles fitted to the large aircraft did not deploy all at the same time, but at intervals of one and a half seconds, so that the rip cords and the parachute canopies did not become entangled with one another.

On the morning of 9 July 1931 over the Central airfield in Moscow P. Grokhovskiy, and N. Yefremov carried out a parachute jump with the help of the 'deployment equipment'. Later on that very same day, in the presence of Ya.I. Alksnis, from an altitude of 500m a group of 11 parachutists led by Grokhovskiy completed a jump. Parachutes made from a cotton and silk material were used, along with static lines. Among the members of the group was one woman; L. Kuleshova, who became the first Soviet woman parachutist. All the volunteers were employees at the design bureau. The participants in the experiment landed successfully. Five days later the second

A diagram showing the design of the 'automatic Red Army soldier deployment device'. One of the soldiers falls down, and the rip-chord would pull the parachute canopy out of his knapsack. A second cradle is in a semi-rotated position, the parachutist inside it will be the second to leave the aircraft.

The earlier variant of the cradle in a ground-based jig.

The cradle attachment and the hinge.

group of volunteer personnel testing the TB-1 'deployment equipment' included Grokhovskiy's wife. It was the first time she had jumped, and the very first time she had actually flown!

The combat testing of this device fitted to the TB-1, which took place at the end of August in the Leningrad Military District revealed a number of defects. For the paratroopers the cradles were closely associated with coffins: you lie down on your own, it's cold, and dark, you can't see anything, and you don't have any way to contact the crew or the other parachutists, and then suddenly you are on your way down. One of the paratroopers then added: "I was always haunted by the thought that this plywood coffin would suddenly collapse or fall off". The principle by which the G-5 parachute was opened came under criticism. Moreover, the canopy would deploy immediately and the parachutist, as he descended, would be exposed to enemy fire for a long period of time. Grokhovskiy, who was not particularly tall, had based the dimensions on himself. Tall parachutists were only able to fit into the cradles by tucking their legs in.

The testing commission concluded that this approach "had a negative influence on the morale of the parachutists". L.G. Minov, who had led the parachute training for the paratroopers and the commanders in the detachment where the tests were undertaken, wrote: "This proposed deployment device cannot be recommended for service with the airborne detachments, in view of its extreme complexity".

Grokhovskiy tried to rehabilitate his idea. The cradles were refined to some extent, affording those inside some sort of visibility. A small opaque windscreen was fitted to the front. These 'deployment devices' were used at the end of 1931, when 24 parachutists were deployed from two aircraft. The number of personnel is testimony to the fact that they could only have been accommodated in cradles under the wings, while the full G-39 assembly envisaged a further four locations for cradles in a ventral position. It is possible that this was linked to ensuring the security of the bomber's centre of gravity.

On 2 December 1931 M.N. Tukhachevskiy ordered that the G-39 enter series production. This gave rise to a protest from the NII VVS since the assembly had not passed state testing. This evidently had gathered its' own

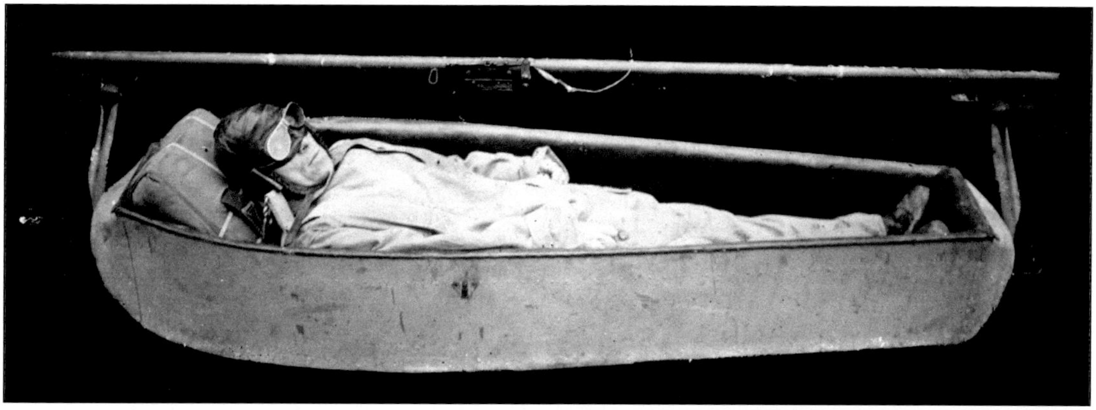

A paratrooper lies inside the cradle with a G-5 under his head.

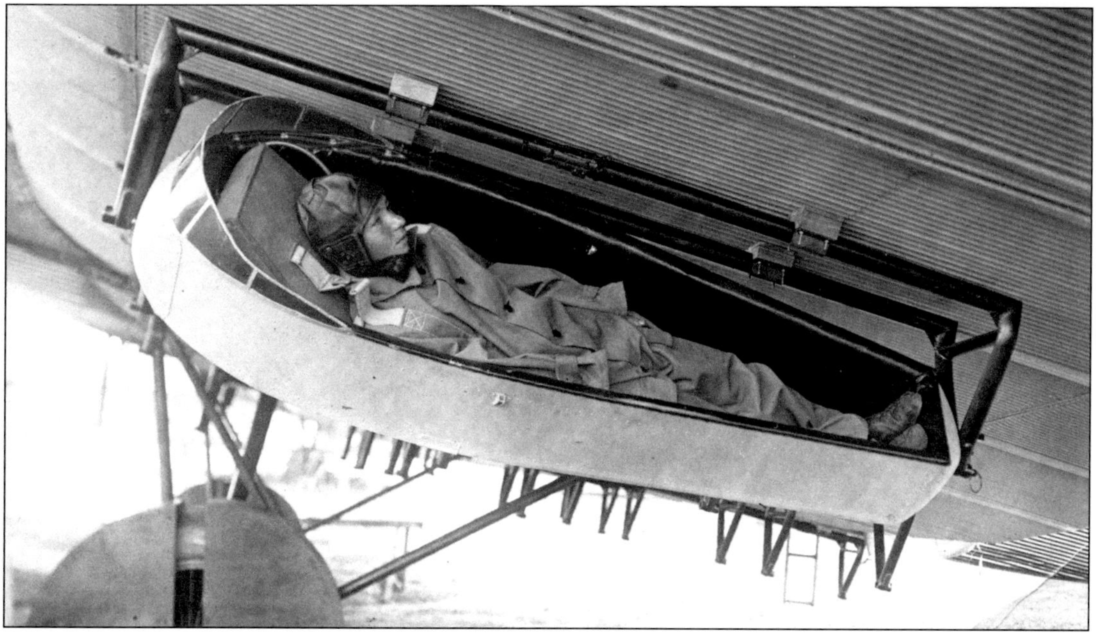

A modified variant of the cradle with a windscreen, under the wing of a TB-1. Note the attachment brackets for the other cradles underneath the aircraft but the cradles themselves are not installed. The paratrooper is wearing most likely a G-55 suit with the straps sewn into it: the locks for detaching the straps after landing can be seen on the soldier's shoulders.

momentum. In total only 50 cradles were manufactured, that is to say four incomplete assemblies, and at that point the work was stopped.

In fact, the 'deployment devices' were rejected. Grokhovskiy however did try to return to similar ideas several times that were designed for the R-5, he made the housings for the paratroopers enclosed (they were fitted with trap doors that opened downwards), he also fitted windows to provide forward, and downward visibility, and even holes for firing.

A group of TB-1 bombers from the 55th Squadron with G-39 cradles, Leningrad Military District, 1933.

10

Underslung Descent Pods

There was another way of enhancing the passenger carrying capacity of these bombers. At almost the same time as the 'cradles' Grokhovskiy worked on the descent pods. The small internal volume of the fuselage in this case was augmented by attaching casings, either under the wings or under the fuselage. The paratroopers would be accommodated inside these cases in a group, or groups. In a fully enclosed cabin it was not so draughty, and it was warmer, than in the cradle. A window provided light and enabled some orientation as to the terrain. The paratroopers could converse amongst themselves and were able to communicate with the aircraft crew. They jumped out of hatches, as they would out of an aircraft, one after another. The members of the detachment were more spread out using this approach.

The casing had to have as much capacity as possible, and yet be as small as possible, as well as having a highly aerodynamic shape. The first of these pods was manufactured in 1931 for the TB-1. A KP-1 pod that had a mixed structure was attached to the fuselage using bolts and was designed for 13 people. Its empty weight was 295kg, and its payload was 1,300kg. In order to carry the pod in flight, all defensive machine guns was removed from the aircraft. Owing to the increase in weight and aerodynamic drag for the carrying aircraft the speed and ceiling were reduced, manoeuvrability deteriorated, and the length of the take-off run increased.

Inside the pod there were two narrow benches, on which the paratroopers would sit in an upright position. In front of them, with his face to his subordinates, sat the commander in his own seat. Between him and the paratroopers a hatch was built into the floor with a lid that was held on by two hinges that opened inwards. In order to communicate with the crew of the aircraft there were two smaller hatches in the ceiling. The cabin was attached to the aircraft using 16 bolts.

In the course of testing ten paratroopers were dropped on two occasions from this device. The commander opened the hatch, and the paratroopers jumped onto it two at a time, sliding forward on their own benches. On average it took one and a half seconds for one person to jump clear.

The testing revealed a series of defects. The commander needed just the most basic of instruments, as well as a reliable communication with the aircraft crew (not just via a hatch in the ceiling). A gap that was found between the carrying aircraft, and the cabin increased aerodynamic drag.

For the paratroopers however the KP-1 was more comfortable than in the 'cradles'. The design was refined. There were now 16 seats in this pod, but the weight had also increased. On the second attempt in 1932 the pod passed the threshold during the course of state testing. On 7 October (according to another document this was on 8 October) 1932 the commission that was chaired by the Assistant Commander of the Leningrad Military District Forces Florovskiy officially accepted the cabin into service with the VVS as the KPS-16.

In 1932 Moscow's Factory No.28 produced a batch of ten pods based on blueprints taken from a prototype example. The weight of the KPS-16 was 469kg. At the beginning of the following year a series of changes were introduced, after lightening the cabin by up to 397.5g (with a cowling this increased to 418kg). Externally this variant was characterised by the number and shape of the windows. The pilot model was presented on 1 June 1933. The first flight with this pod took place on 27 June. TB-1 No. 669 was flown by the Commander of the detachment Sofronov. The flight weight of this aircraft along with this pod was 7,935kg. The parachute jump was conducted over Tushino airfield, and the aircraft landed on the Central airfield.

A prototype of the KP-1 airborne pod suspended under the TB-1 bomber.

In total 50 pods were manufactured for the TB-1. After some short-term upgrading work the weight of the pod increased again to 428kg. These modernised examples were sometimes known as KPS-17s, although the number of paratroopers it could carry was reduced to 15. This pod design cost approximately 7,000 roubles.

Combat testing was conducted in the 3rd Special Purpose Brigade in Detskoye Selo between 26–28 July 1933. The aircraft took less fuel on board, and so the take-off weight was limited to 7,509kg. The KPS-17 created more aerodynamic drag, and the additional weight played its part. The aircraft reached an altitude of 1,000m in 27mins. After testing the pod, the parachutists came to the conclusion that it was very cramped, and cold inside (it is not warm at altitude by any means even in the summer). The following day following the conclusion of testing close to the village of Veneryas 13 paratroopers jumped out of pod armed with a grenade, along with a mannequin. The parachutists threw grenades from the air down to plywood sheets in the ground.

Interestingly it was only in September 1933 that the VVS headquarters commissioned the TsAGI to analyse the design of Grokhovskiy's pod in terms of the centre of gravity, and the strength of the carrying aircraft (a TB-1). The military were potentially interested whether the weight of the pod could be reduced by the institute, making it all-metal and use the plastic as well. Similarly, the calculations were limited for the pod itself, and they needed to find out if the bomber would not be destroyed by vibration generated by the pod sitting on its attachments.

Operations with these pods in service revealed a series of shortcomings. On 14 June 1933 during the course of a jump on the outskirts of Kharkov, a soldier from the 3rd Independent Special Purpose Battalion, I.I. Ivanov, was killed. After he had jumped out of the pod he began to spin, which led to the parachute straps becoming entangled. The canopy failed to open, and he was killed. The appointed commission concluded that the narrow hatch was actually manufactured in such a way that a paratrooper was only able to exit the hatch by lying half on their side, which causes a rotational movement. Jumping from the cabin at an altitude of less than 1,200m was banned (in order to give parachutists time to untangle the straps should they become wound round each other). At the same time parachutists needed to develop a technique for jumping from the KPS-17, and the designers had to redesign the hatch.

Paratroopers boarding the KPS-16 pods suspended under a TB-1bombers, Leningrad Military District, 1933.

A TB-1 in flight with an airborne pod.

In total during the course of exiting the cabin designed by Grokhovskiy there were four fatal incidents as well as several others that actually ended favourably. In all of these cases the paratrooper had begun to spin, or somersault after falling free of the aircraft.

A similar cabin for the TB-3, which was also designed by Grokhovskiy could accommodate 35 paratroopers. The plan for 1933–34 envisaged production of 100 of these cabins but development was protracted and in December 1933 the Head of the RKKA VVS Ya.I. Alksnis proposed that these cabins be excluded from any economic considerations (they were to cost two and a half million roubles). He was of the opinion that they were

Paratroopers next to a TB-1 with a KPS-16 pod. The paratroopers are dressed in warm winter suits and warm felt boots, the latter were also issued to pilots in cold weather.

A paratrooper jumps out of a KPS-16 pod.

A line-up of paratroopers in front of TB-1 aircraft fitted with KPS-16 pods.

An early variant of the underwing two-seat pod cabin designed for the R-5 reconnaissance aircraft. As the base of the pod rotates down on eyelets the paratrooper would slide out backwards.

An R-5 fitted with a G-61 pod during state testing, NII VVS, February 1936.

A 'record' flight of an R-5 with G-61 pods on 8 December 1936 from Podlipki airfield. The noses of the pods are open, and the faces of 14 passengers can be seen.

The G-61 pods were also used in GVF and in Polar Aviation under the Principal Directorate of the Northern Sea Route. This photograph shows a civilian P-5 biplane (an unarmed R-5 reconnaissance aircraft) fitted with G-61 pods.

A pod carried ventrally under a TB-7 heavy bomber, July 1939.

A D-20 pod suspended underneath a DB-3B long-range bomber, July 1939.

not only expensive but had a significant negative effect on an aircraft aerodynamics and increased its weight. In their place he proposed that the TB-3 be upgraded in order to enhance its passenger carrying capacity.

The G-61 project was a stepping-stone from the cradles to the airborne descent pods. They represented streamlined boxes. In the documentation they are actually designated as 'airborne descent pods'. An R-5 biplane would carry two of these plywood boxes (pods) made of wood, under the lower wing. The pod had a wing shaped profile and created the necessary lift. In the first variant there were two cells in each of them, with a paratrooper in each cell. The personnel would lie down in these cells with their head facing the front. In a later design four paratroopers could be accommodated in separate cells; in total the aircraft was able to carry eight men in separate pods. Underneath these cells a hatch was made that opened outwards, and the aft section of the pod was designed to be detachable. The pod had glazing in the front made from celluloid. In one of the variants in the front of the pod holes were even envisaged for firing whilst airborne. Testing of this modification of the G-61 took place in 1935, and Grokhovskiy announced that his new invention was a gift to the VIII Conference of Soviets.

On conclusion of testing the G-61 was introduced into service and entered series production. Factory No. 47 in Leningrad issued an order for 500 assemblies; this order was delivered in 1936.

In February 1936, a modified (and evidently series production) variant of the G-61 underwent state testing at the NII VVS, The G-61 underwent 30 flights in the course of testing. With empty pods the aircraft behaved like a standard R-5. The pod ensured an additional lifting surface of seven metres squared. The aircraft was able to carry eight paratroopers, or eight casualties on special stretchers, or 640kg of cargo. It was also planned to place the blocks of the parachute-cable barrage (another of Grokhovskiy's inventions) into the box cells. Dropping of the personnel and cargo were initiated manually (by the operator) using the bomb release mechanism in the aircraft rear cabin. This opened the hatches underneath, and they were closed again using springs. This enabled cargo parachute bags to be packed into compartments or into pods, and also enabled leaflets to be dropped.

A medical pod designed at OKPB VVS for a TB-1 aircraft. The parachute has been stowed in a cylindrical container that is suspended closer to the aircraft tail.

Inside view of the medical pod.

The medical pod after parachute landing, 1932.

Loaded with ballast the aircraft had a take-off weight of 3,309kg (the R-5 in the light bomber variant weighed 3,351kg when loaded with bombs). The maximum speed fell to 187.5km/hr (as a bomber the maximum speed was 194km/hr). The aircraft ceiling fell to 3,000m (that is to say to approximately 1,500m). The most difficult thing, however, was the deterioration in the aircraft flight performance characteristics, and rate of climb, the aircraft was very slow to gain altitude.

On 8 December 1936 an R-5 took off from an airfield in Podlipki, which was carrying 14 paratroopers in two pods. The aircraft was flown by Grokhovskiy himself, and another passenger was sitting in the aft cockpit. In order to set a similar 'passenger carrying record' two parachutists each were accommodated in the two compartments closest to the fuselage.

In 1937 two civil P-5s (which were actually R-5s with all the armament removed) fitted with G-61 pods, which were used during the search for S.A. Levanevskiy's missing crew who had flown on a long-range flight from the USSR to the USA via the North Pole. These aircraft had been modified with the help of factories No. 89, No. 241, and the Scientific Research Institute of Civil Air Fleet (NII GVF). On each side the three cells closest to the fuselage were occupied with additional fuel tanks. In total the aircraft carried 840l, which increased the flight range up to 2,000m. In the two outer empty cells that remained a spare radio set had been accommodated, as well as enough food supplies for two months, and armament, sleeping bags, warm clothing, and spare parts. By 12 September, B.V. Bitskiy had taken off in the first modified machine, which in a number of documents is designated the PG-61, heading for Arkhangelsk. Short test flights were carried out to Bykovo on 16 September in the second aircraft; pilot Kotov completed four flights. The maximum speed had reduced to 185km/hr, and on take-off the aircraft was inert, and would react sluggishly to the movements of the control surfaces. Nothing untoward however revealed itself in flight.

References can be found stating that a P-5 with G-61 pods was used during the course of the war with Germany in the Karelian–Finnish Air Group of the Civil Air Fleet (GVF) to drop reconnaissance personnel behind enemy lines.

This was how a medical pod was to be transported in case of a landing delivery.

In the Experimental Institute under the People's Commissariat for Heavy Industry (NKTP) work was also underway on a G-45 'soft' descent pod but the author was not able to find any details concerning its design.

Underslung pods resurfaced at the end of the 1930s. The slow, and cumbersome TB-3s were already obsolete, and the fuselage in the new generation of bombers that flew faster, and higher were again not well suited to transporting as many paratroopers as their lifting capacity could handle.

In March 1939 at the NII VVS a pod for the four-engine TB-7 (this was later designated the Pe-8) underwent testing. This pod was designed and manufactured at Factory No.156 (which was the former factory of experimental designs of the TsAGI) and had an extended aerodynamic shape: it was 5.6m long, and 12.7m wide. Despite the dimensions the pod weighed just 127kg. It was attached underneath the bomb bay with the bomb bay doors removed. There were two hatches inside the pod, one of them near the front that was in the floor, and another in the aft section. The doors for the forward hatch opened outwards; they were raised again using a hand operated winch by the bomber's own flight engineer. The aft hatch opened inwards.

The pod could accommodate 18 paratroopers with PN-4 parachutes, or 14 paratroopers with PD-6 parachutes, in both cases they were unarmed; as an alternative 12 fully armed paratroopers could be accommodated with PD-6 parachutes. The paratroopers would sit along the sides of the pod, facing each other.

During the course of testing Captain Datsko's crew completed 12 flights using the pod. On take-off, landing and during manoeuvres the presence of the underslung pod went unnoticed. Only a slight pitch down moment was recorded, which was eliminated by adjusting the trim tabs. The speed of the aircraft fell by 12km/hr and the time taken to climb to a range of altitudes increased by zero point five to three minutes (this difference grew as the altitude increased).

For the paratroopers in the pod it was cramped, and there was not enough legroom. It was difficult to move around the pod. The hatches were very small for anyone in winter clothing and with a parachute. The effort that the pulley exerted turned out to be insufficient, and the doors could not be closed in flight.

Several of these flights were made using ballast, and then with mannequins, and test parachutists. The maximum number of the latter was eight people. They were able to jump through the two hatches in eight seconds.

This pod did not enter series production.

In July 1939, testing began of the DB-3B bomber with a D-20 descent pod, developed under the leadership of A.I. Privalov. The specification for this had been issued in October of the previous year. This pod was manufactured solely from wood and it could accommodate ten people. It had small doors, and oxygen equipment with enough oxygen for two hours of flight for all ten occupants. The D-20 pod was series produced at Factory No.468 in Beskudnikovo. In 1942 some 450 examples were ordered, but how many were actually manufactured is not known.

An alternative to these underslung pods were the underwing pods for the DB-3. They were incorporated into the plan for 'D' group at Factory No.289 for 1940–41. Whether anything of this nature was actually done is not known.

A prototype factory in Voronezh started to manufacture a DK-12 pod for 12 people designed by A.S. Moksalev for the DB-3F aircraft from the summer of 1941 but was evacuated to the Omsk region in the autumn. There was also a DK-16 pod that could accommodate 16 combatants.

It was planned to use similar pods to evacuate injured paratroopers. In 1932 a medical pod that could accommodate nine people was manufactured at Grokhovskiy's workshop. In the documentation it is described as a 'parachute' pod, that is to say the plan was to drop it from the aircraft. A G-39 medical pod is listed in the plan for 1933 that could accommodate eight casualties, and two medics. It is possible that this is one and the same design.

A prototype of a medical pod was manufactured and tested. It is described in the NII VVS documentation as "fragile and unreliable", and "more like a model". Fitting of this pod took almost an hour.

After it had been deployed to the required position the intention was to use it as a mobile first aid post. It was mobile because the G-39 could be loaded onto a flatbed lorry or towed as a trailer by using its own chassis. The plan was to deliver the chassis separately, since the pod was attached to the TB-1 minus its wheels. The reason for this was possibly because of the very heavy weight of the assembly, which was beyond the capabilities of a twin-engine bomber. After the casualties had been placed inside the pod could be airlifted behind Soviet lines by the bomber that would have landed close to the location of the assault.

There is reliable evidence to the effect that the medical pod was dropped from an aircraft using a parachute, this occurred at least once, outside Leningrad in September 1932.

11

Pods, Bags and Cages

In Russia, the first cargo parachute and the packaging that went with it, was proposed by G.E. Kotelnikov in 1924. This rigid cylindrical box was designed for a cargo of 300kg, and a circular canopy with a diameter of 12m was sewn from a cotton material and was attached using straps to the parachute at a single point. The designer however had no intention of using it for military purposes at all, but for delivering post to inaccessible areas: therefore, in the application for the invention the assembly is called an "airborne postman". It is unlikely that Kotelnikov's cargo parachute was tested, there were simply no aircraft available in the country at the time that were capable of lifting a weight like that.

Thoughts began to turn seriously towards dropping cargoes using parachutes in the USSR at the end of 1928. There was no discussion at that time of airborne assaults of any kind. It was just that the military wanted to find a way to deliver armament, ammunition, medical supplies, and anything else pulled from the supply line to detachments and forces behind the lines quickly. The task of providing effective assistance to an advancing cavalry, that is to say troops participating in a raid, as well as to partisan detachments, reconnaissance groups, and agents behind enemy lines, as well as to forces in inaccessible areas in the event of an overstretched front, detachments that were surrounded and crews of aircraft that had either been shot down, or had been in an accident was set.

In April 1929, at the NII VVS the principal requirements for a cargo parachute were developed. It needed to be light, compact, simple and cheap and ensure a safe landing for the various goods supplied. The Scientific and Technical Committee in July of that same year incorporated two types of cargo parachute with special packaging for their contents, into their five year plan. The various designers were quick to follow suit with their designs.

N.P. Blagin was the first to design a 'postal parachute' that was manufactured and tested at the NII VVS in the first half of 1929. Grokhovskiy however soon took the lead. His 'cargo parachute bags', which were also known as 'Grokhovskiy's device for drooping cargoes from an aircraft' underwent testing between 18–20 March 1930. The cargo was successfully dropped. The bag had two compartments: the cargo was in one of them, and in the other one was a parachute made from percale. An R-1 aircraft was able to carry four packages on bomb racks underneath the lower wing. The canopy was opened forcedly, since it was deployed using a cord attached to the bomb rack under the wing.

The new parachute packages were tested in August 1930, in the Moscow, and Leningrad military districts at almost the same time. The 28th Squadron carried out their first parachute drops in the area around Petergof. Squadron Commander Bondaryuk was in charge of these tests. To begin with the attempts were unsuccessful, the canopy would not come out of its cover, or the rip cords would tear. After the standard twine was replaced with a stronger spun material everything went more smoothly, the parachutes would open normally. An assortment of cargoes were packed inside the bags, right up to two dozen light bulbs; these did not break on landing.

In contrast however during the course of exercises in the Moscow Military District in September of that year the result was worse than expected. The 28th Squadron completed two sorties with cargo bags. On the first of these sorties only one of the parachutes opened out of the three, and only two opened on the second sortie. In one of the bags, which landed without any problems, were the radio valves.

In the exercises described above in the Moscow Military District during the course of a drop at the Klochkovo farmstead, all the cargo parachutes worked fine, delivering their armament and ammunition safely to earth.

Airdrop cargo bags (most likely of G-3 type).

Type 3A 'cargo-carrier' designed by Blagin suspended under the fuselage of an R-1 biplane.

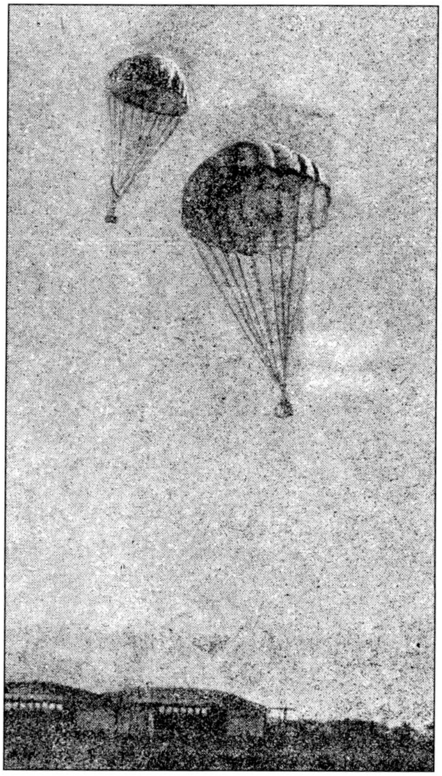

Dropping Blagin's cargo bags by parachute.

Under the leadership of Grokhovskiy, the G-52 'cardboard airdrop device' was created. This was a cigar shaped box made from cardboard, a G-2 parachute made of percale was packed into one of the ends of this box with a diameter of three and a half metres. This box could carry up to 30kg of cargo, such as six Russian 1891-model 7.62mm 'three-line rifles' or 5,000 rounds of ammunition, in cans. A R-5 biplane was able to carry ten of these 'cigar'-shaped objects. In that same year, and even without having undertaken state testing, it was introduced into service as the PG-2k. The Deputy People's Commissar for Naval, and Military Affairs M.N. Tukhachevskiy ordered that the drop device be put into series production. In the specification, however, the load the box could carry was to be restricted to 20kg.

The G-2, and G-3 'soft bags' designed by Grokhovskiy were made to carry one and the same cargo but the first was designed for a landing delivery, and the other could be dropped using a parachute such as the G-2, in the same way as the PG-2k. Don't let the continuation of the designation surprise you, with Grokhovskiy this nearly always happened. Three 76mm artillery shells could be carried in a G-3 bag, or three DP machine guns, or three boxes of machine-gun round belts. On 31 January 1931 by way of an order issued by the RVS of the USSR the G-2 parachutes, and G-3 bags were introduced into service.

That same year they entered series production. The UVVS ordered 1,000 G-3 bags for 1931. By the beginning of October some 800 parachutes had already been manufactured, but these turned out to be useless for the actual cargo bags. The bags made from a rubberised material were ordered by the *Rezinoobyedinenie* (Rubber Manufacturing Plant), but it was not possible to manufacture these in time due to the manufacturing plant being overloaded with other projects. Agreement was reached with the worker's cooperative in Stalingrad, but a great deal of time had been lost and the first prototype bag was only produced there in the middle of October. The situation with the G-2 bags was more favourable: by 22 September 100 bags had been delivered. Interestingly the political Directorate of the RKKA submitted a request to be supplied with these parachutes, as they wanted to

G-6 airdrop bags under the lower wing of an R-5 reconnaissance aircraft.

use them for emergency delivery of propaganda materials. The reason why the political workers actually ordered 143 bags precisely is not known.

The G-2 and G-3s did not remain in service for long, and they were rejected in 1934. Grokhovskiy produced the G-57 bag, which was slightly different, to replace the G-2, and the G-57 was also designed to carry 30kg of cargo. A batch of G-57s was produced at the *Kauchuk* factory.

In a modified variant the G-3 was introduced into service following testing as the PDM-4. Initially, it was also produced for carrying on the R-5. This bag though could not be suspended from external hard points on a TB-3, they had to be carried internally and dropped by hand.

Blagin's competing group produced the 3A type *gruzovoz* (cargo parachute), which had an excellent lifting capacity. This was made up correspondingly of a larger box (known as a 'packing cylinder'). In fact there were several types of cylinders – for different types of cargo, including liquids. The total weight with cargo was up to 83kg. Seven 76mm shells could be carried in the package, or four Lewis light machine guns (these evidently were 1915 'infantry' models) or six PD light machine guns, sixty-four 1914-model grenades, six hundred 7.62mm rounds, or 60kg of provisions. A 76mm recoilless cannon was dropped in two bags (one of them housed the barrel, and the other the tripod, lock, and sight). Some 50kg of petrol or oil, and 60kg of water could be carried in a fluid tank (this would be in the event of an operation in an area affected by drought, for both people and vehicles).

An R-1 aircraft could carry two of these boxes, and an R-5 could carry four. Blagin's parachutes successfully passed testing and began to be series produced.

The advent of indigenous cargo parachutes and the packaging for them made the purchase of a licence from the American Irvin company for a cargo parachute designed to drop a machine gun from an aircraft redundant. A German cargo parachute designed by Kuntzer was tested at the NII VVS in the first half of 1929 but did not make a good impression.

Grokhovskiy's collective went further, however. In October 1932 a small G-4 soft bags was introduced into service as well as the rigid (made of plywood, with an oval cross-section) G-5 pod (this was actually a PD-Kor).

PD-MM 'soft bags' under the wing of an R-5 aircraft.

Paratroopers unpack a soft bag that has been dropped by parachute in the course of exercises, Brovary, 1935.

A P-5 aircraft (an unarmed R-5, that was operated by GVF) with 'plywood cargo bags', summer 1935.

A cargo cage designed to hold one tonne of cargo and which is designed to be dropped by parachute, attached under a TB-1 bomber.

An R-1 aircraft with PD-BB airdrop tanks, July 1932.

They were both designed for a 150–160kg cargo. The lifting capacity that Grokhovskiy stipulated however was again thought to have been overestimated, and for a PD-Kor this was set at 135kg. It was dropped using a percale parachute with a diameter of 12m. This pod was often used even without parachutes to transport a larger amount of cargo than could be carried in the rear cabin of an R-5. This biplane would usually carry two 'cigars' under the lower wing. In 1934 during the course of an operation to rescue the crew members of the *Chelyushkin,* V.S. Molokov carried people inside these pods, one person in each of the cells.

Later, the plywood cylindrical PDTs pod appeared that was designed to carry 120kg. In that same year 1932 the G-6 pod was presented for testing that was designed for 80kg (this was a circular rigid pod), as well as the G-7 for outsized cargoes (this was cylindrical), as well as a cardboard G-8 for carrying provisions.

The soft PDMM bag (this was originally designated the PD-MM) was dropped using a percale parachute with a diameter of 8m. Its maximum lifting capacity was set at 80kg (subsequently this figure was also thought to have been overestimated). The rigidity of the packaging was enhanced by adding long wooden strips to the outside. An earlier model of the 76mm recoilless gun (DRP) could fit into the PDMM in one piece, along with its tripod. A later model of the BPK gun was dismantled and packed into two boxes. Alternative variants were: eight cartridges for the DRP, six DP light machine guns, 24 disc magazines for the DP, 100 hand grenades, and 12 rifles between 800 to 3,000 rounds of ammunition, 50 revolvers and pistols, and a kit for an entrenching tool made up of 30 pieces. In the bag's cargo cell a metal tank can be accommodated with a capacity of 60liters of fluid. The inside of the compartment for the DRP positioning was lined with board. Following testing, the PDMM was accepted for procurement and production of a combat series was sanctioned. The design was modified several times, after which it became widespread. An extended variant of the bag appeared later on, for longer cargoes, the lifting capacity however remained the same.

Fuel tanks which could be dropped by parachutes, suspended under fuselage of an R-5 aircraft.

The provisions to feed the paratroopers were also dropped from the sky, and moreover this was not just restricted to dried food. Special thermos containers were designed that were dropped by parachute. Inside the rigid 'cigars' was a cylindrical metal thermos with a handle on the outside.

In 1933 the RVS of the USSR issued a requirement for the standardisation of parachute packages. As a result, after a short time less than a dozen of these types of packages were left in service with the VVS. New examples however continued to be developed. NII VVS documents indicate that on 20 September 1935 'descent pods' equipped with parachutes, designed by Khrustalyov, were accepted for testing. The pods were intended to be carried under an R-5, and pilot Kalilets was due to carry out test flights. The author was not able to establish what happened to these pods beyond this point.

During a landing delivery there was no need to drop anything by parachute. In June and July of 1935 'plywood cargo bags' were tested, these were rigid cigar shaped boxes with an oval cross-section that were designed for the R-5 aircraft. Four boxes could be suspended on bomb racks in a minimal amount of time. The bomb racks did not require any kind of adjustment for this to happen. Each 'bag' was designed to carry 105kg of cargo given that the bag weighed 27kg. It was planned that four boxes of rifle rounds (which amounts to 810 pieces in each), as well as 20 'three-line rifles', two machine guns (a single DP light machine gun and a single Maxim with a stand) as well as two disc magazines for the DP and two boxes of machine-gun belts for the Maxim would be accommodated in this package. In place of the cargo, personnel were able to climb into the box. They would lie down with their heads facing forwards, and a small celluloid window was made for paratroopers to provide them with forward and downward visibility.

'Cargo cages' also saw the light of day, these were large boxes that could carry up to a tonne of varying equipment. The first of these the KG was manufactured and tested in 1932. The carrying aircraft for this equipment was a TB-1 bomber. A percale parachute was accommodated not in the cage itself but in a separate cylindrical casing that was suspended from the bomb racks. As the cylinder fell it drew on the rip cord pulling out

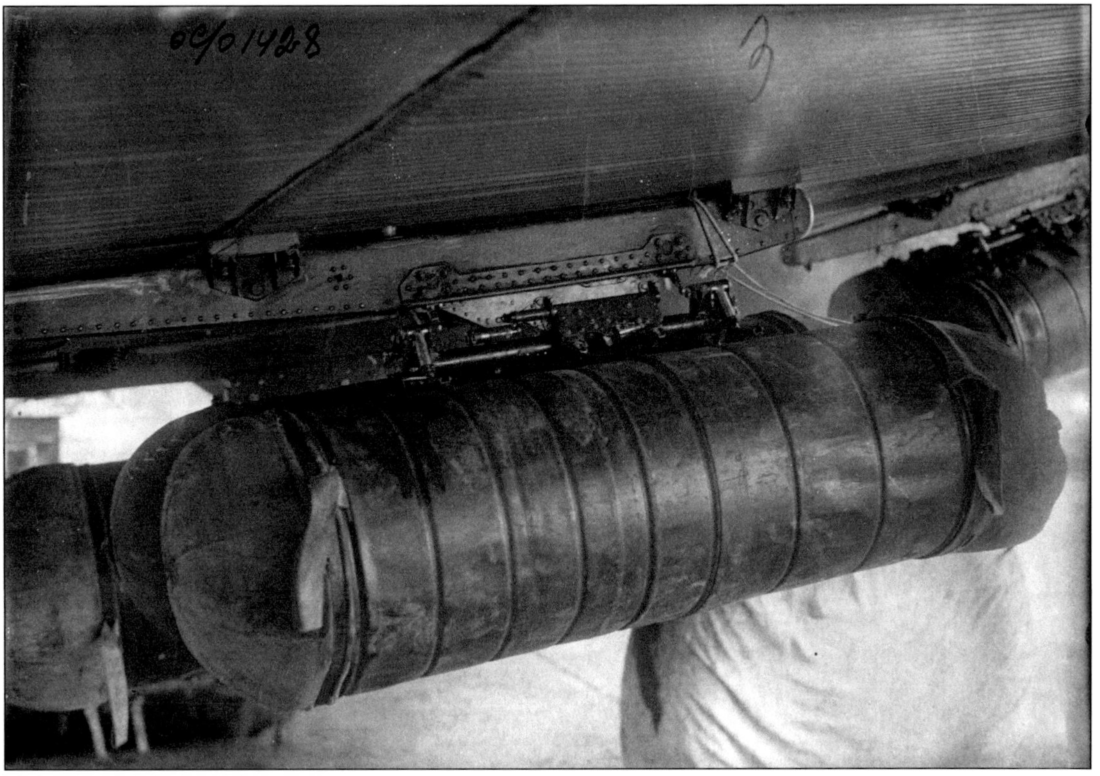

A PDBB-100 tank, that was designed to be dropped by parachute, mounted on a paired SPD-200 rack of the cargo bridge under a TB-3 bomber.

A 1,000l tank designed to be dropped by parachute, attached under a TB-1.

The PBS-100 pod designed for free (without a parachute) airdrop.

PBS-100 pods on bomb racks under the wing of a R-5 aircraft in course of testing in August 1938.

the parachute. The cage itself was dropped using a separation method – as the parachute filled with air it literally pulled the pod out from underneath the aircraft. This enabled the impact to be reduced, as well as the minimum drop altitude. A new method was tested using a barrel full of sand, which was secretively dubbed 'article Kh-43'. Testing was carried out despite a categorical ban that had been put in place by Alksnis, who was in receipt of a negative conclusion from the specialists. The drop however was completed successfully. Alksnis complained to Tukhachevskiy, but the latter forgave the designer.

Underslung medical pods mounted under the wing of a P-5 aircraft which was a part of the *Narkomzdrav* (People's Commissariat for Public Health) Squadron named after Kalinin.

During the course of state testing between September–October 1932, the KG cage was dropped on three occasions. Between September–October 1934 in Detskoye Selo a G-33 cage was tested carrying three tonnes of cargo, which was attached under the wing centre section of a TB-3 using a universal bracket.

In the summer of 1931, during testing, PP-BB tanks for dropping fuel and lubricating materials were supplied with parachutes. The capacity of these tanks was 66liters. The canopies were the same as those used for the PD-MMs, percale parachutes with a diameter of eight metres. All the tanks however either fell off, or broke. Attempts were made to rescue the situation, Grokhovskiy even claimed that these examples had been brought along by accident and were not intended for testing. A new batch of PP-BB tanks were brought, and the drops were completed successfully. In the end under the designation PDBB they were accepted for procurement for the VVS and series production of them began. The intention was to suspend them underneath either the lower wing or the fuselage of an R-5.

The result of the development of this design was the PDBB-100 tank. In 1939 it was modified for carrying under the SSS biplane which was similar to R-5 but had different design of the bomb racks. In the second half of the 1930s larger tanks appeared that were designated PDBB-250, and PDBB-400, these were also series produced. An example of an even larger tank existed, which was dropped by parachute, and which had a capacity of 1,000 liters. This was suspended under the fuselage of a TB-1. There is no information available however concerning testing of this tank.

All these tanks were metal. At the end of October 1935 however at the NII VVS a 'soft petrol tank' was tested that was designed by Khrustalyov. This tank held 130liters of fuel and was also dropped using a parachute. The author was not able to find details of the design of this 'soft container'.

A prototype example of a 4,000liters tank was manufactured, which was intended for the TB-3. There were no plans to drop this tank by parachute. The aircraft was to land after which the tank would be detached, and the fuel would be drained out of it. It was also possible to fuel the tanks, and vehicles from the aircraft itself without detaching the tank.

PDMM cargo bags under the fuselage of a DB-3F bomber.

At the end of the 1930s cargoes were actively dropped from low altitudes without parachutes. This could be very effective if the cargoes were to land on snow, sand, or on ploughed land, or into some bushes, especially when shock absorbing is provided for the package itself. In August 1938 PBS-100 pods underwent testing, which were designed to be dropped without a parachute from low altitudes. This was developed in 'D' brigade of the KB-29 design bureau.

The pod represented two cigar shaped willow cradles that had been placed one inside the other. A layer of wood shavings was laid between the cradles. On the outside the pod was covered in a closely woven fabric and had stabilisers on the back that streamlined the descent. Despite the large dimensions (a length of 2,390mm, a diameter of 535mm), the PBS-100 was very light, weighing less than 30kg. Moreover, up to 100kg of ammunition provisions, or clothing could be accommodated in it. For example, one of variants for loading the pod envisaged the accommodation of eight cans loaded with rifle bullets plus five discs for the DA machine gun. If clothing was loaded into the pod, which was not breakable, the internal cradle was removed, and the shavings were tipped out.

During testing the PBS-100 was dropped from an R-5 aircraft. The machine was piloted by Senior Lieutenant Nikitin. The R-5 carried four pods on bomb racks under the wings. The drop was carried out from an altitude of 10m at a speed of 175km/hr. The advantage of a drop without a parachute lies in the greater degree of accuracy and the low cost of the specially designed box. For carrying the PBS-100, the high-speed aircraft of that time could be used – the R-10 reconnaissance aircraft, the DB-3 bomber, and the PS-84 transport aircraft (a copy of the American-made DC-3).

All the airborne bags, pods, and tanks for fuel were suspended on bomb racks and dropped using the bomb release lever. The possibility of them being suspended externally was only envisaged for slow aircraft, otherwise the cargo would be torn away in the oncoming airflow. Moreover, not all the bomb racks were suitable for this purpose. The large bombers were designed to take a small amount of large calibre bombs on external hard points but the Der-19 and Der-20 racks were not suitable for the bags. These had to be stowed in the fuselage and were

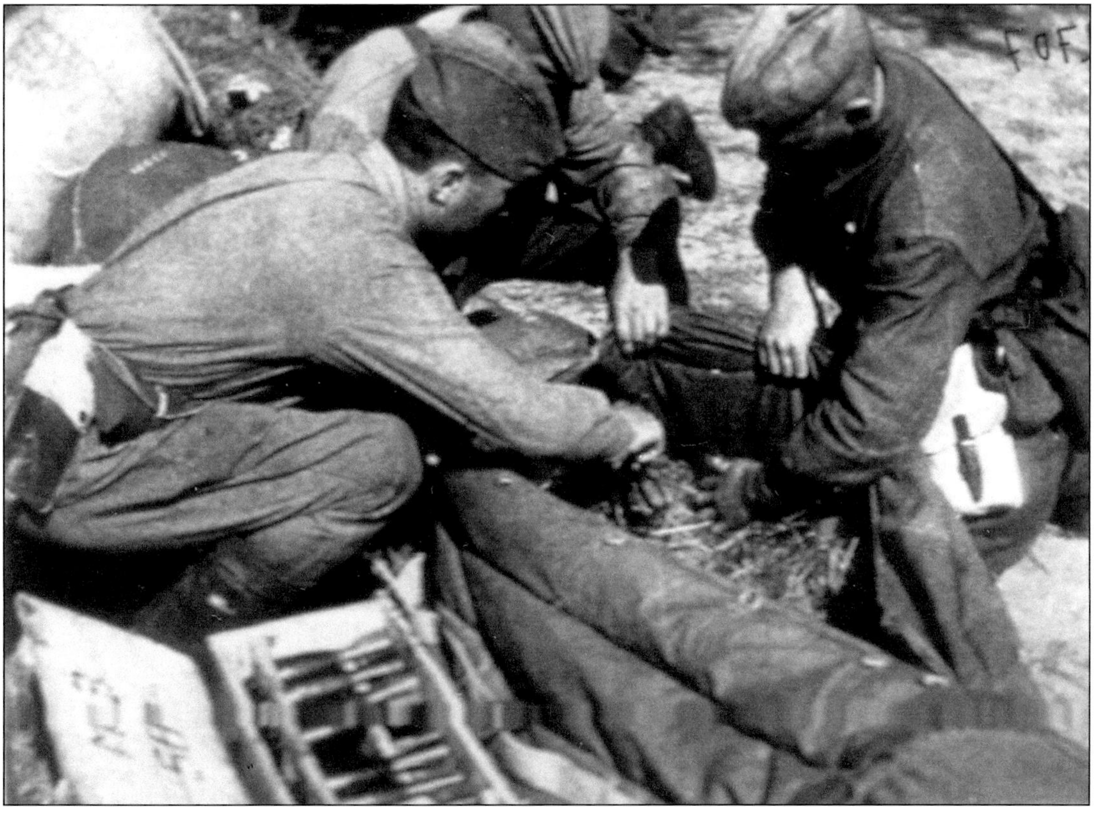

Unpacking a dropped parachute bag; note a box with mortar shells for a 50-mm mortar.

dropped through doors, or through hatches in the turrets. In order to use the lifting capacity of this aircraft to the full a number of racks for small calibre bombs would be required.

Therefore, for the large aircraft so-called cargo bridges began to be manufactured, these were detachable assemblies on which were a large number of bomb racks. A TB-3 bomber would have two of these bridges with a lifting capacity of up to 1,200kg with six locks fitted onto the principal bomb racks under the wing, and under the fuselage – with a further one designed to hold 1,600kg with four locks.

The bridge that was designed for the DB-3 bomber enabled either 12 PDMM parachute bags, or the same number of PDBB-100 tanks to be carried, or four large PDBB-400 tanks, or finally four universal descent pods weighing 300kg each. All this was to be dropped by parachute.

Cargo platforms appeared later for transporting cargoes without the need to drop them, since this would be the landing delivery. The platform for the DB-3 bomber was attached ventrally. It was used to carry machine guns, rifles in boxes, ammunition, provisions, and clothing, as well as spare parts and 50mm mortars. Motorcycles could also be loaded into it, as well as a 45mm anti-tank gun, up to a maximum weight of 1,400kg. This platform was under development in 'D' Brigade from the beginning of 1939. No information however is available concerning the manufacture of even prototype versions of this platform.

12

'Personnel Cages'

Within the OKPB, work was underway on alternative delivery systems to parachutes. The first of these to be put forward was the 'air droppable cabin cage'. Drawings revealed a large box shaped object with windows, standing on runners. These runners were spring mounted using rubber cord shock absorbers, similar to those used on aircraft operating at that time. A cage weighing 1,000kg could accommodate 14 people. It was to be suspended under a TB-1 bomber, and after it had been dropped from the aircraft it would descend under a single large parachute canopy (it goes without saying that this would be made of percale). The advantages of this approach would be the possibility of deploying combatants who were not accustomed to being dropped by parachute (since they would not actually have to do anything) and the compact nature of the landing, which offered a greater degree of safety for those on board. However, nobody actually came up with any means of controlling the cage in

A project for an 'air-droppable cabin cage' designed for 14 soldiers.

flight, whereas a parachutist can actually to some extent control his motion. Similarly, a prototype example was manufactured but the UVVS rejected it even before the start of testing.

Project G-49 envisaged the dropping of a similar personnel cage without any parachute at all from a low altitude and at a speed of between 100–150km/hr. There is no evidence anywhere of the provision of any kind of shock absorbers for the personnel inside the cage.

The G-73 assault cage was listed in the plan for 1933 and was designed for 16 people. This was intended for the TB-1 bomber. It is possible that this was the variant mentioned above of the KPS-16 production pod. The difference being that people jumped out of the KPS-16 and the aircraft actually brought the cage back, while the G-73 was to be dropped in its entirety. A percale parachute would be deployed with a diameter of 30m, and the pod detached from the aircraft using the separation method. That is to say the G-73 was in fact a 'personnel cage'. Equally there is no information available concerning any kind of shock absorbing provision, nor is there any information about the manufacture of a prototype example.

N.P. Blagin designed his own system that fulfilled a similar purpose, and which was known as a 'collective launch parachute' back in 1929. Six people should have been able to fit into his pod. A prototype example was manufactured which was dropped with ballast instead of people, but for some reason this broke up. It was not repaired any further.

13

The Aviabuses

What is an aviabus? It is an original airborne and landing system, which was invented by P.I. Grokhovskiy at the beginning of the 1930s. The aviabus was designed to deliver personnel, military vehicles, and various other cargoes to the ground without using parachutes. It was dropped over a flat location from low altitude. The main body in the shape of a short wing with a thick profile created a small amount of lift, which served to slow down the descent very slightly. The energy would later be dissipated as the aviabus moved along the ground. The 'summer' variants would ordinarily have two wheels at the front, while at the back they would have aircraft style tail skids. The 'winter' designs were either fitted on skis, or just landed on their belly. If the aviabus had wheels fitted or skis then shock absorbers were envisaged: these were either rubber plates or cords, leaf springs, or sprung shock absorbers. There were hydroaviabuses as well, these were actually open or enclosed craft that were dropped onto the surface of the water.

The aviabus was considered a means of delivering the first wave of paratroopers. This was motivated by the fact that a parachutist is in the air for a relatively long period of time. All the time that they are hanging underneath their canopy they are under fire from the ground. In that space of time the enemy could organise their defences, occupy convenient positions, and repel an attack by paratroopers. With the aviabuses however it was completely different. In a moment bombers would suddenly appear over a suitable landing site, carrying aviabuses on their external racks (either under the fuselage or under the wing). They fly very low, drop their cargo and then vanish behind the tops of the trees in the nearby forest. The aviabuses would trundle along the ground, and while they are still in motion hatches would open and gunners appear out of them. Once the aviabus has stopped soldiers would jump out and spread out towards the target, immediately going on the attack. The combatants would then clear the landing site of the enemy and occupy defensive positions, ensuring that the second wave of paratroopers is able to land. If the enemy are absent from the landing site then the operation begins as soon as the defensive positions have been occupied.

In the future, the use of cargo aviabuses was examined alongside the personnel variants. They were to be used to deliver ammunition, provisions, medical supplies, radio equipment, an entrenching tool, fording equipment and armament. The only thing that the designers were reticent about adding to the list were explosives. There is nothing in the documentation about using the aviabuses for delivering chemical weapons or incendiary mixtures. On the other hand much is written about heavy weapons: it was planned to load the aviabuses with heavy machine guns, small mountain and recoilless guns, tankettes, motorcycles and cars. The latter could also be loaded with machine guns, and small calibre automatic or recoilless weapons, which would support the infantry with covering fire. The creation of special self-propelled aviabuses was also envisaged that could carry snowmobiles, armoured vehicles, and light tanks, which could be dropped ready filled with fuel, oil and water and also loaded with ammunition and with a crew inside. They were to go on the attack immediately after landing.

The hydroaviabuses could ensure a rapid deployment of naval and river assault troops in what would be unexpected locations for the enemy. They were designed to support the deployment of troops onto the coast with fire from the machine guns they were fitted with. This group could then capture a lighthouse, a hydroplane base, quayside or bridge over a river.

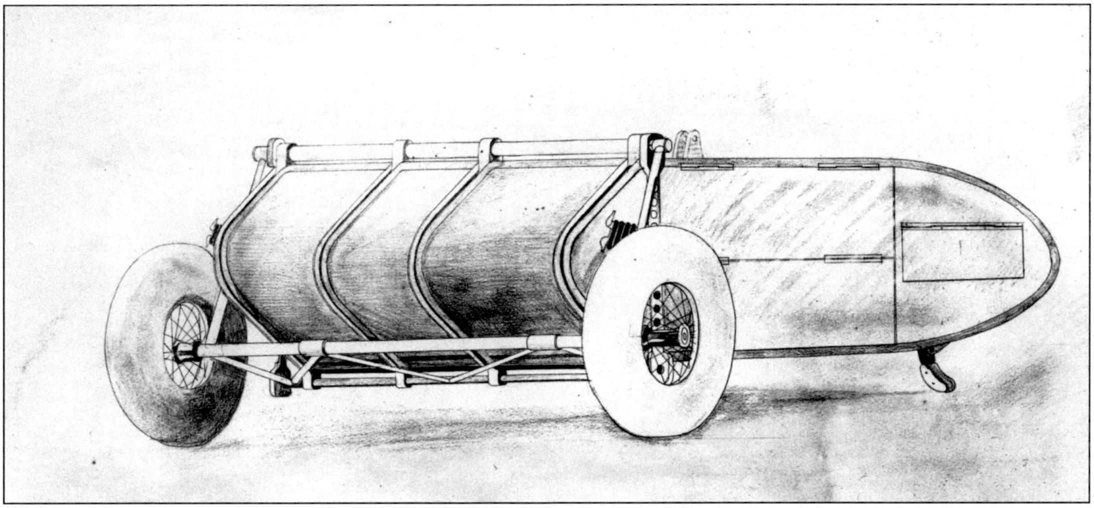

A project of wooden, 16-seat aviabus.

Two small, metal winter-use cargo aviabuses, suspended underneath an R-1 aircraft.

The aviabuses provided the possibility of not using airborne paratroopers who had undergone additional training, but ordinary rank and file infantry without any special clothing or equipment. An individual sitting or lying down inside would not have to do anything until the moment they touched down. Apart from that paratroopers would land without becoming scattered, as one team, whose combat potential was enhanced through cooperation.

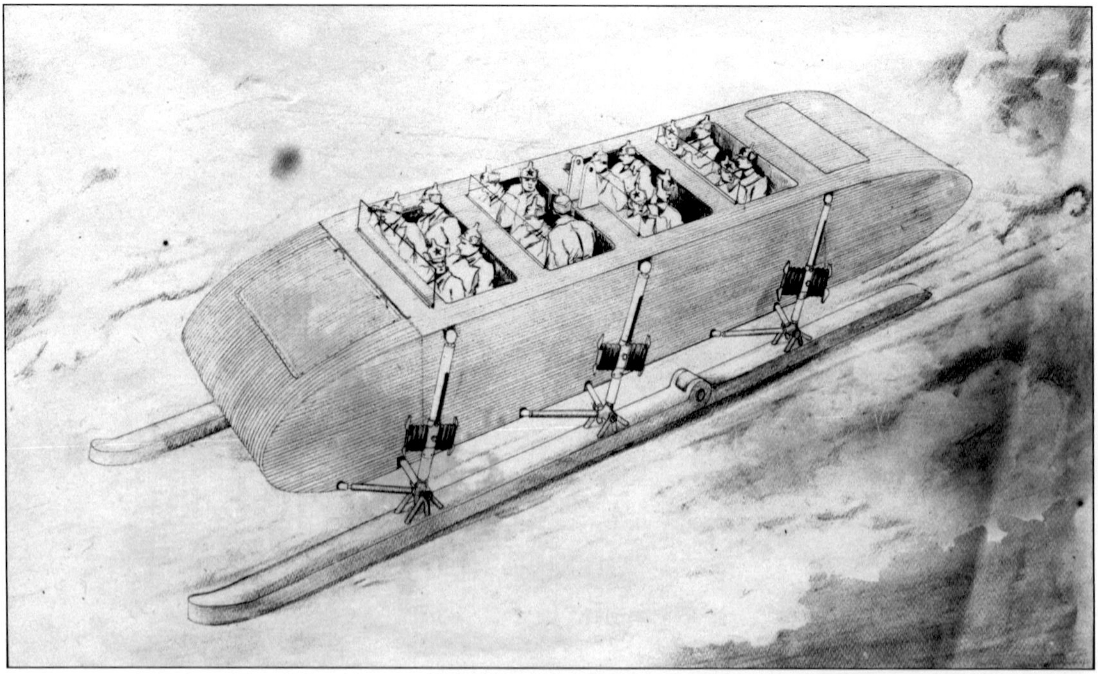

A project of airdrop sledges designed to accommodate 16 soldiers and to be dropped without a parachute.

Grokhovskiy appointed I.V. Titov to lead the work on the aviabuses. It was Ognyev who designed the first examples.

Experiments began in the autumn of 1930 when the first aviabuses were tested. They were small and capable of fitting under the wing. In actual fact, however, these were the larger models. The carrying aircraft was an R-5 biplane. The apparatus was attached to the beams for the bomb racks under the lower wing. They were dropped along with ballast (sand) onto the Moskva river. The first hydroaviabus immediately sank, but then floated to the surface but in doing so it had capsized "onto its belly". The second survived a few jumps but was destroyed in the course of the next drop onto water.

Sometime later small designs were tested that were to be carried under the wing of an R-1 aircraft, and which were configured for the 'winter' variant. They were manufactured in the workshops on Sinegubinskaya Street. Preliminarily one of the aviabuses was tested in a wind tunnel at the TsAGI – they wanted to see how it would behave in flight. In the tests the aviabuses were dropped onto a snow-covered field, ballast was placed inside in place of a cargo – this was made up of sandbags. After they touched down onto the snow they bounced for some time and one of them at the end of its landing roll turned over after hitting a bump.

At the NII VVS a scathing preamble was doing the rounds: "Only morons spend their money on boxes like that!" Grokhovskiy though was not put off. The next year saw a whole gamma of designs being produced for cargo, and passengers. There are references in various documents about three and five seat machines that were designed to be carried under an R-5. Their design was similar: an enclosed body of a mixed (wood and metal) structure, a pair of wheels on the front and two skids at the back. The spoked wheels were taken from the training Avro 504K (U-1) biplane. Interestingly although this aviabus is mentioned everywhere as being designed to carry three combatants its payload was just 150kg. Even if Grokhovskiy had based this on himself (and he was not a large man) then clothing, footwear, and the minimum weaponry would have to be factored in for an ordinary Red Army soldier (for example it was proposed that a Red Army soldier would carry a Mauser with him and two grenades). When all this is multiplied by three it is unlikely that Grokhovskiy would accommodate this in just 150kg.

A loaded G-51 platform underneath a TB-1 bomber.

This aviabus that was allegedly designed for three people was manufactured (several examples were evidently produced) and underwent testing. According to the report it was dropped five times. The altitude for these drops did not exceed eight metres. After sliding for between 30–100m depending on the prevailing conditions on the ground, the aviabus would come to a stop. In July 1931 this design was demonstrated during the course of exercises by forces from the Leningrad Military District in which the first airborne forces were active participants. The tests were conducted in the presence of the Deputy People's Commissar for Military and Naval Affairs M.N. Tukhachevskiy, who was overjoyed with these exotic innovations.

That very same year an aviabus drop was demonstrated before the upper leadership of the country on the Central airfield. The aviabus was dropped from a TB-1 aircraft. There were no people in it but after touching down dogs and chickens escaped from the hatches.

An aviabus designed for five people, and also manufactured from a mixed construction, looked more realistic. With a weight of 550kg it was designed for a payload of 600kg, that is to say for five fully equipped soldiers with their armament and their ammunition, and possibly a light machine gun into the bargain. This apparatus was naturally a little larger in reality, and the wheels were taken from an R-5.

In several documents the aviabus designed for five people is described as having been intended for the R-5 but this is not very likely. The point being that the maximum load for this biplane is around 800kg. Even if the electrical equipment were removed from this aircraft as well as the radio and the aft turret with its pair of machine guns this would not bring the aircraft up to 1,150kg. Apart from that how was this aviabus to get airborne under an R-5, is that not an issue as well? It could not be carried under the wing since the asymmetric nature of the load and the drag would be colossal, and it was beyond the capabilities of this aircraft to lift two of these aviabuses with a weight of 2,300kg. There are beams for Der-19 bomb racks under the fuselage of the R-5 but the ground clearance is minimal.

Therefore this aviabus was obviously designed for the twin-engine TB-1 bomber, which at that time was the most powerful aircraft in the RKKA VVS. It is suitable in terms of weight and could be accommodated

A loaded G-51 platform underneath a TB-1 bomber.

A G-68 aviabus under the lower wing of an R-5.

A cargo aviabus designed to carry 1,000kg.

comfortably under the fuselage between the undercarriage pyramids. It is possible that it was actually this apparatus that featured in the documents under the designation G-45.

The first drop with this aviabus occurred over the Central airfield in Moscow. The 'briefcase' survived the impact with the ground. The second drop was carried out with ballast and was also successful. A stray dog was drafted in for the third test after tempting him with sausage. The flight probably left an indelible impression on the dog; only after the apparatus had stopped did the hatch open and the dog shot off out of the awful metal cage and away from the mean bystanders as fast as he possibly could. Nobody ever saw that dog on the Central airfield again.

On the next drop a decision was taken to test the aviabus with people inside. Grokhovskiy himself climbed into the G-45 along with his Deputy I.V. Titov, Similar to the others, no comforts were envisaged for the passengers in this box. A half-length fur coat each was all that was laid down for the two commanders on the floor, and they were separated by a plywood bulkhead. Another document states that they were also tied down. The drop was carried out at a speed of approximately 170km/hr from a TB-1 that was flown by A.F. Anisimov. The landing was not a very smooth one at all, the apparatus bounced several times, after which it rolled around the airfield. Titov hit his head badly and lost consciousness for a short time, blood running from his nose. Grokhovskiy fared better. Titov was given something to wipe his face after which the crew were captured next to the apparatus on a movie camera. The fifth drop with the G-45 was again carried out without people inside.

On 2 December 1931 M. N. Tukhachevskiy ordered that the G-45 enter series production, and moreover the document stipulated that the lifting capacity of the apparatus was one tonne. This obviously did not refer to the G-45 but actually to the larger G-45A (or the G-45a), which was incorporated into the plan for 1932. This apparatus was proposed as a 12 seat passenger and cargo aviabus with a weight of 1,000kg. The intention for the G-45A aviabus was that it also be carried under the fuselage of the TB-1 bomber. It had a wooden body and

A TB-1 dropping an aviabus from under the fuselage.

P.I. Grokhovskiy and I.V. Titov after landing in a G-45 aviabus.

paired wheels at the front; four skids, which were similar to claws were manufactured, two on each side. Work to manufacture ten of these aviabuses began straight away at an experimental factory.

The full weight of the G-45A when loaded was set at approximately one and a half tonnes. The flight weight of the bomber moreover rose to 6,100kg. Furthermore, the aircraft was most likely specially lightened, with the armament removed and the fuel capacity reduced. The author was not able to find any Information concerning changes in the TB-1's flight performance characteristics with this pod suspended underneath but, with assemblies under the fuselage that were similar in dimensions and weight, the aircraft lost considerable amount of speed, and its practical ceiling and lifting capacity were significantly reduced. As if that wasn't enough the manoeuvrability, which was not excellent to start with, deteriorated still further. The take-off roll was made much longer, and the engines had to be maintained almost at full throttle right up until the moment the aviabus was released, which put them at risk from overheating.

An R-5 aircraft with two G-68 aviabuses under the wings, 1932.

The drop was carried out at a speed of 130km/hr: the pilot was not able to lower the engine rpm since the aircraft in this case would lose altitude rapidly. At the prescribed altitude of 10m this was simply dangerous. In 1932 a 12 seat G-45A was to have been presented to the NII VVS, but it still had not materialised by the end of the year.

In that same year of 1932, it was planned to demonstrate the G-45 on the Central airfield to the state and military leadership, but the author has not been able to locate any documents to this effect.

Parallel to the G-45 and the G-45A, the G-51 cargo aviabus platform was developed that was designed for a payload of 1,000kg (according to the NII VVS documents this figure was 750kg). It was similar to the G-45 but did not have any sides or a lid of any kind. The cargo would be loaded onto a platform, covered in a tarpaulin, and tied down securely with ropes. The G-52 was attached to the TB-1's ventral bomb racks. The platform underwent factory testing at 'Grokhovskiy's circus' and then in 1932 it was tested at the NII VVS. The list of inventions that were tested details an anonymous "cargo aviabus designed for a payload of one tonne". Judging by the photograph it was very similar to the G-45A. Evidently, this was still the G-51. It was written off as being "unbelievably overweight"; the apparatus was destroyed on the first drop after which it was rejected by the commission.

It was also planned to carry cargoes in small G-68 aviabuses. This was a wide, flat 'suitcase' type design with two wheels at the front and two pairs of skids at the back. Wood and plywood were the main materials used in its design. The standard lifting capacity was set at 150kg. Two of these apparatuses would be suspended on bomb racks under the lower wing of an R-5. The first drop of a G-68 was carried out by the famous pilot V.P. Chkalov, Two boxes were in the aviabus that were filled with light bulbs. Ahead of the flight Chkalov said: "I will drop your suitcase but first bring some bags and use them to collect some trash". The pilot however was wrong. After it touched the ground the apparatus continued its landing roll for another 100 metres, and then stopped. The cargo remained intact. The G-68 aviabuses were then presented for official testing at the NII VVS where it was damaged in the course of the first drop, and Grokhovskiy himself withdrew them from testing as incomplete.

Dropping an aviabus designed for summer use that was fitted with wheels from a TB-1 aircraft.

In Grokhovskiy's future plans, a 16 seat 'summer' aviabus was also envisaged, which was of a wooden construction (it is possible that this was a development of the G-45A, and in some documents the designation G-54A can be found), these represented a metal aviabus sledge, and a cargo aviabus for heavy equipment.

A drawing of the 16 seat aviabus on wheels is found in an album of reports belonging to OKPB. Seemingly the G-68 was used as a basis, and its dimensions were increased significantly.

The author was able to find a drawing of the aviabus sledge that was drawn by an artist. Some 16 combatants sat in groups of four in four cells, protected from the oncoming airflow only by a windshield. Interestingly the combatants are armed with 'three-line rifles' with bayonets affixed. Neither the artists nor the designer had given any thought to what would happen with these bayonets should one of the combatants not be sitting in their place. It was more important for them to underline the full combat capability of the detachment immediately on landing. The sledges were fixed onto long runners that were attached to the main body using legs fitted with shock absorbers. Each of these runners consisted of two sections, linked by a hinge. This was done so that the runner did not break whilst moving over an uneven surface.

Details of the design of this heavy aviabus are not known. What is known is that in terms of the concept it should have been able to deliver a 76mm mountain gun, or a tractor to the ground, or a car such as a 'Ford A', or a T-27 tankette or even a light tank (although it is not known which of them). The carrying aircraft for this large aviabus was to have been the four-engine TB-3 bomber. Moreover, this was 'not up to the job' of carrying a light tank.

The military commissioned Grokhovskiy to create an 'aviatankette', which was an aviabus but on caterpillar tracks that was lightly armed, and had its own engine, and armament. It was to be dropped along with its crew and be able to move straight away, immediately after landing. It has to be said that this was not an easy task to set. Overall the machine would not weigh less than a T-27. In full configuration this tankette could only be carried by a TB-3. Furthermore, at altitude the oil and water in this vehicle would freeze. They had to be dropped separately in PDBB tanks, and would be pre-heated and only then would the engine be started. Since the attachment for the aviabus along with its engine was also an external one these same problems would be encountered with them. Evidently the creation of the 'aviatankette' was not taken seriously.

A hydroaviabus underneath a TB-1 aircraft.

From 1934 onwards, the attitude to the aviabuses began to change. Enthusiasm gave way to scepticism. The constant problems in the course of testing undermined faith in their reliability. Apart from that the design characteristics of the aviabuses began to work against them. An aviabus turned out to be much heavier than a parachute harness for the same cargo and significantly more expensive. Parachute equipment progressed rapidly in those years. Under the leadership of Grokhovskiy a system was created for dropping artillery armament, motorcycles, cars, and T-27 tankettes, which was introduced into service.

Dropping the aviabus from low altitude appeared dangerous for the carrying aircraft. At an altitude of between 8–10m the aircraft could be fired upon even from a pistol and an R-5, and especially a TB-1 were by no means small targets. Therefore, work on the aviabuses began to be wound down. During a demonstration to the members of the Government on 8 August 1944 the aviabuses did not feature at all.

Grokhovskiy however did not give up on the idea of dropping cargoes from low altitude without a parachute. In 1935 he worked on a whole series of these projects. In the G-48 design he planned to drop a T-26 tank from low level. In this case he designed the equipment for another kind of carrying aircraft: the TB-3 was not able to carry this equipment. It is possible that he was counting on the six-engine TB-4 or the military variant of the *Maksim Gorkiy* or perhaps on another multi-engine flying monster.

From 1936 in the Soviet Union, work on similar topics was stopped altogether. The Germans were gaining ground in the race. During the Second World War the Germans produced the *Dobbas* droppable container, which was a freshwater aviabus but without wheels. In profile it was the shape of a large droplet and the sides were straight. The *Dobbas* was suspended on beams for external bomb racks on He 111H and Ju 88A bombers and was dropped without a parachute from low altitude. A box was envisaged for dropping military equipment, anti-tank guns and small field guns, as well as motorcycles with sidecars. Furthermore, the barrels of the guns would protrude through the window in the forward section of the box. The Germans tested the *Dobbas* but did not deploy it on the front line.

Dropping a hydroaviabus onto the Moskva River from a TB-1 aircraft.

Grokhovskiy turned out to be a visionary: cargoes, as well as military equipment are dropped from low level nowadays. It was just that the technical capabilities were not there for the development of this equipment at the time and owing to his lack of education he himself was not able to foresee all the 'pitfalls'. The aircraft with suitable lifting capacity had yet to be developed, and the same could be said of the high-strength materials, and modern calculation methodologies.

Today the separation method is used on a regular basis – a drogue parachute, as it opens drags some military hardware or a pallet with a cargo on out of the fuselage. These experiments were carried out in the 1960s, and in the 1970s the Americans used this method to supply Ke Sanh airfield in Vietnam that was surrounded.

It is therefore by no means ruled out that the aviabuses may return to us in some new form, in the same way that the Gatling gun returned in the form of a chain gun.

14

Drops onto Water

It was not only the hydroaviabuses that were designed to be dropped onto water. For example, Grokhovskiy created the G-48 motorboat for 14 people. This was a relatively large launch that was rounded in shape, which it was planned would be dropped together with its crew. In the front, behind a glass windscreen was the driver, the engine was located at the back. The soldiers sat on transverse seats and there was no roof. Along a vertical axis was a steel bar, to suspend this craft underneath an aircraft (judging by the drawing this would have been a TB-1). Apart from the paratrooper's armament the craft was armed with three 7.62mm DA aviation machine guns, two in the front, and two at the back. It cannot be said with any confidence whether the G-48 was actually manufactured and tested, but there was a 'Grokhovskiy's assault craft' at the NII VVS in 1932. During the course of its first drop onto the Moskva River it "was destroyed and sank".

Blagin designed a slightly smaller craft for six combatants and 170kg of cargo. Another document states that it was planned for this craft to be armed with three machine guns. This craft however was to have been dropped by parachute. A prototype example was manufactured and presented for testing in the summer of 1931, so earlier than the G-48. The drop was carried out just once, the parachute opened, but then deflated, and the craft was destroyed as it hit the water and went to the bottom. After this evidently the work was stopped.

A project of G-48 motor boat which was designed to hold 14 soldiers and to be dropped without a parachute onto water.

The idea however did not die. In the Second World War years in many countries rescue craft were either dropped from aircraft with parachutes or by parachute, (and moreover these craft were not inflated) down to sailors who found themselves in the water after their ships had sunk.

Grokhovskiy's plan for 1933 mentions dropping a small torpedo boat with an M-34 engine (evidently this was the GAM-34 motor boat engine) from low level at a speed of approximately 100km/hr. Since there were no torpedo launches with an approximate weight in service with the Soviet fleet this was just an interesting idea that in reality was never realised.

15

Assault Gliders

At the end of 1942, Soviet assault gliders were first used just outside Stalingrad to solve an actual objective of transporting military cargoes. The idea itself though was nothing new. The concept of a military 'transporter glider' appeared in the first half of the 1930s. The VVS OKPB worked on these craft, and later on, at the Experimental Institute of the NKTP under the leadership of P.I. Grokhovskiy.

In October 1931, Grokhovskiy proposed an idea to the designer B.D. Urlapov that they carry out preliminary calculations for an assault glider design. The towing aircraft was to have been an R-5. Nobody had produced gliders such as these anywhere in the world at that time.

The first variant of this design envisaged a traditional monoplane layout with a fuselage, in which the pilot and the combatants would sit. The payload was set at 1,000kg. Grokhovskiy rejected it, specifying a payload of 1,700kg.

Urlapov selected a layout for the second time that was closer to a flying wing. The only person sat in the fuselage would be the pilot with his controls, the passengers and cargo would be accommodated in the thick profile wing (with a maximum thickness of 600mm), which created a large amount of lift. The aft section of the fuselage represented a thin tail boom with a standard monoplane tail fin. According to the calculations this aircraft would be able to carry a pilot, and 16 soldiers.

Grokhovskiy organised an aviation section in his design bureau under this project with a staff of eight people. The head of this section was a student Urlapov who had not yet completed his studies, and who back then was just 20 years old.

Work began on a preliminary design for this glider, designated the G-63, at the beginning of 1932. This was a cantilever monoplane of a wooden construction with a wingspan of 28m. A drop shaped cockpit was attached to the front of the wing centre section for the pilot. This was open to the elements and the pilot was protected from the front by a windscreen. A compartment was envisaged behind the pilot where a small amount of cargo could be stowed, or another person could sit. The drop shaped nose section provided a smooth transition to a boom with an oval cross-section on the end of which was a fin and a stabiliser. The stabiliser was attached to the fin by bracing wires, and the fin in turn was attached to the wing in the same way. The elevators and rudder both had balance horns.

In the wing root on both sides there were eight cargo cells with a length of 2,100mm, a width of 660mm, and a height of 550mm. Each cell was designed to hold one person or a package containing 100kg of cargo. OKPB documents for 1932 state that the glider was designed for 16 people plus 500kg of cargo. If the glider were used for transporting people, the paratroopers inside it would lie on their stomachs facing the direction of flight. The leading edge of these cells was made transparent (it was manufactured from celluloid). Several documents indicate that there was a plan to put holes in this leading edge to enable paratroopers to fire using their weapons – rifles and light machine guns. The leading edge of the wing where it met the cells was made to fold backwards opening the hatches for people to embark, or disembark, or for cargo to be loaded.

The G-36 had what was for that time a traditional fixed undercarriage with two main pyramid type undercarriage legs and a metal tail skid. Shock absorbing for the undercarriage was rubber. The standard flight weight for the glider was assessed as 3,000kg.

The designer of the G-31 and G-63 gliders, B.D. Urlapov.

The 'airborne barge' project was demonstrated to the Head of the VVS Ya.I. Alksnis and gained his approval.

Manufacturing of the glider was completed at Factory No.47 in Leningrad. It was manufactured in less than eight months. The empty weight of the glider was 1,289kg. At the beginning of 1932 the machine in a dismantled form was readied for transfer to Krasnogvardeysk (Gatchina). There was trepidation about testing this glider at the Commandant's airfield in Leningrad, since the 'sky train' needed a long take-off run. The wing centre section, tail section of the fuselage along with the fin, and the wing outer sections were transported separately. The greatest difficulties lay in transporting the wing centre section that had a wingspan of 12m. The wing centre section was loaded onto a truck and a four-wheel trailer in such a way that the cockpit was jutted out to the side. The width worked out at approximately 6m. The route had to be closed while the glider was being moved, and in one location the tall parapets of a bridge had to be cut off. The move though was successful.

In the course of a day the G-63 was assembled and on the following day was demonstrated to the People's Commissar for Military and Naval Affairs K.E. Voroshilov, and his Deputy M.N. Tukhachevskiy who had arrived from Leningrad with their entourage. Grokhovskiy himself provided the commentary.

An R-5 reconnaissance aircraft was used to tow the glider. All the weapons had been removed from this aircraft and a truss made from pipes was fitted to the aft section of the fuselage, which protruded beyond the rudder. The glider could be towed at a speed of 150km/hr.

On the first flight the towing aircraft was flown by B.V. Bitskiy, while Urlapov sat in the back seat and was responsible for disengaging the glider should anything untoward happen. Grokhovskiy himself flew the glider. The aircraft took the glider into the sky successfully. The take-off roll was around 120m. At an altitude of 4–5m Grokohvskiy disengaged from the towing aircraft, climbed a little higher, then glided for a while, and landed. The flight had revealed the aircraft lack of stability as it would lurch from side to side. Longitudinal fluctuations also occurred that were caused by the poor design of the shock absorber in the towing gear.

The reason behind the G-63's directional instability was thought to be the introduction of a bearing into the design of the towing gear and this was replaced by a rigid coupling. The second flight confirmed the validity of

A group of OKPB VVS employees who participated in the design of the G-31 glider.

A G-63 glider in flight.

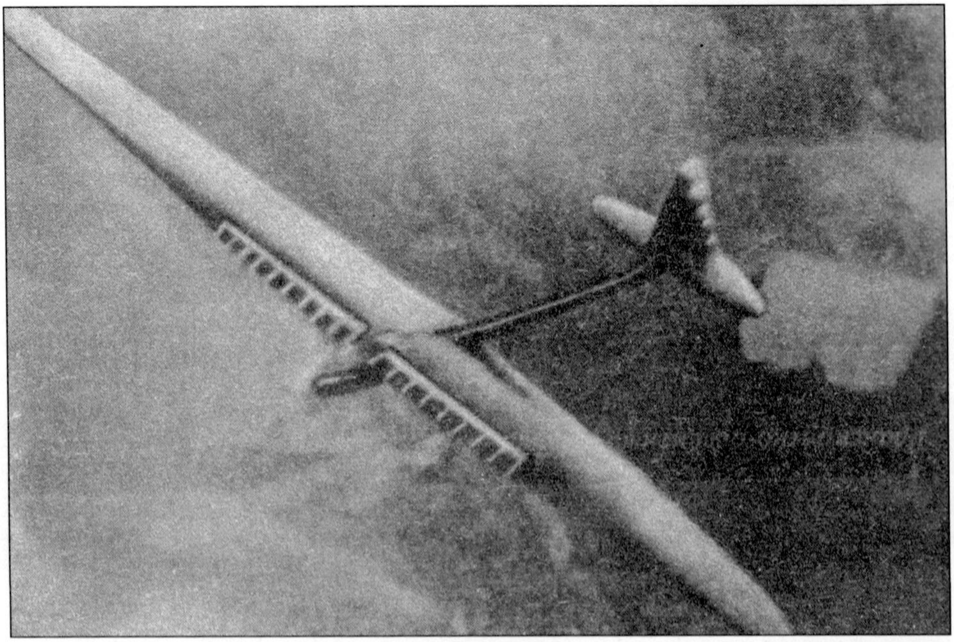

A G-63 glider in flight.

this decision, the same crew also flew the aircraft on this sortie.

The third flight took place with the aircraft fully loaded with ballast in the shape of 32 sandbags. This time however Grokhovskiy disengaged from the glider at a very high altitude and was not able to land back on the airfield. After crossing a river with some difficulty, he landed the glider in a marsh. Bouncing on the hillocks the glider broke a wire somewhere and came to a stop. No damage was noted and the G-63 was pushed back onto the airfield manually by a company of Red Army soldiers.

Following these flights, the glider was handed over for state testing. These tests were undertaken by military test pilots. V.S. Vakhmistrov was appointed Chairman of the Commission. The G-63 was due to be piloted by V.N. Stepanchenok, and the towing aircraft by pilot Kotelnikov. In the rear cockpit of the R-5 sat Urlapov. With these new pilots some quite sharp jerks were evident on take-off and this caused the towing mechanism to fluctuate once again but Stepanchenok was able to handle the controls. He disengaged at an altitude of 500m and performed a series of turns and figures of eight. A series of successful flights followed this one.

The commission concluded that the G-63 had been a success. The following was written in the report on the test programme: "The tests that have been carried out on the experimental towed 'sky train' confirm the possibility, and the expediency of the deployment of special cargo and passenger gliders in airborne operations".

At the end of 1932 the G-63 suffered an accident during one of its flights. It was decided that the repair would be carried out alongside a modernisation. The glider underwent repairs and a refit in Leningrad from May to August 1933. The new variant was designated the G-31. The cockpit had been expanded, and a seat for a second pilot had been fitted to it. The rudder had been expanded and the range of deflection for the control surfaces and the ailerons was changed. The empty weight of the glider had risen to 1,490kg.

On the G-63's first flight, Stepanchenok took off and immediately disengaged from the glider, turned and landed on the edge of the airfield. The glider was loaded with ballast in the shape of 12 sandbags. Stepanchenok commented on the poor handling of the G-31, which was in his opinion linked to the small area of the ailerons. On the next flight 16 sandbags were loaded on board. In order to shift the centre of gravity forwards a tank was fitted in the nose section of the fuselage that held 50 liters of water. The glider was flown by M.A. Nyukhtikov and Grokhovskiy sat in the co-pilot's seat. The take-off run was long – the G-31's take-off speed was higher than that of the towing aircraft: The R-5 would take to the air first to be followed by the glider. In flight, the G-31

An R-5 towing aircraft with a protective frame behind the tail fin.

Details of the protective frame mounted behind the tail fin of the R-5 towing aircraft.

Pilot V.A Stepanchenok who test flew the G-31 and G-36 gliders.

would stay below the towing aircraft at all times and would jerk it from side to side. When the cable jerked, the R-5 would slow down and loose altitude. After the third such sharp jerk on the cable Nyukhtikov disengaged. On landing he clipped the roof of a single storey building and came down in a courtyard. Nyukhtikov was not injured, but Grokhovskiy was thrown onto the wing and was stunned.

The G-31 was later repaired, and Stepanchenok completed further successful flights in this glider. Following these flights, the machine was converted into a powered glider.

In July 1934, a second example of an assault glider was manufactured in Moscow, which differed from the G-63, and the G-31. This glider was named the *Yakov Alksnis*. Permission to use of the Head of the VVS name was granted by Tukhachevskiy, but he had not asked permission from Alksnis. The undercarriage for the new glider was lower, and the attachment points for the brace struts had changed and drop shaped cowlings had been fitted to the wheels. The new undercarriage was made more rigid and was strengthened. The cable to the control surfaces was taken inside the fuselage. For winter operations it was planned to replace the wheeled undercarriage with skis. There were two pilot seats, and the pilots sat in a tandem arrangement. The aircraft was brightly painted in blue and white colours.

Testing of the *Yakov Alksnis* to begin with was successful. Stepanchenok flew the glider. It was planned to demonstrate this aircraft at the Air Fleet Day celebrations on 18 August at Tushino. Apart from an evaluation of the handling characteristics, special boxes for armament and ammunition were evaluated within the confines of the test programme. The point being that the design that had been selected for stowing the payload had a series of shortcomings. The system of long and narrow cells made loading and unloading difficult. Stowing of large sized armament, such as guns was not possible, even though the lifting capacity of the glider would have enabled it in theory. The paratroopers were not able to jump out of the glider in the air since the hatches for the cells were built into the leading edge of the wing. There was a plan to partially offset the first shortcoming by creating special boxes and tanks, which were manufactured to the exact measurements of the cells, and which had special attachments.

During the course of testing experiments were conducted into how the 'sky train' would behave if an

A G-31 glider and an R-5 towing aircraft in the hangar.

The *Yakov Alksnis* glider on the Central airfield in Moscow, August 1934.

The *Yakov Alksnis* glider in flight.

The Yakov *Alksnis* glider on the airfield.

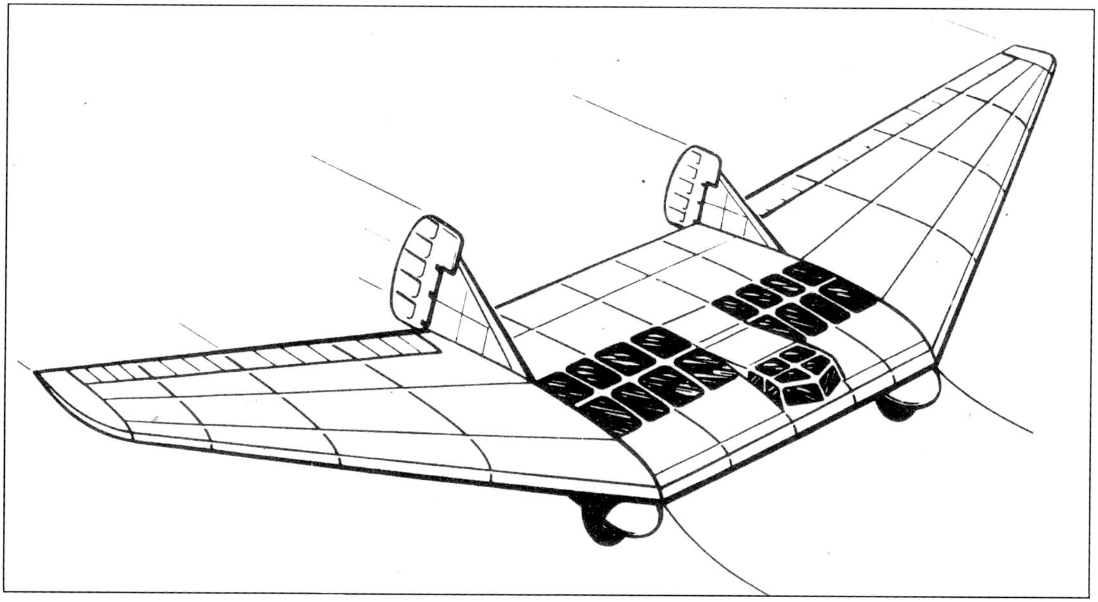

A 50-seat G-64 glider (possibly also designated as G-51).

This illustration shows positioning of the crew, paratroopers and cargo in a G-64 glider.

Designer's view of a train of G-64 gliders being towed behind a G-52 towing aircraft.

inexperienced glider pilot were to take the glider up to a high altitude and the tail of the towing aircraft began to pitch-up. The R-5 was piloted by pilot Dubrovskiy and Urlapov sat in the rear cockpit. In the cockpit of the *Yakov Alksnis* was Stepanchenok.

Whilst carrying out this manoeuvre, Stepanchenok overdid it: the tail of the towing aircraft not only started to pitch up but was actually in a vertical position with the nose pointing downwards. Urlapov pulled on the release lever but the lock did not release. The biplane began to descend downwards pulling the glider down with it. Stepanchenok also tried to open the lock from his end but it did not work. It then turned out that in a twisted position the ring would not disengage from the lock. Stepanchenok put the *Yakov Alksnis* into a steep dive and overtook the towing aircraft slightly. The cable sagged; at that moment the glider pilot pulled the stick towards him sharply. The cable snapped as a result of the jerk.

The R-5 recovered from the dive at such a low altitude that it took the top branches off the trees. The glider actually flew over the tall brick chimney of a forge and caught it with the cable. The cable wound itself round the chimney, but actually slid off. The *Yakov Alksnis* landed successfully.

At the beginning of August however the glider pilot's luck changed. The R-5 was flown by M.N. Kaminskiy and Urlapov sat once again in the rear cockpit of the glider. So a young, inexperienced pilot sat in the glider, while Grokhovskiy sat in the co-pilot's seat. The *Yakov Alksnis* took a long time to take off, the young pilot was not able to put the aircraft into the air. Then it became clear that the situation was dangerous for the towing aircraft. The glider slid to the side and crashed into the roof of a single storey barracks. The crash disrupted the planned demonstration of the glider at the aviation celebrations in Tushino. By the end of August repair work on the glider had begun and it soon returned to flying again. The *Yakov Alksnis* was used for some time to test various developments produced by the Experimental Institute.

In 1933, Alksnis issued an order to examine the possibility of converting the G-31 into a powered glider. It was planned that with its maximum payload on board it would be towed as a self-contained glider but would actually fly by itself when empty. Grokhovskiy entrusted this work to Urlapov as a matter of priority. A variant

A project of five-engine G-52 towing aircraft in the transport version.

was developed with an air-cooled M-11 radial engine with a nominal rating of 100hp. The engine was mounted on a frame made from steel tubes in the nose of the fuselage. The aircraft was fitted with a two-bladed wooden, fixed pitch propeller. The engine controls and the required instruments were fitted inside the cockpit. The undercarriage was reworked using the undercarriage on the *Yakov Alksnis* as an example with cowlings on the wheels. In winter the wheeled undercarriage could be replaced with skis.

The G-31 was again converted in Leningrad. After that it was tested in the course of 1935 and partly into 1936. The designation remained as before, but the engine designation was added to it, so it became the G-31 M-11. In the institute's plan for this work it is listed as the G-31B. T.T. Malomuzh flew this aircraft. The powered glider took off confidently without a towing aircraft both on a wheeled undercarriage, and on skis. The take-off run was approximately 450m. The aircraft cruising speed was around 130km/hr. In the opinion of the pilot this machine was sufficiently stable and handled well. Malomuzh however thought that the G-31 M-11's power to weight ratio was insufficient.

According to documents that have survived, it was planned in the future to fit the G-31 with two M-11 engines and increase the number of paratroopers up to 18. Evidently in this case the engines would need to be fitted onto the wing. Instead in 1936 the M-11 was replaced by a more powerful American Wright *Cyclone* F-3, an air-cooled, nine-cylinder radial engine fitted with a supercharger. A two bladed propeller was again fitted but this time it was a metal, variable pitch propeller. The cylinder heads were covered in a narrow Townend ring cowling, and the cowlings on the wheels were removed. The speed rose to 150km/hr and the practical ceiling also rose. The imported *Cyclone* was replaced some time later with an M-25, which was a Soviet copy of this engine. This variant is known as the G-31 M-25. The powered glider was tested up until the end of 1936; work on this project was brought to an end in connection with the disbandment of the Experimental Institute of the NKTP.

Grokhovskiy was engaged in other glider projects to transport people and cargoes. In the plan for 1932 the G-5 topic is listed in terms of a 50-seat glider that would operate with the twin-engine R-6 aircraft. This glider would itself later feature under the designation G-64. No details concerning the design of this glider are known. It is possible that this was the same glider that went on to become the G-51. This machine is described in very general terms in materials dating from 1934.

The G-51 was designed to drop paratroopers and to deploy troops behind enemy lines. Alternatively, it could be used as a bomber, dropping bombs of varying types as well as chemical spraying devices to spray poison agents. This was a flying wing 'tailless' design with a twin tail. A thick profile wing was used as before, in which passengers would be accommodated along with the crew (the two pilots). The top of the pilot's cockpit, which was fully glazed, as were the sides and the forward section, protruded upwards (though not forwards) from the leading edge of the wing. The passengers and cargo were accommodated in the wing centre section in cells in the wing leading edge, these cells had one hatch on the top. The wing centre section itself was rectangular in plan view. It

A project of the G-53 'airdrop fighter'.

had reinforced ribs at both ends to the top of which the vertical tail fin was attached, while the undercarriage was attached to these same ribs from below. It is evident from drawings that have survived that the wheels are hidden inside enormous cowlings. The machine was controlled using control surfaces and elevons. It was planned to tow the G-51 using three cables, attached to the sides of these same reinforced ribs.

The G-51 could be used to transport people and cargo, as well as being used as a bomber with a payload of up to 40tonnes (!). In the latter instance it would disengage at an altitude of approximately 500m at a distance of around 50km from the target. The machine would glide silently up until the moment the bomb was dropped, the poison agents had been discharged, or the incendiary mixtures had been deployed (evidently this took the form of a granulated yellow phosphorous – a 'Fire Rain' system). According to Grokhovskiy's assurances the glider could poison a strip 500m wide and 100km long or set an area 80km long and 100m wide ablaze. After that was completed, the pilots were to jump out by parachute "abandoning the glider to the flames".

The G-51 also could participate in 'sky train' sorties, which consist of eight gliders flying one behind the other at a distance of 50m from one another. None of the aircraft available at that time would have been able to tow this 'train', so a special G-52 towing aircraft was used for this purpose. It made use of individual components from the TB-3 heavy bomber including the wing and the engine mounting. A fifth engine was added to the four engines of the TB-3 and in total they should have been capable of producing 5,000hp. The aft section of the fuselage formed a twin-boom arrangement with a twin tail. The tail booms were linked at the end by a single stabiliser. The undercarriage differed significantly from the design of the TB-3, since it did not have any bracing struts and the wheels were covered in cowlings.

Grokhovskiy dreamed of mass glider assaults. In Experimental Institute documents there are references pertaining to estimates of assaults involving 40,000 men, who would be deployed using 100 'trains' with eight gliders in each.

The G-53 'assault fighter' project was also in existence at that time. Ordinarily a fighter is just designed for a single person, the pilot. Grokhovskiy's design bureau however considered how it could be used to deliver paratroopers. A glider in the form of a flying wing would be attached underneath a fighter (in a surviving illustration this was similar to an I-5 biplane). The attachment of the glider, which had its own undercarriage, to

The I-5 biplane fighter which was planned to be used in the G-53 project.

the fighter would allegedly take just 15 minutes. The glider could accommodate 12 paratroopers lying down and facing forwards. The leading edge of the wing was made transparent so that they would have some understanding of what was happening. The paratroopers would exit the aircraft through narrow hatches in the specified location (it is possible that this was achieved according to the principle of the 'automatic Red Army soldier deployment system') and the fighter would return along with the glider. In a second variant the glider would be dropped at low level (at an altitude of between five to six metres) and the locks would open automatically after a probe protruding under the aircraft had hit the ground.

The G-53 was also assessed as a potential bomber with a payload of 1,500kg but it was most likely viewed as a glide bomb. After it had been dropped it would glide towards the target in a straight line without a pilot and would maintain its heading with the help of gyroscopes.

As far as future Experimental Institute designs were concerned, all these projects remained on paper. In the institute's documentation there are no numerical calculations presented for the dimensions, weight, and proposed flight performance characteristics. It is possible that these were not realised, and were limited to general considerations, and ideas. For example, in relation to the 'train' made up of G-52 towing aircraft and eight G-51 gliders a thought that immediately comes to mind is the enormous dimensions of the airfield that would be needed for them to take off. This issue was probably not thought through like so many others.

In August 1934 one issue that was discussed at the Committee for Defence was dropping small submarines onto the water in large hydrogliders (these were essentially flying boats that landed on water). This would significantly increase their range, enhance manoeuvrability, and could ensure the element of surprise in an attack. No realistic steps were ever taken however in this direction.

The practical solution therefore was limited to the G-63/G-31 and *Yakov Alksnis* gliders. Work on these projects ceased following the liquidation of the Experimental Institute of the NKTP. Assault gliders were forgotten for several years and were only remembered when news broke of successful operations by German military glider pilots in May 1940.

16

Communication Systems

From the very beginning the intention was to supply the paratroopers with radio communications. This was to have been provided by light radio sets that could be dropped from aircraft in parachute bags and crates. Subsequently it was decided that these should be augmented by more powerful apparatus, capable of working as a telephone over a range of up to 150km, and as a telegram machine over a distance of up to 400km. It was envisaged that they would be carried in vehicles.

Communications between detachments of paratroopers were to be provided by a field telephone. The cables however would be laid using a far from traditional method. Instead of a telephone engineer towing a coil of cable on their back an R-5 biplane would be used, which would unwind as the aircraft flew along. To begin with a PG-2k boxes would be dropped from an aircraft by parachute containing a UNA-F field telephone. The cable would begin to be drawn out from this equipment. The length of this cable could vary. Thus the cable in the PRK-5 assembly there was a coil of cable 5km long. There were drums containing 10km (PRK-10), and 30km (PRK-30) of cable. As the cable ran out the aircraft would drop a second field telephone, and where necessary a telephonist.

The system was developed at the Leningrad branch of the OKPB. Testing of the first variant of the assembly, named the 'airborne cable dispenser' was undertaken at the NII VVS between 20–25 March 1932. A cable six kilometres long was laid from an R-5 aircraft, dropping two telephones at each end. This entire operation took just five minutes.

This system was refined and updated several times. One of the later variants was demonstrated to the People's Commissar G.K. Ordzhonikidze. A second telephone system along with a telephony operator was dropped near a village and allowed the Commissar to have a conversation with the representative of the Village Soviet who was very surprised.

Other projects as well as more powerful telephone cable dispensing systems were in existence. The lengths of the lines in these cases were measured in kilometres.

During the Second World War a similar assembly for laying field telephone cables was in service with the *Luftwaffe*. The cable was unwound from a Fi 156 *Storch* liaison aircraft at low level.

In order for paratroopers to send signals over a short distance, as with other ground-based forces it was planned to use signal guns (flare guns) with different colour rockets. Popham's flags, an indispensible accessory on any airfield at that time would also come into play. These were flags formed of strips of a white material from which different signals were set out. The most famous of these was the letter 'T' denoting 'cleared to land'. By changing the symbols on the runway for aircraft in the circuit some quite complex messages can be sent. In a combat environment the strips can quickly discolour, turning grey, and they can be hard to make out in the terrain. In the absence of signal flags, the plan was to form signal characters from items of clothing, torn up newspapers, and even the combatants themselves.

The messages that were unfurled, trophy documents, and maps were to be picked up by the grapnel. Grapnel was in form of a small anchor that was towed behind a reconnaissance aircraft on a cable. The documents were packed and suspended on a cord hung between two poles. Sometimes in place of the poles, pyramids were formed of rifles fixed with bayonets. An aircraft at low level would deploy the grapnel and capture the cargo. Then the flight observer would retract the cable into the rear cockpit along with the package. For the crew this was a very

A telephone set in a parachute bag is dropped from an aircraft fitted with a G-8 'cable dispensing' system.

Catching a message from the ground using a grapnel from an R-1 aircraft.

Soldiers from the 3rd Special Purpose Brigade pack communications equipment and ammunition into parachute bags.

complex task requiring specific training' and often the 'cat catchers' would catch on to something else and crash into the ground or into trees.

This idea was later developed further: in 1939 research was conducted into the possibility of capturing a cargo from the ground that weighed up to 100kg, including a human being, using various aircraft. Interestingly this not only included an R-5 biplane but bomber aircraft, which for their time were relatively fast such as SBs and TB-3s. Nothing further however is known about the results of this research.

There were also plans to use messenger pigeons. Paratroopers were planning to drop them in a G-57 cylinder that could accommodate ten birds. This would have landed under a parachute. An example of a liaison vehicle with a pigeon loft was manufactured in prototype form for paratroopers that made use of the wheels from a 'Ford A' vehicle.

The raiding paratroopers were able to get their orders and other documents including maps with the help of the 'parachute messengers'. In the course of an assault raid the messengers can liaise between the detachments getting around on bicycles or motorcycles.

Grokhovskiy was planning at one time to lead the paratroopers from an airborne command post based on an ANT-9, giving commands from the air via a powerful megaphone that was being lowered down 500m on a cable. If you can imagine a huge three-engine aircraft flying at low level with a commander shouting out orders from it!

Subsequently the design of the TB-3 flying headquarters aircraft appeared. The plan was for this aircraft to have working facilities and a powerful communications hub. Following a landing behind enemy lines a large antenna mast was to be mounted from out of the fuselage of this aircraft, an electric generator would be started, and the command post would be ready. A main airborne assault could be controlled from this command post, but no prototype was ever manufactured – it is possible that this was because there were insufficient numbers of TB-3 aircraft even for heavy bomber squadrons.

17

Long Tailed Saboteurs

It was not only people who were to be dropped by parachute. Para-saboteurs were to be assisted by specially trained animals – 'secret service' dogs'. They were trained to identify targets for setting up explosive operations: railway bridges and the personnel posted around them, bridges, and oil storage depots, as well as aircraft, and vehicles. It was thought that long tailed saboteurs could be of use specifically in disrupting any movements along railway lines in the period when forces were concentrating in a specific area. Other operations were entrusted to the dogs in the sense of action against aircraft and fuel, oil, and ammunition dumps on airfields. The dogs were to sniff out various vehicles and their oil tanks: they were trained to search for oily rags on actual military hardware – cars, tractors, and steam locomotives. In the future military leaders wanted to entrust arson and poisoning operations to these dogs. When it comes to arson however it's more or less straight forward, a fuel storage depot or fuel dumps can be set alight using a quantity of a flammable mixture, the same goes for aircraft made of wood or which are of a mixed construction. Evidently it was planned to use reservoirs for poisoning operations. Grokhovskiy's design bureau worked on special ammunition designed to infect the drinking water supply. The plan was to drop them from an aircraft into the water intake points for the water treatment works in large cities. It is possible that the devices for the dogs were actually a modification of this 'asset'.

At the Experimental Institute there was a small kennel with specialist dog instructors (today they would be known as dog handlers). It was there that these long-tailed saboteurs would be trained. For the most part they were Alsatians, big strong dogs.

The four-legged saboteurs were able to act independently or under the leadership of an instructor. To begin with they were deployed close to the asset that they were due to take out. Later on, the dogs would look for their targets both visually, and using their sense of smell. After choosing a site the dog, on which the 'explosive combat saddle' (which was actually a belt) was placed was to move closer to the asset and pull on a pin on their shoulder. The 'saddle' would fall off and a timer would be set, allowing the animal time to get away to a safe distance. Then the explosive charge would go off…

The weight of the explosive charge in the 'saddle' according to various documents was between six and eight and up to 10kg. It is possible that there were several body sizes dependent on the size and weight of the dog. It was planned to acquire new explosive charges in the future, more powerful ones, which would enable the 'saddle' to be made more effective whilst maintaining this same weight. The possibility of using these dogs to deliver chemical weapons was also examined. Moreover, the animals would most likely be killed after they had set this weapon off, since there were no plans to fit them with gas masks.

In a second scenario the dogs would be dropped along with a human commander. They could be dropped in secret away from the object of their attack. They would then march to their objective. Closer to the target the commander could send the requisite number of animals on the mission, either all of them at once or one at a time. In the documentation this was known as "deploying dogs by hand". After they had completed their mission the dogs that survived were to return to their masters. He would then take them to a site where an aircraft would land that would take the group of saboteurs back behind the front line. This variant was considered the principal one and would take no longer than two to three days. A different scenario however was possible.

The dog handler would deploy ahead of time to an agreed inaccessible location and would await the delivery

Dropping a dog by parachute from an aircraft.

of a cargo that was necessary to carry out their next mission. He could be sent new 'explosive saddles', or food for the dog, or for himself. Reinforcements could also be sent, new dogs to replace those lost or seriously injured in attacks. A speed march would then take place to a new target and some more targets would be blown up.

In order to drop service dogs, special container kennels were developed for a single animal, which would open automatically on contact with the ground. An R-5 biplane could carry six containers on bomb racks under the lower wing, this was a whole canine airborne assault. In the course of testing a dog named *Neron* completed 17 parachute jumps. Following state testing in December 1934 the G-58 was introduced into service of the RKKA. On tests the dogs were either dropped by parachute into unfamiliar territory, or they were taken there in vehicles, or 'deployed by hand'. Various targets were chosen for the attacks. In all cases the animals "demonstrated excellent work". The Chairman of the test committee was the Deputy Head of the VVS Headquarters V.K. Lavrov. In the report on the results of these experiments he wrote: "The tests demonstrated the flawless work on the part of the dogs ... The possibility of deploying dogs deep behind enemy lines predetermines a high degree of success in sabotage operations".

In the same way that Grokhovskiy considered a 'personnel cage' an alternative to an individual parachute drop, he also invented a cage for dogs. Object G-56 was designed to drop several dogs at one time: this was produced at the Experimental Institute in 1934 and moreover there were two variants of the cage design: with cells for each dog, and as a communal cage. In the latter case the G-56 could accommodate up to ten dogs. The author has not been able to establish which aircraft this cage was designed for.

It was not only dogs that were trained to carry out sabotage operations. Under the same designation of G-56, a cage was envisaged that was known as a 'bacteriological parachute cage' or KPB to give it its Russian designation. This was a box that would be used to accommodate 500 rats infected with the plague. It was to be dropped deep

A dog wearing a tethered parachute system.

behind enemy lines. The cage opened on contact with the ground and the hungry rats would run out and would start to bite anything in their way. In general, this also amounts to sabotage ...

After the liquidation of the Experimental Institute, the mass deployment of animal saboteurs was forgotten. The idea of deploying dogs in airborne forces however was not rejected. There were plans to use them in reconnaissance, military guard operations, and also to seek out casualties and explosives as well. In the latter case the task that was set was simplified – the dogs went up along with the mines.

A belt harness system was developed for dogs, as well as for humans. A parachute would be packed into a knapsack similar to a pack loaded onto a horse and attached to an animal's back. They were dropped one by one from an aircraft cabin with the canopy opening forcibly using a rip cord. The parachutes for the dogs were the same as those used for people but were smaller.

18

Wheels and Tracks

Almost from the very start, thoughts turned to how to enhance the mobility of airborne troops on the ground. It would be tempting to deploy paratroopers quietly to point 'A' where there are no observation posts, communications lines, or enemy combat units. This would minimise losses, afford some 'flexibility' in timing and would ensure the element of surprise was not lost in an attack. The paratroopers would then have to complete a speed march and would attack the enemy at point 'B', who would not be ready to defend themselves. If the paratroopers did not have to complete this journey on foot but could actually travel there on something then the distance between 'A' and 'B' could be extended significantly, and the gain would increase.

At the beginning of the 1930s, thought was given to transporting and dropping horses – for cavalry, artillery, and for carts. There is a legend that says that Grokhovskiy promised to deliver the cavalry along with the machine-gun carts to the chief 'cavalryman' in the RKKA, Army Commander (he was not yet a Marshal) S.M. Budyonniy. It is not very difficult to suspend a cart underneath an aircraft: in essence it does not weigh very much. It is however not very strong. A cart like that though would most likely survive a flight and a landing. It is much more complicated when it comes to horses, however. There were no Soviet aircraft in existence at that time that were capable of carrying a horse inside the fuselage, and so they could only be carried externally. In terms of its power to weight ratio a TB-3 would be capable of carrying five or six animals. To invent harness systems with soft collars was possible, but for a live horse! They do get agitated and could begin to struggle and, given their weight, they could affect the aircraft stability. There were discussions around the fact that a horse could die of fright. It is by no means warm at altitude and these immobile animals could get very cold, they would need to be wrapped, or protected from the oncoming airflow.

This idea was later rejected after correctly assessing the future mechanisation of the Army. At the same time the proposal concerning the delivery of machine-gun carts by air was also rejected. It was true that up until that point some estimations had been made and a horse had undergone testing in the wind tunnel at the TsAGI. The aim was to determine which direction it was best to transport the horse in: head in the direction of flight or against the direction of flight.

It was much easier to carry a bicycle: it was more compact and lighter, it does not ask to be fed and watered, and will stay in one place without moving around. Bicycles could be loaded into the fuselage via hatches and doors. This was how this was achieved on exercises in 1930 close to the station at Siverskaya just outside Leningrad. The bicycles for the paratroopers were carried in the fuselages of JuG-1 bombers. At a later stage a harness link system was developed for bikes for attachment underneath the aircraft using cords. In the future there were plans to cover these in order to reduce the aerodynamic drag.

Standard bicycles were used in the exercises near Siverskaya, which were used by the cyclists in the Russian and later the Red armies. By the spring of 1932 there was talk of special bicycles for paratroopers. They were to be stronger than standard bicycles, but lighter too. A light machine gun was to be fitted to the frame. In accordance with one of the variants of the specification for a similar design the bicycles would need to be able to fire whilst on the move. Moreover, the gun would be immobile in relation to the frame and a soldier would need to direct fire by turning the whole bike, just like a pilot in a fighter aircraft would. Theoretically, it would be possible to attach a machine gun to the handlebars but the DP light machine gun that was then in service with the RKKA was too

A military bicyclists detachment are offloaded with their bikes from a TB-3 bomber during the Kiev manoeuvres in 1935. The white strips on their cap bands denote the fact that these troops are fighting on the side of the 'blues'.

cumbersome and heavy for this. Subsequently the German Opel made a bicycle for the bicycle mounted troops in the *Wehrmacht* with a special bracket on the handlebars, but a much lighter and more compact submachine gun was mounted on this bracket. The second variant of this specification appeared more realistic: in a combat environment a paratrooper would dismount, the bike would fold up on the ground, and would become a stand for a machine gun that has been removed from its attachment. Later on, as motorisation gathered pace the role of the bicycle mounted troops began to fade. The standard for an airborne brigade in 1941 however still envisaged a bicycle mounted reconnaissance company.

In the Leningrad-based OTB back in the mid-1920s, consideration was given to transporting cars as well as armoured cars and tanks by air. It was this bureau that issued a specification and financed the manufacture of A.N. Tupolev's aircraft that later became known as the TB-1 and the TB-3. They however were long in the making and up until that point Soviet aviation had not possessed aircraft with a suitable lifting capacity. Serious work on the design of attachment assemblies that were intended to enhance the mobility of assault troops began in the summer of 1930 when the new TB-1 bombers entered service that were able to carry up to a tonne of cargo. The command of the Leningrad Military District took the initiative. The commanders turned to the Military Aviation Academy, the TsAGI and the OTB with a request to design an attachment assembly for carrying a light 'Ford A' car. The main problem was the short timescales – a small series of assemblies were to be ready by the end of August, by the start of the autumn exercises.

The Academy responded by saying that they could start work on this, but they would only have a prototype example ready by 20 October. The TsAGI decided first of all to undertake a cycle of research on the influence of an assembly on the aerodynamics of the TB-1 and requested that a model of the vehicle be provided in 1:20 scale for wind tunnel testing, it was only the OTB that actually started work straight away.

The 'Ford' was attached to a special bridge frame under the wing centre section of a bomber. This was lifted in place using hoists. In order to enhance the air flow from the vehicle the windscreen and the front wheels were removed. The wheels were also used as a balancing cargo to ensure a safe centre of gravity (otherwise as the cargo

A G-9 attachment of a Harley Davidson motorcycle with a 3.5hp engine suspended under the wing of an R-5. A parachute is stowed inside the metal container.

The People's Commissar for Heavy Industry G.K. Ordzhonikidze inspects the mounting of a Harley Davidson underneath an R-5, August 1934. Note the different design of the parachute container which is either a G-36 or a G-36A.

An inspection of the motorcycle after it had been dropped by parachute.

An R-5 with a motorcycle attachment proposed by the 3rd Special Purpose Brigade.

According to the design proposed by the 3rd Brigade, a motorcycle was attached vertically, while the parachute was placed into a soft knapsack and not in a metal container which used G-9 and G-36 designs.

was loaded it would shift significantly aft). They were stowed in the forward turret of a TB-1. No further changes were made to the car itself. The total weight of the fully equipped 'Ford' (in the sense of being filled with water, fuel, and a load in the vehicles cabin) was 1,175kg, which was somewhat more than the maximum permitted weight if the bomber were to retain a full complement of defensive weaponry. This was compensated for by a reduction in the reserve of fuel in the aircraft tanks. The flight weight of the TB-1 with the assembly fitted was 6,720kg.

In the space of less than three weeks a batch of ten bridges had been designed and manufactured at the OTB. Testing was carried out using TB-1 No. 621, which was serving in the 57th Squadron. Pilot B.V. Glagolev made more than 20 take-offs and landings with the car underneath the fuselage. The take-off run did increase slightly, and the bomber did start to accelerate more slowly. The flight itself did not present any problems although the speed did not exceed 140 km/hr. It was more difficult to land the aircraft since at speeds of between 125–130km/hr the aircraft would lose its stability. The aircraft had to land on a very flat trajectory and needed to be held above the ground for some time. The landing roll was also lengthened, but this was within acceptable limits. Approximately ten aircraft were fitted with attachments for carrying vehicles and these aircraft did participate in the autumn manoeuvres organised by the Leningrad Military District.

It was at this same OTB that the first attachments for transporting motorcycles by air were produced. To begin with the military were planning to carry them, in the same way as they did for bicycles, in the sufficiently specious fuselages of three-engine JuG-1 aircraft. Sidecars had to be removed from motorcycles that had them fitted otherwise they would not fit through the door. On 20 August 1930 the OTB informed Leningrad that they had manufactured an external attachment assembly for carrying motorcycles underneath the fuselages of JuG-1 aircraft. In this case the sidecars would not need to be removed. The attachment of this cargo (when two motorcycles were attached together) would take around 15mins, and offloading (which was also done immediately) would take between five to seven minutes. The OTB also developed a small series of strap-based systems and used these in manoeuvres in September 1930. They were later to be discarded as the JuG-1 was withdrawn from service with bomber aviation.

Dropping a motorcycle by parachute.

The work on the attachments for transporting cars and motorcycles was carried out at the NII VVS under the leadership of Grokhovskiy. In contrast to the OTB design these designs envisaged the military hardware being dropped by parachute. The G-9 design enabled two Harley-Davidsons to be attached using the bombs racks under the wings of an R-5 biplane. Each motorcycle was attached to a special frame and was provided with two parachutes (which together weighed 656kg). The two assault parachutes were linked together via an aperture in the centre of the canopy and would deploy one after another.

An R-5 with two motorcycles would lose something in terms of speed and incur a significant loss in terms of manoeuvrability. After dropping one motorcycle the aircraft would demonstrate a strong tendency to want to turn. During state testing in 1932 the two Harley-Davidsons that were used were damaged. On one of them the saddle and the rear light were damaged during the first drop and on the third drop the other the frame was bent and the wheel fork broke. The second motorcycle got off fairly lightly on the first drop – the inner tube was pushed out, but on the on the second jump a handlebar was bent, the fuel tank was crumpled, and the saddle was damaged: the stem on the shock absorber fitted to the front fork broke. Some examples of the G-9 were nevertheless manufactured. Grokhovskiy subsequently created the modified G-36, and G-36A attachments for the Harley-Davidson and the G-35 for the indigenous L-300 motorcycle.

In 1935, a modified motorcycle attachment that was designed in the 3rd Special Purpose Air Brigade appeared. It differed from the previous one in terms of the fact that the motorcycles were enclosed in protective frames and were mounted vertically and not horizontally. Silk parachutes were used. This design underwent testing in the Brigade, and then in June 1936 at the NII VVS.

The R-5 biplane carried two motorcycles under the lower wing. Two people could mount them in the space of 12–15mins. Up until that point some five to seven minutes would be spent fitting auxiliary components to the bomb racks.

The R-5 was flown by pilot Ya. Lipkin. The flight weight of the aircraft was 2,700kg, this meant that the aircraft

Two motorcycles with sidecars are packed into a parachute cargo cage designed to carry 1,000kg, and which has been suspended underneath the fuselage of a TB-1 bomber. This set was designated PD-M2.

An L-300 motorcycle at the factory in Leningrad.

This L-300 motorcycle is exhibited at Vadim Zadorozhny's Technical Museum in Arkhangelskoye near Moscow.

An IZh-9 motorcycle.

The IZh-9 motorcycle exhibited at Vadim Zadorozhny's Technical Museum in Arkhangelskoye near Moscow.

had been specially lightened although this was not shown in the documents. The aircraft behaved normally on the take-off run but the take-off roll itself had increased to 390m – double what it would usually be. The maximum speed of the flight had fallen by more than 40km/hr. The ceiling fell by approximately 1,000m. The aircraft was stable in flight however, demonstrating acceptable manoeuvrability. An attempt was made to fly with just one motorcycle, but this turned out to be very difficult for the pilot because of the asymmetric nature of the drag.

The motorcycles were dropped by parachute on four occasions, each time this was successful. The minimum drop altitude was set at 130m. The attachment could also be used in a landing delivery, although the landing speed increased to between 15–20km/hr and the landing roll to 265m (as opposed to a 220m landing roll without the attachment fitted). The most annoying thing though was that on the landing roll the aircraft would pitch down and there was a danger of it ground looping.

In 1931, Grokhovskiy began to undertake experiments dropping motorcycles with sidecars (the PD-M or PD-M1 system). In this case the TB-1 bomber would carry a single motorcycle ventrally under the fuselage. A percale canopy would be used with a diameter of 12m, which could be encased in a special cylinder. A year later the PD-M system underwent state testing. Later on, the PD-2M attachment was produced at the OKPB that was capable of holding two 'Harleys' with sidecars, which would be stowed inside an overall cowling pod. A cargo cage was used for the latter, which was designed for 1,000kg. This again was carried ventrally under the fuselage of a TB-1 bomber. A parachute with a diameter of 25m lay inside a cylinder that weighed 31.5kg. Following testing the PD-2M was accepted for procurement into the RKKA.

In the future it was hoped that modified motorcycles could be obtained for the paratroop detachments with enlarged fuel tanks (with enough fuel to cover between 200–250km). Two machine-gun mounts were to be mounted onto the sidecar for firing forwards and backwards (this however would be with the one machine

An AM-600 motorcycle with sidecar.

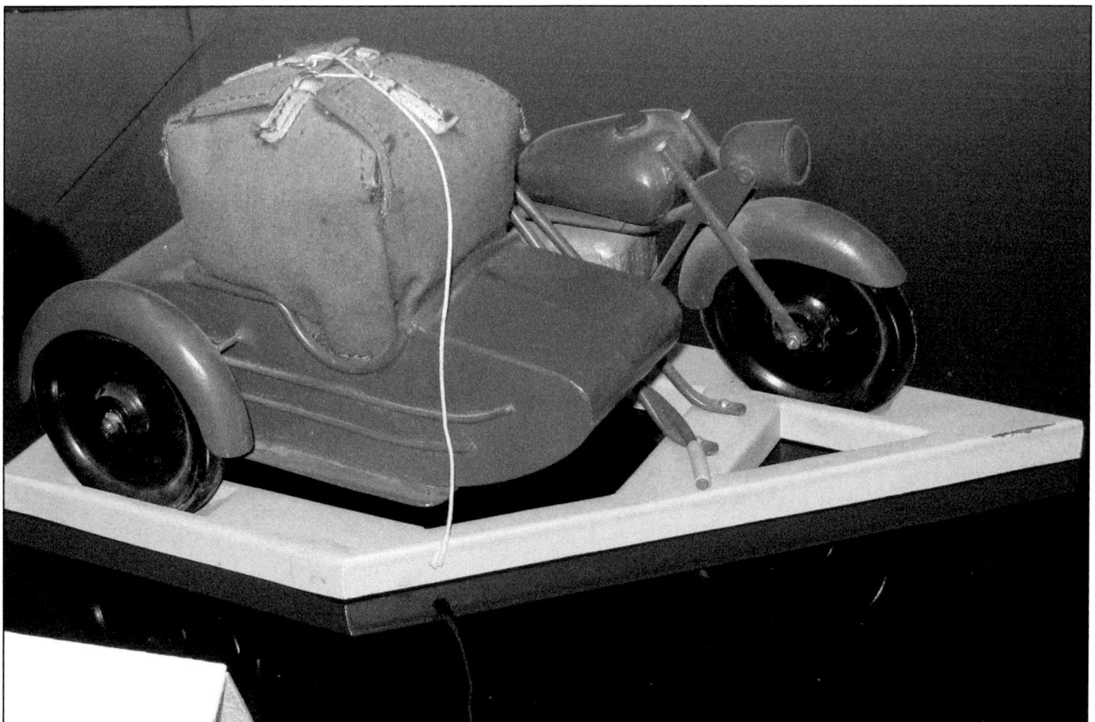

A model of a motorcycle and sidecar that are fitted with a D-11 attachment and a protective frame.

A motorcycle and sidecar on a D-11 attachment under a DB-3F bomber.

gun with eight disc magazines for both mounts). The attachments envisaged engagement of both ground, and air targets. Two incendiary grenades and three poison smoke grenades would be kept in the sidecar. In some documents, specifications were recorded concerning the possibility of using soft tracks. How this was to be achieved on a standard motorcycle however is not known.

A.I. Privalov was subsequently engaged in producing harnesses for dropping motorcycles using parachutes. At his design bureau in Factory No.468 the D-11 attachment was created for a motorcycle and sidecar. The carrying aircraft for this was a DB-3F. The first variants of this attachment were not very successful, and several motorcycles were completed destroyed. The design was steadily developed. In a number of instances, the motorcycle landed successfully but the canopy dragged the motorcycle as it was billowing in the wind and it got caught on various obstructions. At the end of 1939 there was a proposal to use an ARD-1 automatic disengagement device, which separated the straps from the cargo 15 seconds after the relaxation of the tension on the straps. Testing of the modified D-11 variant at the NII VVS was completed successfully in April 1941.

The motorcycles could be carried using the cargo bridges created for the DB-3, and PS-84 aircraft in that same KB-29 DESIGN BUREAU. Work was underway there on a similar attachment for the TB-3. Therefore, four IZh-9 or AM-600 motorcycles fitted with machine guns could be carried on a bridge manufactured to fit an external attachment mounted ventrally under a DB-3.

The design of the G-54 'avia-motorcycle' designed by Grokhovskiy was something completely different. It would be hard to conceive of a more unrestrained flight operation. It is even hard to imagine how exactly to relate to it – as a landing device, or a transport, or combat vehicle. The vehicle itself was tracked – the single, soft track ran along the axis of the 'avia-motorcycle' as per contemporary snowmobiles. Two small wheels were attached to the outer edges at the rear, similar to a child's bicycle, so the machine did not fall over. It moved using a small eight horsepower engine and furthermore used the thrust from a pusher propeller. A DA light machine gun (according to the description) was mounted above the controls. The drawings however instead of this machine gun depict

A sketch of an G-54 'avia-motorcycle' in flight.

A G-54 'avia-motorcycle' is ready to start moving on the ground after the wing has been removed.

The first type of car that entered service with the Soviet airborne troops was the American 'Ford A'. They were used in the standard variant with a cabriolet body as well as the pickups (shown in the photo). In the USSR these cars were produced at Gorkiy (now Nizhniy Novgorod) factory under NAZ-A designation later changed to GAZ-A. These cars were carried by TB-1 and TB-3 aircraft and could be dropped by parachutes.

something small of an unknown design. Maybe this is not a machine gun at all but some sort of a fantasy system. According to the calculations the dry weight of the G-54 was to have been around 60kg. This thing though had to fly as well! It was fitted with a detachable wing for this purpose. The flight weight of this machine was set at 200kg.

The concept was that the 'avia-motorcycles' would be dropped with their drivers on board from a carrying aircraft and would glide for a short time, with a low-powered engine lending a helping hand, and would then land. The flight speed was assessed as being 100km/hr, while the landing speed was 20km/hr. The motorcyclists would detach the wings once on the ground and go into battle, spraying the enemy with machine-gun fire.

Which carrying aircraft though would be capable of carrying a G-54? Judging by the drawing, its wingspan was around three metres. This would mean that it could only be dropped from the bomb bay of a TB-3 abeam the direction of travel. The TB-4 had a wider bomb bay but there was a longitudinal beam running the length of it that meant it could not carry outsized cargoes. The only other option would be to store the 'avia-motorcycle' externally. But then this would mean that the driver and passengers would freeze in flight. In actual fact how many G-54s would a TB-3 carry?

A similar situation arises with respect to controlling the 'avia-motorcycle' in flight. No flying controls or other surfaces are visible in the drawings. There are tail fins on the ends of the wings, but no actuating components are visible, if they are indeed mobile. It is possible that none of this was actually thought through at all.

Thank God that Grokhovskiy was engaged in more realistic projects. In his calculation for the TB-1 he designed a PD-A (G-38) parachute attachment for a small 'Ford A' car. The vehicle was far from ordinary. It had been converted into a pickup at the OKPB with a collapsible body in place of the back seats. There were two seats in the front and two benches at the back, with enough room for three people. There was also a canopy that was only attached at points above the front seats. A DRP was mounted on a tripod in the car's back, that is to say the

The Head of the Technical Department of the Headquarters of the 3rd Special Purpose Brigade tests the DT machine gun mounting on a 'Ford A' car.

The NAZ-A pickups suspended under a TB-3 bomber, with the attachment for the landing delivery.

A modified 'Ford A' pickup on a PD-A (G-38) attachment suspended under a TB-1 bomber. Note the cowling in front of the car's radiator and the wheel cowlings.

Dropping a 'Ford A' vehicle by parachute, 1932.

A lightened pickup on a GAZ-A chassis. Such cars were used by the paratroopers of the 3rd Special Purpose Brigade.

Two lightened pickups suspended underneath a TB-3 bomber, 1935.

A project of special three-axle truck designed for airborne delivery, to be dropped without a parachute.

vehicle was effectively converted into a self-propelled gun. Alternatively, a heavy machine gun could be mounted in its place. The vehicle received reinforced shock absorbers, hub caps on the spokes and a cowling in front of the radiator.

The machine was dropped using a 30m percale canopy. The parachute along with its attachments and the box weighed 240kg (of this the cylindrical box accounted for 35.5kg). The car was dropped several times on the Central airfield in Moscow.

During a demonstration of the new equipment to the Deputy People's Commissar for Defence M.N. Tukhachevskiy in July 1931, Grokhovskiy wanted to land in this vehicle and then approach the rostrum where the leadership were standing and give his report. Tukhachevskiy however outlawed this dangerous move. This it turned out was no bad thing. The parachute did not deploy fully and the vehicle smashed full force into the corner of a hangar. The wheels flew off in different directions. Grokhovskiy who was watching events from the TB-1 launch aircraft said sadly: "It's beyond repair".

The Joint State Political Directorate carried out an investigation to rule out foul play. As strange as it may seem the *chekists* did not find anything untoward. On the other hand, it turned out that the car that had been destroyed, which Grokhovskiy claimed was his own, had been stolen! This 'Ford' was registered to a garage at the headquarters of the Leningrad Military District and was presented to the inventor along with a driver for the duration of testing of airborne equipment in this location. Grokhovskiy though had not given the vehicle back after travelling to Moscow by car. He however did not suffer any negative consequences for this.

A modernised variant of the attachment for the 'Ford' designated the G-38A successfully completed state testing just outside Leningrad in October 1932, when two vehicles were dropped one after another from a TB-1. Later, the G-38 was produced in several guises, preferably based on an analogous design by Blagin (this was also based on a 'Ford A'). G-29 attachments were developed for the TB-3 that were designed to hold two pickups at one time, as well as another G-29 for a cargo carrying vehicle. In 1934 at the Experimental Institute work was underway on an attachment for dropping a truck (which make of truck though was not specified) from under a TB-3 without a parachute and from low level. Without any significant strengthening of the vehicle itself this

The first armoured tracked vehicle that was used by airborne forces was the T-27 tankette. This photo shows the tankettes on parade on Red Square in Moscow on 7 November 1932.

Grokhovskiy demonstrating his design of the attachment for the 'English-type tankettes', August 1934. Initially an actual Carden Lloyd tankette was dropped, which was acquired in Great Britain, since it was lighter than the T-27.

A T-27 tankette on a PD-T (G-43) parachute attachment under a TB-1 bomber.

experiment would only lead to the pieces of the vehicle being recovered across a wide area.

If during tests at Siverskaya the standard vehicles were being loaded while Grokhovskiy would drop modified vehicles under a parachute, then the headquarters were preparing the specifications for specially designed airborne vehicles. The chassis from a three-axle Ford was the preferred model for this vehicle (*Timkens* had been purchased in the USA for the Red Army and later on, 'Ford AAA' cars as well) albeit with significant modifications. The body needed to be highly streamlined, the suspension strengthened, and the wheels needed to be 'solid' that is to say packed with a foam rubber, and bulletproof. It was envisaged that the rear wheels would be fitted where necessary with soft 'Overall' tracks and moreover this actually turned the vehicle into a half-track. The capacity of the fuel tanks was to correspond to an amount sufficient for 400–600km.

It was envisaged that the mandatory armament for all these airborne vehicles would be machine guns, and also in some cases DRPs or small calibre (between 20–30mm) automatic guns. The fitting of the DRP onto the vehicle was first undertaken by L.V. Kurchevskiy, since Grokhovskiy had manufactured the special self-propelled machine that had used a 'Ford-A' chassis described above.

In the future, the military were thinking they could partially fit airborne vehicles with armour, turning them in actual fact into armoured cars. Grokhovskiy's design bureau in 1934 worked on a special assault vehicle, which in many respects met the requirements listed above. The basis for this vehicle was a three-axle 'Ford' (either a 'Timken' or an 'AAA'), behind the cabin on this vehicle a small body was fitted that had bullet-proof armour. Some 15 soldiers could be accommodated inside this body, who would be able to open fire from rifles, and light machine guns via oblong firing holes in the sides. In the illustration the body is low, so the gunners evidently sat on the floor. The driver's cab though was open to the elements! The windscreen is shown in a folded down position onto the bonnet. A strong frame passed above the body and the driver's cab with longitudinal channel beams that were interlinked with the vehicle's frame using circular rods. It was by this frame that the truck was suspended from an aircraft. It was envisaged that a combat vehicle such as this would be dropped from low level (from an altitude of approximately two metres) over a flat terrain, such as the steppe, and furthermore it would be dropped along with its crew.

The idea of course was very tempting. From beyond the horizon at low altitude a squadron of heavy bombers would appear, they would drop armoured trucks that continue the advance across the terrain. Behind enemy

Dropping a tankette by parachute from a TB-1 bomber.

lines a reinforced motorised infantry company would advance, covered in armour. The enemy forces would be anticipating any kind of an attack and the vehicles would rush forwards, firing as they went ...

Aircraft would appear and disappear, and an armoured column would be rushing towards enemy lines at full speed. What though would be able to transport this armoured 'Ford' and how was it to be carried on an external harness? The point being that it would be difficult for a four-engine TB-3 bomber to carry a ZiS-5 truck with a carrying capacity of three tonnes: it is a very heavy weight and the drag would increase significantly. Even transporting light tanks presented fewer difficulties than this would generate: It is possible that the military were counting on the giant TB-4, and K-7 aircraft and the even larger TB-6 and G-1 (D-1). The first two however were only manufactured as prototype examples, and the rest were delayed somewhere at the design and model stages.

Flying a heavy bomber at an altitude of two metres for a rank and file pilot is a reliable way to send everyone on board to kingdom come. What then would happen to the vehicle that would hit the ground at a speed of between 120–130km/hr? It could summersault, fall onto its side or simply be smashed to pieces. Overall it was considered a brilliant idea, but one which had clearly not been thought through.

However, a much simpler approach was subsequently realised. To begin with the main type of vehicle for paratroopers was the 'Ford A' and its' Soviet copy the NAZ-A (which was later designated the GAZ-A). These fell into the 'car' category (with a collapsible tarpaulin top) and a standard series pickup. In the 3rd Special Purpose Brigade some of the vehicles were armed with 7.62mm DT machine guns (tank machine guns, harmonised with DA infantry ones) and mounted on the windscreen frame for firing at both ground, and air targets.

For motorised detachments in the 3rd Special Purpose Brigade a batch of lightened vehicles that used a GAZ-A chassis were manufactured. They resembled Grokhovskiy's modified pick up. Everything that could be removed from these vehicles was removed. Two people sat in the front and a further six on longitudinal benches in the back (they sat back to back facing outside so the possibility of firing on the move was retained). The benches were manufactured from thin wooden battens and were reminiscent of garden benches. A vehicle such as

A T-27 underneath a TB-3 bomber on an attachment which was designed by the OTKB for a landing delivery.

this would transport a detachment of paratroopers consisting of seven men plus a driver. A TB-3 bomber would be able to carry two of these vehicles, suspended ventrally under the fuselage one behind the other.

Attempts at mechanising the airborne forces showed no sign of stopping in order to supply the paratroopers with motorcycles and cars. This not only concerned enhancing the mobility of the combatants but also reinforcing a detachment's fire-power. This could be achieved by supplying armoured military hardware, with machine guns or a gun armament.

In 1932 Grokhovskiy's design bureau manufactured an example of a G-43 (PD-T) system for dropping 'the English tankettes'. This referred to T-27 tankettes that were manufactured in the USSR between 1931–33 on the basis of a design developed by the Carden-Loyd company.

The Soviet variant was slightly larger and heavier than the original owing to the reinforced armour. This was a comparatively small machine with a crew of two and armament consisting of one 7.62mm DT machine gun. Several tankettes, including those that were later to operate in the 3rd Brigade, were also fitted with flamethrower.

The weight of the T-27 was 2,700kg, which nevertheless still exceeded the limit for the TB-1 bomber. Specialists thought it would not be possible to get this vehicle into the air. The tankette was lightened by 344kg, after removing everything that could possibly be removed; even the fuel, oil, and water were drained from the cooling system. The aircraft also had to be lightened. Specifically, one of the aft turrets was removed as well as all the machine guns. Apart from that the fuel capacity was significantly reduced. The vehicle was dropped using a 30m percale parachute via the detachment method. The canopy was packed inside a cylinder that was hung on the bomb racks. The cylinder would fall, and the rip cord would pull the parachute out of the cylinder, and the parachute as it opened would in turn 'pull the tankette out' of its attachment.

State testing was undertaken just outside Leningrad between September–October 1932, and the tankette was dropped twice. In December of that year the PD-T was tested again at the NII VVS. It would become a precursor for a large number of similar devices, which were designed to drop light tanks, armoured vehicles, and cars.

Also, in 1932, at the Leningrad OTB an attachment was designed for the T-27 that was intended for the four-

A TB-3 fitted with M-34R engines under which an attachment for a T-27 tankette is mounted.

One of the tankettes in the 3rd Special Purpose Brigade opens fire with its flamethrower during exercises in the mid-1930s.

engine TB-3 bomber. The lifting capacity of the bomber in this case was clearly sufficient but this design could only be used on a landing delivery; no provision was made for dropping the tankettes by parachute.

A prototype example of a G-33 universal cargo cage was manufactured at the OKPB in 1932. This was a large box with a truss structure (fitted with open girder webs), which stood on runners. The main legs for these runners were fitted with shock absorbers. A tankette could be accommodated inside the cage, as well as a light tank, a tracked tractor, or a car. The thinking was that the cage would be dropped using a large parachute via the separation method. It was envisaged that this would provide the possibility of ensuring a low-level airborne assault for which the enemy would be unprepared. The deployment of the canopy in this case would be supported

A T-26 tank in the twin-turret variant which is armed with 7.62-mm DT machine guns. Evidently it was for this lighter variant that the G-40 parachute system was designed.

A T-26 tank with a single turret that is fitted with a 45-mm gun.

If the attachments for the T-26 tank were only at the project stage, then for the T-37A amphibious tank several variants of attachments were designed for both landing delivery and parachute drop. This illustration shows T-37As on the move.

not only by the oncoming airflow, but also by the slipstream from the aircraft engines.

Testing of the G-33, however, did not take place. The author is of the opinion that a tankette or a tracked tractor, much less a tank, would be out of the question as a cargo for this aircraft (and what is more this is before the weight of the cage is added in).

That same year the 'shock resistant parachute cargo frame' was proposed. This was a low-sided platform. It did not have tracks but wheels. The payload would be the same, but the platform was not designed to carry a tankette or a tank. The principal difference between the cage and the 'frame' was that on all the designs mentioned above the supporting truss or the bridge was the initial attachment to the aircraft and then hoists on these bridges or trusses would lift the vehicle, but with the platform the cargo would initially be loaded onto the platform and then this was put in place together with the platform. The 'frame' since it had wheels also made transporting cargo around an airfield easier.

In 1934, at the Experimental Institute work was undertaken on the G-48 attachment assembly for the T-26 tank, and furthermore the plan was to drop this from low level without a parachute at a speed of between 100–150km/hr. One year earlier a G-40 design was developed at Grokhovskiy's design bureau: this was designed to drop a light tank (which type of light tank was not specified) on two parachutes with a diameter of 30m. The plan also included dropping a T-26 using a single 62m parachute and an amphibious tank (evidently a T-37A) using a 40m parachute.

The T-26 was a Soviet variant of an English Vickers Mk.E and was produced from 1931 in several modifications. The lightest of these weighed 8,000kg. Moreover, the normal loading on a TB-3 was 2,000kg. If less fuel was taken on board this could be raised to 5,000kg but no more. It is possible that the designer was again counting on future giant aircraft. When work on the multi-engine monsters came to an end these projects too were shelved.

So from the T-37 (T-37A) onwards, everything looked more realistic. This amphibious tank was developed in 1932 based on the knowledge gained from a similar design produced by the English company 'Vickers' as well as several indigenous prototype examples. From 1933 onwards, it was in series production. The tank had a crew of

A T-37A amphibious tank suspended under the fuselage of the TB-3 bomber.

A project of G-61 'High-Speed Light Assault Tank'.

The battalion commanders and those of higher rank were allocated with M-1 cars. These automobiles could be carried underneath a TB-3 aircraft on a PG-12 attachment and dropped by parachute using a PG-12P. Pickups that were designed on the basis of the M-1 were also used in the airborne forces. From 1940 onwards, the GAZ-11-40 began to be produced at the factory in Gorkiy, with the same body but with a more powerful engine and four-wheel drive.

The light M-1 vehicle suspended on a PG-12 attachment under a TB-3 aircraft.

A pickup based on the GAZ-A prepares to take its place on a PG-12 attachment under a TB-3.

A D-12 armoured car on a PG-12 attachment suspended under a TB-3 aircraft.

A D-12 armoured car on a PG-12 attachment suspended under a TB-3 aircraft.

two and was armed with a single DT machine gun. The feasibility of suspending the T-37A under an aircraft lay in the fact that the amphibian weighed not much more than a T-27 tankette – 3,200kg.

These though were production vehicles, which were designed without taking into account the specifics of the airborne forces. The G-61 airborne high-speed light tank was designed in 1934 at the Experimental Institute and was created especially taking into consideration the requirements of transporting a tank on an external attachment assembly underneath a TB-3. The tank needed to be light, compact and create minimal aerodynamic drag. Therefore, the main body of this tank was given a highly streamlined shape reminiscent of a boat. The upper part of the driver and mechanic's cabin would fold down while it was being transported – this consisted of three plates mounted on hinges. The armament (a single recoilless gun and two machine guns) was accommodated in the side turrets that could be lowered and raised into a combat position. A gunner would sit in each of these towers; in total the crew consisted of three people. The G-61 tank moved on a single track and two side mounted wheels. The wheels (which were not powered wheels and were not steerable) were fitted with brakes, and it was this that made it possible for the tank to turn. When moving along a good road the forward part of the track could be raised upwards so that the G-61 tank could move faster. Evidently, the G-61 did not even reach the serious design stage, remaining just another of Grokhovskiy's fantasies.

Another of the Experimental Institute's products, however, turned out to be highly successful and was in service with the VVS for a relatively long period of time. In 1935 the PG-12 attachment assembly was introduced into service (this was known as the "1935-model universal frame"). It was series produced as the PG-12 (for landing deliveries) and the PG-12P (for dropping by parachute). The latter could be fitted with a G-42 parachute (designed for a payload of up to one and a half tonnes) or the G-43 (that was designed for two tonnes). Both of these featured a mesh design with diameters of 35m and 40m respectively. The carrying aircraft was the four-engine TB-3 bomber: the frame was mounted under the fuselage between the undercarriage legs. In total 150 of

A TB-3 aircraft with a D-12 light armoured car suspended underneath it.

these PG-12s were produced out of the 500 originally ordered. These attachment assemblies had arrived in the military districts by October 1936.

The PG-12 attachment (bridge), weighing 165kg, enabled cars, armoured vehicles, and light tanks (weighing up to three tonnes) to be carried and vehicles weighing up to two tonnes could be dropped by parachute, that is to say it was not possible to drop a tank. A cargo platform designed around a truss was attached to the PG-12 and was fixed ventrally under the fuselage using a series of rods. A pickup could be mounted on this platform (this was based on the GAZ-A and M-1 cars) or the GAZ-AA trucks (these had the upper part of the cabin cut off, and this was replaced by a collapsible canvass top). An attempt was made to load a T-37 amphibious tank and a D-12 armoured car from the ranks of armoured vehicles. The latter was a variant of the D-8 armoured car but did not have a turret. It weighed 1,580kg which was approximately half that of a tank. The D-8 was later used in the airborne units and was armed with two DT machine guns (one of which was coaxial tank machine gun while the other was mounted on a rotating turret), and the D-12 fitted with a single DT (coaxial). In addition to the DT there was also a possibility of mounting an anti-aircraft Maxim in the aft section of the main body, the D-A armoured personnel carrier (that could accommodate six combatants in the back) also served in these units. The only inconvenience lay in the fact that the hardware had to be towed onto the platform after it had been suspended under the fuselage. Everything had to be specially prepared, and seats were drilled in the armour for the attachment bolts.

As strange as it may seem, the hardest thing to do was to fly with the GAZ-AA since the truck created the greatest degree of aerodynamic drag and forced the pilot of the carrying aircraft to fight the aircraft tendency to dive. The speed of the TB-3 with an external attachment was reduced by 10–20km/hr.

In October 1936, the heavy cargoes bridges, which had been manufactured by the Leningrad aircraft Factory No.47, began to be distributed around the military districts, in which there were formations of heavy bombers. In addition to the GAZ-AA the old AMO-F-15 trucks were also loaded onto the PG-12 in military units.

At the end of 1936, the PG-12 had been modified at KB-29 design bureau – it was fitted with quick release joints, making its assembly quicker. The weight of this equipment however reached 180kg. A modified example, which had been manufactured by the *Podyomnik* factory was tested in April 1937. A crew led by Captain Avtonomov flew the TB-3 fitted with M-34R engines.

Two D-12 armoured cars after they had been detached from their carrying aircraft during the Kiev manoeuvres in 1935. This was the landing delivery at Brovary.

Initially, this was designed for the old modification of the TB-3 fitted with M-17 engines. It had to be modified at the NII VVS taking into account changes in the undercarriage on the new variant of the bomber.

Attaching a T-37A tank took between 35–45mins and removing it after it had been delivered by parachute took another 15–20mins. Seven flights were conducted with this tank and the aircraft speed carrying this cargo fell by 12km/hr. The conclusion of the report by the NII VVS stated: "This bridge can be introduced into service".

The *Podyomnik* factory manufactured 150 production modernised PG-12Ps; the total cost of them was 4.5 million roubles. The plan was for them to be used to transport the T-38 tank, and not the T-37A. In essence the amphibious T-38 tank differed little from its predecessor but had become 100kg heavier.

In February 1938, a BA-20 armoured car was test loaded onto a PG-12P under a TB-3 fitted with M-34R engines. This armoured car that used a chassis from an M-1 car had a crew of three and was armed with a 7.62mm machine gun. The machine weighed 2,520kg. The flights were conducted by a crew led by Lieutenant Gulyayev from the 9th Air Brigade. The take-off weight of this aircraft with the armoured car was 18,940kg. The BA-20 was however not dropped by parachute but was delivered in landing missions on 20 separate occasions.

There were alternative designs for attachments in existence for transporting light tanks and armoured cars. For example, in 1935–36 the Military Aviation Academy Design Bureau developed their own design of attachment to transport a T-37A tank underneath a TB-3 (without dropping it by parachute).

In 1936, TsAGI proposed free attachment assembly. This was designed by Venevidov, Sviridov, Savelyev, and Boguslavskiy. The assembly was manufactured at the Factory of Prototype Designs at the TsAGI. With the help of the factory the bomber was able to carry a T-37A or up to three 76mm guns. These were attached to the standard bomb racks underneath the fuselage. Specifically, the T-37A was suspended on four Der-20 bomb racks.

The design passed factory testing and, in June 1936, it was submitted for state testing at the NII VVS. The aircraft was flown by a crew led by Captain Kurban. The results turned out to be disappointing. The cargo caused a very great deal of vibration, which affected the bomber's centre of gravity right up to the point that it started to lose its stability. Control of the bomb release mechanism was lost due to vibration. It was decided not to drop the actual tank itself, and in its place a platform loaded with ballast (made up of sandbags) was attached to the aircraft. Around 20 percent of the attempts to make a drop were abandoned. Testing was brought to an end as it

The GAZ-AA with a cargo capacity of 1.5 tonnes was the most widespread type of truck in the airborne troops. From 1938 onwards, the GAZ-MM was manufactured that was almost identical externally but differed in a more powerful engine and a modified suspension. The same vehicles were in service at the brigade level, equipped with paired and quadrupled anti-aircraft Maxim machine guns that were mounted on the truck body.

was considered dangerous for the aircraft and its crew.

The transportation of amphibious tanks without dropping them by parachute was envisaged for a number of other designs. In 1935 the 3rd Special Purpose Brigade created and manufactured its own attachment design for the T-37. It weighed 280kg. The bridge designed by the Military Academy of Mechanisation and Motorisation (VAMM, which was subsequently known as the Armour and Tank Academy) was a competitor in this design, but their device was much heavier at 325kg.

In 1936, the 3rd Special Purpose Brigade produced a new version of the bridge, which was intended as an attachment for the T-37A and the T-38 and was designed for a TB-3 aircraft fitted with M-34R engines. This represented a system of pipes and cables and weighed 116.5kg. Ahead of the fitting of this assembly the external bomb racks under the wing centre section had to be removed. The bridge underwent flight-testing in April 1937.

It also took between 22–25mins less to attach a tank than with the PG-12 than it did using the VAMM bridge. The aircraft was flown by Lieutenant Gerasimov. In the course of the first flight the rear cable became unwound, but the strain was taken up by the rear thrust pipe. The aircraft landed successfully with the tank fitted. In total 13 flights were completed; all of these apart from one were on a ski undercarriage. The bridge was acknowledged as having successfully passed state testing. At the VAMM in 1936, work was also underway on a system that would enable an amphibious tank to be dropped onto water without a parachute. With this in mind a special attachment was made for the TB-3 aircraft fitted with M-34R engines. This work was led by Zh.Ya. Kotin, the drop was carried out at low altitude (from an altitude of approximately five metres) at a speed of around 150km/hr. This needed to be tested and it was. The T-37A disengaged successfully but was seriously damaged on contact with the water and sank. Ahead of the next test, the base of the amphibian was strengthened using a longitudinal wooden beam (a 'keel') with a metal plate attached to it: this in fact formed a second base. This though did not help. The tank was dropped from an aircraft flown by Senior Lieutenant Antokhin. The keel was destroyed on contact with the water, the T-37 remained afloat for between 18–20mins and then sank (the water got into the main body of the tank via the slit for the driver-mechanic's position).

In September 1937, a modified TVD-2 attachment was tested. This weighed a little more than 240kg. For this experiment an aircraft fitted with M-34R engines was again chosen. The flight weight of the bomber with the attachment and the tank together was 17,600kg. In the course of testing the commander was pilot Tyagunin. Their assessment of the specifics of the aircraft handling was sufficiently terse: "It does not affect flight".

In September 1937, the tank was dropped from an altitude of between five to six metres at a speed of 160km/hr. The required open space of not less than 500m was located on the lake. Disengagement was achieved using an SBR-9 bomb release mechanism. After it had touched the surface of the water the machine bounced some 25–30m. The spray reached up to the aircraft but did not present any danger to it.

Three different variants of shock absorbing devices were tested. They were all very simple and straightforward: a steel beam encased in wood on the base of the tank, a steel plate where pine twigs were placed between it and the base of the tank, and lastly, just placing bunches of branches underneath the tank. In the first scenario the bottom of the amphibian caved in and some of the rivets burst; the tank floated for around 20mins and sank. The wooden beam broke in two. In the second scenario the tank sank after the armour in the aft section burst open, and in the third one the aircraft also sank after losing one track. The fountain of water reached up to the aircraft, but it was not affected. The idea was considered futile and work on the TVD-2 was stopped.

In December 1938, the *Podyomnik* manufactured the first batch of a dozen DPT-2 attachments. This design had been developed by engineers Troitskiy, Rogov, and Zuyev. This was a development of the DPT-1, which had only existed thus far in prototype examples, and was more reliable and safer than the PG-12, ensuring less of a load on the components in the aircraft fuselage. The assortment included the T-38 amphibious tank, the BA-20 and the FAI armoured car, and the T-20 *Komsomolets* artillery tractor, the 5AK mobile radio station that used a GAZ-A pickup chassis. The new attachment enabled a GAZ-AA truck to be used with a standard cab (without the cut down top) and even the off-road three-axle GAZ-AAA. The FAI that has not been mentioned above represented a light armoured car that used a GAZ-A chassis. This vehicle had a crew of two or three and was armed with a single DT machine gun; it weighed exactly 2,000kg. The *Komsomolets* tractor that used the old PG-12 chassis could not be carried anywhere since this machine even without a cargo weighed 3,460kg.

Testing with the DPT-2 was carried out between January–March 1939 using two TB-3s. The attachment it turns out was less complicated than that of the PG-12. The speed and ceiling with a cumbersome external load did suffer of course. With the tank fitted the bomber could not accelerate beyond 190km/hr, and with the GAZ-AA this reached 198km/hr. Furthermore, up to 150km/hr the aircraft when fitted with the G-38 attachment was unstable. The ceiling with the pickup fitted was 3,250m, and with the tank this was 2,300m; in the latter case this fell by almost a half in comparison to the figures that were obtained without the attachment fitted. With the truck fitted the TB-3 was reluctant to enter into steep banking turns. A runway of 800 by 600m was needed for landing with a tank or a truck fitted.

The T-38 tank on test was dropped ten times. It was dropped onto the ground admittedly, but this was successful. It seemed that nothing was easy when it came to a landing delivery. The vehicles and tanks that had been unloaded after the flight could not pull away, the engines would not start. It is far from warm at altitude even in summer; the lubrication in the vehicles that had been suspended outside the aircraft had congealed. The author has not been able to find any reference as to whether the cooling system was filled with water or not; this could freeze completely and burst the radiator. All the report states is that the hardware would start after approximately 15–20mins after offloading. It is possible that warm water was carried in separate thermos tanks. The VVS did have these tanks available for topping up the engine cooling systems for the large aircraft.

Overall, the DPT-2 was accepted. The report on the testing stated " ... it demonstrates considerable advantages in comparison with the old PG-12 attachment". In 1939 the DP-2 was introduced into service.

A short time later, the DPT-2 was augmented by the GP-1 platform which was designed for a cargo of up

A GAZ-AA truck on a PG-12 attachment suspended under a TB-3 bomber. The upper part of the of the driver's cab has been removed and replaced by a tarpaulin cover.

A T-37A amphibious tank on a PG-12 attachment suspended under a TB-3 aircraft.

A BA-20M armoured vehicle that could be delivered by air using the PG-12P and DPT-2 attachments. This photo shows a commander's variant with a handrail radio antenna in the upper section of the body.

A TB-3 bomber carrying a BA-20 armoured vehicle.

A T-37A tank suspended under TB-3 bomber on an attachment that was designed by the 3rd Special Purpose Air Brigade, April 1937.

to three and a half tonnes. This was also compatible with the PG-12 bridge that was manufactured previously. Specifically, the platform underwent combat testing from January–March 1939 in the Kiev Special Military District along with the PG-12, and the DPT-2 (using two TB-3s). Subsequently it was planned to fit this platform with a cowling to reduce the aerodynamic drag it generated.

Up until the beginning of the war, this new attachment was not in widespread use. In April 1940 there were just seven DPT-2s in the VVS stores, as well as seven GP-1s, and DPT-1s. This though was distributed around various districts. The personnel in the aviation units did not receive any special training on how to fit them or how to transport large size cargoes.

The NKTP received a specification in 1941 to manufacture 20 attachments for a TB-3 that were designed for a cargo of 3,300kg. Evidently this referred to the DPT-2 or to some other modification.

The transfer of other types of military hardware was envisaged in various designs. For example, the military variant of the *Maksim Gorkiy* aircraft (this was never actually produced) according to the specification that was approved in March 1936 would be used to transport T-27 tanks, T-37 tanks, and BAI and FAI armoured vehicles. The BAI armoured vehicle is a large and heavy (weighing almost four tonnes) three-axle vehicle that used an American 'Timken' truck chassis. This was the only time when any intention of taking this vehicle into the air was ever mentioned. This specification is also interesting in the sense that the T-27 tankette it was planned would fit inside the bomb bay (the bomb bay was large enough). This was the first instance of this ever happening in Soviet practice. Another specific feature was that the plan envisaged two vehicles each being loaded in different combinations (with a total weight of between 5,250kg to 6,560kg). The aircraft would be fitted with something akin to a lift, a platform that would be raised and lowered using a cable mechanism.

In accordance with the specification dated 4 May 1938, a platform (again an external one) was to be developed for the T-38 amphibious tank) the *Komsomolets* armoured tractor and the GAZ-AA and GAZ-AAA and 'four-wheel drive pickup'. Some 45mm and 76mm guns could also be accommodated in the cradles. A decision taken by the Committee for Defence dated 28 February 1941 from the NKTP specified that a batch of 12 attachments be manufactured for the TB-7 before the end of the year, which were designed for a weight of up to 4,500kg. No

Free dropping of a T-37A tank (without parachute) from a TB-3 aircraft onto water, September 1937.

A T-37A tank is being lifted with a hoist on its TVD-2 attachment under a TB-3 bomber.

information however is available even concerning the design of these attachments.

This concerned military vehicles that were far from the ordinary. Snowmobiles can be very useful to paratroopers in winter. Three such projects are known about. Two of them were the brainchild of Grokhovskiy. The first were the small snowmobiles that used three skis (a steering ski at the front and two main skis at the back). The engine evidently was an M-11 with a two-bladed wooden propeller. The snowmobile had a crew of two: a driver and a gunner. The seat for the latter had a ShKAS or a DA machine gun fitted. The intention was for this machine to be dropped without a parachute from low altitude along with its crew. The main advantage of this equipment was thought to be the possibility of engaging in fighting immediately after landing. If the vehicle is dropped by parachute some considerable time is required to deflate large canopies or to disengage the harness system from the military equipment or to remove the vehicle from the assault platform.

The other pair of snowmobiles known as 'Project G-67' evidently were designed to be much larger. They had an armoured main body made of steel eight millimetres thick (this was sufficient to protect it from bullets) and an air-cooled engine rated at 250hp. The G-67 armament consisted of guns and two machine guns, and a crew again of two. The TB-1 bomber was to carry the snowmobiles under the fuselage and drop them onto snow from low level and furthermore this would be achieved with the driver and the gunner on board. Moreover, the engine and the propeller would be stowed in a vertical position in order to reduce the dimensions as well as the aerodynamic drag. After landing they would be turned vertically upwards and the engines started. No information is available concerning the manufacture of a prototype example of the G-67.

Finally, the third design did not have anything to do with Grokhovskiy. It was manufactured as a private aviation initiative by two aircraft technicians D.I. Nikolayev and S.P. Bashilov in 1932. These assault snowmobiles were also to be carried using a TB-1 bomber. In this case there was no mention anywhere of dropping these snowmobiles from low level. It is possible that this apparatus was to be delivered in a landing mission.

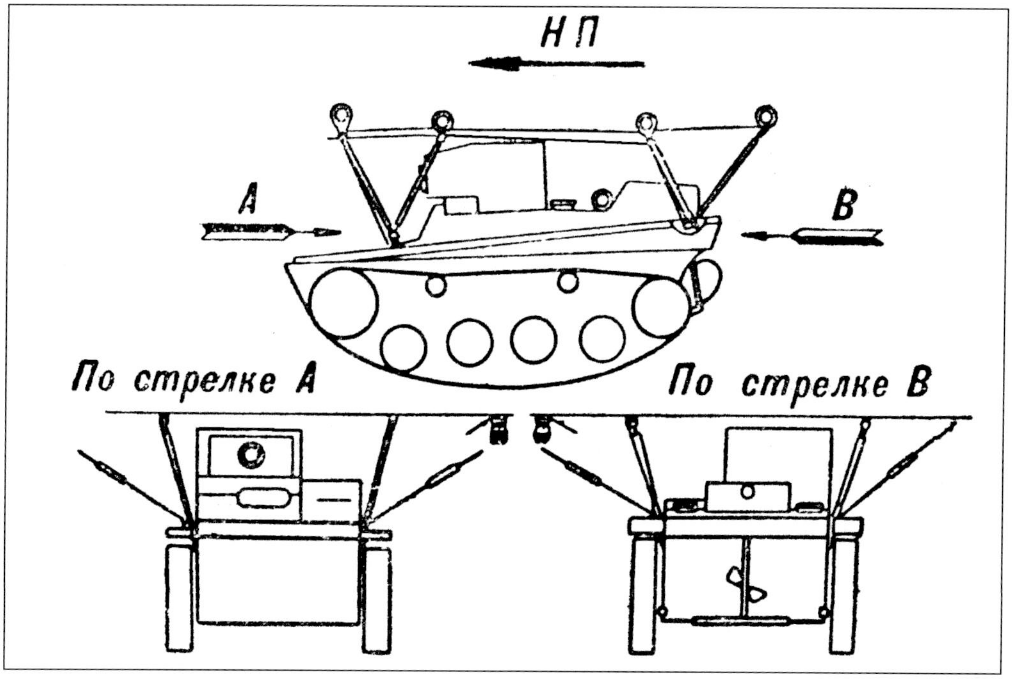

A scheme of attaching a T-37A tank on a DPT-2 attachment under a TB-3 bomber.

A T-37A amphibious tank suspended on a TVD-2 attachment. Note the plate that protected the underside of the tank, under this was a wooden beam.

A T-37A suspended on a TVD-2 attachment, without the underside protection.

A T-38 amphibious tank armed with a 20-mm ShVAK cannon.

A T-38 tank armed with a 7.62-mm DT machine gun.

A T-38 amphibious tank suspended on a DPT-2 attachment underneath a TB-3 aircraft, March 1939.

A GAZ-AA truck with a 45-mm anti-tank gun mounted in the back of the truck, suspended on a DPT-2 attachment.

The FAI-M armoured car could be transported by air using a PDT-2 attachment.

A restored D-8 armoured car at the 'Motors of War' festival, summer 2018.

A T-20 *Komsomolets* armoured artillery tractor could be transported under a TB-3 aircraft using a DPT-2 attachment.

This photo was taken in summer 1942 during the exercises involving airborne troops. Between the DB-3F and TB-3 bombers are the line-up of the vehicles which the TB-3 could carry. The T-37A and T-38 tanks and GAZ-MM truck with removed roof top remained from the pre-war set of airborne equipment. A quadrupled anti-aircraft machine-gun mount is installed in the back of the truck. The British 'Universal Carrier' and BA-64 armoured vehicles, and GAZ-64 'jeeps' were added to the airborne set.

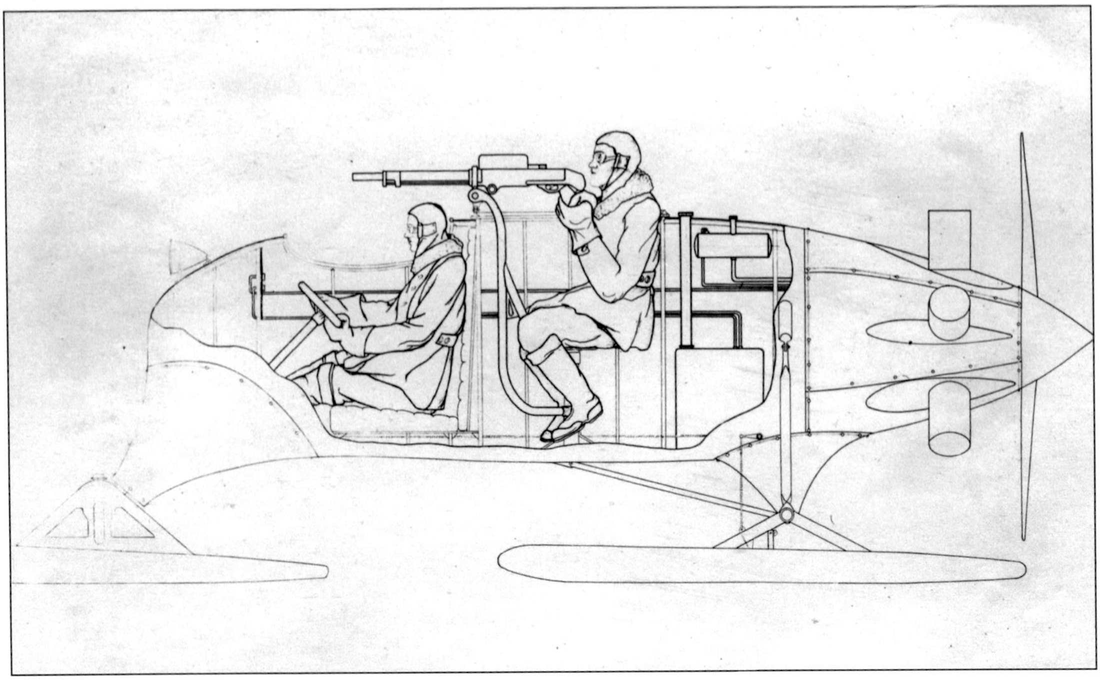

A project of the two-seat snowmobile designed to be dropped without parachute, which was prepared at the Experimental Institute.

19

'Flying Tanks'

The programme to manufacture 'flying tanks' in the USSR does stand out somewhat from what has been described above. The point being that the entity that commissioned and manufactured this work was not the UVVS, which the airborne forces were subordinate to at the time, but the Mechanisation and Motorisation Directorate of the RKKA (this was later renamed to the Automotive and Tank Directorate). The aim of this was not to support the airborne troops but to enhance the mobility of the detachments that were armed with tanks.

This idea was the brainchild of American tank designer, Walter Christie, at the beginning of the 1930s. He proposed fitting wings and a tail fin to a tank and making its powerful engine drive a propeller. In this way the tank was transformed into an aircraft of a kind, although it was not capable of flying fast, or at high altitude. Christie would share his ideas with journalists enthusiastically, who would then set to work writing emblazoned prose on how armadas of 'flying tanks' would cross the front line, drop their wings and go on the attack behind enemy lines. "An awful and deadly weapon of war" the newspapers would write. The designer promised to create a tank weighing between four to six tonnes and armed with a 76mm gun. The crew would not need to leave the tank to jettison the wings he added.

This prospect was also of interest to the Soviet military, as well as to aircraft designers. Designs began to appear one after the other that were developed on the basis of Christie's concept. What was probably the first design was the project designed by A.N. Rafayelyants and V.V. Nikitin, which was known by an amalgam of the designer's surnames as the *Rafnik*. This dated back to July 1932 and the *Rafnik* represented a large monoplane with a wingspan of 17.5m. The tank was suspended between the tall undercarriage legs in such a way that its turret fitted into a slot in the wing centre section. The landing gear tread was four metres. The legs were fitted with rubber plastic shock absorbers.

Frames would extend backwards from each leg and these extensions would be joined underneath the stabiliser. A tail skid was attached to them at this point that had a tail wheel fitted to it. The stabiliser itself was a floating stabiliser and the aircraft had a single fin.

In the drawings, the tank is very reminiscent of a wheel-track BT-2, which at that time had only just entered series production.

This was by no means a surprising choice since the running gear on the BT-2 was created using a licence for the M1940 American tank that was designed by Christie himself. The engine compartment however was illustrated as being much higher up. This was explained by the fact that Rafayelyants and Nikitin decided to use the M-17 aircraft engine (with a maximum output ranging from 680hp, to 730hp depending on the compression ratio) and the BT-2 was fitted with an M-5 (to be more accurate this was a conversion of the American *Liberty* engine into a tank engine variant) rated at 400hp. The engine was to drive a two-bladed pusher propeller that was placed on the elongated forward section of the crankshaft. A guard for the propeller was attached to the back of the engine.

The pilot (who was also the driver) sat in his usual position in the forward section of the tank. In flight the engine was fed by two fuel tanks in the wing centre section. The speed of the 'flying tank' in the air according to the calculations was approximately 150–160km/hr.

After landing, one of the tank crew would pull a lever and the undercarriage legs would retract rearwards about a hinge in the aft brace strut, folding away forwards and upwards. The tank would sit down onto its tracks

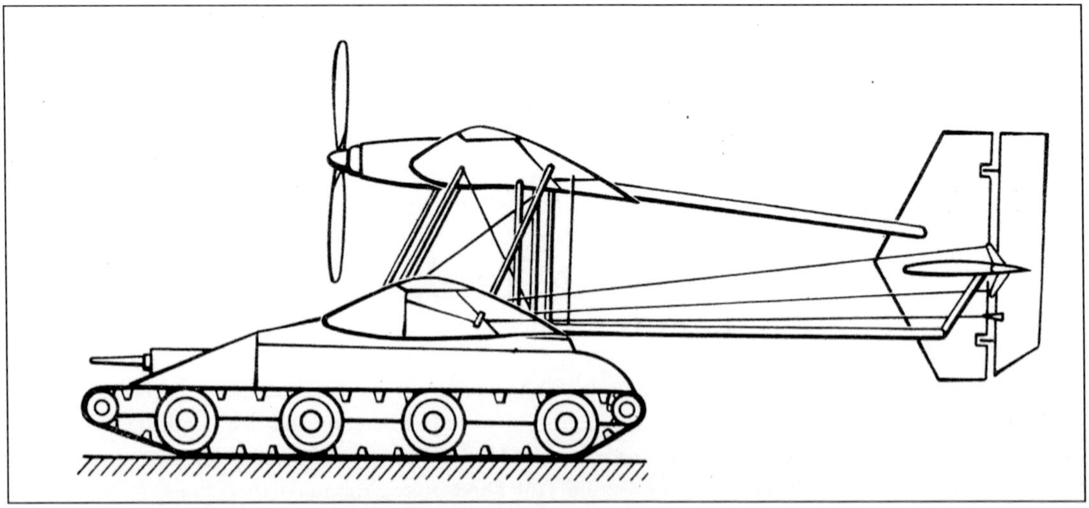

A project of the Walter Christie 'flying vehicle'.

A lightened half-track tank without a turret, which was demonstrated by Christie as a prototype for the 'flying vehicle'.

and at the same time the locks that connected it to the airframe would open. The combat vehicle would move forward. The propeller moreover was not removed but was just placed into a horizontal position.

Interestingly, Rafayelyants and Nikitin thought that the tank would return to the airframe after the battle, reconnect with it and again take to the skies, maybe to fly back to base or to another sector of the front line. From the proposals for the *Rafnik* it is known that its range was 300km, and in an overloaded configuration the figure was up to 400km. This would be an excellent manoeuvre for the forces along the front line – 'a vertical encirclement' or 'the airborne cavalry'.

The second flying tank, evidently, was conceived of a design by a group of employees at the TsAGI, namely R.S. Ermonskiy, A.I. Solovyov, and V.I. Matsyuk. They proposed delivering the tank to the scene of a battle using a glider, which would be towed by a towing aircraft. The tank itself was modified only in the sense that it was fitted with attachment points for a wing and a tail boom along with a tail fin, although this was incorporated into the force diagram.

The glider represented a monoplane with a high aspect ratio wing with a wingspan of 35.8m (according to

The American Government Commission standing next to the lightened Christie tank after a demonstration jump.

a separate document this was 36m). This was situated above the tank in a 'parasol' design mounted on a pylon made of tubes and was additionally linked to the aircraft using brace struts. The wing was a single spar wing that was made solely of wood with a plywood skin that was fitted with ailerons as well as fixed leading-edge flaps and slotted trailing edge flaps. The fin was covered in a canvass. The wing was connected to the tail only via the tank itself.

The vertical fin was made to be a twin fin and incorporated two rudders. The stabiliser was not fitted with an elevator. Conversely, on the port and starboard side of the wing additional stabilisers would extend rearwards that were fitted with control surfaces. The length of the whole apparatus was 12.45m.

The intention was for the craft to take-off and land on tracks or on the tank's wheels. The glider would be controlled by the main gunner, in as much as the driver would accelerate the tank up to maximum speed on take-off and just prior to landing would preliminarily set the tracks in motion.

The weight of the tank itself in the first variant of the design was between six to eight tonnes and the glider weighed two tonnes. Furthermore, the TB-3 heavy bomber fitted with four M-34RNB engines was able to act as a towing aircraft. It was true that this tank had to be lightened slightly (up to 19tonnes) and fitted with a three-bladed variable pitch propeller. At a later stage the design was reworked, and it turned out that standard fixed pitch wooden propellers could be fitted.

After landing, the tank crews would open eight locks that would separate the wing and the tail. The advantage of this was the use, in essence, of a standard tank. This vehicle did not need to be fitted with a powerful engine to be able to move across copious tracts of ground. The one disadvantage however lay in the fact that take-off and landing was performed using the tank's chassis. According to the author's estimations the craft would need to move at a speed of 100km/hr on take-off! For the tanks of that period this was inconceivably fast: on tracks they would develop a little over 50km/hr and on a wheeled chassis this would be up to 75km/hr. Subsequently designers settled on a speed of 80km/hr, which looked more realistic.

The most exotic project, however, was presented in September 1932 by the famous helicopter designer, N.I. Kamov – a 'helicopter-tank'. It was true that if this design were studied carefully one would realise that this was not a helicopter, but an autogyro. If the competitors were to take Christie's tank as the starting point to some

A Soviet BT-2 tank, the running gear of which was made under licence from Christie.

degree, then Kamov's machine bore no relation to it.

This was a purely tracked machine and pairs of rollers were linked to aviation type oil pneumatic shock absorbers. The underside of the tank was made to sit low down and was broad with a width between the tracks of three and a half metres. A superstructure would extend upwards from here with an oval shaped cross-section in which the engine was housed, along with one of the two crew members. The designer chose what was at that time the newest indigenous aircraft engine the M-34 with a maximum output of 800hp. Back then it had only just undergone testing and did not stand out in terms of being particularly reliable. The engine drove a pusher propeller, behind which was a rudder. A shaft also extended from the engine that would spin up the main rotor just prior to take-off. Thus the aircraft that Kamov had designed was a so-called 'jumping' autogyro with a reduced take-off run.

The three-bladed main rotor with a diameter of 20m was mounted on the top of the superstructure using a wide bushing that had been invented by Kamov. Two variants of the blade design were considered: one made of steel and one made of an aluminium alloy. The diameter of the rotor head enabled a circular turret to be placed on top of it with two machine guns inside. A second such turret, also fitted with a paired machine gun, was fitted above the superstructure. A further two-gun barrels extended from the superstructure itself, and these fired rearwards to port and starboard of the pusher propeller. How a crew of two was to control all this armament is not altogether clear.

Overall the tank was short, wide and tall (the height was judged to be four point three metres). The flight weight, according to the calculations, was between 4,000–4,500kg, including 650kg of fuel.

A short time later Kamov proposed turning the autogyro into a real helicopter. The total output for the M-34 engine was transferred to the lifting rotor, which was larger than that on the autogyro, and was 30m in diameter. The flight performance characteristics for the helicopter, according to the calculations turned out to be worse and by the end of September the designer had rejected this variant.

Kamov was subsequently engaged solely with the autogyro. It was proposed that the 'helicopter-tank' (the autogyro) would take-off from a small runway (a take-off run of no more than 50m was promised) and would fly

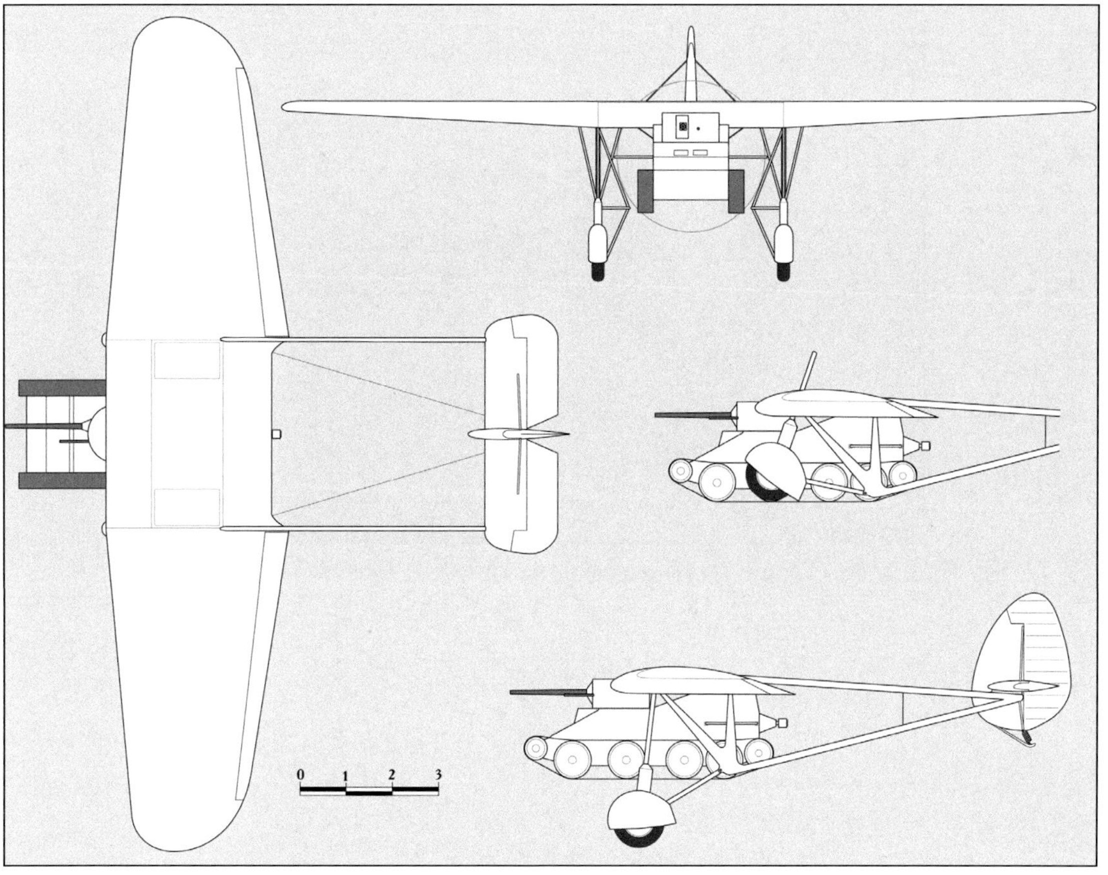

The project of *Rafnik* designed by Rafayelyants and Nikitin, 1932.

at a speed of 150km/hr. It was able to land almost anywhere, since it had a 'miniscule' landing roll of around five metres. After landing the crew would fold the blades on the lifting rotor backwards (this was done manually, but without getting out of the aircraft) and it was able to go into battle. It was proposed that the tank could travel at a speed of 35–40km/hr on land. If it encountered any kind of a significant obstacle the vehicle could get into the air again and hop over it. This was how it was envisaged the vehicle would be able to attack behind enemy lines. In their report the Design Section of the Experimental Aircraft Design Sector (KOSOS) of TsAGI on the 'helicopter-tank' stated: "this idea is an excellent and very productive one".

In general, everything worked out very well. The stumbling block however was the tank. Kamov had to design the whole aircraft 'from scratch'. He compiled a long list of specialists who would be required and intended to start by manufacturing a small autogyro for testing and to develop the rotor head that would be needed for it. In the end this turned out to be a very complicated task.

The other two designs proposed the use of an existing, or a modified tank. No such tank existed at that time in the USSR however. The weight of the *Rafnik* according to the consolidated data was 4,550kg with the airframe, while the tank itself weighed 4,000kg. Yermolonskiy and his colleagues gave a slightly higher figure from the tank itself of between 6,000–8,000kg, and moreover this was without an engine that was capable of driving an airscrew. The designer had to use a 'BT type tank'. This being the case there was only one type of tank to choose from, this was a BT-2 that has already been mentioned above, but this weighed more than 11tonnes.

As a result, the designers were being asked to design a complex made from a special tank and the airframe to go with it, and moreover the programme was being led by the tank crews. During the formulation of the specification for the designers they were irrepressible in their desire to attain everything straight away without

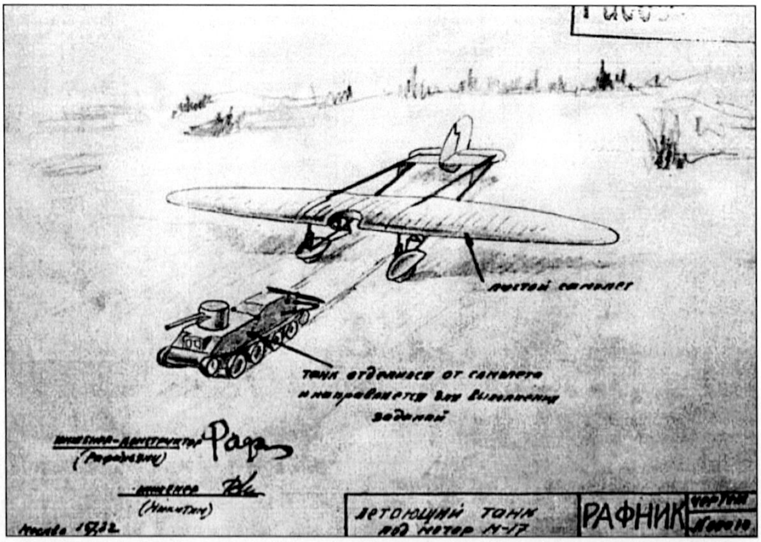

A sketch from the project documentation, showing the detachment of a Rafnik tank from the glider structure.

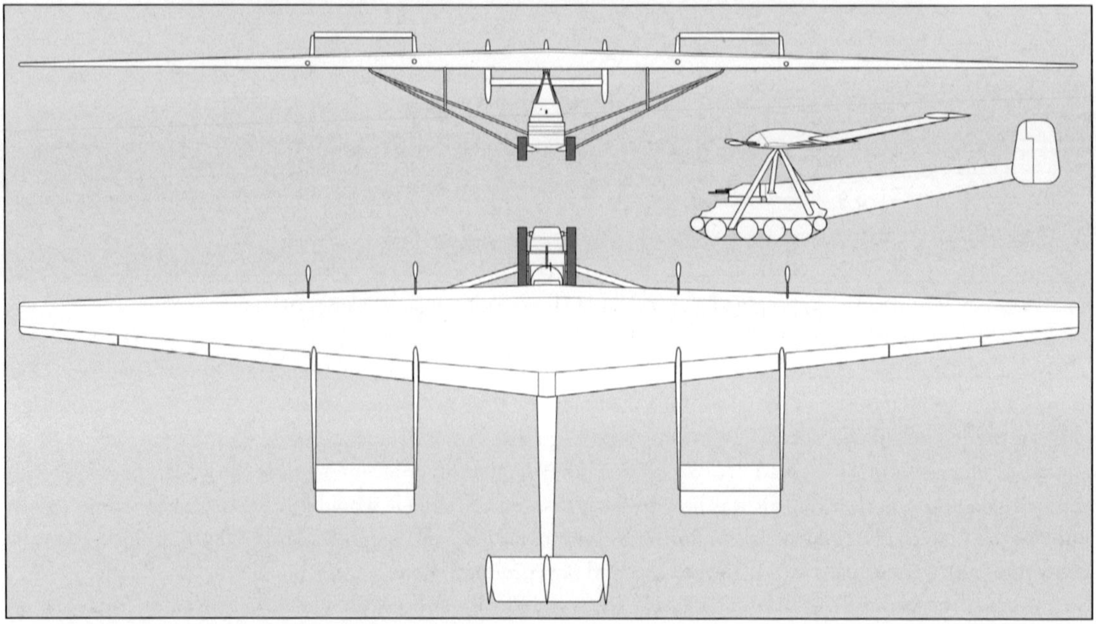

A glider project for carrying a tank that was proposed by Yermonskiy, Solovyov, and Matsyuk at TsAGI in 1932.

thinking about how realistic the task actually was.

They needed a half-track vehicle with a weight of between three and a half to four tonnes with bulletproof armour (with a thickness of up to eight millimetres) a crew of two people, and either an M-17, or and M-34 engine. With the wings fitted this vehicle had to weigh no more than six tonnes. Moreover, however in September 1932 armament consisting of 45mm guns and two 7.62mm machine guns were written into Rafayelyants's specification, that is to say this tank would be more powerful than the BT-2 that had a 37mm gun and a single machine gun. The BT-2 though had a crew of three, which made working with the armament easier. They dug their heels in however, probably because the task of creating a special tank had been entrusted to designers who had little understanding of it. The work came to a standstill.

A decision was made at this time to find out what Christie himself was doing. The employees of the *Amtorg*

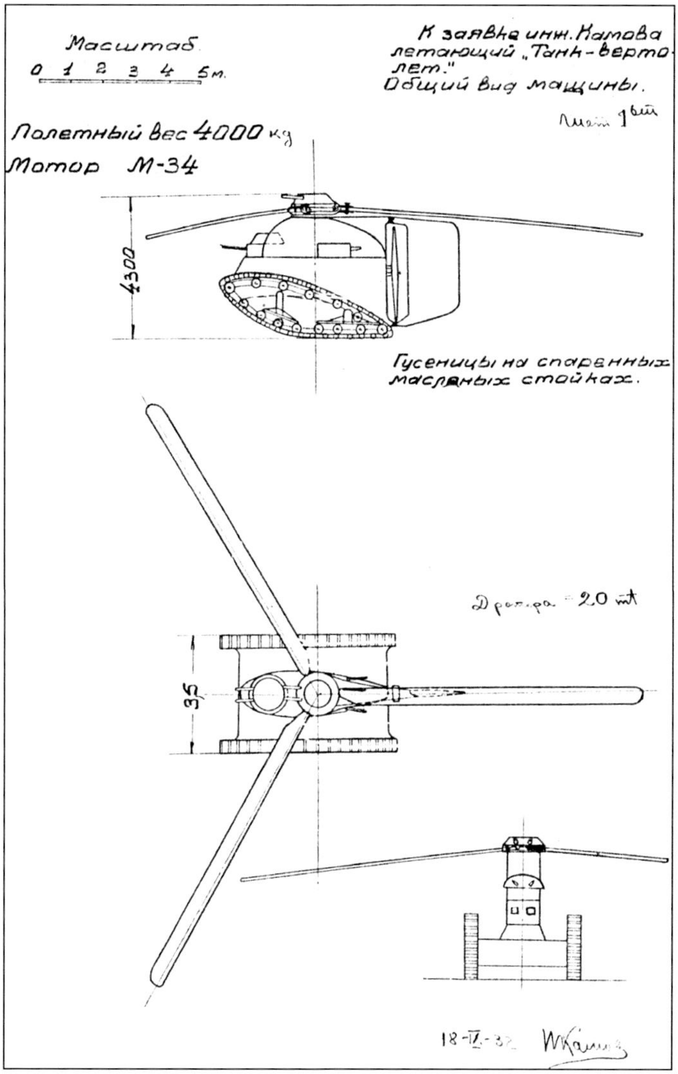

A 'helicopter-tank' (autogyro) project designed by Kamov, 1932.

corporation, which at that time performed the function of a Soviet trade representation were entrusted with gathering information on this. They found out that Christie had actually prepared a design in which a biplane cell, from which beams would extend rearwards to accommodate a fin, would be placed on a very much lighter half-track tank that was designed without a turret. A puller propeller was situated on the leading edge of the upper wing and was rotated by a power take off shaft driven by the tank's engine. Take-off and landing was on a track chassis.

Christie demonstrated this to an American Government Commission without any armament fitted, the weight was allegedly six tonnes and it was fitted with an aviation power plant in the shape of a Hispano-Suiza engine rated at 650hp and announced that this was a prototype for a 'flying vehicle'. This tank however could not fly but just jump over trenches. Soviet specialists assessed its weight to be approximately four tonnes or less.

Christie later came to the conclusion that the original concept that was based on using a tank engine for flight was a mistake. An engine rated at between 650–700hp given the existing wing area could lift a cargo into the air that corresponded to the weight of the tank, but the additional weight of the airframe would have been beyond its capabilities. Christie then took a chance on a carrying aircraft that would be fitted with its own engine. The

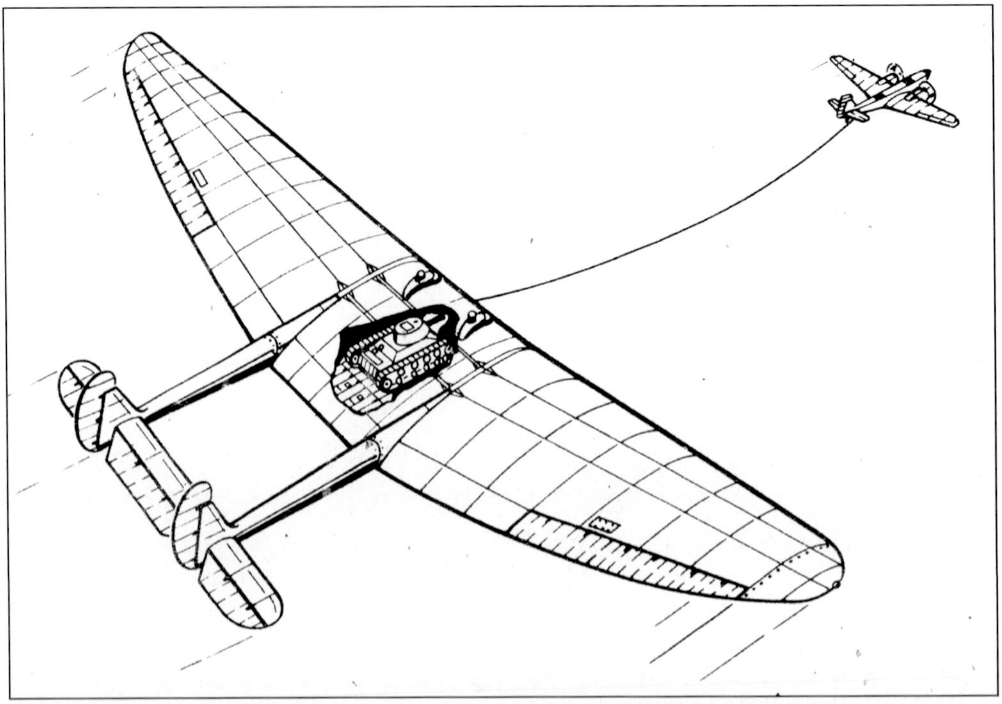

A project of the G-67 glider that was designed to carry tanks, which was prepared at the Experimental Institute of the NKTP under the leadership of Grokhovskiy. In contrast to the other designs, the tank in this case is accommodated in an enclosed cabin inside the glider and should not be adapted for transportation by air.

tank's engine would only assist on take-off or when rotating the tracks ahead of a landing.

According to a message from New York dated 24 August 1932, the American designer reached agreement with the Miller company concerning joint development of a special aircraft, for which Miller would produce an engine rated at between 800–1,000hp. In turn, in their acquisition of examples of this wheel-track vehicle *Amtorg* paid $25,000 less than the asking price due to the lack of turrets on these vehicles, as well as armament, and also because of the fact that the documentation was incomplete. They were then prepared to pay this sum in exchange for the blueprints for the connection equipment linking the tank to the airframe, and for an example of a Miller engine. The Americans asked for $50,000 for the blueprints alone and refused to enter into negotiations on the engine. Therefore, no agreement was reached with them.

By spring 1933, all the work on the 'flying tank' had gradually come to an end. In its place work to create external attachment assemblies for transporting military hardware underneath heavy bombers that has been described above, was activated.

At around the same time Grokhovskiy proposed the G-67 project, which was named the 'glider-tank', and represented a glider for delivering a light tank. In drawings it was illustrated as a glider with a 'frame' like design with twin tail booms that were linked at the back by a stabiliser. The tank was hidden in the wing centre section and evidently was not incorporated into the load bearing structure of the glider but was merely a cargo. The crew of the glider sat in two cockpits in the leading edge of the wing, which had canopies that protruded upwards. In the plan for OKPB for 1932 the G-26 is also mentioned – in the form of a similar glider for transporting 'Ford' cars (evidently these were 'Ford As' in the car or pickup variant). These two designs were taken up later at the Experimental Institute and work continued until the end of 1934).

During the course of the war with Germany, in December 1941, the O.K. Antonov Design Bureau, which at that time was located in Tyumen, designed an A-40 glider (this was actually a flying tank) that would be attached to a T-60 tank. Just one flight was completed with this machine, which ended with one of the engines on the TB-3 towing aircraft overheating.

20

Artillery

The firepower of the paratroopers, it was planned, would also be increased by providing them with artillery. The first to attempt to transport artillery guns by air were the Americans. In 1931, during exercises to beat back an assault by the marines in the Panama Canal Zone, they delivered a battery of four 76mm guns from one shoreline to another along with the artillerymen and shells. Seven aircraft were needed for this to happen. The American military however did not set the task of dropping the ordnance by parachute.

In the USSR rigorous work was underway on supplying airborne troops with artillery. One of the first documents that examined the requirements of airborne troops stated: "Artillery not only enhances fire power but can deceive the enemy in terms of the calibre of the rounds". In order to solve the latter task a large amount of artillery shells were needed; more than the military units had onhand in the front line.

For the paratroopers the priorities were compactness and light weight. To begin with the emphasis was on dynamo-reactive (recoilless) guns. In the Soviet Union these were developed by L.V. Kurchevskiy. A series of his designs were introduced into service with the RKKA. Specifically, for airborne operations the short barrel 76mm DRP was very well suited when mounted on a collapsible tripod stand (this was sometimes known as a DRP-4). This could either be stowed inside a single parachute bag or into two (depending on the barrel with its sight and mounting). After it had been dropped this could be unpacked and brought up to combat readiness relatively easily. A gun such as this could be delivered anywhere in a combat configuration along with a means of transport, such as a car or a motorcycle and sidecar.

The more powerful DRP with this same calibre of 76mm was in service in airborne brigades. These were battalion BPK weapons that were mounted on a two-wheel gun carriage (these wheels were wooden). This weapon weighed 180kg and had a firing range of up to seven kilometres. The ammunition incorporated fragmentation and armour piercing, as well as shrapnel burst warheads. The BPK could be dismantled into several components, which would be dropped in two soft parachute bags. This gun can be seen in the documentary film *The Battle for the Dniepr*: a crew is seen unpacking bags and starting to put a DRP weapon together in front of the viewers.

Recoilless guns were very light, but their shells had a slow flight speed. As a result, in terms of accuracy, range and armour piercing qualities they conceded significantly to classical artillery. Apart from that as they were fired, they would produce an enormous cloud of gas or dust. It was therefore decided to augment them with small calibre automatic guns also mounted on tripod mounts that had been specially lightened, or onto vehicles. There were no such indigenous systems available at that time. Imported guns were considered: there were examples of Swiss 20mm *Oerlikon* guns in the USSR (for aviation the L and S modifications were acquired which were characterised by the length of the barrel) and the German 30mm *Rheinmetall* RM 6 (this was given the simple designation RM). It was proposed that they would be used in battle with enemy armoured military and transport vehicles (including steam locomotives) and would augment the machine guns used in action against enemy aviation. The Soviet Union did not start to acquire foreign automatic weapons in any number however as much as the country began to roll out production of these weapons within its own borders. The indigenous systems only appeared in the second half of the 1930s and were intended first and foremost for aviation and the Air Defence System.

Neither the DRPs, nor the small calibre automatic guns were able to replace classic artillery, however. In 1931 at the OKPB a PD-O (G-37) system was created for transporting and dropping 1909-model 76mm mountain

A 76-mm recoilless gun is unpacked and assembled after it was dropped in two parachute bags. Note the packaging that had been used are lying alongside.

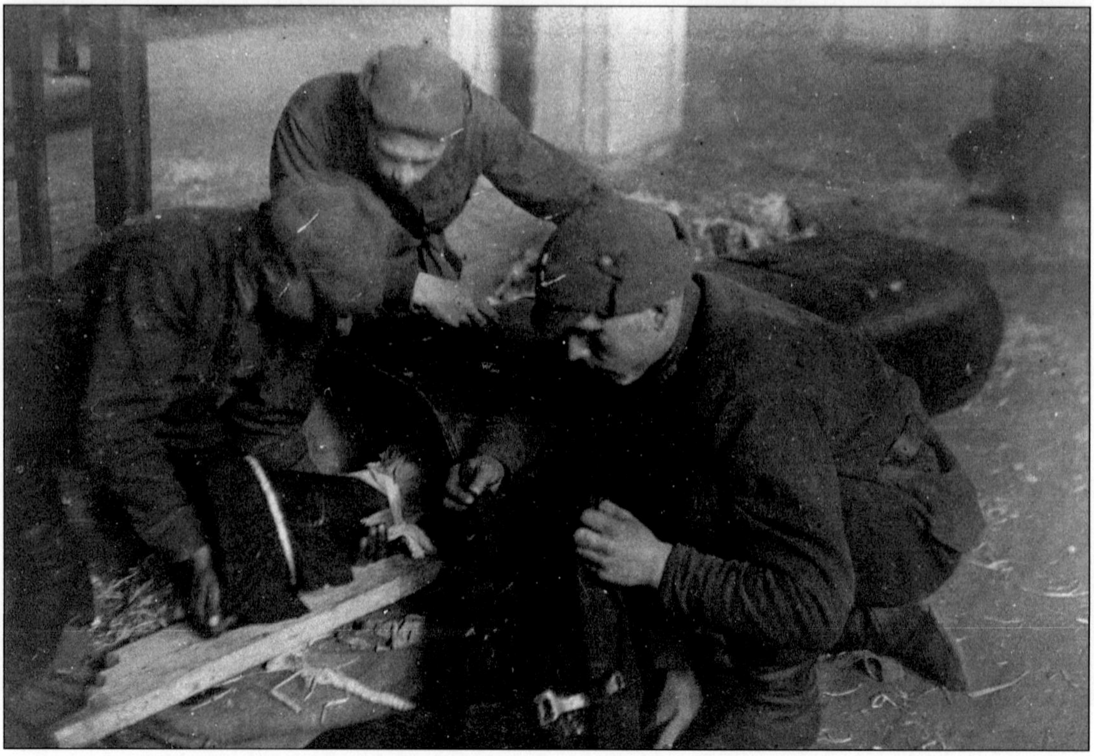

Packing the barrel of a DRP recoilless gun into a cardboard pod for dropping by parachute.

An R-5 aircraft with DRP recoilless gun packages under its lower wing.

guns by parachute. Back then this was the most compact and the lightest production gun of this calibre available in the USSR. The gun was carried between the undercarriage legs of a TB-1 bomber, the parachute would be stowed in a cylindrical, conical shaped box attached to the Der-13 bomb racks ventrally underneath the fuselage. The guard on the weapon was removed. This whole assembly weighed approximately a tonne and the diameter of the percale canopy was 25m. On tests the gun was dropped several times successfully from a bomber. During a demonstration to the Deputy People's Commissar for Defence M.N. Tukhachevskiy in July 1931 the gun broke free of the parachute and was destroyed.

The option of dismantling the mountain gun into various components and transporting them in packages was examined, but Grokhovskiy would drop these weapons in one piece. It was chosen because of its comparatively light weight. Later there was a shift to more powerful and heavier systems, but the mountain guns were not introduced into service with the airborne detachments.

A new G-37 parachute attachment for the 1927-model 76mm short barrel field gun. In terms of its design this gun was analogous to the previous model. The attachment successfully underwent state testing just outside Leningrad between September–October 1932. Furthermore, two drops were achieved from a TB-1 aircraft using the separation method. The first to drop would be the box with the parachute, and the canopy would deploy under its own weight, which once it had opened would pull the weapon out from its attachment located between the pyramid undercarriage legs of a bomber.

Grokhovskiy tested an earlier variant of the gun, a 1927-model, with wooden wheels that was horse drawn. At that same time in 1932 a new modification of this gun began to be manufactured with metal wheels covered with rubber that was designed to be towed behind a truck at high speed. These guns then became standard for the airborne brigades, operating in four-gun batteries.

The G-32 design that appeared later envisaged transportation underneath a TB-3 of either two or more heavy 1930-model 76mm guns (these were the well-known 1902-model 'three-inch' gun following modification) that

A 76-mm BPK battalion recoilless gun, which was in series production and in service with the airborne troops.

made use of a universal frame (that is to say the future PG-12 mentioned above). There is no information available however on the realisation of this project, the 1930-model guns did not enter service with the airborne units.

In 1932, the designers at the Leningrad Special Designs Bureau were also engaged in transporting guns by air (but without dropping them by parachute). In the plan for that year developments are mentioned concerning some 3-inch (76mm) guns and 18-inch howitzers! It is possible though that the latter was some sort of a specific type of DRP: if that were the case its weight would be within acceptable limits.

Between 1935–36, at the VVS Academy Design Bureau, an attachment was developed for some sort of 76mm gun that would go under a TB-3. This underwent state testing at the NII VVS.

In reality, however, any serious options for dropping artillery only came about after the PG-12 attachments were introduced into service in 1935. The GP-1 cargo platform that was of a truss construction was also attached to the PG-12 as mentioned above and this enabled a variety of outsized cargoes to be transported and dropped by parachute. One platform could carry one 1927-model 76mm field gun, 45mm anti-tank gun with limbers or two 1927-model guns (also with limbers). The total weight of the cargo on the platform could reach up to 3.2 tonnes. The platform had wheels and could be towed around an airfield by a car or a tractor. The GP-1 could interface with another later DPT-2 attachment that was introduced into service in 1939.

The introduction into the assortment of weapons delivered behind enemy lines of an anti-tank gun appeared highly logical. The role of armoured vehicles in any future war was constantly growing. Paratroopers needed protection from tanks and armoured cars. Two types of 45mm anti-tank guns were used: the 1932-model and the 1937-model. The first of these was based on licence production of a German 37mm gun. In 1937 this gun was modernised the bolt was updated, and the wheels were replaced. The latter was the main outward sign by which they could be differentiated visually. The 1932 guns had motorcycle style wheels with spokes, while on the 1937

Paratroopers on exercise taking out the components of BPK recoilless gun from a bag dropped by parachute, Brovary, 1935.

guns the discs were welded from forged parts. In the airborne forces the preference was for the older variant since it was slightly lighter. According to the standards for 1936 an airborne brigade in wartime would rely on anti-tank battalion made from three batteries with six guns in each.

The TB-3 heavy bomber could deliver two 45mm guns with limbers using a PG-12 attachment or could actually drop them by parachute using a PG-12P. The crews furthermore would be accommodated in the fuselage of the aircraft. Another variant was often used however – a gun with a limber would be loaded into the body of a GAZ-AA truck. In this case the TB-3 would deliver the entire battery along with the tractors, the ammunition and the personnel. An attachment assembly was also used for a 45mm gun that was designed for an R-5 aircraft.

The TsAGI attachment assembly mentioned above that was tested at the NII VVS in June 1936 envisaged the transportation and dropping by parachute of three 76mm guns attached to bomb racks. Interestingly the designers chose the so-called 1913-model 'short' guns. Each gun would make use of a single Der-20 and a single Der-19 bomb rack. In the very first flight as soon as the aircraft reached a speed of 160km/hr the gun would begin to shake so much that the gun shield corners began to strike the fuselage. As a result, the beam on the Der-20 bomb rack failed.

Flights, however, continued, and a second gun was added to the first one, and then a third was added as well. The reader may recall that testing with the TsAGI was never finished before it was declared dangerous. The designers suggested that the guards be removed from the guns thus eradicating the danger of them hitting anything. It was proposed that they be carried separately in the fuselage. Apart from that without guards the aerodynamic drag generated by the cargo, which was considered excessive, would be reduced slightly. The military however spoke out against removal of the guards, claiming that it reduced the combat readiness of the guns. This was rejected by the TsAGI and the 1913-model guns did not enter service with the airborne forces.

In April 1941 testing was concluded of the new D-16 attachment at the NII VVS, this was designed to drop two types of guns by parachute: a 45mm anti-tank gun and a 76mm field gun. It was fitted with an ARD-1 automatic disengagement device. The D-16 however did not enter service prior to the outbreak of the Great Patriotic War.

After the entry into service of the American DC-3 aircraft and their Soviet copy the PS-84, it became possible to transport 45mm and 76mm guns inside the fuselage, but in a dismantled form. First, they would not go

A crew of artillerist-paratroopers pull a BPK recoilless gun into position, 1935.

The 1909-model 76-mm mountain gun was the lightest cannon in service with the Red Army at the beginning of the 1930s. It was for this same reason that it was chosen for experiments in transporting by air and dropping by parachute.

A 1909-model 76-mm mountain gun with the shield removed, suspended on a PD-O (G-37) attachment under a TB-1 bomber.

Dropping a 76-mm mountain gun by parachute.

A 1932-model 45-mm anti-tank gun.

through the narrow passenger door any other way, and secondly the aircraft floor could not withstand the high concentrated loads. Only on a prototype example of the military transport modification of the PS-84K did it become possible to load the guns in their entirety via a large cargo hatch. The PS-84K carried two guns with limbers inside the fuselage.

In 1936, the paratroopers received 82mm battalion mortars. The latter was a new innovation at the time, which had just entered service with the RKKA units. It was as though the 1936-model battalion mortars had been specially designed for the airborne forces. They were light (just 67.5kg), compact and easy to pack away, and easy to handle, and were also reliable. The three components of the weapon (the barrel, base plate, and bipod) could be carried by its own crew of three. The mortar could be dropped by parachute or delivered using a landing method. Mortar batteries were incorporated into the airborne troop line up. According to the standard for 1936 a brigade would have 27 mortars, or three batteries. In that same year this weapon entered service with the airborne troops, but this did not always coincide with the supply of armament. For example, the 47th Brigade had actually received issue mortars by the end of 1936, but there was no ammunition for them. Arrival of both the training and combat ammunition was severely delayed, which in turn delayed the training of the forces themselves.

A short time later, the modified 1937-model 82mm mortars began to enter service with the airborne forces. The base plate on this mortar was round, as opposed to rectangular.

Subsequently, the 1938-model 50mm company mortar began to be used. This weighed just 12.1kg. This type of mortar entered series production in 1939. In a stowed position this mortar could be folded and carried by a mortar operator. With the assistance of belts, it could be carried and dropped along with the operator by parachute. These mortars started to be used for the first time in the war with Finland in the winter of 1939–40. In 1940 the new 1940-model 50mm mortar that was simpler to operate and cheap to produce began to be manufactured.

Experiments were carried out around the transportation of the 1938-model 120mm field mortar carried ventrally under the fuselage of a DB-3F bomber. It weighed 275kg. No information is available concerning the entry into service of this weapon with the airborne forces in the pre-war period.

This is the line-up of artillery armament with which the Soviet airborne troops approached the start of combat operations against Germany.

A 1937-model 45-mm anti-tank gun was easily recognisable by its pressed wheels, in place of motorcycle-style wheels with spokes.

A 1927-model short-barrel 76-mm regimental gun with a limber. The later variant is shown, which has the metal wheels in place of wooden ones.

A 1927-model regimental gun (the early variant with wooden wheels) underneath a TB-1 bomber. This attachment was for landing delivery as the parachute is absent.

(20-10b) The 76-mm regimental guns have been offloaded from a TB-3 aircraft and prepared for towing, Brovary, 1935.

Three 1913-model 76-mm short-barrel guns (one of them has the shield removed) on a TsAGI-proposed attachment, June 1936.

Two 1932-model 45-mm anti-tank guns with limbers mounted on a GP-1 platform with the wheels removed.

A single 1927-model 76-mm regimental gun (an early variant with wooden wheels) and a single 1932-model 45-mm anti-tank gun, both fitted with limbers, mounted on a GP-1 platform and suspended on a PG-12P attachment.

A 1932-model 45-mm anti-tank gun fitted with D-16 parachute which is mounted on the gun carriage.

A 45-mm antitank gun with protective frame and D-16 parachute suspended underneath the DB-3F bomber.

A DB-3F bomber with an anti-tank gun under a cowling underneath the fuselage.

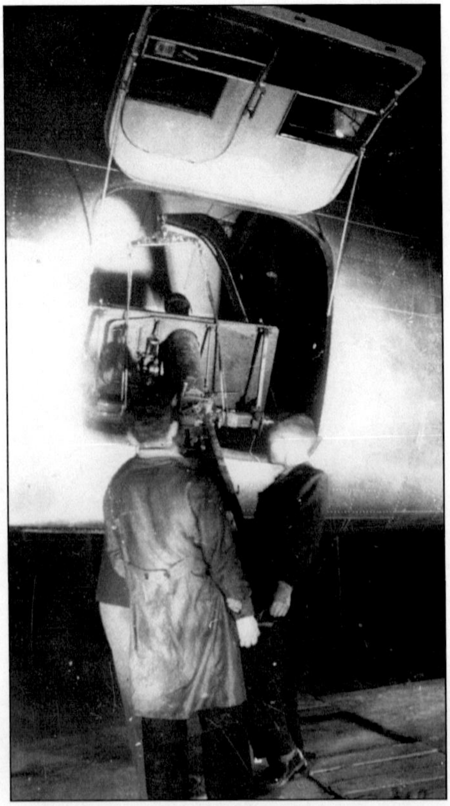

Loading a 76-mm regimental gun (a 1934-variant with metal rubberised wheels) into a PS-84K aircraft.

Two 45-mm anti-tank guns with limbers inside the cargo cabin of a PS-84K aircraft.

A 1937-model 82-mm battalion mortar.

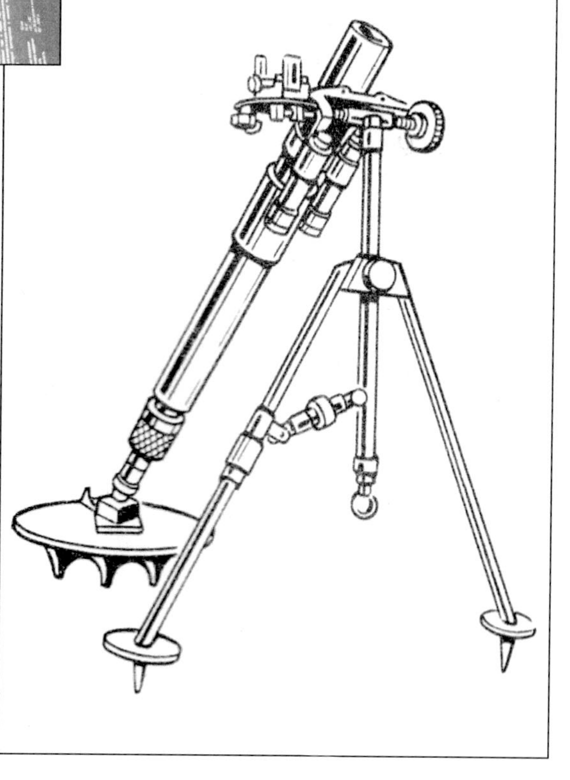

A 1938-model 50-mm company mortar.

A 1940-model 50-mm company mortar.

21

The Reliance on Bombers

There was almost no military-transport aviation in the RKKA VVS line up at the beginning of the 1930s. Based on the considerations of that time cargo and passenger aircraft movements up and along the front line relied on requisitioned civil aviation aircraft. Airborne operations should ideally have been carried out using bombers that one way or another were adapted to these missions without losing their capability of performing their principal function. In the spirit of this concept almost all the bombers created in the USSR up until the outbreak of the Great Patriotic War were capable at least to some degree of carrying people and cargoes. The section below details only those aircraft that were in service at that time in the RKKA VVS.

1. The Farman F.62 *Goliath* (FG-62)

The first bomber that was used in the RKKA VVS to drop paratroopers was the French twin-engine biplane the Farman *Goliath*. Four aircraft of this type were acquired in France at the beginning of 1926. This was a large wooden aircraft fitted with Lorraine Dietrich 12E engines rated at 450hp each, the aircraft had a crew of four and was armed with five 1924-model Lewis machine guns.

This machine did not have any real value in combat in as much as they were purchased with a set of French bomb racks, and these were not compatible with Russian examples of aerial bombs. They operated in the 1st

A twin-engine Farman *Goliath* bomber (FG-62) from the 11th Air Brigade in Voronezh at the beginning of the 1930s.

Heavy Squadron in Trotsk (now known as Gatchina) in actual fact as training aircraft. Following the entry into service of the German JuG-1 (K.30C) *Goliath* bombers they were used in a variety of aviation units as training and transport aircraft.

Since the aircraft had a relatively capacious fuselage it started to be used to train aircrew how to make parachute jumps. It was this same *Goliath* from the line up of the 11th Aviation Brigade that took part in manoeuvres in the Moscow Military District in 1930, after having performed the world's first parachute descent. The FG-62 did not undergo any modifications for transport missions, although periodically it was used in various exercises to carry command personnel and groups of mediators. At the beginning of the 1930s, the two remaining machines were deployed to the Leningrad Military District where they began to be used to train parachutists.

2. The R-1

The reconnaissance and light bomber aircraft the R-1 was the most numerous aircraft in the RKKA VVS in the second half of the 1920s and 1930s. This was a Soviet variant of the famous English aircraft the De Havilland DH.9a, a wooden biplane fitted with an American *Liberty* engine rated at 400hp. This was adapted to local materials, technology, equipment, and armament. As with the original R-1 it had a crew of two and was armed with two or three machine guns.

It was manufactured by the GAZ-1 factories in Moscow (the former *Dux* factory) and the GAZ-10 *Lebed* factory in Taganrog, initially these aircraft were powered by American *Liberty* engines and then by their Soviet copies in the shape of the M-5. The R-1 was periodically used to carry passengers (up to two people in the rear cockpit) as well as small cargoes. In the initial phase of the creation of the airborne troops in the USSR a series of special attachments were created especially for this aircraft. It was on this machine that the 'automatic Red Army soldier deployment system' designed by Grokhovskiy was first tested as well as other examples of boxes dropped by parachute. The R-1 aircraft dropped armament, and ammunition to participants in the first parachute assault in 1930. It was later used for similar purposes on more than one occasion.

The capabilities of the R-1 were significantly limited by its low lifting capacity. Therefore, the majority of the attachments for transporting and dropping cargoes were manufactured for the R-5 and the TB-1.

In 1931, the question was raised concerning the conversion of some of the old R-1s into medical aircraft for evacuating the wounded. Furthermore, the aircraft could carry one casualty in the fuselage on stretchers. No work on this modification however was ever carried out. In 1932 production of the R-1 finally ceased.

An R-1 reconnaissance aircraft, a Soviet variant of the DH.9a biplane.

3. The R-5

In the first half of the 1930s, the R-1 conceded its place to the new R-5 reconnaissance aircraft, which was also a wooden biplane, but one that was already a full-fledged indigenous design. The creator of this aircraft was N.N. Polikarpov. It was true that the aircraft did make use of a BMW VI engine. However, this engine soon began to be produced at Rybinsk under the designation M-17. This aircraft was manufactured across a range of variants from 1930 up to 1936. Close range as well as long range reconnaissance aircraft were manufactured as well as ground attack aircraft, light bombers, training aircraft, and torpedo bombers (these were single seat aircraft). On 1 January 1938, some 2,644 R-5 aircraft were listed on the inventory of the RKKA VVS. At the time it was the most widely produced combat aircraft type.

The maximum bomb load for the R-5 was 500kg, and when some of the equipment was removed and the aircraft was not fully loaded with fuel this could be raised to 800kg. The aircraft had a crew of two and armament consisting of two or three 7.62mm machine guns. This machine could be used in airborne operations without requiring any modifications to deliver cargoes and to drop bags and pods by parachute, as well as cages with canine-saboteurs inside. All this was achieved using standard bomb racks. Attachment assemblies were in existence for transporting heavy machine guns under the wing as well as 45mm guns (without the option of dropping them by parachute). With a small amount of modification, the R-5 could be converted into a 'cable dispenser' and an assault glider towing aircraft.

This biplane in its original form was poorly suited to the task of delivering parachutists. Only one other person could be accommodated in the aft cockpit, aside from the gunner. Unmodified R-5s were just used for training jumps using parachutes. The lifting capacity of the bomber was realised with the fitting of the G-61 racks, when apart from the crew the aircraft could carry a further six combatants.

The R-5 could be used also for evacuating the wounded. Under the lower wing furthermore G-69 underslung stretchers were fitted, or alternatively four guns could be carried with one person for each of them. The stretchers were made of wood and were covered in a tarpaulin. The aircraft would often carry just two stretchers.

An R-5 reconnaissance aircraft taxies out to take off.

In wartime the VVS also intended to use the P-5, which was an unarmed R-5 that operated in civil aviation. Some of these aircraft were fitted with underwing cargo attachments (including those for use in parachute assaults) and G-61 racks. PR-5 aircraft also served in the GVF. They were converted from P-5s by the aircraft repair factory in Bykovo (just outside Moscow). A new more capacious fuselage was developed for these aircraft. The pilot and the four passengers sat in closed cabins. A door was cut into the port side for the passengers. In place of people some cargo could be carried in the cabin. It could also be accommodated in the baggage compartment under the pilot's cockpit. Several R-5s were fitted with underwing cargo boxes, which were known as 'canisters' or 'cigars'.

An R-5 aircraft on the factory airfield in Taganrog, 1930.

Pilots near an R-5 aircraft, the mid 1930s.

An accident with an R-5 from the VVS Transport Detachment of the 57th Rifle Corps, Mongolia, 1939.

In wartime the VVS planned to use PR-5 passenger aircraft for military purposes.

4. The Junkers JuG-1 (K.30C)

Between 1925–28 in the USSR three batches of three-engine all metal JuG-1 bombers (they were originally known as the K.30C) were acquired from the Junkers company. This was a military variant of the G.24 passenger carrying monoplane. Three L5 engines rated at 310hp each, a crew of four or five and armament that consisted of five machine guns.

Two heavy squadrons were equipped with these aircraft in the Leningrad Military District, which were based to begin with at Trotsk (Gatchina) then in Krechevitsy just outside Pskov, as well as several naval aviation detachments in the Baltic, and Black Sea fleets. The spacious fuselage, which the JuG-1 had inherited from its passenger carrying predecessor enabled it to transport up to seven or eight people, or up to 650kg of cargo.

During the course of preparations for exercises by the Leningrad Military District in 1931 cable harnesses were designed and manufactured to enable motorcycles either with sidecars or without them to be carried ventrally

A three-engine JuG-1 bomber on Krechevitsy airfield, August 1929.

Aircrew and technical personnel from the Air Force Special Purpose Squadron, which was used for air transportation, standing next to a JuG-1 at Moscow Central Airfield.

An accident with a JuG-1 from the 57th Squadron which took place when the aircraft was on landing approach at night in the area near Trotsk (Gatchina), August 1927.

under the fuselage of the JuG-1. They were used during the exercises.

Shortly afterwards, the JuG-1 began to be replaced by the TB-1 indigenous bomber. The German machines that were still airworthy were for the most part handed over to Civil Aviation.

The few JuG-1s that remained in the VVS were used as transport and headquarters aircraft. For example, one aircraft with a full complement of armament was used for some time as a personal aircraft for the Head of the UVVS P.I. Baranov. He flew in this aircraft to inspections of aviation units and in the course of various units, but he never flew it, since he himself was not a qualified pilot. Another JuG-1 was at the disposal of the RVS of the Special Red-Banner Far East Army (OKDVA) and served as a transport aircraft for command personnel at least up until the beginning of 1933.

After the withdrawal of the JuG-1 from service with the VVS and their conversion to passenger aircraft, they remained for some time on the inventory for mobilisation, so they could possibly be used in military transport and airborne operations. In the event of an outbreak of war they were to serve in the 4th (in Irkutsk) and the 5th (in Tashkent) detachments.

5. The TB-1

The heavy bomber the TB-1 was, for a relatively long period of time, the mainstay of the Soviet airborne fleet. This aircraft was created in 1925, initially as a specially designed aircraft to drop aerial mines and torpedoes. The prototype example of the all-metal monoplane had English Napier *Lyon* engines.

This aircraft was launched into series production only in 1929 as a heavy bomber with two German BMW VI engines rated at 680hp (these were later replaced by M-17, M-17Bs or M17F engines rated at 700–730hp). The aircraft had a crew of five and was armed with six machine guns. In terms of its lifting capacity the TB-1 overtook the JuG-1 by one and a half times, but the narrow fuselage of the bomber did not have sufficient capacity, to be used for the majority of the time solely for airborne assaults. For example, with a full complement of crew it was not able to carry more six people on board, who would be accommodated in very cramped conditions. During parachute jumps the personnel were not able to climb out of the bomber quickly. Therefore, given the capabilities of the aircraft the emphasis was put on delivering paratroopers in a landing mission.

The majority of these aircraft were designed at the NII VVS, the VVS OKPB and at the Experimental Institute under the People's Commissariat for Heavy industry. The TB-1 aircraft fitted with different types of attachments were able to carry tankettes, cars, and pickups (including self-propelled recoilless guns), motorcycles both with sidecars, and without them as well as mountain and field guns. These could also be dropped by parachute. As mentioned above the first of these attachments that entered service in 1931 was the OTB that was designed to carry a 'Ford A' car albeit partially dismantled. A parachute drop was not envisaged for this equipment. Later the attachments designed by the OKPB namely the PD-A, PD-T, and PD-O appeared that were capable of dropping a cargo by parachute. With cars and tankettes suspended underneath the aircraft were normally lightened by virtue of the removal of some of the armament, and a reduction in the reserve of fuel.

Parachute bags and various types of fuel tanks were suspended on external bomb racks. The KP-1 pods were used to drop paratroopers. These were series produced and were used in front line forces. The 'cradles' designed by Grokhovskiy were attached underneath the wing and the fuselage, they were manufactured in large batches and underwent combat testing but were not introduced into service.

A twin-engine TB-1 bomber at the Moscow Central Airfield awaiting ferry to a service unit.

A twin-engine TB-1 with a ski undercarriage.

For a landing operation, a single TB-1 was able to carry either a 'Ford A' and four light machine guns, or a 76mm DRP that made use of a 'Ford' chassis, or two motorcycles with sidecars, a single 76mm DRP and a single light machine gun, or two motorcycles without sidecars and two light machine guns.

The first TB-1s were used in exercises for a landing delivery in 1931 (this included transporting vehicles), a parachute descent was carried out in 1932. Up until 1934 this bomber was the main means of delivering paratroopers and their equipment to the landing site.

The TB-1 was also considered as a medical aircraft. Up to seven casualties could be accommodated inside its fuselage without any modifications, this was much less than the lifting capacity would permit. Stretchers however would not fit inside its doors and hatches.

After the roll out of series production of the four-engine TB-3 bomber, the twin-engine aircraft were withdrawn from the bomber brigades and transferred to special, transport and training units. Many of the TB-1s were handed over to a number of fighter and bomber regiments as transport aircraft in ones to twos. They did, however, retain their role as an airborne assault aircraft for some time. Up until the end of 1937 the 22nd Squadron, 3rd Special Purpose Air Brigade operated these aircraft. Several dozen transport TB-1s survived in various aviation units until the German attack on the USSR in June 1941.

6. The TB-3

The main type of aircraft that operated in the RKKA VVS in the 1930s in the airborne assault role was the four-engine TB-3 heavy bomber. These aircraft began to enter service in the spring of 1932, but they only began to enter service with the 3rd Air Brigade that specialised in airborne operations in 1934. On 1 July three such aircraft entered service with the 24th Squadron's Brigade.

This aircraft was a large all metal monoplane with non-retractable undercarriage. These aircraft were manufactured between 1932–38 at three factories, several modifications were produced with BMW VI, M-17, M-17B, M-17F, M-34, M-34R, M-34RN, and M-34FRNV engines rated between 700–1,200hp. The crew consisted of between eight to ten men, and for the aircraft that were used purely as transport aircraft this figure was between four and five. The armament across the different variants ranged from four to eight machine guns. On aircraft serving in transport detachments and squadrons the armament could be partially or completely removed with the aim of lightening the aircraft.

It was not only aircraft from the 3rd Air Brigade that were used to deliver airborne paratroopers but also aircraft from other units and formations, which were considered heavy bombers.

Aircraft with an earlier, more widespread modification that were fitted with M-17 engines could, according to the official standards, carry 32 soldiers or 24 parachutists. In reality up to 30–40 parachutists could be

The first series TB-3 manufactured at Factory No. 39 in Moscow, the end of 1932.

A four-engine TB-3 bomber fitted with M-17 engines, January 1937.

A group of TB-3s flying over Amur river, the mid 1930s.

Paratroopers climb into the bomb bay of a TB-3 with the help of step ladders. They will subsequently jump out through the open bomb bay doors.

accommodated in the aircraft if it were not completely full of fuel. The personnel would sit on wooden benches or simply on the floor. The airborne troops would jump from the bombers through the door and bomb bay, as well as by climbing onto the wing via the pilot's cockpit. They would slide down the wing in the same way as they would slide down a mountain.

In 1933, the RVS of the USSR ordered that the: "Airborne assault capabilities of the existing aircraft must be enhanced". The Head of the VVS Ya.I. Alksnis ordered that ways be found for bringing the internal capacity of the TB-3 up to 35–40 men. For the convenience of the airborne troops he ordered that a second door (on the port side) and a second-hand rail be installed (also on the port side), and that the hatches in the wing be flanged, after removal of the underwing B-2 turrets (known as 'trousers' and after the hatch covers had been made into sliding covers.

In the 3rd Special Purpose Brigade in 1933, experiments were conducted with different variants of loading an aircraft fitted with M-17 engines with personnel. In the end the following was observed: 34 men with parachutes, and 48 without parachutes. Furthermore, 14 combatants would sit on the floor in the nose section of the fuselage, and 16 would sit in the radio compartment (the maximum number who could get into this compartment was 24, but this fills the compartment to the max, like the Moscow metro during the rush hour). A further ten paratroopers would sit on benches in the wings. This was without parachutes. Only seven, 15, and nine men could fit into these locations respectively with parachutes. Furthermore, they needed to get into some uncomfortable places, which it would then be difficult to get out of. For the paratroopers this prolonged the process of leaving the aircraft and had a negative effect on grouping as the troops landed.

Later on, a temporary wooden decking was installed in the bomb bay and the combatants would sit on the boards. They would then jump through the bomb bay.

On demonstration jumps, Grokhovskiy would accommodate some of the paratroopers on the actual wing of

A TB-3 fitted with M-34RN engines and equipped with a bridge for carrying and dropping cargoes, 1939. Note a variety of parachute bags and tanks suspended on the clamps of the bridge and on the external bomb racks.

the TB-3. They would stand on the wing, holding on to handrails that extended along the side. It was possible to accommodate approximately 40 people that way. Naturally the aircraft in this case flew relatively slowly but even so the flight speed was in excess of 100km/hr, which of course was just dangerous for the men standing on the wing while the aircraft was climbing to a sufficient altitude for the parachutes to open.

On several of the early series aircraft fitted with M-17 engines, a second door was cut into the starboard side to expedite the process of leaving the aircraft, the underwing turrets were also removed, and additional hatches were put in their place. Sometimes a further additional hatch on each side would be cut in the lower wing surfaces. These hatches would be closed using thin plywood covers, or just by using plywood panels. This work was carried out specifically in the 3rd Air Brigade. Parachutists would jump out of the aircraft at intervals of eight to ten seconds. Furthermore, the TB-3s retained their entire bomb load and at any point they could also be used as bombers. All the aircraft in the 3rd Air Brigade were dual purpose machines.

Aircraft fitted with M-34R and M-34RN engines were less practical when it came to airborne assaults since they did not have doors or hatchways in the underwing turrets. According to the specification however the aircraft could carry 41 soldiers, or 34 paratroopers on account of their enhanced lifting capacity. However, the dropping of the latter would take up to 40 seconds. Usually a TB-3 fitted with M-34R engines would take 35 paratroopers or two pickups on an external attachment, and 12 combatants.

Small cargoes were carried on the TB-3 in the cockpits, in the passageways, underneath the fuel tanks and in the compartments behind the wing tanks. Furthermore, wooden guards or plywood panels were placed onto the corrugated skin, and sometimes shelf space was manufactured on two levels. In the bomb bay the hatchway was expanded using a net, which was spliced from rope with a diameter of between 10–12mm, boards were placed above it. The packages containing cargoes were linked together and were also separated from each other using ropes.

TB-3 heavy bombers fly to the paratroopers drop zone in the area around Kiev, 1935.

The maximum weight of the cargo carried according to the specifications for the M-17 engine modification was 3,346kg, and for the M-34RN this figure was at 4,206kg. The take-off weight furthermore was 19,000kg and 21,000kg respectively.

The TB-1 and the TB-3 were, in the same way, originally created for the Leningrad OTB as aircraft for transporting heavy cargoes using external attachments. The specification for the T1-4RT3 envisaged vehicles, artillery guns, and even small torpedo boats being carried. A series of specific design solutions sprang from this, a more spaced out tricycle style undercarriage, and a large clearance between the fuselage and the ground.

After the aircraft were converted into heavy bombers these specifics were retained and were used rationally. The outsized cargoes were carried using an external attachment between the undercarriage legs. As mentioned above the first of these designs were developed for carrying the T-27 tankettes (the G-43 created at the VVS OKPB, and a frame attachment designed at the Design Bureau under the 3rd Air Brigade). Subsequently production truss type designs such as the PG-12 and PG-12P were used, and from 1939 onwards the lighter and more convenient DPT-2 was used.

When the attachments were used, the TB-3 was able to deliver both cars and trucks, armoured cars, tankettes, and light amphibious tanks, mortars, anti-tank, field, and anti-aircraft armament (with up to two guns per aircraft). Field guns were sometimes loaded with the guards removed in order to reduce drag. The speed of the TB-3 was reduced by 10–12% when the aircraft was carrying an external attachment, the practical ceiling was also reduced, increasing the take-off and landing rolls.

The PG-12 and DPT-2 attachments could be augmented by the GP-1 cargo platform. It was proposed that ammunition would be carried using these attachments as well as guns, bombs, aero engines, cars, anti-tank, and field guns, engineering equipment, inflatable A-3 craft, and many other cargoes weighing up to 3,500kg.

In January 1934 P.I. Grokhovskiy proposed using the TB-3 as a towing aircraft for a large assault glider. Subsequently experiments were carried out in this regard, these aircraft were never used however as tugs in combat.

An aircraft designed at the second half of the 20s would rapidly become obsolete. This slow, cumbersome, clumsy, low flying aircraft became more and more vulnerable to fighters and enemy anti-aircraft artillery. Back in 1936 doubts had emerged concerning the suitability of the TB-3 for airborne operations. As a result of exercises

This TB-3 has delivered a T-37A amphibious tank, 1935.

in the Moscow Military District Brigade Commander E.I. Tatarchenko, who was a participant in these exercises wrote: "This aircraft can only be sent deep behind enemy lines given absolute air superiority at least for the course of the operation. On the other hand, the aircraft could be restricted to night flying. In the short summer nights however the TB-3 cannot fly far behind enemy lines due to its slow speed".

There was, however, nothing to replace these giants that were becoming obsolete. New heavy bombers did appear but in the best-case scenario these were in prototype form. Not one of the NII VVS aircraft was able to carry heavy equipment. This is how the TB-3 bomber began to lose its capabilities. A mass re-equipment of the heavy bomber units was therefore carried out with the twin-engine DB-3, and the four-engine aircraft that remained in the formation were for the most part dedicated to transport missions.

In the light of these trends, on 24 June 1938, the Head of the OKDVA VVS Pumpur issued an order for the conversion of the TB-3s in the 25th Heavy Bomber Squadron into transport and assault aircraft. These were old aircraft that were fitted with M-17 engines. The underwing 'B' turrets were removed from these aircraft and in their place, hatches were cut that were 1,100x900mm in size, and closed using flap covers. Not only were the multiple bomb racks removed in the bomb bays but the actual attachment brackets as well. Inside the compartment was covered in plywood and an internal bridge was manufactured. Furthermore, fully-fledged operations with the TB-3 as a bomber had already been rendered impossible since the internal bomb rack had been completely removed. It was envisaged that 20 parachutists could be accommodated in this aircraft. This could not however be a large-scale conversion since the 25th Squadron had just four aircraft!

As mentioned above a ventral descent pod had been developed and manufactured for the TB-3s, but this was not series produced.

The cargo bags, box and fuel tanks were usually loaded into the fuselage of a TB-3 and dropped out of the aircraft manually. There were very few types that were compatible with the Der-19 and Der-20 bomb racks mounted under the fuselage. The latter had only a small number of fasteners that were designed for carrying very heavy cargoes.

In order to increase the number of attachment points, the aircraft was fitted with M-34RN engines under

A later series TB-3 fitted with M-34RN engines carries an armoured car.

the wing centre section that could be fitted with a cargo bridge consisting of eight beams with 24 attachment points per beam. The central bridges were designed to hold a cargo of up to 500kg, while the rest were designed for 300kg. The bridge was designed by 'D' brigade at Factory No.289 and underwent testing in 1939. The aircraft was flown by Captain Sokolov's crew.

The bridge made it possible to carry cargoes and then drop them by parachute up to a total weight of 4,200kg in different cargo bags. For example, an aircraft could carry eight PDBB-500 parachute tanks, 14 PDBB-250 tanks, 24 PDBB-100 tanks, or the same number of PDMM-100 bags. Some 12 AM-600 motorcycles could be carried along with their armament. During the course of testing 12 flights were completed. The speed was reduced by 10–12km/hr and the take-off and landing rolls increased and handling deteriorated (the report noted: " ... it requires a great deal of attention"). The opinion however was that the bridge had passed testing.

The TB-3 could also be used to evacuate the wounded. According to the standards an aircraft fitted with M-17 engines and which had not been modified could carry a single casualty lying on a stretcher, 20–21 in a seating position, and one accompanying medic. From 1939 onwards, an attachment for accommodating three stretchers began to be fitted in lines inside the wing centre section, alongside the fuel tanks. Moreover, some six or eight casualties could be transported lying down. Those seated would be accommodated in the fuselage and inside the wing panels. In 1939, a special modification was planned of five TB-3s that were fitted with M-17 engines into a medical variant although the preference was for a conversion of the PS-84 aircraft. A later modification of this aircraft fitted with M-34RN engines could carry four casualties in a lying position and one accompanying medic.

Fuel could be carried in a TB-3 in canisters and barrels inside the bomb bay (with an accompanying reinforcement of the main body) in PDBB tanks with varying capacities that could be jettisoned, as well as in the aircraft own tanks. A prototype variant fitted with B-1000 tanks (with a capacity of 1,070liters each) was in existence with the tanks fitted inside the bomb bay. A ZiS-6 fuel bowser would fill both tanks in 10–12mins. Drainage was either achieved by gravity or using a ground pump. An aircraft fitted with a B-1000 tank underwent testing in 1938 (which included filling ground-based fuel tanks and BT-7 tanks) but these tanks were not manufactured owing to a series of shortcomings that came to light during testing. In 1939 testing of a 4,000-liter

A TB-3 fitted with B-1000 tanks refuels BT-7 tanks, 1938.

tank fitted onto a GP-1 platform was undertaken but this too was not accepted into series production.

By the beginning of the 1940s, several TB-3s still remained in the VVS fleet, more than 500 examples, and around 80% of these were considered serviceable. A decision was taken to select the airworthy machines for transport units and for civil aviation, and the rest would be written off. Owing to a shortage of contemporary aircraft in the fast developing RKKA VVS in the summer of 1940 this decision was overturned. The opposite happened, it was proposed that the TB-3s be withdrawn from assault and transport units, and that they be repaired and used to augment bomber regiments, and squadrons. In February 1941 an order was issued on the formation of five new bomber regiments operating these machines.

By that time the parachute assault function it was decided would be transferred to the PS-84, a Soviet copy of the American DC-3. They were in service with the VVS as well as the GVF by the beginning of 1941. This aircraft however was not suited to carrying and dropping heavy armament by parachute. Work was undertaken successfully to create attachments for a DB-3F bomber, but this twin-engine bomber conceded significantly in terms of its cargo carrying capability to the TB-3. It was not able to transport trucks, or light tanks.

The old four-engine bomber remained the principal means of delivering airborne troops right up to the German invasion of the USSR.

7. The SB

In designing the high-speed SB bomber, no requirements were put forward for it to carry people or cargo. The aircraft was conceived purely as a combat aircraft for front line aviation. In their quest to attain the maximum speed the designers made the fuselage very narrow and cramped. With this same goal in mind they rejected the idea of installing external bomb racks.

The SB was a twin-engine all-metal monoplane and series production began in 1936. It was manufactured in large numbers by two factories, and was fitted with M-100, M-100A, M-103, M-104, and M-105 engines rated at outputs ranging from 750 up to 1,100hp. There were no plans to use this aircraft as a transport, special attachments were not developed for it, and the aircrew and ground crew did not undergo the prerequisite training.

On 1 April 1939, there were 1,725 SBs serving in the RKKA VVS in different variants. As the VVS began to be updated with new aircraft, the search was on for a new use for the old bombers. Some of them were transferred to training installations, but aside from that thoughts began to turn to whether they could actually be used for transport missions. The old series SB aircraft were used without any modifications in several transport detachments and squadrons. For example, in July 1940 three aircraft were listed as serving in the transport detachment under the 29th Air Brigade.

In practice, the operating environment sometimes forced these bombers to be used as transport aircraft, in the main for transporting and dropping cargoes in small packages. These cargoes were carried in the bomb bay, and on occasion a temporary floor formed of boards would be installed. Aircraft manufactured after the 98th series also had external bomb racks under the central section of the wing, on which PDMM bags, and PDBB tanks could be fitted. The use of these external attachments however did limit the aircraft speed to no more than 250km/hr, but on the other hand the bags would actually be blown off the bridges. The total weight of the cargo was between 500–900kg.

Sometimes reconnaissance personnel and saboteurs would be accommodated in the bomb bay. The SB could also be used to transport a single wounded soldier.

In accordance with the plan for 1940–41, design group 'D' at Factory No.289 worked on a transport variant of the SB, taking the "design produced at the NII GVF" as a basis. This related to a postal aircraft that represented an SB with the armament and the navigator's cockpit removed, the glazing was covered over with metal and the bomb bay was converted into a cargo storage area (the bomb bay doors were shortened). These aircraft were series produced in Moscow as the PS-40 (with front-mounted engine radiators), and PS-41s (with the radiators in ducts

A 1938-built SB bomber fitted with M-103 engines and frontal air coolers.

A later version of the SB (so-called '200 series') with air coolers mounted in ducts of the engine cowlings, 1939.

in the engine fairings). A small number were manufactured as PS-41bis with fuel tanks under the wing. All these aircraft would normally be used to carry post as well as urgent cargoes. Special military transport modifications of the SB however never materialised. The PS-40 and PS-41 aircraft were mobilised following the outbreak of the war with Germany and were incorporated into a separate liaison air group.

An SB bomber with parachute bags suspended on the external Der-19 bomb racks under the wing. The PDMM-100 bags are grouped in three per attachment.

A PS-41 aircraft on an airfield.

8. The DB-3

In contrast to the SB, the specifications for the DB-3 concerning the possibility of them being used to land airborne troops were put forward almost from the very beginning. They were however sufficiently modest.

This long-range bomber, which was a twin-engine all-metal monoplane was in series production from 1937. Three factories produced them in several modifications and they were fitted with M-85, M-86, M-87, and M-88 engines with outputs rated from 760 up to 900hp. On 15 July 1940 there were 1,050 DB-3Ss serving in the RKKA VVS in different variants. The last modification of this bomber was the DB-3F, and in 1942 this was re-designated to an Il-4. This aircraft was in production until the beginning of 1946.

According to the specification issued in 1938, the DB-3 was to be designed to carry seven people without any conversion but in very cramped conditions that were not able to jump using parachutes, or alternatively it would carry seven casualties in a seating position. On 3 November 1938 the tactical-technical requirements were approved for the special assault variant of the aircraft. It was designed to be able to carry an underslung pod for paratroopers, or a special box (including one that could be dropped by parachute) on external bomb racks under the wing, or a cargo bridge, or cargo platform under the wing centre section.

The bridge was designed for 12 PDMM parachute bags or the same number of PDBB-100 tanks, or four IZh-9 or AM-600 motorcycles fitted with machine guns, or four large PDBB-400 tanks, four universal descent pods designed to hold 300kg each. All this could be dropped by parachute.

In a landing delivery, a cargo platform was to be suspended underneath a DB-3. Machine guns would be carried on this platform (including heavy machine guns without dismantling them first), as well as rifles in boxes, ammunition, provisions, clothing, spare parts, and mortars. Motorcycles could also be loaded as well as 45mm anti-tank guns up to a maximum weight of 1,400kg. The *Podyomnik* factory began to develop this platform from the beginning of 1939. Information concerning development of prototype versions of the platform and the bridge and their testing however is absent.

On 25 October 1938, the requirements for a 10-seat descent pod for the DB-3 were affirmed. This pod was designed with a hatch with small doors to enable paratroopers to jump out by parachute. The plan was to provide the personnel with sufficient oxygen for two hours of flight.

In July 1939, testing of the DB-3 with a D-20 descent pod did actually begin, the pod was developed under the leadership of A.I. Privalov. It was manufactured entirely from wood and could accommodate ten people. It did indeed feature small doors as per the specification, as well as oxygen equipment with a reserve of oxygen for all ten people for two hours flying. Series production of the D-20 was rolled out at the factory in Beskudnikovo. In 1942 some 450 examples were ordered but how many were produced is not known.

In spring of 1941, testing of the D-11 attachments designed for motorcycles with sidecars and the D-16 for 45mm anti-tank, or 76mm field guns, was concluded. Subsequently experiments were carried out around delivering and dropping 1938-model 120mm mortars from a bomber. To reduce the aerodynamic drag the cargo was occasionally enclosed in plywood casings.

The DB-3 was also considered as a potential towing aircraft for the 'transporter glider' (an assault glider) that was actually realised during the course of the war.

A long-range DB-3B bomber fitted with M-86 engines.

A long-range DB-3F bomber fitted with M-88 engines and a new nose section of the fuselage, 1940.

At the end of 1937 for the requirements of 'Operation Zet' (an air bridge into China) two bombers were converted: one of them to carry passengers, while a second was converted into a tanker to deliver fuel.

9. The SSS

The SSS aircraft represented a modification of the R-5 biplane that was created in 1934. The aircraft was specially adapted for the ground attack role and had a powerful machine-gun armament, an internal compartment for small bombs, and an external attachment for 250kg bombs, RRAB-250 cluster bombs, chemical spraying and smoke-generating apparatus. An M-17F engine was fitted to the SSS that was optimised for low and high altitudes.

The aircraft was manufactured from autumn of 1935, and in total 350 of these biplanes were produced.

To begin with these aircraft were used only for their intended purpose, but in 1939 a decision was taken to fit

An SSS ground attack aircraft.

them with different attachments for carrying cargoes or for dropping cargo by parachute. The devices used for the R-5 were not suitable for the SSS owing to the difference in the types of bomb racks used. After some modification the ground attack aircraft was capable of delivering cargoes for military units that had been surrounded, as well as for paratroopers and partisans.

10. The R-Z

Under the leadership of D.S. Markov, the R-Z biplane that was produced was a development of the R-5 aircraft concept, and borrowed a range of its design solutions but was more compact and fitted with a powerful M-34NB engine. Series production of these aircraft began in the spring of 1936. In total more than 1,000 examples of these aircraft were manufactured, which served in the VVS as reconnaissance aircraft and light bombers. From 1939 onwards, cargo platforms began to be fitted to these aircraft that had been produced previously for the R-5.

Prototype of R-Z reconnaissance aircraft and short-range bomber during testing at NII VVS.

An R-Z serving in one of the regiments in the Far East, 1939.

Aside from the R-Z the intention was to use the P-Zet aircraft for transport along the front line, similar postal aircraft were manufactured for civil aviation without armament and a payload of 275kg. A PT was produced in the shape of one prototype example, which was a P-Zet variant fitted with large plywood cargo boxes above the lower wing; this aircraft could carry 495kg.

11. The DBA

Fitted with four M-34FRN engines, the DBA heavy bomber was developed under the leadership of V.F. Bolkhovitinov. From a technological perspective this aircraft was similar to the TB-3, but had a smooth outer skin, enclosed cockpits and glazed turrets. The undercarriage was made to be semi-retractable: after take-off the undercarriage legs would fold in half, lifting the undercarriage into large cowlings known as 'trousers'. The armament consisted of five ShKAS machine guns and a single ShVAK cannon, and the standard bomb load was 3,000kg.

The first prototype variant of the DBA was manufactured in 1935. After conclusion of testing and modification the well-known pilot S.A. Levanevskiy in August 1937 used this aircraft (without armament) for a flight from the USA via the North Pole. The flight was not successful: the aircraft and its crew vanished without trace.

The modernised DB-2A was produced following this incident (this was actually a '1937-model of the DBA'). One of the examples of this aircraft was manufactured in Moscow and a further five in Kazan. The latter was used in an VVS transport squadron under the 1st Special Red-Banner Army that was based on Khabarovsk-Bolshoy airfield.

DBA aircraft were capable of carrying the same number of paratroopers as the TB-3 and retained their capability to deliver military hardware on an external attachment.

A DBA (DB-A) heavy bomber, 1937.

12. The TB-7 (PE-8)

Work to create the heavy four-engine bomber the TB-7 began in July 1934. In the ANT-42 design several design solutions were used that were taken from the earlier ANT-38 and which were produced according to the specification VSB-1. On the one hand the TB-7 was an advanced all-metal cantilever monoplane with enclosed cockpits and retractable undercarriage, on the other hand it had a structure formed of a truss made from tubes that was very complex technologically and was outmoded. The specification for this aircraft was updated several times, which delayed the production of the aircraft somewhat. The first prototype example of the ANT-42 took to the skies in the hands of M.M. Gromov on 27 December 1936.

As with all heavy bombers of that time, this aircraft had a dual purpose, as a transport and airborne assault aircraft. The standard bomb load for this aircraft was 2,000kg, while the maximum was 4,000kg. It was within these parameters that the ANT-42 was to have transported a range of military hardware as well as paratroopers. According to the specifications that were affirmed on 4 May 1938 the TB-7 should have been fitted with a universal ventral attachment that would have enabled a T-38 amphibious tank to be carried, or a T-20 *Komsomolets* tracked armoured tractor, GAZ-AA (two-axle) and a GAZ-AA (three-axle) trucks, a car or pickup, or 76mm or 45mm guns. It was envisaged that the attachment a cargo platform would be fitted to the attachment for boxes and barrels. The guns would have been accommodated in packs in the trucks or on the platform itself.

The specification also stipulated the transport of between 50–55 paratroopers. They would not be able to all fit in the fuselage, so a pod was created that would be carried underneath the aircraft and which has been described above. This pod could accommodate 12–18 parachutists (depending on the type of parachutes and the availability of weaponry). However, only one prototype example of this pod was manufactured, and this was tested in March 1939.

Series production of the TB-7 began in that same year at Factory No.124 in Kazan in a four-engine variant fitted with AM-34FRN engines and an ATsN-2 centralised supercharging unit in which a fifth engine was fitted, an M-103. Production was then stopped but in 1940 it resumed once more. Use of the ATsN-2 was quickly rejected after the aircraft had been fitted with four AM-35, and subsequently AM-35A engines.

In accordance with an order issued by the Committee for Defence dated 25 May 1940, the factory manufactured a prototype example of the TB-7 fitted with AM-35A engines in a transport and airborne assault variant. This aircraft was presented for state testing at the NII VVS on 20 March 1941.

This aircraft differed from the bomber in terms of its strengthened spars in the wing centre section and the main body of the centre fuselage compartment. In the bomb bay, the height of which had been increased slightly by virtue of the fact that it featured a downward projection, the attachments for the platform were fitted, which was designed for a cargo weighing up to 4,000kg. This evidently would need to be lowered down to the ground for loading and unloading. The dimensions of the bomb bay enabled the guns mentioned in the 1938 specification to be stowed inside, but it is doubtful that cars and tanks could have been accommodated inside. There is no mention in the documents of any kind of an external attachment.

In the absence of a bomb bay platform, seats for 32 paratroopers were fitted. A further eight places were

A four-engine TB-7 heavy bomber with a pod under the fuselage in course of testing at the NII VVS, March 1939.

A transport version of the TB-7, March 1941.

installed in the compartment where the ATsN-2 was previously fitted. Thus the specification was not completely fulfilled, the aircraft provided 40 seats and not 50. In the tail section of the fuselage two doors were made that opened inwards. It was through these doors that the paratroopers were to jump out of the aircraft.

The crew was the same as that of the bomber, ten men. The defensive armament did not change either: two 20mm ShVAK cannons, two 7.62mm ShKAS machine guns and two 12.7mm BT machine guns.

This aircraft successfully passed state testing, but the TB-7 was never series produced in this modification. The prototype example was later converted into a bomber.

The TB-7 (which would actually go on to become the Pe-8) entered service with the VVS in spring 1940 but only matured into a combat capable aircraft during the course of the Great Patriotic War.

22

The Stronghold Dropped from the Air

Ideas were streaming from the OKPB. One of the most exotic projects (that remained a design on the drawing board) was the G-38 armoured gun emplacement, a kind of airborne pill box. A gunner was housed inside a drop-shaped armoured casing armed with a 7.62mm DA aircraft machine gun and ammunition. The parachute canopy would open immediately on detachment from the carrier aircraft. After having dropped several of these a kind of reinforced line is created in the sky that is able to fire at both air and ground targets. The impact on landing was cushioned by four spring-loaded feet on the underside of the casing. The weight of the gun emplacement was such that a group of Red Army soldiers would be able to carry it themselves, or it could be carried on a pickup.

In materials dating from 1933, there is a reference to variants of the G-38 with a small calibre automatic or anti-tank gun inside. A crew consisting of one person could serve either one or the other. One of the documents states that the gun and the machine gun could be fitted together into the same armoured gun emplacement, again with a single gunner.

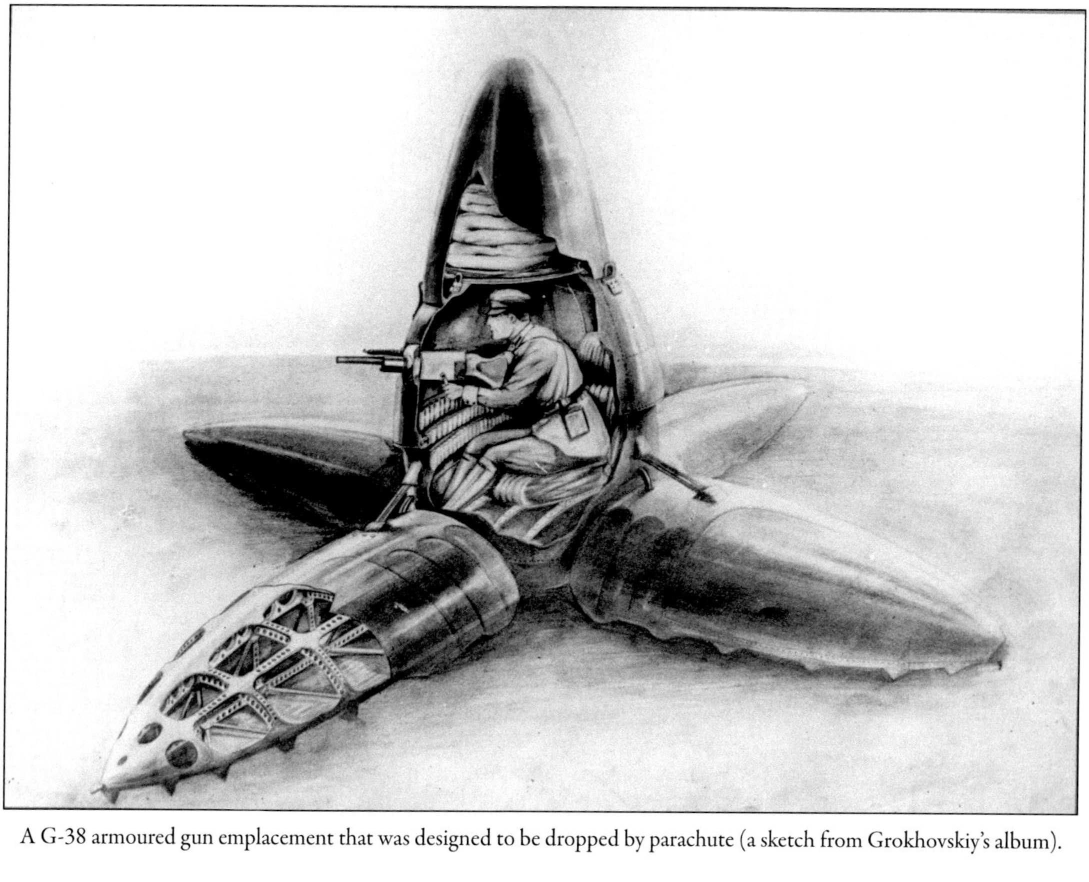

A G-38 armoured gun emplacement that was designed to be dropped by parachute (a sketch from Grokhovskiy's album).

This emplacement, though, could fire when on the ground. In the air, however, it is doubtful that it would be able to fire. That is to say the person inside it could open fire but would they be able to hit the target? The armoured gun emplacement would unavoidably swing and spin under the canopy. Firing creates a recoil effect and the weight of the G-38 was considerably less than that of the aircraft, so it would have more severe problems with stability.

No information is available concerning the manufacture of a prototype example of the gun emplacement that could be dropped by parachute. Grokhovskiy's materials in essence only contain drawings. No information is provided concerning dimensions, the thickness of the armour, or the weight of the structure.

23

The Assault at Siverskaya

The world's first large-scale airborne assault was competed during exercises held by the Leningrad Military District in September 1930. It reflected the concept of a 'raiding assault', in which the participating forces would move around apace behind enemy lines. With this in mind a detachment of airborne troops was to make use of cars, motorcycles and bicycles.

The 55th and 57th Squadron from the district's Air Force were used for the assault, which had already received their new TB-1 bombers but which for the most part flew old JuG-1 aircraft. These forces were augmented by TB-1 aircraft and their crews from the 11th Air Brigade, based in Voronezh. These aircraft became part the 57th Squadron for the duration of the exercise.

In August, a non-standard motorised airborne detachment began to be formed, and on 6 August E.D. Lukin was named as the commander. To begin with, there were 46 men in this detachment. The personnel were selected from soldiers and commanders from the 2nd and 11th Rifle Divisions, as well as from units that were immediately subordinate to the district headquarters. They were assessed for their readiness to undertake these flights based on their medical condition and a "special initiative and self-reliance". The preference was for 'all-rounders' who were capable with all kinds of weaponry, up to and including a light machine gun. For the commanders, it was mandatory to know how to fire a machine gun. Gunners, machine-gunners, artillerymen, demolition specialists, signals personnel, and four chemical weapons specialists with spray equipment in their backpacks joined this detachment. As far as armament was concerned the detachment had revolvers, carbines, rifles, light machine guns, and recoilless guns. To begin with the detachment was given a one and a half-tonne truck and two cars. Later on, a further ten cars were added along with motorcycles, and bicycles.

The organisation of the detachment included a rifle company and three platoons, a sapper, and signals platoon, and a light vehicle platoon. In total there were 16 cars and ten cargo trucks in the detachment as well as three armoured cars, four motorcycles, and two T-27 tankettes. The firepower of the detachment was augmented by 14 light and four heavy machine guns, as well as four grenade launchers and two 76mm recoilless guns. In the course of the preparation the number of combatants and rank and file soldiers and the composition of the armament changed somewhat.

According to the exercise scenarios, the 'reds' would land behind the 'blues'' enemy lines by virtue of a landing delivery, which using the transport dropped by air would go on the march and to the surprise of the 'enemy' they would then take the city of Krasnogvardeysk (now Gatchina) in a single thrust.

The landing would take place at a specially prepared site near Siverskaya station, which was code named 'point S'. Military engineers had been deployed to this location in advance and they cut down the trees, removed the stumps and levelled out the landing site. So, things were made a little easier for the landing troops from the start since the aircraft would land on a pre-prepared strip and not just on a large field.

In total, ten TB-1 bombers and seven JuG-1s were used to carry the paratroopers and the equipment, each of which would make a number of flights. The assault took from eight in the morning until 1300 hrs in the afternoon of 3 September 1930. The 'Ford A' vehicles were only delivered underneath a TB-1. The tarpaulin roofs on these vehicles were drawn back. The vehicles were delivered in a partly dismantled form, minus the front wheels and the windscreen, which was stowed in the aircraft forward cockpit. This was linked to the need to maintain a safe

R-1 aircraft of the 1st Wing of the 28th Squadron catches a message using a grapnel, September 1930.

centre of gravity for the bomber. Some of the cars had been converted into self-propelled recoilless guns with 14 rounds of ammunition and a crew of three. The armoured cars and tankettes remained back at base since there was no way yet of transporting them by air.

The Junkers with a spacious fuselage, which had been 'bequeathed' from the G.24 passenger aircraft, was best suited to carrying infantry. It was able to carry up to eight men over and above its standard crew who would be equipped with armament and equipment, while the TB-1 could carry no more than six men. Motorcycles and bicycles were also carried on the JuG-1. The bicycles were simply folded on the floor inside the fuselage. When it came to the motorcycles the initial plan was for them to be stowed in the same way, and the motorcycles with sidecars would be separated and loaded individually. As mentioned above however the OTB developed an attachment system for motorcycles and sidecars under the wing centre section. They were attached to the Der-6bis bomb racks using a system of cables. Loading took around 15mins and unloading was almost twice as fast. Aircraft from the 55th Squadron were fitted with this attachment. These were used to carry American Harley-Davidson and English Norton motorcycles.

In the first wave of the assault 78 men were deployed, as well as six motorcycles and sidecars, and four without sidecars (all the motorcycles were carried by the JuG-1), 20 bicycles, five recoilless guns and 70 shells, 27 machine guns, 28 rifles, four radio activated mines, and six fuel canisters. The flight weight of the JuG-1 with the different load variants would range from 2,445kg up to 2,540kg, and that of the TB-1 from 2,915kg up to 2,935kg.

In total, during the Siverskaya operation 151 paratroopers were dropped, 19 cars, 12 motorcycles and sidecars, and seven without sidecars, 41 bicycles, ten recoilless guns, and 140 shells, 41 rifles, 59 light machine guns, four radio sets, eight packages, with demolition equipment, and 12 fuel canisters. For example, the Commander of the 57th Squadron Alekseyev made two flights in the TB-1. Each time he carried a 'Ford A' vehicle, a recoilless gun and 14 shells, as well as three paratroopers. Other pilots who carried vehicles, did not take recoilless guns on board, but did carry up to six paratroopers: five of them sat in the nose of the fuselage, while one sat in the aft turrets. Another variant was tested by N.P. Zhuravlyov's crew: a 'Ford', a radio set, some fuel, and four paratroopers. One of the TB-1s was not able to make a second flight owing to the failure of one of the engines.

The timetable for the assault was not followed. The weather got in the way with low cloud and periodic rain. The unloading took significantly longer than planned. Because of this the intervals between the landing aircraft were 25mins instead of 10mins as per the plan. The landing site was barraged with the equipment that was being unloaded. In one case this almost led to an accident.

The delay led to the assault being discovered by aerial reconnaissance on the part of the 'blues'. The landing site was initially attacked by six I-2 and I-2bis fighters from the 11th Squadron, which notionally stormed the airfield and intercepted all the aircraft carrying cargo, and one hour later they raided the airfield three more times, using groups of light bombers.

Nevertheless, the paratroopers assembled the vehicles and marched towards Gatchina, having captured the town as envisaged in the plan for the manoeuvres.

It was during these exercises that a landing mission was used to deliver reconnaissance troops. The 28th Squadron provided communications with these forces. They were given a mission: first and foremost, to locate them in the terrain, not only by day but also by night. The pilots were given a signal from the ground: by day this would be spreading newspapers, waving items of clothing, whereas by night it would be fires, or lamps. The second mission was to receive messages for delivery to their airfield. Some of the reconnaissance groups were given radio sets, but they were not very powerful. They could receive messages over a distance of 15–17km; but the distance to the front line was sometimes greater. Therefore, a decision was taken to use an intermediary, an aircraft. The flight observer would receive a message from the ground and send it to the radio station on the airfield. A transmission from the air would be heard over a greater distance, up to approximately 25km. Another variant was tried, a message was sent from an aircraft by messenger pigeon.

This communication method was by no means the only one. Reconnaissance personnel would use different methods to send messages to aircraft. Specific signals were set out on the ground, which would be photographed from the air, and reports and documents would be sent with the help of 'cats', that would be trailed from aircraft on a cable. The 28th Squadron tried ten times to receive something from the ground using this method. Furthermore, two of the 'cats' broke free along with the cargo. This was not as bad as it could have been. Working with the 'cats' there were often cases where the cable would snag on the bushes and trees and would not break. If the flight observer did not disengage it in time the aircraft would 'nose dive' at low level and crash into the ground.

During exercises held by the Leningrad Military District in September 1930, officers from the German *Reichswehr* were present and demonstrations of the airborne operations were provided for them.

24

The ANT-9 – Misplaced Hopes

This three-engine aircraft has always been considered a purely passenger aircraft, the flagship of *Aeroflot*. In actual fact though the specification for this aircraft was issued by the UVVS and it was the directorate that provided half of the finance for the design and manufacture of a prototype example. Why then did the military need this? The ANT-9 was considered by the military as a potential military transport aircraft, as well as an 'auxiliary bomber' or a '3rd class bomber'. The latter related to an aircraft that in peacetime would carry passengers, and in wartime it would transform into a bomber. The capability for this conversion was built into the bomber from the very start.

According to the specification the aircraft was to have a crew of three and a payload of 750kg. The AGOS (Aviation, Hydro-aviation, and Prototype Manufacturing) section at the TsAGI created this aircraft under the leadership of A.N. Tupolev. It was there that the aircraft was given the designation ANT-9. As a result, an all-metal monoplane was produced that used the wing and the tailfin from an R-6 (the ANT-7). This aircraft was fitted with three French Gnome-Rhone 5A *Titan* radial engines rated at 230hp each. There were nine seats in the passenger compartment.

On 1 May 1929 a prototype example of the ANT-9 was exhibited on Red Square and it was in Moscow that the aircraft underwent factory, and state testing. The aircraft then completed a long-range flight under the name of the 'Wings of the Soviets' around the capital cities of Europe.

Series production began in 1930 but with American Wright J5 engines rated at 300hp. The first ten of these aircraft manufactured in 1930 were fitted with these engines as well as some of those produced in 1931. Subsequently aircraft were manufactured with indigenous M-26 engines (rated at 360hp) and which were fitted with superchargers. The production of the ANT-9 from 1932 was transferred to aircraft Factory No.31 in Taganrog, but a year later it had stopped at this location as well, and the final aircraft that used the surplus airframes that had previously been manufactured were subsequently completed at factories Nos. 84 and 89. These two latter enterprises no longer manufactured the three-engine ANT-9, but a twin-engine variant the PS-9, fitted with two M-17 engines rated at 600hp. This took place because the M-26 was very unreliable: this engine would struggle to reach 500 engine hours. No finance was provided for new Wright engines. In total around 100 aircraft were produced.

The UVVS intended to acquire dozens of these aircraft. The intention was to hand them over one at a time to the aviation detachments that were attached to the airborne units, while the rest would be used to transport commanders, together with small cargoes. The military however soon became disillusioned with the capabilities of the ANT-9. It appeared to be completely unsuitable as a '3rd class bomber'. As a transport aircraft it did not possess any distinct advantages over the TB-1, or the TB-3 for that matter. Ten passengers is very few: it was customary on exercises to carry 11 or 12 paratroopers, and according to the calculations provided by the NII VVS the ANT-9 could carry three crewmembers and 13 paratroopers. L.G. Minov proposed bringing the number of paratroopers up to 14, that is to say two sections of seven paratroopers each. Following a series of accidents however that were caused by overloading the aircraft a ban was introduced on accommodating more than ten people aside from the crew in the aircraft, and furthermore the 10th person would evidently just be sat on the floor in the aisle.

The ANT-9 was not able to carry external cargoes, it would have been difficult to drag anything into the

The aircraft designer, A.N. Tupolev.

Manufacturing of an ANT-9 aircraft prototype in TsAGI workshops, spring 1929.

fuselage through the narrow door in the fuselage, since it was the wrong shape. In order to increase the number of paratroopers the aircraft could carry and to shorten the time taken to drop the entire group P.I. Grokhovskiy suggested fitting the ANT-9 with an 'automatic Red Army soldier deployment device'. He even designed a G-60 device for it (there is no evidence as to how many people this was designed for). The intention was to fit five aircraft with this device, but no attempt was made to fit this to any of the aircraft.

In April 1931 at the TsAGI, in accordance with a suggestion put forward by the UVVS, work began on a medical variant of the ANT-9. The plan was to remove six of the seats and replace them with six stretchers laid out in two lines. Three seats would be left in place for any casualties able to sit or for two casualties and a medic. Two cupboards were envisaged for medical instruments, medicine, and linen. A prototype example of this medical

The ANT-9 prototype fitted with three Gnome Rhone *Titan* engines demonstrated on Red Square in Moscow, 1 May 1929.

A series ANT-9 fitted with Wright J5 Whirlwind engines. The VVS RKKA received only this version of the ANT-9.

aircraft was to be handed over on 11 January 1932 but an inspection of a mock-up of the re-equipped cabin only took place on 11 January 1932. It was planned that the Military Aviation Academy would modify three aircraft in this way, which were designed for the OKDVA VVS. However, this idea was only revisited again in 1939 after two PS-9s had been modified by that time.

As a result, the VVS only took delivery of seven ANT-9s, all fitted with the Wright engines: six in 1931 and

A group photograph of the participants of military parachutists' muster in Yevpatoria, standing in front of an ANT-9, 1932.

one in 1932. Periodically, however, plans arose to replenish the military aviation fleet with aircraft from the GVF. For example, within the confines of measures to enhance troop alignments in the Far East in 1932 there was a plan to withdraw eight aircraft from the civil aviation fleet to form a special airborne detachment. The idea was to form this detachment in March of that year in Omsk, and in April the detachment would be re-deployed to Chita. This project however was never realised.

A special military transport version of the ANT-9 was proposed, that would be fitted with three M-26 engines and was designed to carry ten people in collapsible seats, plus 100kg of cargo. This design was never even carried through.

The military did make active use of the ANT-9 for landing and dropping paratroopers between 1931–33. There were a small number of these aircraft but at the same time there was only a small number of paratroopers at that time too.

In the summer of 1931 aircraft from the 95th Transport Detachment that formed part of the Turkmen air group supported an operation against the *Basmachi* in southern Turkmenia. Among these aircraft was a single ANT-9. The aircraft ensured provision of supplies to sparsely populated areas both to the air group itself, and to the troops on the ground as well as evacuating the sick and injured. The ANT-9 was fitted with bomb racks under the fuselage and was also used as a bomber. As mentioned above, in September 1931 this aircraft participated in a landing delivery of armed troops in Turkmenia, in the course of which a machine-gun section was deployed.

Later on, the three-engine Tupolev served for the most part as command posts, and from the end of 1937 as training aircraft for training navigators at the school in Ryazan. The last of these was written off in 1939.

In civil aviation almost all the ANT-9s were transformed into twin-engine PS-9s. In the war they were due to join six military aviation transport detachments in Moscow, Monino, Voronezh, Kharkov, and Krechevitsy. In total the plan was to withdraw 66 aircraft of this type. These aircraft were to be fitted with a 7.62mm DA machine gun in a turret above the pilot's cockpit (and with 350 rounds of ammunition in disc magazines) and they would also be fitted with a 13-SK radio. The crew would remain unchanged from the passenger variant: a pilot and flight

A group of instructors from the Higher Parachute School walking out to an ANT-9 aircraft to undertake demonstration jumps during a sporting event, 18 February 1933.

A paratrooper jumps clear of an ANT-9 aircraft.

engineer. The latter would also act as a gunner and radio-operator.

The military aviation transport detachments were to have ensured the supply of air brigades, serving front line cavalry, and mechanised units in raids behind enemy lines, as well as forces that had been surrounded, and partisans and saboteurs. The PS-9s were also only supposed to fly over enemy territory in groups and with a fighter escort. These plans however were never realised.

By June of 1941 only two-dozen PS-9s remained in the GVF and these operated at the furthest extremities of the country.

25

Separate Detachment No. 3

In September 1931 exercises had already taken place in which landing and airborne assaults had played a part. Prior to this on 18 March of that same year a decision was taken on the formation in the Leningrad Military District of Separate Detachment No. 3 with a compliment of 146 people under the command of M.V. Boytsov. The Chief of Staff was I.P. Chernov. The detachment was to be deployed to Krasnogvardeysk (now Gatchina), and it was subordinate to the 1st Air Brigade Command. In contrast to the motorised airborne detachment of the previous year that was disbanded following the exercises this new unit was considered a permanent one, although it was non-standard. Some documents make reference to this detachment as an 'airborne parachute detachment'. In the future the numbers of combatants serving in this unit was set to rise. There were however problems with the parachutes, they only had 45 chutes, and for the most part these were Irvins of various types. This problem was made all the more complicated by the fact that by way of an order from the Head of the VVS dated 9 February 1931 training jumps using combat parachutes (these were safeguarded) were banned even though there was a shortage of two canopy training chutes.

The detachment made specific demands of its personnel. They recruited physically and mentally well-developed individuals who were able to operate a variety of weapons. One fifth of the personnel serving in this detachment had to have knowledge of foreign languages and be familiar with the traditions of neighbouring countries. The list of requirements for the personnel specifically noted the need for "a readiness for self-sacrifice in the interests of the detachment". Selection of the commander echelon was also interesting. "A Commander ... needs to have an innate passion for engaging in dangerous undertakings". Apart from that they needed to know the structure of the armed forces of any potential enemies, know foreign statutes, and manuals, and naturally they had to know their own – by heart!

In the second half of the June L.G. Minov arrived in Krasnogvardeysk with a group of instructors and parachute riggers. Some 55 men were sent there for training, of these nine were rejected by a medical commission. The remaining 46 up until 15 August underwent a training programme. Up until that time there were approximately 45 combatants and commanders amongst the paratroopers – one of them requested he be dismissed after his first jump and be allowed to return to his previous posting, which was duly granted.

For the detachment, the OKPB workshops were ordered to build four reinforced pickups on 'Ford A' chassis, which were adapted for dropping by parachute. This vehicle was designed to carry eight people and a heavy machine gun. On a good road it could travel at a speed of between 40–50km/hr. The orders were also placed for a headquarters car fitted with Popham's flags and dovecote, eight attachments for Harley-Davidson motorcycles, six attachments to carry recoilless gun packages, 101 parachute bags for light machine guns, 150 packs for hand grenades, 26 packs for demolition equipment (including four for powerful high explosive mines for blowing up bridges), 64 packs for an entrenchment tool, and 16 first aid kits.

The first group of parachutists had completed their training by the end of June. On 15 August 1931 the first demonstration assault was carried out around Krasnoe Selo. Two ANT-9s carried ten paratroopers each. Nineteen paratroopers jumped out of these aircraft since one remained on board the aircraft. The reason for this was that the soldier had snagged something in the aircraft and his reserve parachute knapsack that was attached to his stomach had deployed. The paratroopers did not engage in any combat activity, similarly they had jumped

Commander of Separate Detachment No. 3, M.V. Boytsov.

Paratroopers stand alongside an ANT-9 in Krasnogvardeysk, 1932.

this time without their armament.

On 20 August, a similar assault was organised in Krasnogvardeysk itself, near the airfield. Twenty paratroopers landed successfully after they had been taken up to altitude in two ANT-9 aircraft. In fact, in both cases group jumps as well as the methods for jumping out of the aircraft were developed, which ensured a sufficiently well grouped landing. By 21 August, the tally for the detachment's personnel already amounted to 237 parachute jumps.

At the beginning of September, 'Detachment No. 3' was redeployed to Kiev for participation in manoeuvres organised by the Ukrainian Military District and was included in the Airborne Motorised Group. The parachutists had to interact with armoured cars and mechanised infantry. On 10 September the detachment were ordered to

A paratrooper jumps from an ANT-9 aircraft.

drop 30 men in the area around Mogilevka. Three ANT-9s took off from Kiev. Twenty-nine men jumped out of these aircraft but the reserve parachute of one of the combatants opened inside the aircraft and he did not take any part in the assault. The paratroopers used Blagin and Irvin cargo parachutes to drop two recoilless guns as well as machine guns and ammunition.

On 15 September, in that same location just outside Mogilev, a demonstration assault took place for the commanders and units who had gathered on the ground to watch. A group of 29 paratroopers were sent from Kalinovka airfield (approximately a 20min flight away) using three ANT-9 aircraft. The group 'captured' the airfield, on which a squadron of TB-1s then landed. The bombers delivered the troops, machine guns, two recoilless guns, and vehicles.

The success of these exercises was overshadowed somewhat by a tragedy, which took place immediately after the exercises had finished. A TB-1 that belonged to the airborne detachment, and had a pickup slung underneath it, took off to return to base. The aircraft was severely overloaded. Aside from the vehicle it was carrying a variety of equipment. Seven people were on board the aircraft. One of the engines however failed (it emerged later that a connecting rod had sheared). The pilot decided to turn back and land back at this same airfield, but he had underestimated the pitch down moment the external attachment had created. The aircraft flew into the ground: everyone on board was killed.

At the end of September similar exercises took place near Leningrad. By this time detachment No. 3 had returned to Krasnogvardeysk.

In order to deploy the paratroopers two squadrons of TB-1s were prepared from the 3rd Air Brigade, which were fitted with descent pods, or 'automatic deployment devices', in total this amounted to 20 serviceable aircraft. The cradles and pods were fitted with the help of the technical staff as well as aircrew from the squadrons themselves. The documents indicate that the crews from the 55th Squadron did not like flying with the cradles. The TB-1s were augmented by three military ANT-9s: two from the special purpose squadron and one from the training brigade of the Military Aviation Academy. The paratroopers and aircraft were concentrated on Krasnogvardeysk airfield.

A paratrooper pulling the parachute, 1932.

During the course of the exercises the deployment of reconnaissance troops in civilian clothing behind 'enemy' lines was practised. They were deployed using the landing delivery method from an R-1 aircraft.

The parachute assault was initially set for 27 September, but a strong wind interrupted proceedings and it was postponed until 29 September. The parachutists were dropped from ANT-9s and TB-1s. Political Instructor Kuznetsov's parachute who had jumped from the 'automatic deployment device' from a 55th Squadron bomber did not open. He fell from an altitude of 500m to his death. The canopy of one of the other paratroopers only opened at an altitude of 50m. Some of the parachutists sustained injuries and bruising. It was not only people who were dropped from these aircraft, but bags with different cargoes, including recoilless guns.

The parachutists captured the landing site on which the aircraft carrying the troops landed. The assault moved away from the landing site on a predetermined route on a speed march. The success of this assault was only marred by one incident: on the night camp the paratroopers from the 3rd Motorised Detachment Company left their ... light machine gun behind ... in a village barn. As a result, the troops bickered for a lengthy period about whose turn it was to tow the heavy DP, and as a result nobody would take it. When the Commander found out about this, he drove the platoon back as a joke. The machine gun was discovered but the detachment did not reach their objective on time.

On 29 September an ANT-9 ground-looped on landing at Krasnogvardeysk that belonged to the Military Aviation Academy. The port undercarriage leg and the spar in the port wing broke. The reason it was discovered was the fact that the aircraft was significantly overloaded – it was carrying 12 people and a recoilless gun.

A demonstration descent was arranged for the commanders who had gathered on the airfield with a three-seat aviabus (with nobody on board) dropped from a TB-1.

The following year Separate Detachment No. 3 took part in demonstration exercises arranged by the Leningrad Military District in which the People's Commissar for Military and Naval Affairs K.E. Voroshilov took part. An exhibition of armament and equipment used by airborne troops was specially arranged for him. In September 1932 the parachutists operated in these exercises alongside ground forces. After dropping from the sky, they would inflict a surprise attack on one of the divisions of the XIX Rifle Corps, and then attack behind the lines of the mechanised corps. In cooperating with the mechanised brigade, the paratroopers could also advance towards a notional enemy rifle regiment.

26

The Future Wings of the Airborne Troops

The suitability of bombers and standard passenger aircraft to transporting military equipment could not fully compensate for the lack of special military transport aircraft in the RKKA VVS. Therefore, in the first half of the 1930s in the Soviet Union prototype manufacturing work was undertaken on a series of military transport aircraft starting with the comparatively small T-1 up to the giant D-1 (the G-1). Some of them remained at the design stage or even the technical specifications stage, others were manufactured in prototype form and underwent flight testing.

In 1933, the Revolutionary Military Committee tasked the UVVS with preparing technical specifications for the production of special transport and airborne assault aircraft (these are actually one and the same thing).

1. T-1 and T-2 Specifications

In July 1933, the VVS airborne service represented its approach towards the creation of future transport aircraft. In this document the specifications for the aircraft designated T-1 and T-2 were formulated.

The T-1 represented an aircraft with a flight weight of between 6,000–8,000kg that was designed to carry 22 people or a corresponding weight in cargo. The aircraft was to have more than one engine, and furthermore the designers were required to ensure the aircraft could fly on one engine. The conversion of the aircraft from a passenger to a cargo variant was to take no more than half an hour. The aircraft would be designed to carry 10m long tubes (possibly for field pipelines). The cruising speed was set at 250km/hr with a landing speed of no more than 85km/hr. The plan was for the engines to be started using their own on-board starter systems (of any type), which would not require a ground feed.

The T-2 was significantly larger, its weight reached up to 20tonnes and it could carry up to 50 people. Apart from personnel the loading of transport or of military hardware weighing up to four tonnes was envisaged (such as armoured cars, amphibious tanks, or trucks). Furthermore, the document specified the provision of automated loading.

The author has not been able to find any evidence that the T-2 was actually manufactured, but an aircraft designated T-1 was certainly produced.

2. T-1 (TS)

In November 1931, Soviet representatives familiarised themselves on Tempelhof airfield in Berlin with a prototype example of the Junkers Ju 52 aircraft in its initial single-engine variant. To begin with the aircraft was examined on the ground and all the interesting components were photographed. Then the aircraft was displayed to those present in a flying display. The report along with the photographs was sent to Moscow.

The documents were slow to progress through the channels before they caught the attention of Soviet specialists who thought that a similar aircraft would be useful to the RKKA VVS. A small group of lecturers at the Zhukovskiy Military Aviation Academy led by A. Mozhayev made the preliminary estimations. Mozhayev drew up a petition for the UVVS proposing that a "universal transport aircraft" be developed. The Head of the RKKA VVS Ya.I. Alksnis approved this proposal. Mozhayev gathered a group of designers together consisting of eight individuals, among whom specifically were S. Kozlov, V. Bolkhovitinov, E. Andreyev, A. Kovalkov, and P.

A demonstration of a Junkers Ju 52 transport aircraft (in the initial single-engine variant) in Berlin, 17 February 1931. This photograph was taken by a member of the Soviet trade representation who had been invited to this event. This aircraft was considered a prototype for the future Soviet T-1 (TS) transport airplane.

Osipenko. Some of the specialists (Kovalkov and Osipenko for example) came from the NII VVS.

Mozhayev prepared a design for the aircraft that was simply designated the TS ('transport aircraft') along with a short description. The group members discussed this and made a few corrections. The document arrived at the UVVS in this form and was sent from there to the NII VVS for approval. In May 1933 an order arrived from Alksnis, who had acknowledged the importance of manufacturing a military transport aircraft and who had given permission for it to those who were working at that time on this task (they were all VVS personnel). Mozhayev's group carried out the principal calculations and produced a model for testing in a wind tunnel. This model was tested in the institute's wind tunnel. Based on the results of the wind tunnel tests the design was modified and new calculations were made. The final layout of the aircraft was established in November 1933.

By that time Mozhayev's group had already received their full official status. The All-Union Society of Inventors (VOIZ) took on the finance side of this work. On 21 July 1933, the Central Council of the VOIZ passed a decree on the creation of an aircraft using their own funds. The aircraft was described in the propaganda as a gift from the society to the Red Army. Mozhayev was made Chief Designer. The VOIZ reached agreement with the academy, after drawing up an agreement to engage the services of the Academy's specialists and the use of its facilities and equipment. The design was carried out in the academy's design bureau, which at that time was led by S.G. Kozlov (one of the members of Mozhayev's group).

In accordance with the initial specification the T-1 transport aircraft fitted with a single M-34R engine and armament consisting of between one to three machine guns was to have a maximum speed of 180km/hr and a practical ceiling of 3,500m, and a range of 1,000km.

The aircraft represented a large, single-engine monoplane. In order to enhance the flight performance characteristics, the wing was fitted with Zap-type flaps with 'servomotors' (most likely with an electromagnetic drive). The flaps were designed to shorten the landing roll to 300m. The undercarriage was fixed and interchangeable, in the summer they would be fitted with a wheeled undercarriage and in the winter with skis. One significant difference from the Junkers was the arrangement for carrying cargoes that was based on boxes. The aircraft had a detachable cargo compartment in the wing, which was interchangeable with an alternative airborne platform. The raising and lowering of this equipment was achieved with pulleys.

The aircraft could be divided into components that enabled it to be transported in a dismantled form along a railway line or using road transport.

The aircraft was designed to carry a cargo weighing up to 2,000kg, and furthermore it was proposed that up to 1,000kg would be carried on an external attachment. The cargo could consist of aero engines, fuel in tanks or in another box, chemical spraying equipment, smoke generators, poison agents in a special box, rounds, bombs, ammunition, guns, medicines, provisions, airfield equipment, and tools. The largest cargo that was designed to be carried by the T-1 was the 76mm field gun. In place of the cargoes, paratroopers could be carried in the fuselage – up to 16–20 men. According to the specifications they all had to jump out of the aircraft with their parachutes in no more than six seconds. The T-1 medical variant could accommodate four casualties lying down on stretchers or between 10–15 in a seated position, with one accompanying medic.

The crew was made up of a pilot and a gunner-navigator who would be accommodated in an enclosed cockpit. Although the pilot was on his own dual controls were fitted so that the navigator could take over from the pilot for a short time should that prove necessary.

The T-1 carried armament consisting of two 7.62mm ShKAS machine guns. One of them, a synchronised machine gun, was to be fitted in the fuselage (alternatively consideration was given to housing this gun in the forward section of the wing); the ammunition for this gun was set at 500 rounds. The sight and the trigger button for this gun were fitted in the pilot's cockpit. In a second was mounted on an easily detachable turret above the fuselage, and the navigator would fire this gun; the ammunition for this gun was the same at 500 rounds. The turret was removed for flights around the home front, saving weight.

As the employees of the NII VVS familiarised themselves with this work, it led to a series of remarks which, in February–March 1934, were partially incorporated into the drawings. A large number of employees from the academy's design bureau were drafted in to prepare the working drawings – more than 60 people.

According the plan drawn up by the VOIZ, the design had to be completed by 1 April 1934. This requirement was fulfilled. On 10 April the design was affirmed albeit with some remarks. For example, rubber shock absorbers for the undercarriage had to be replaced with oil-pneumatic shock absorbers. A prototype example now had to be manufactured. The VOIZ did not have its own aircraft manufacturing plant. Attempts were made to reach agreement with Factory No.1 in Moscow but this enterprise did not take on the work to manufacture the T-1 since it was overloaded with its own work. Factory No. 18 in Voronezh first asked 350,00 roubles, and then raised the quote to 450,000 roubles, saying that it may request a further 200,000 roubles. Nobody was able to appropriate that kind of money.

Mozhayev turned to the VVS Command requesting a commission be set up to 'deconflict' the situation that had arisen. On 25 July Alksnis wrote a resolution on his letter: "There is interest in this aircraft and it has to be seen through to the end". On 23 August 1934 the UVVS drew up an agreement with Kharkov Aviation Plant of Prototype Manufacturing (KhAZOS).

In the end agreement was reached for 300,00 roubles plus ten percent for unforeseen expenses. For this KhAZOS was to manufacture three prototype examples of the T-1, as well as a separate wing, fuselage, fin and a 'half-size' undercarriage for static testing. The first example had a rubber shock absorber while on the second example oil-pneumatic shock absorbers were fitted to the legs. The components for static testing had to be handed over to by 1 December 1934. Later in June 1934 engine mounts and flaps were added to the list of components for testing. A full-size mock up of the cargo compartment also needed to be manufactured.

On 26 August, the Principal Directorate of the Civil Air Fleet, to which the KhAZOS belonged, requested of the VOIZ that they transfer all the documentation and send eight engineers to Kharkov. They also wanted to obtain an engine, wheels, instruments and some other materials and semi-finished products from the VOIZ. The guys in Kharkov did not stay within the allotted budget. In comparison with production in Moscow the manufacture of an example at a less well-equipped enterprise in Kharkov it turned out was more expensive to the tune of 100,000 roubles. The VOIZ did not have sufficient funds. They could only stretch to no more than 390,000 roubles. Mozhayev again approached Alksnis. He added a resolution to Mozhayev's correspondence: "We are in need of a transport aircraft and we need it to pass through the prototype stage as quickly as possible". With the help of the UVVS agreement was reached with the Council of People's Commissars to grant the VOIZ a sum of 600,000 roubles for the T-1.

The UVVS, however, decided to take over this work from then on. On 14 September the Deputy Head of the VVS Tkachev affirmed a new plan for this work. From 29 October the VOIZ handed over all responsibility to the military.

In November 1934, static testing began of the components. The first prototype example of the T-1 in accordance with the agreement was to be handed over by 1 July 1935. This aircraft however was not ready. Not for the first time this was linked to changes in the specifications for the aircraft.

In July 1935, new technical specifications were prepared. The maximum speed had been increased up to between 250–300km/hr given a landing speed of no more than 70–80km/hr while the flight range was increased up to 1,500km. The M-34R engine was now used to turn a metal variable pitch propeller.

The wheels had to be fitted with brakes, which was designed to reduce the landing roll to 150–200m. Since the aircraft was to operate from front line airstrips the take-off run was also drastically reduced to 200–250m.

The equipment on board the aircraft included an RR radio set, a fixed-loop radio-compass, and an aircraft intercom system. The electric generator for the radio worked off the engine, and not from the aerovane. The aircraft did not have lamps, but underwing lights were envisaged.

Evidently work on the T-1 ceased at the end of 1935 when the commission under the People's Oversight Committee recommended to the VVS to reduce the number of prototype projects and concentrate their funds on the most important designs.

3. G-37

The G-37 aircraft (which was initially a G-35 'Universal flying wing') was designed as a special transport and airborne assault aircraft at the VVS OKPB between 1932–33. The leading designer was V.F. Rentel. In some documents this aircraft is referred to as the G-1.

This machine represented a twin-engine cantilever monoplane fitted with twin tail booms. It was fitted with two engines developing 450hp each and which were located in the forward ends of the tail booms. The undercarriage was fixed and was accommodated inside cowling 'breeches'. One specific feature of the G-37 was the box like nature of the cargo. Under the wing centre section passenger pods could be carried, and either a cargo box (a 'pod') or an example of large military hardware. In each case it was envisaged that they would be dropped by parachute using the separation method. The passenger pod would be dropped in this case with the people

A G-37 neat a hangar, with a cargo container suspended underneath.

A view of the nose section of a G-37 fuselage.

A G-37 takes off without container.

The tail part of a G-37. The aircraft had a twin-boom layout, each of the booms had a vertical fin, with the booms joined by a horizontal tail.

The G-37 starboard power plant and undercarriage leg with fairing.

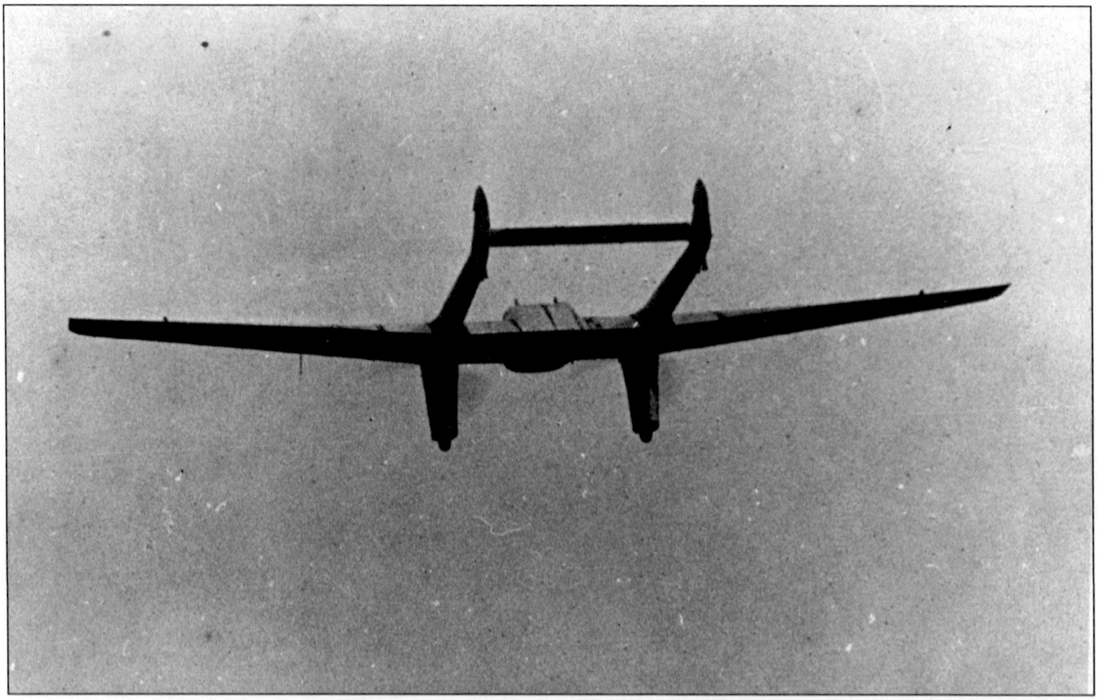

A G-37 in flight over the Moscow Central Airfield.

The People's Commissar for Heavy Industry, G.K. Ordzhonikidze, inspects a G-37 aircraft.

inside, representing a variant of the 'personnel cage'. Interestingly in the first variant of the project the crew would be accommodated along with the paratroopers in the jettisonable pod. After it was dropped the aircraft was left with nobody at the controls and would crash. Thus the G-37 was considered a 'single-use' aircraft.

This was considered unacceptable. At a meeting in the office of the Head of the VVS on 24 November 1932, it was decided that the pilots would be moved into a separate cockpit on the leading edge of the wing. At a later stage more powerful engines were selected, M-17s rated at 600hp each. Some 622,000 roubles were allocated for the manufacture of a prototype example of the G-37. By February 1933 the design stage was complete and approximately 95 percent of the effort was on manufacturing the first components for the aircraft.

One prototype example of the G-37 was manufactured in Leningrad. Factory testing was conducted by V.P. Chkalov who flew this aircraft to Moscow. During the course of testing a test drop of the pod was carried out by parachute.

The G-37 did not pass state testing and was not series produced. The only prototype example was used later at the Experimental Institute of the NKTP for experiments into dropping a variety of cargoes by parachute.

In October 1933 Grokhovskiy gave an interview to a correspondent from *Pravda* newspaper in which he explained about the design of the "propaganda-aircraft named after the Central Committee of the All-Union Communist Party of Bolsheviks", which was a development of the G-37 with four engines, a pilot's cockpit in the leading edge of the wing and which did not have a release system for releasing the passenger cabin in flight. The aircraft allegedly was designed for a maximum speed of 300km/hr and a practical ceiling of 6,000m.

4. ANT-14

Development of the ANT-14 passenger aircraft began at the Central Aero and Hydrodynamic Institute under the leadership of A.N. Tupolev in spring 1930. His design was a development of the ANT-9 that had already been produced but with increased dimensions and the number of engines was also increased. This was an all-metal cantilever monoplane with a high wing. Four Gnome-Rhone 9Akx engines rated at 480hp each were accommodated on the leading edge of the wing, and a fifth such engine was housed in the nose section of the fuselage. The fuselage itself had a rectangular cross-section with a rounded top and underside. The undercarriage had tandem main bogies. In winter the bogies could be interchanged for skis.

The 32 passengers sat in eight rows of paired seats with a central aisle. The aircraft had a crew of five: two pilots, a navigator, and two flight engineers. The first three sat in an enclosed cockpit in the nose section of the fuselage, behind the central engine. The workstations for the flight engineers were located in the wing centre section under a transparent canopy, which enabled them to observe the engines in flight.

If in the ANT-9 many components were used from the 'cruiser' R-6, then the ANT-14 borrowed components

An ANT-14 aircraft on a ski undercarriage soon after the commencement of testing.

The only example of the produced ANT-14 was named *Pravda* and joined the Propaganda Squadron named after Maksim Gorkiy.

The ANT-14 was often used for demonstration parachute jumps at various aviation events and parades.

and assemblies from the TB-3 heavy bomber. The aircraft used the wing from the TB-3 (with a wing centre section that had been extended by zero point eight metres), as well as the undercarriage and part of the fin.

The first flight of the ANT-14 took place on 14 August 1931. The second flight took place the next day. The aircraft was flown by M.M. Gromov. For a flight weight of 17,530kg the aircraft had a maximum speed of 236km/hr and a range of approximately 1,200km. The ANT-14 was distinguished by its acceptable stability and handling.

In 1932 the Principal Directorate of the Civilian Air Fleet tried to order 30 ANT-14 aircraft from the industry,

A sketch of the ANT-14 fitted with tubes to enable paratroopers to leave the aircraft, basing on the proposal of the Experimental Institute of the NKTP.

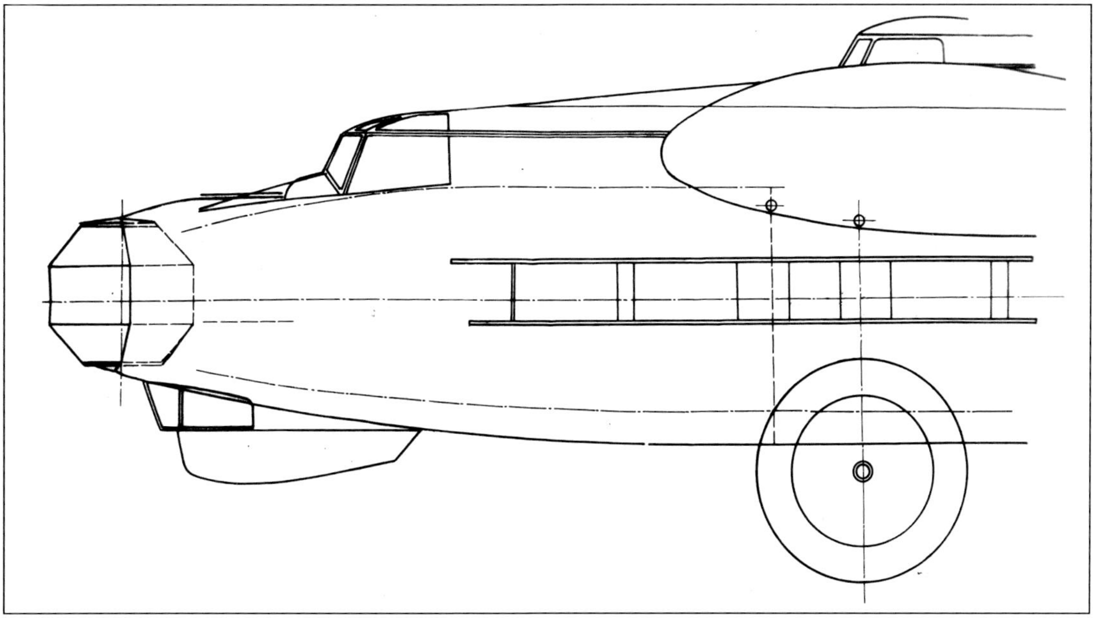

This was how the nose section of the ANT-14 military variant was to look. The aircraft was planned to be fitted with four M-22 engines.

but the requisition was not received by the Principal Directorate of the Aviation Industry (GUAP), because the military were overloaded with orders.

The aircraft however was not just conceived as a passenger aircraft. In 1933 an outline design was completed for a military modification of the ANT-14 fitted with four M-34R engines and a new tail section. These aircraft it was planned would be manufactured at Factory No.22 in Fili. In September 1933 the leadership of this enterprise approached the Principal Directorate of the Aviation Industry for permission to produce a prototype example. An airborne assault variant of this aircraft was developed at the OKPB that was designed to carry 50 paratroopers, who were to jump out of the aircraft through angled pipes.

The paratroopers would 'dive out' underneath the fuselage. It was proposed that this would take less time than jumping out of an aircraft through an open door. A model of this device was manufactured but this was s scaled down experimental model that was tried on the TB-1. All work was brought to an end after the decision was taken not to launch the ANT-14 into series production.

The prototype example of the ANT-14 that was named *Pravda* at the beginning of 1935 became part of the *Maksim Gorkiy* Propaganda Squadron. It completed a significant number of propaganda flights and in 1935 it delivered an *Osoaviakhim* delegation to an aviation celebration in Bucharest. Several times at aviation events the group parachute jumps would be undertaken from an ANT-14. Subsequently it was used for pleasure flights over Moscow. In total this aircraft carried up to 40,000 passengers. After the ANT-14 had used up its service life it stood for some time as an exhibit in Gorky Park in Moscow.

5. D-1 (G-1)

This was the most colossal project of the first half of the 1930s. According to the technical specification the D-1 was a multi-role aircraft. In contrast to the TB-3, TB-4, and TB-6 whose primary function was as a bomber this machine was first and foremost a transport aircraft. Furthermore, the emphasis was not on supplying the front line and not on the rapid deployment of forces, but on airborne operations. The D-1 was designed to deploy large numbers of airborne parachutists and landing forces. This was the reason for the letter 'D' in the prefix, which denoted *Desantniy* (airborne). This aircraft could of course be used to deliver both people and cargoes to the front line, as well as for their "delivery ... to an area of disturbance in an enemy alignment". The D-1 was designed to carry between 180–200 people or 30tonnes of cargo. In terms of its lifting capacity it eclipsed somewhat the world's largest aircraft that at the time were German: it surpassed the Junkers G.38 by four times, and the Dornier Do X flying boat (in fact it was a ground effect vehicle) by one and a half times. A series of design specifics followed on immediately from the aircraft primary purpose, large open spaces inside the wing, and the capability to carry cumbersome military equipment externally.

The aircraft was also used in a role as a heavy night bomber, but this function was considered secondary. Defensive armament consisted of three guns, four large calibre and ten standard machine guns. The specification stipulated a maximum speed of 250km/hr at an altitude of 3,000m, a practical ceiling of exactly 4,500m and a flight range with 15tonnes of bombs of 2,000km. The aircraft according to the specification would be fitted with ten M-34FRN engines.

The aircraft was designed at the Design Bureau under the Zhukovskiy Military Aviation Academy under the leadership of S. Kozlov. His deputy was V. Bolkhovitinov. The aircraft was designated the G-1 at this location (it is hard to say whether this was derived from *Gigant* (Giant) or *Gruzovoy* (Cargo)). The preliminary design was ready in the summer of 1932, and by December of that year more than 80 percent of the blueprints had been completed.

In terms of its design, the G-1 had a layout that was similar to a 'flying wing'. A thick spar wing with a trapezoidal shape in plan form. The maximum cord was equal to 15m, and the wingspan exceeded 60m. Between the spars formed of a truss was a servicing passage, along which crewmembers could walk fully upright. Both artificial and natural illumination was envisaged in the wing (the natural light being provided by windows in the upper surface).

Since the specified engines were not available, others had to be used,which were less powerful, so the quantity was increased. The aircraft had a highly original engine mount. Twelve engines stood in six pairs, nose to nose, on the leading edge of the wing. Each pair of engines worked through a common gearbox, which via an angular drive would turn a long shaft that ran upwards. There on tall legs stood secondary angular drives that would actually turn the propellers. The propellers themselves were twin-bladed steel props with a diameter of four and a half metres. In order to service the upper gearbox a detachable ladder was fitted to one of the legs. An engineer was able to climb out onto the wing via one the hatches in the ceiling.

Access to the engines was provided both from inside the wing, and eternally. A part of the wing root was designed to fold back. The section folded back and turned into working platforms. In order to change an engine, the wing root it would extend into the servicing passage and a hoist that ran on rails moved along the ceiling of this passage. A hatch was envisaged in the floor of this passage under each engine for lowering an engine down into it.

The fuel tanks were located in this same place, in the wing, but were separated from the engines by fire-resistant bulkheads. In total there were 24. The reserve of fuel was very high, 24 tonnes, since the calculated flight duration exceeded 20hrs. All the fuel tanks were made to be detachable; they were installed via hatches in the lower part of the wing. The fuel tanks in one wing were all linked via a common pipeline that had a filling point under the wing. The fuel would be fed into it from a tanker using a powerful pump under pressure; according to the calculations it would have taken four hours to completely fill the aircraft. Each of the engines had its own oil tank, and in total there were 12, holding a total of 2.5tonnes of oil.

The aircraft did not have a fuselage as such. A 'gondola' or 'cabin' extended along the aircraft axis from the wing nose part, which was where the pilots sat as well as the navigator and several other crewmembers. In its aft section was where the designers wanted to accommodate the 'most sensitive equipment'. Seats were to be placed at the top behind the gun turret for the pilots, and lower down in the actual nose itself. Behind the upper cockpit was the navigator's astronomical navigation position as well as an armoured extendable cylindrical commander's 'combat cabin'. The commander would only be in this cabin in times of danger however because usually he would sit to the right of the pilot below him in a collapsible seat. It would be there that he would have all the communications systems and fire control systems at his fingertips. The chief engineer's position would be underneath this 'combat cabin'.

To the rear of the wing two massive tail booms extended backwards and were joined at the back by the stabiliser. The aircraft had two tail fins, one on each of the tail booms.

The control surfaces were to be controlled with the help of hydraulic or electro-mechanical actuators. To be more precise: the latter was available in the Soviet Union, but they were unreliable, but the former was not available at all.

The G-1 undercarriage was a four-point design: the two main undercarriage legs and two tail-skids. The main undercarriage legs had four-wheel bogies, but the wheels were fitted in tandem in two pairs, each pair had its own leg and its own set of struts extending forward and rearward. The undercarriage leg was joined at the top by a lever system, which transferred effort down to the shared shock absorber that was hidden inside the wing.

The paratroopers as well as the cargo were housed inside the wing centre section. During offloading they were lifted upwards by special lift platforms. These same platforms were used to enable the paratroopers to jump out. One of the documents also indicates that in the future there was a plan to launch the paratroopers using compressed air (in the same was as a torpedo launch system works). The aircraft could carry infantrymen with all their equipment and armament, as well as parachutists, light rifles, and machine guns, an entrenching tool, explosive materials, ammunition, provisions, fuel and oil in a different box, artillery armament of various calibres and designs (including anti-aircraft artillery), light tanks, tankettes, light cars and trucks, and armoured vehicles. The aircraft would also carry the wounded.

The crew of the G-1, depending on the mission they were carrying out, could vary from nine to 18 people. There was also a plan for a more fully-fledged compliment of personnel. The composition of the aircraft crew and the list of responsibilities were closer to that of a small naval ship, let alone an aircraft. On board were a commander who had been relieved of any other duties, two pilots, a chief engineer, four engineers and five technicians, a chief artilleryman, two aircraft engineers and engine specialists, a radio operator and from five to ten gunners. The entire crew apart from the rear gunners would climb up on the ladders to the hatches in the engine passageways, from where they would disperse to their workstations. On the ground 69 people were needed to service one of these giant aircraft.

Internal communication between the crewmembers was provided by an intercom system (an internal telephone) that had 12 subscribers, a pneumatic dispatch system, colour light signals, and a siren. The chief artilleryman and the commander also had an electronic system aside from this that was analogous to a ship's telegraph system. This had repeaters at every workstation. A rotating arrow on a dial would indicate the direction of fire. With the help of this equipment it was possible to give a command to concentrate fire in a specific direction. A signal panel was fitted in the commander's position that showed the condition of various systems. Communication between other aircraft in the group was provided by radio, and by launching coloured rockets, and ... by flags that were run up the antenna cables, just as they are on board ship! The latter according to the designers ensured a covert transfer of messages from one aircraft to another when flying in a formation. Enemy radio-operators could not tap into them at all, since no radio equipment was used.

The firing points were housed right in the nose of the central gondola, in the forward extremities of the tail booms, passing under the wings and extending slightly beyond its leading edge, above on the wing sections, on the top and half way along the tail booms, and in the ends of these same booms, behind the stabiliser. In the nose and on the ends of the tail booms cannons were fitted, while all the other points were fitted with machine guns. The firing was controlled from the two cabins: in the forward cabin by the commander and in the aft cabin by the senior artilleryman. The document entitled "The prospects for the combat deployment of the G-1" dated 27 October 1932 indicates: "It is however unlikely that the enemy would risk ... taking on a G-1 using a single aircraft, since this aircraft would probably be shot down". The designers thought that the giant aircraft could repel an attack by up to nine fighters at once, successfully engaging in combat with any number of enemies, which would be less than the number of firing points.

The G-1, however, in defending itself was not only capable of bringing its cannons and machine guns to bear. The tail section housed 'self-defence tanks' that could spray poison agents. Small bombs would be dropped from special cells with time fuses, these were the prototypes of the future aviation grenades. Finally, though the G-1 could put out a smoke screen behind it, for which it had a special tank containing two tonnes of the required mixture. This would allow the aircraft to hide from anti-aircraft artillery and fighters. This mixture could be either as standard S-4 or a poison mixture.

The G-1 bomber had a maximum payload of 25 tonnes and a standard load of 15 tonnes, as per the TB-6 (ANT-6). The maximum range with a 5,000kg bomb load according to the calculations would be 2,200km. The largest bombs that the aircraft could use were the FAB-2000s, but their standard calibres were 250 and 500kg. It was envisaged that the aircraft would carry RRAB single use cluster bombs.

The RRAB expanded as the 'rotating aviation cluster bomb'. Small bomblets would be stowed inside, or sometimes ampules containing poison agents or incendiary mixtures. After it had fallen out of the aircraft the bomb would start to spin under the influence of the angled fin blades that worked as a turbine. When it reached a set speed of rotation the locks would open, and the contents would be spread out under centrifugal force. There were three sets of these munitions, which were known as the RRAB-100, RRAB-250, and RRAB-500.

As a bomber, the G-1 was immediately equivalent to ten TB-3s. In low cloud the plan was to extend an armoured cabin ('an armoured cradle') down on a cable a kilometre long with a bombardier and a sight. A similar design named the 'Gerasimov pod' was tested on a TB-3.

In place of bombs, the aircraft could carry chemical spraying equipment carrying a total weight of poison agents of up to 20tonnes, the contents would be sprayed out under pressure. From an altitude of 1,000m the aircraft could hit an area between one and half to two square kilometres in size. It was planned that a number of aircraft would carry out a chemical attack at low level. The total standard flight weight for the G-1 was set at approximately 40tonnes.

On 11 August 1932, an outline design for the G-1 project was reviewed by the Revolutionary Military Committee of the USSR. The work of the academy's design bureau was approved, but the manufacture of a prototype example of the aircraft was conditional on preliminary tests of the main engine gearbox in the engine mount, which was to have been manufactured in November 1932.

As a stipulated preliminary. the deadline for completing the manufacture of a prototype of the G-1 aircraft began from 1 August 1933. A further million was added to the 500,000 roubles that had been previously allocated. For the production of a prototype example of the G-1 some 100,000 roubles had been allocated for a variety of materials, as well as 120,000 for the jigs and tools.

Since there was a serious deficit of M-34 engines at that time and the M-34FRN that had been stipulated in the specification did not yet exist, a decision was taken to try a very new engine mount, using two M-27 engines. Based on the designer's surname the main gearbox is sometimes referred to in the documentation as "the comrade Dzyuba's unit". Since the aircraft manufacturing factories were overloaded, other factories belonging to different departments had to be drafted in. The components for the prototype engine mounts were manufactured at various Moscow enterprises, including a fixture-production factory belonging to the *Orgametall* trust and *Vladimir Ilyich* Electromechanical plant in Moscow. The propeller hub was ordered from the Automobile Factory named after Stalin. These enforced approaches to factories that were not specialist aircraft manufacturing plants led to departures from the drawings and specifications in terms of used materials and precision of the parts manufacturing.

By 1 December 1932, a prototype example of the engine mount had been readied for testing. This began on 23 January 1933. Following a number of failures however on 9 April production was stopped. In place of the two M-27s a pair of M-17s that were less powerful were used instead. With these engines the 'component' had amassed 58hrs of operating time by 20 June.

By 15 February 1933, all the working drawings had been completed for the tail fin, 98 percent of the drawings for the undercarriage was also complete, 94 percent of the fuselage, and 70 percent of the wing sections, and 50 percent of the ribs in the wing centre section. By 1 April 1933 the academy was to have handed over a model of the aircraft. Whether this was actually manufactured is not known.

Work on the G-1 (D-1) was stopped in the first quarter of 1934. The reason was trivial, the money that had been allocated had run out. It was estimated that a prototype example was 70 percent complete by this time. According to the estimations of the designers a further 508,000 roubles would have been needed to complete the aircraft, and the powers that be refused to allocate this.

6. TB-4 (ANT-16)

The majority of the fantastic specifications that were written 'on a whim' did not have any real basis or any realistic chance of being produced, at least to the specified timescales. Only a very few designs for the giant combat aircraft were actually realised. One of them was the Tupolev TB-4. The origins of this aircraft appearance were the same as for the TB-1 and TB-3.

Back in October 1929, the OTB were interested in the possibility of manufacturing an aircraft with a high lifting capacity of between 25–30tonnes. The role of this aircraft was specified as "carrying combat hardware (tanks, guns, and so on)". The estimations carried out at the Central Aero and Hydrodynamic Institute demonstrated that at that time this was unrealistic, but an attempt could be made to create an aircraft capable of carrying around 10tonnes. The UVVS entered into the dialogue between the OTB and the TsAGI as they had decided to create a 'super-bomber' from this flying giant. In November 1929 the military officially ordered the AGOS TsAGI to design and manufacture a prototype example of the heavy bomber under the designation TB-4.

It was initially proposed that the aircraft would receive four M-35 engines rated at between 1,500–1,800hp each. It was around these engines that the outline design for the ANT-16 was produced, which was completed in October 1930. Then it was realised that the aircraft would actually have to be manufactured but the required engines were not available and were not to be anticipated in the near future. The search began for alternatives. Variants were considered in which different indigenous and foreign engines would be used. All these conceded to the M-35 in terms of output. In order to ensure the required total amount of thrust, the designers were forced to decide to increase the number of engines up to six. Using imported engines was banned under a decree issued by the Council of People's Commissars. By April 1931 a conclusion had been reached that the best variant would be to fit six M-34 engines.

Work on manufacturing the prototype aircraft had begun by that time. In terms of its layout the bomber in many ways echoed the TB-3, but the size of all the components had been significantly enlarged. Structurally however it differed significantly. For example, the undercarriage arrangement was totally different. The four engines stood in a row in the wing, while a further two in a special gondola on trusses above the fuselage. A seventh engine was also envisaged this was an auxiliary engine that drove the so-called 'central power generating station' designed by Siemens (this was an auxiliary power unit).

The number and location of the firing points changed more than once during the design stage. Subsequently during the course of the design stage, the arsenal followed the specification: two cannons and eight machine guns.

The bomber was designed to be serviced by its crew of ten men. This crew composed of a forward artilleryman (an artillery technician, who was actually a reserve bombardier), the commander of the aircraft (the navigator), the chief bombardier (the second navigator), the two pilots, a senior technician, and two juniors (who also acted

A TB-4 (ANT-16) during state testing, September 1933.

The upper tandem engine mounting was considered a temporary solution prior to the delivery of more powerful engines.

as gunners at the same time), the radio-operator and photographer (the TB-4 was to be fitted with the Potte-1B photographic equipment) and an additional artilleryman.

As with all bombers of that time, the TB-4 was designed as a potential means of delivering airborne troops. It had a large clearance underneath the wing centre section and a considerable lifting capacity that enabled it to carry tanks, three-axle armoured gun cars, and heavy artillery armament. The author has not been able to find any information thus far concerning the development of special assault attachments for this aircraft.

It was proposed however that the entire first series of ten aircraft would not receive any bomb armament but would as it turned out be used as military transport aircraft. From the eleventh aircraft onwards, the plan was to fit equipment designed for carrying special cargoes, hoists together with the platforms that they are there to operate.

On 3 July 1933 M.M. Gromov first took this bomber into the air. In September the TB-4 was handed over to the NII VVS for state testing. It was here that the aircraft was flown by P.M. Stefanovskiy, who later wrote in his memoirs about the new aircraft: "It just bowled me over!".

The aircraft however did not satisfy the military. Its statistics were far from those stipulated in the specification. The aircraft did not fall within the parameters in terms of speed, practical ceiling, or range. It turned out the aircraft was relatively complicated to fly, and the same could be said of its technical servicing. The ANT-16 had far from a full complement of armament and equipment.

It was considered that in the current configuration this aircraft was not suitable for the RKKA VVS. It was suggested to Tupolev that he introduce a number of significant changes to the design. In response to this the designer created what was actually a new aircraft–the ANT-20.

7. *MAKSIM GORKY* – A Military Variant

This aircraft did not figure in the plans at all to begin with. Since it had not managed to demonstrate the flight-performance characteristics set out in the specification for the TB-4 heavy bomber (the main reason for this was the lack of suitable engines) A.N. Tupolev increased the size of the wings and added a further two engines. Thus the design for the ANT-20 was conceived, and this was also designated in a report on the manufacture of a prototype as the 'TB-4-6M-34R'.

The ANT-20 *Maksim Gorkiy* before the start of flight testing.

The ANT-20 after cowlings had been fitted to the undercarriage bogies.

Given that the length of the fuselage was the same as that of the ANT-16 (the TB-4), this aircraft was designed to have a larger wingspan and a larger wing area. The wingspan was to reach 63m (as opposed to 54m for the ANT-16). The cord of the wing however had not changed since the aspect ratio had changed, which should have had a positive impact on the flight range. Two more engines were added on the wing. The fuselage was widened, and a beam that ran along the aircraft axis was removed and the bomb bay was redesigned, enabling bombs of 1,000 or 2,000kg calibre to be stored internally, as well as large size cargoes.

The aircraft maximum flight weight was assessed as 45tonnes. The aircraft was to have been fitted with eight M-34R engines with a future transfer to the more powerful M-34FRN (in reality these only appeared in 1936).

Although this aircraft was first and foremost considered a heavy bomber, work was undertaken in parallel on military transport, passenger, and 'propaganda' variants. Thus the transport aircraft was designed to transport heavy and cumbersome military hardware – tanks and artillery armament. In the main the intention was for the aircraft to carry this hardware externally, between the undercarriage legs, but a proportion was accommodated inside as well. For example, estimations were drawn up for carrying a T-27 tankette inside the bomb bay.

This was the first design for transporting armoured military hardware inside the fuselage. A platform that was two metres by four metres would be lowered from the bomb bay, which was designed to lift cargoes of up to six tonnes.

On 5 November 1933 the authoritative commission led by Ya.I. Alksnis examined this new design and approved it. A decision was taken to reject the ANT-16 and to gamble on the ANT-20. This aircraft, which at that stage existed only as a design on paper was destined to become the standard for the future series production TB-4. Thus two aircraft featured at different times under this designation, which were at once similar, and yet different. It was proposed that series production of the giant bombers would be rolled out at Factory No.18 in Voronezh.

The design that was developed at the TsAGI according to the calculations was to have a top speed of 215km/hr, a ceiling of 4,180m, and a range at a normal weight of 1,300km. The aircraft was designed to carry a defensive armament consisting of four (this was later changed to two) cannons, and seven machine guns.

A model was manufactured of the bomb bay with a platform. In September 1934 an actual T-27 tankette was driven onto the platform and was successfully lifted using an electrified KD-3 hoist linked to a pulley.

Manufacture of a second prototype example of an ANT-16 was stopped. Evidently the numerous components that had already been manufactured for this aircraft were used for the prototype ANT-20, since by the end of the year it was assessed as being 60 percent ready.

The *Maksim Gorkiy* in flight over Moscow.

A model of the military version of the ANT-20.

The 'propaganda' variant however gradually became more important. It was in this guise that the ANT-20 began to be manufactured. By March 1934 it had already been given its own name *Maksim Gorkiy* (which in documents was often shortened to the MG). This was explained by the fact that this giant aircraft was to have become the flagship of a propaganda squadron named after M. Gorkiy. There were no plans to fit this aircraft with military equipment.

The *Maksim Gorkiy* propaganda aircraft was ready by 1 May 1934. It had cost what for the time was an enormous amount of money, six million roubles. On 17 June the aircraft completed its first flight. A report written by the NKTP stated: "This giant aircraft surpasses all existing ground-based aircraft anywhere in the world. The aerodynamic qualities put this aircraft in line with the best examples made by global aviation industry".

Testing the lifting mechanism for the platform with T-27 tankette.

In accordance with the specification, the BAI heavy three-axle armoured car was added to the list of vehicles that the military variant of the ANT-20 could carry.

A PS-124 (ANT-20bis) on the airfield of the Factory No. 124 in Kazan, spring 1939.

This aircraft, however, did not last long relatively speaking. On 18 May 1935 the giant collided with an I-5 fighter in the air. Everyone on board the *Maksim Gorkiy* was killed, along with the pilot of the fighter.

The catastrophe rocked the entire country. Funds began to be collected for the manufacture of first ten and then 16 ANT-20 aircraft. These aircraft were even given names: the first one was to be called the *Vladimir Lenin*. A special decree was issued on 4 August 1935 in respect of this by the Council for Labour and Defence (STO).

At that time, however, the views of the military concerning the merits of enormous supersized bombers gradually began to change. The UVVS gradually began to distance itself from the idea of using fleets of enormous slow bombers. Several factors came into play at the same time to cause this. To begin with the level of development of aircraft manufacturing and especially of engine production at that time was not able to provide acceptable flight performance characteristics for these giant bombers. Secondly the economic factor had no small part to play. An armada of bombers would cost enormous amounts of money but even more would need to be spent on airfield equipment and special equipment. Against a backdrop of a constant deficit in terms of budgetary provision for the VVS there was a basis for rejecting such prohibitive expenses.

From 1935, the accent for all the prototype aircraft manufacturing shifted to aircraft that were smaller, but the requirements for their flight performance characteristics increased sharply. This had given the country the well-known SB. The time for the TB-4 though had already gone.

It was decided, therefore, that all 16 giants would be transferred to civil aviation. In terms of their principal function they were now considered passenger aircraft. In wartime, however, it was planned that they would be mobilised and used as heavy night bombers and military transport aircraft. In accordance with this approach the installation of gun and bomb armament was envisaged in the design, although this was never actually fitted. The OPB-1 bomb sight and the aircraft intercom system were to be fitted straight away. The new aircraft were to differ from the *Maksim Gorkiy* in that they would be fitted with six and not eight engines. The plan was for the upper engine to be removed. The engines themselves were to be modifications of the M-34RN. A ski undercarriage was planned to replace the wheeled chassis. The American Sperry auto-pilot system was included on the list of modern equipment, as well as modern gyroscopes, fixed-loop radio-compasses, and launch tubes for the PAR-13 parachute signal flares.

On 4 August 1935, by way of a decree issued by the STO, the production of the 16 MG aircraft was entrusted to aircraft manufacturing Factory No. 124 (formerly *Kazmashstroy*) in Kazan, which had not yet been built.

On 31 March 1936, a new specification was affirmed for a military variant of the MG. It was conceived as

A PS-124 (ANT-20bis) in course of the state testing at the NII GVF, August 1939.

a dual-purpose aircraft – both a long-range bomber and a transport aircraft, used both by day and by night, as well as operating in inclement weather conditions. The military specified a maximum speed for this aircraft at an altitude of 275km/hr and at low level this would be 250km/hr. The landing speed was equal to 100km/hr, and the practical ceiling was 6,000m. The maximum range for this aircraft was set at 3,000km, but when carrying 4,000kg of bombs this reduced by a half down to 1,500km.

The engine mount consisted of six M-34RN engines. The universal engine mounts enabled six M-34R engines to be installed in place of these engines, and the latter power units did not have superchargers. The propellers were metal with variable pitch. In contrast to the civil machine, the military stipulated that the MG have an emergency fuel transfer system from all fuel tanks with a consumption of not less than 1,000kg/min.

The crew for this military MG was to have been 12 men: a commander who was relieved of his other functions, two pilots, a navigator bombardier, three flight engineers, a radio-operator, and four gunners.

Defensive armament for the aircraft consisted of five 20mm ShVAK cannons (two of these were fitted in a paired mounting in the nose section of the fuselage) and four 7.62mm ShKAS machine guns, these were provided for the commander, and navigator, and another one would be mounted on top of the fuselage, and one would move from side to side (firing through a window). The overall reserve of ammunition would be 2,400 shells and 6,000 rounds of ammunition.

The normal bomb load of a military MG would be 4,000kg. When performing transport missions this could rise to 80 individuals all carrying a weapon or up to 8,000kg of cargo. Furthermore, it was envisaged that the paratroopers and the cargoes would be dropped by parachute. The load configurations included armoured cars, light amphibious tanks, tankettes, and armoured cars.

The fulfilment of the specification was protracted. In order to make the task easier the number of aircraft that were to be manufactured was reduced to five, and then the military rejected the proposal to fit any military equipment in these aircraft, as well as the prospect of fitting any of this equipment in the future.

In reality, the only passenger ANT-20bis (this was actually a PS-124) completed in Kazan was in May 1939 and was designed for 64 seats. The aircraft was fitted with six M-34FRNV engines with VISh-4 variable pitch propellers. In August 1939 the aircraft successfully completed state testing and was accepted into operation. This aircraft flew on the *Aeroflot* route from Moscow to Mineralniye Vody. During the Great Patriotic War this aircraft was lost in a landing accident in Tashkent in December 1942.

8. ANT-26 (TB-6) and the ANT-28

In fact, in 1929 at the TsAGI under the leadership of A.N. Tupolev estimations began to be made for an aircraft that was even larger than the ANT-16. This aircraft continued the line of enormous single-engine monoplanes with a thick profile wing, corrugated skin, and fixed undercarriage, and which bristled on all sides with barrels of machine guns and cannons. It was the engine mount that caused the majority of the problems since no engines of a suitable output were available in the country at that time for an aircraft of this weight.

The TB-6 heavy bomber with six M-44 engines (rated at 2,000hp each) was listed among the specifications that were issued in July 1932 by way of an order from the Council of Labour and Defence. This aircraft was featured in the plan for prototype aircraft manufacture for 1933–34. An aircraft with this designation was found in similar documents that predate this, but judging by the parameters that were recorded this related to a variant of the TB-4 designed around four M-35 or FED engines. The next step was then taken up the 'heavy' bomber ladder. The maximum speed of this aircraft was to be 250km/hr with a practical ceiling of 7,000m. The maximum bomb load was set at 22,000kg and the normal bomb load was 15,000kg. The aircraft was designed to carry bombs of up to 2,000kg. Armament consisted of four cannons and between seven to eight machine guns (including three 'heavy' large calibre machine guns). The aircraft was to have a maximum range of up to 4,800km and with 15tonnes of bombs this was reduced to 3,300km. The aircraft was recorded as belonging to an 'experimental' category, that is to say there was either some doubt over the requirement for this machine, or the country's ability to actually produce it. There was however a deadline for handing over a prototype example of 1 December 1935.

A model of the TB-6 (ANT-26) in the museum of Tupolev Design Bureau.

A sketch of the ANT-26 in flight.

A full-scale mock-up of the nose section of the TB-6 heavy bomber.

Work on the TB-6 at the TsAGI began in October 1932. It was not possible however to bring the powerful M-44 engine up to flying condition, there was a need to look for a replacement. Thus in place of six M-44s the TB-6, which had been designated the ANT-26 by Tupolev received 12 M-34s. The replacement was not like for like: six engines of 2,000hp each in total provide 12,000hp and 12 M-34s produce significantly less, 9,600hp. It was true that the designers were counting on obtaining engines that at the time were not in existence but had nevertheless been written into the plan in the shape of the M-34FRN. With these engines any losses in terms of output would be compensated. With 12 M-34FRN engines though the engine mount would be significantly heavier than with six M-44s, and the aerodynamics would deteriorate. The AN-1 diesel engines suggested by the UVVS as an alternative did nothing really to help the situation. The standard bomb load had to be reduced to ten tonnes and the widespread use of steel that was envisaged in the specification was rejected, but even this did not help. There was no other option than to increase the surface area of what was a huge wing.

Eight engines were moved to the leading edge of the wing, and a further four were accommodated in two tandem mounts on top of the aircraft on trusses, but these were not positioned above the fuselage, but above the wing. The wingspan was 95m, and the take-off weight was around 70 tonnes. The aircraft had a triple tailfin and it was possible that they were afraid that a single huge fin would be very complicated to produce and to service. The large fin was attached to the fuselage and two smaller fins were mounted on the stabiliser approximately one third of the way along it.

Tupolev wrote into the design an even higher maximum payload than was stipulated in the specification, 25,000kg. In a huge bomb bay bombs of one or two tonnes could be carried.

During the design stage a number of changes were made to the aircraft structure, equipment, and armament considering the experience gained with the creation of the TB-4, MG and the modification of the TB-3. The undercarriage had two huge two-wheeled tandem bogies as per the TB-3, but the wheels no longer shifted out to

A model of the ANT-26 in the bomber variant (TB-6).

the side (both wheels on one bogie moved along one track). The undercarriage bogies were protected by shields on the sides and the undercarriage legs were also enclosed in cowlings. The tail wheel was housed in a robust drop shaped fairing. The aircraft later received undercarriage that was similar to the MG with wheels located side by side within the bogies. The entire undercarriage leg and the upper part of the wheel were enclosed in a long cowling which then transferred into a firing point further up (similar design was subsequently used on the TB-7, later redesignated as the Pe-8). The tail wheel cowling was removed since it was considered redundant. Finally, an attempt was made to introduce retractable (more precisely, semi-retractable) undercarriage. The leg folded half way along its length and its lower part rotated through 90°, raising the wheel into a niche of the enormous cowling.

The dimensions and shape of the vertical and horizontal fin were changed. The size of the rudder was either increased or made smaller. In the final variant the middle fin was made taller and the tips of the tailfin were rounded.

The engine mounts were modified in an attempt to make them more aerodynamic. The coolers were modified several times and were withdrawn inside the ducts.

This though does not compare with the variations of armament tried on the enormous bomber. As with the MG to begin with the emphasis was on RM guns, or *Oerlikon* guns and DA machine guns that were later replaced by more modern ShKAS machine guns and ShVAK cannons. In one of the first variants of the design a structure was placed above the fuselage and behind the wing that in terms of its shape was reminiscent of the conning tower on a submarine, this was used to accommodate one of the firing points. A shielded gun mounting was placed was placed in the nose section of the fuselage. At one point there was an intention to place this mounting at the back of the aircraft. There were also firing points on the wings. In contrast to the design for the military MG these were not placed onto the upper wing surface, but they were extended forward on projections from the leading and trailing edges. The mountings on the wings were shielded. There were always two forward firing points across all the variants, while there were either two or four rear firing points. In certain instances, additional machine guns were envisaged that would fire through the windows in the fuselage.

As with all heavy bombers of that time the ANT-26 could be used to carry paratroopers and a variety of military equipment. The lifting capacity enabled the aircraft to almost take whole tanks and armoured vehicles that the Red Army had at that time in service (with a partial reserve of fuel the aircraft could even take a three-turret T-28 tank with a weight of 27.8 tonnes), as well as heavy artillery and given the dimensions of the bomb bay the majority of this could be carried inside the fuselage.

Several models of the ANT-26 were manufactured for testing in the TsAGI wind tunnel and a large glider model was then manufactured with a wingspan of 24m (that is to say around a quarter of the full-size aircraft).

A model of the transport version of the ANT-26, which was later converted into the ANT-28. It is quite likely that the plan was to use power plants buried in the wing, which would drive the propellers using long shafts.

This was tested in flight in May 1935 and was towed behind an R-5. The towing aircraft was flown by pilot V.V. Ryabushkin and the pilot of the glider was N.P. Blagin who has been mentioned several times above. At the AGOS TsAGI work began on manufacturing a prototype example of the aircraft, but in that same year of 1935 this work ceased since it was considered inexpedient to continue with it.

Along with the ANT-26, its military transport variant the ANT-28 that was designed for transport and for deploying heavy military equipment also vanished into oblivion. This aircraft was distinguished by the structure of the middle section of the fuselage and by special equipment for mechanisation of loading and unloading. Where necessary this machine could also be used as a heavy bomber.

9. G-36 Triplane

The G-36 triplane featured in the plan for Grokhovskiy's design bureau in 1933. This was designed to be a very individual design for a triplane. No images of this aircraft have survived but a description indicates that the machine had "wings that connected at an angle". Some fifty paratroopers or an equivalent cargo could be carried in this aircraft. The weight furthermore of this aircraft turned out to be very favourable and it is surprising that the designer considered an engine mount of just three engines producing 150hp each sufficient. The plan was for the aircraft to be fitted with armament consisting of one recoilless gun and three machine guns.

The outline project was handed over to the UVVS for examination by experts Goroshchenko and Pyshnov. They concluded that the design that the triplane design that the aircraft used was not viable aerodynamically. With this design the fuselage would need to be very rigid and heavy, and the longitudinal stability of the aircraft was unsatisfactory. It is possible that there was vibration from the aerodynamic shading of the rear panels.

Bearing in mind the opinions of the experts an order was issued from the UVVS to firstly test a model of the G-36 in the wind tunnel and then manufacture a small glider based on a similar design. It is not known whether this was actually done, but the question of the G-36 triplane was not raised further.

10. Vakhmistrov's Giant Aircraft

V.S. Vakhmistrov, who worked at the NII VVS, is famous for the series of *Zveno* aircraft and at the beginning of the 1930s proposed a design for the *Aviamatka* transport aircraft. Specifically, this project was not developed, but was just proposed as a basic concept and a few design solutions. The *Aviamatka* represented a huge monoplane that was designed around a 'flying wing' layout that was parabolic in plan form. The engines that had tractor propellers were accommodated along its leading edge. The aircraft was designed in three variants: a flying aircraft carrier, a transport aircraft and a tanker. In the first instance the aircraft would take off from the upper surface

A sketch of the giant aircraft designed by V.S. Vakhmistrov, which should have an ability to carry cargoes inside the fuselage on a special platform.

of the wing of the *Aviamatka* as they would from a ship after having been lifted onto the 'flight deck' from the internal hangars using lifts. In the transport variant a ramp was envisaged in which to allow wheeled and tracked vehicles to load and unload. The hatch itself was located on the lower part of the wing, which in a landing configuration was accommodated at an angle.

Interestingly, the undercarriage had what was for that time a traditional layout with skids at the back. On the ground the wing was at a considerable angle, which meant that anything inside had to be tied down.

Vakhmistrov's proposal in view evidently of the low level of development and the enormous costs of manufacturing a prototype example, was never really a serious contender.

11. K-7

A competitor of the TB-4 and the military MG was the K-7 that was manufactured in Kharkov. The design for this aircraft was developed under the leadership of K.A. Kalinin. He described his concept as follows: "In creating new large-scale aircraft these new projects open new avenues for aircraft design, towards using the wing to store cargo. This means that the trend is to favour a 'flying wing' concept, which actually represents an ideal aircraft". The K-7 was the first actual large-scale aircraft that this designer proposed: up until this point he was known for creating a series of single-engine passenger aircraft that had a very traditional layout.

In 1930, Kalinin presented the leadership with a preliminary project for an enormous aircraft that had both a military and a civil purpose at the same time. This was the same slow, cumbersome monoplane with a thick profile wing as the TB-4, but which looked just fantastic. Kalinin introduced a series of unconventional solutions into the design. A wing with a wingspan of 53m that was divided into three sections: a rectangular section in the middle of the wing centre section and two elliptical wing sections. The internal capacity of the wing centre section that had a maximum height of more than two metres could be used to accommodate people and cargo (including bombs). The intention was to fit fuel tanks into the wing sections. The crew cabin protruded forward from the wing itself. Two booms extended rearwards from the wing with a triangular cross-section and they were joined at the back by stabilisers. Closer to the axis of the aircraft above the stabiliser rose the two elliptical shapes of the fins. The four engines were located on the leading edge of the wing centre section, two each to port and starboard

The seven-engine K-7 aircraft designed by K.A. Kalinin during factory testing, September 1933.

The power plants on the port wing of the K-7 aircraft.

of the crew cabin.

The undercarriage, however, was the most unusual feature. Two huge trucks stood under the wing with a wide undercarriage track between them, and three wheels were located on each of these: the forward rotating wheel with a diameter of 1.6 metres and two main wheels with a diameter of two metres, which were fitted with brakes. They were all fitted with low-pressure tyres. The shock absorbers were oil pneumatic. The undercarriage bogies were protected on the outside by an aluminium sheet. This was linked to the wing by legs and struts. In the forward section that was covered by cowlings, forming a well that ran upwards. A door was envisaged in the skin on the port undercarriage: on entering through this door the crew would climb up into the wing by spiral staircase. In the wing between the spars there was a passageway along which crewmembers could walk at full height. In the parked position the K-7 fuselage was horizontal as with any aircraft fitted with a nosewheel. In the event that the tail beams should hit the ground on landing, small wheels were to be fitted under their tips.

If the first K-7 project was envisaged as a wooden construction, then Later on, Kalinin relied on a welded main body made from chrome-nickel steel tubes.

There was a shortage of alloy steel in the country at the time and it had to be imported first and foremost from Sweden. Some 10,000 roubles had to be spent on this enormous aircraft. Production in the USSR was only just being assimilated and the quality of indigenous production was lower. Interestingly Kalinin intended to cover the huge wing almost entirely in canvass.

Calculations demonstrated relatively quickly that the weight of the giant would be very high for the first four engines with which it was planned the aircraft would be fitted. In the design for the K-7 that was dated 1931 to begin with the aircraft was to be fitted with six, and later seven engines. Their layout looked very original. Four engines as before were on the leading edge of the wing, but they were joined by a further two on the forward sections of both undercarriage bogies, and one more engine in the nose of the crew cabin. The undercarriage bogies were sufficiently tall that even with their large diameter (three point two metres) the propellers did not touch the ground.

To begin with, Kalinin was relying on the M-17 engines, but later on, he switched to powerful M-34s. This it seemed enabled him to get rid of the seventh engine, and furthermore he wanted to free up the nose of the passenger cabin – this was important first and foremost for the military variant of the aircraft since it improved visibility and made bomb aiming easier. It was in this same configuration that a full-scale wooden model of the aircraft was produced on which the navigator's cabin can clearly be seen with expanded glazing. The K-7 was incorporated into the plan for prototype aircraft manufacturing for September 1931 fitted with six M-34R or FED engines. In the next variant of the design they were all in a row on the leading edge of the wing, three on the port side and three on the starboard side. The seventh engine however had returned, although this time it was located on the trailing edge of the wing between the tail booms and fitted with a pusher propeller.

The design gradually became more detailed and more carefully developed. To begin with the system envisaged electromechanical amplifiers (boosters) in the control system. At the level of development prevalent at the time however it was unlikely that indigenous industry would be able to obtain them. The designers had to resort to servo tabs (that were actually trim tabs) mounted on the long booms behind the ailerons, as well as on the elevators, and rudders.

At the start, the wing was designed with five spars and a cell was even manufactured for testing, but the designers later resorted to a three-spar structure. The attachment trusses for the undercarriage bogies were either to be enclosed fully in cowlings, or left open, or enclosed partially. The vertical fin was made larger and was made trapezoidal in shape with a rounded upper section. At the same time the designers rejected the idea of joining the fins at the top with a beam and later struts. The tail booms were made slightly longer to accommodate turrets for the military variant. In total the wingspan was to be 58m, and the length of the aircraft was 28m, with a height of 10.8m. Interestingly how did Kalinin imagine the aircraft would be serviced?

In a passenger variant the K-7 was to have carried 128 passengers, and their seats would be arranged in rows along the wing centre section.

In the military variant, the K-7 was a heavy day and night bomber and transport aircraft. The maximum bomb load according to the calculations was 16,600kg and in a normal configuration this was 9,300kg. With 6,000kg of bombs the K-7 would have a range of 2,400m with external fuel tanks fitted. Subsequently these figures were better defined: in a maximum take-off weight of weight of 43tonnes in an overloaded configuration the maximum bomb load was assessed as 14,000kg. The bomb bays were located in the wing. The beams in the bomb racks that were designed to carry bombs with a calibre of up to 250kg were incorporated into the load bearing elements of the wing, which for that time was a very advanced solution. According to the specification it was planned that the aircraft would also carry bombs externally with a calibre of up to 1,000kg.

Defensive armament for the military variant consisted of four 20mm *Oerlikon* guns and eight DA machine guns, which ensured an all-round capability. Two guns were mounted on the turrets and on the ends of the tail booms and in addition there were two in the gondola underneath the crew cabin. The machine guns were to be fitted in front of the glazing in the cabin (this was a pair of DAs) in the front of the tail booms and two each (both forward and aft) in the undercarriage bogies. In this case the enemy would encounter fire from at least three gun emplacements from any direction. The gunners were to reach the firing points on the ends of the tail booms on electrified carts, that moved with on rails with the help of cables. When necessary it was planned to also move ammunition using these carts.

The crew was to consist of 19 people. The aircraft in the same way as a ship was to be controlled by a commander who had been relieved of all other duties. Apart from that two navigators, two pilots, a radio-operator, two technicians, nine gunners, and even a boatswain formed part of the crew (the boatswain was an auxiliary gunner and medic).

The transport variant was orientated as before around the needs of airborne operations. The K-7 could transport 122 paratroopers in flight with full kit or an equivalent cargo. The cargo could be accommodated inside the wing centre section or on an external attachment between the undercarriage bogies. In the latter case

The K-7 crew being briefed before a test flight, 1933.

the aircraft could carry a heavy and cumbersome cargo: guns, vehicles, armoured cars, and light tanks weighing up to 8,400kg. Alternatively, a descent pod could be attached at the same point as was done with the TB-3. It is possible that this figure of 112 men did actually include this pod. The point being that Grokhovskiy's design bureau prepared a special G-45 airborne equipment assembly for the K-7 in 1933. The aircraft was designed to carry up to 80 combatants with this assembly, or up to 11,000kg of cargo, including a tank, vehicles, and artillery.

Taking into account the design that had been proposed on 28 February, new flight performance requirements were drawn up for the aircraft. The initial requirements had to be amended drastically. Now the maximum speed was described as follows: "not less than 190km/hr", the ceiling was limited to 5,000m (an hour was given for the aircraft to reach that altitude), while the range was 2,000km. The bomb load was reduced again down to 12,300kg.

Certain aspects of the design came under criticism. For example, it was thought that the pilots had a poor forward and downward visibility and that they sat in the plane of rotation of the propellers, which must have been causing considerable noise in the cockpit. The members of the commission who had sat in a model of the aircraft in the navigator and bombardier's seat announced that it was cramped and uncomfortable. They proposed fitting the forward guns with pairs of machine guns, and to fit the planned reconnaissance camera, and armour for the pilots. They also wanted the commander to sit in a rotating armoured turret (a 'cabin') that would extend forward, with a DA machine gun.

The majority of these proposals were ignored by the Kharkov specialists but the guns and machine guns on the tail booms changed places. The gun turrets were planned in the forward ends of the booms, as well as pairs of machine guns behind the tailfin.

A prototype example was manufactured that was not fitted with armament but also without any of the passenger equipment fitted. If the TB-4 was listed in the plan for 1934 among the priority designs, then the K-7 was treated as an 'experimental' design and was considered secondary. In one of his letters Ya.I. Alksnis acknowledged that he supported the creation of the K-7 as an alternative to the TB-4, since he was a little apprehensive of the formation of a monopoly on the part of the TsAGI in creating heavy bombers. The competition was designed to boost the activities of both design bureaux.

It took nine months for Kalinin's giant to be manufactured. The final stages were taken up purely with asphalting the runway, which was surrounded by plantation forests, since the huge aircraft could not be accommodated in a single hangar. The empty weight of the aircraft exceeded the calculated weight by three tonnes, it reached 22,900kg, and the full take-of weight of the aircraft was approximately 36tonnes.

When the engines were started for the first time, the aircraft began to vibrate and the tail booms shook. They needed to be strengthened. Struts were again introduced that supported the fins and the tops of them were linked by another plane, which in fact turned the aircraft into a biplane.

On 8 August 1933, pilot M.A. Snegirev completed the first runs in the K-7 around the airfield. The aircraft took to the air on 19 August; it did not take-off but hopped some five metres into the air and again landed on the airfield. This was enough though to convince engineers of the insufficient rigidity of the fin. It would move up and down over a distance of approximately a metre.

On 21 August, the K-7 completed the first flight in the shape of a circuit. M.A. Snegirev sat in the pilot's seat and the co-pilot's seat was occupied by the designer K.A. Kalinin. The Head of the Principal Directorate of the Aviation Industry P.I. Baranov was present on the airfield, as well as the Commander the Ukrainian Military District I.E. Yakir and the well-known pilot M.M. Gromov. After take-off the servo tab failed, followed by the lower elevator, and it then emerged that the cable had broken. The control was flapping freely, causing the aircraft to vibrate. In order to help the pilot Kalinin had to take the control wheel too. They were able to turn the aircraft using their combined efforts. The designer suggested landing in a field, but the K-7 would not have been able to take off from there as it would have to be dismantled and brought back in sections. Snegirev still managed to complete a circuit and land the aircraft. The entire flight took 12mins. The pilot received a vote of thanks from Baranov, while the designer was given – a sentence.

On 13 September an order arrived to convert the prototype aircraft into a military one, and to cease work on the passenger variant. In November the aircraft had to be ferried to Moscow to hand the K-7 over for state testing. Kalinin did not make the planned timescale, neither did he achieve it within the allocated budget.

Testing resumed on 22 September. After each flight some sort of adjustments had to be made. The speed and lifting capabilities of the aircraft that were recorded during testing turned out to be lower than the design figures. The speed was 213km/hr, the practical ceiling 3,650m. The range was assessed at 2,000km. Kalinin tried stubbornly to "squeeze the last drop" out of them to get them to meet the requirements.

The date of the flight over the ground speed course was postponed several times due to bad weather. Finally, on 21 November it took place. There were 20 people on board the giant aircraft. The aircraft passed the first line at full power. The tail booms were prone to buffeting at high engine rpm and this had been noticed prior to this test. According to the testimony of eyewitnesses it sounded as though the spar tubing in the port tail boom had snapped. The ends of this tail boom as they separated pressed down on the elevator control. At a distance of five kilometres from the airfield the K-7 pitched nose down and headed towards the ground at an angle of 40°. When it hit the ground the undercarriage first broke off, and then the fuselage of the aircraft hit the ground nose first. The undercarriage and the forward gondola were crushed under the wing. A fire broke out and the fuel tanks exploded. The entire canvass skin on the wing quickly caught alight. A few minutes later the two escort aircraft landed alongside the wreckage and vehicles approached. Three of the crewmembers were able to get out by themselves and rescuers pulled out a further four survivors but two died on their way to the hospital. In total 15 people were killed including the commander of the aircraft.

After an investigation into the catastrophe a commission under the chairmanship of the Deputy Chief of Staff of the VVS V.K. Lavrov a conclusion was reached that the main reason behind the accident was the fitting of the seventh engine that had not previously been envisaged. This caused significant vortices to form on the tailfin, which was compounded by the effect of the servo tabs that had been fitted to the long tail booms and the insufficient rigidity in the trusses.

The designer set about designing a modified variant of the K-7. The aircraft to begin with was designed for five

M-34FRN engines but these could not be obtained, and Kalinin transferred to six M-34RNs. As an alternative he tried to order a special batch of M-34Rs with an enhanced compression ratio: the intention was to improve the aircraft excellent characteristics. The NII VVS recommended designing a reserve variant with two M-34 engines, working one propeller. The steel ribs in the wing were replaced by those made of a lighter duralumin; the tail booms acquired a square cross-section. Defensive armament was to consist of three cannons and 13 machine guns. The idea of turrets on the undercarriage bogies was rejected, and they were replaced with towers that protruded forward from the wing (more or less the same as the TB-3).

A new variant was designed with six M-34RN engines. According to the calculations, the maximum bomb load for this aircraft was to be 13tonnes. If the engines were replaced with M-34FRNs the maximum payload would rise to 17tonnes. The military were more interested in the K-7 as a transport aircraft that was able to carry between 150–200 combatants. The designer promised that this second aircraft would attain a speed of 300km/hr and a practical ceiling of 7,000m. In May 1934 work began on preparing the components for the second aircraft.

A year later, this aircraft was more or less 60 percent ready. The question of whether the K-7 could be manufactured at Factory No.18 in Voronezh was raised. Following the catastrophe with the *Maksim Gorkiy* however work on giant aircraft was stopped, but on the other hand funds were still being allocated for their continued development. The conclusion was soon reached however that Kalinin's aircraft did not possess any significant advantages in comparison with the more refined MG. That and the attitude to giant bombers had begun to change.

In April 1936, Ya.I. Alksnis wrote to the People's Commissar for Defence K.E. Voroshilov: "Taking into account the serious disposition of our aviation industry, which is not providing us with the combat aircraft we desperately need, I think that spending time and money on the production of the K-7 is inexpedient". Kalinin's Design Bureau was disbanded in the July of that year. The second example of the K-7 that was more than half finished was conserved, and then dismantled.

27

Special Purpose Battalions

The systematic formation of the Soviet airborne forces dates back to a period from 1932 onwards. The Separate Detachment No. 3 increased its numbers and enhanced its available hardware. On 5 January the Revolutionary and Military Council of the USSR discussed the issue "Of the Leningrad Military District's airborne detachment" and a decision was taken to form a further three detachments based on this formation: in the Moscow, Ukrainian, and Belarusian military districts.

The standard compliment of the detachment consisted of 144 men. Some of these detachments it was planned would be made highly mobile and possess significant firepower. This group would be able to move freely over an area covering between 50–100km and would be defended from cavalry, light armoured cars, and ground attack aircraft.

Although in terms of manpower the detachment was on a par approximately with that of an augmented company, in terms of being equipped with heavy weapons it would even surpass a battalion. A decision was taken to compensate for the small numbers of paratroopers that are dictated by the requirement to drop them from an aircraft, by saturating the detachment with automatic weapons and lightened artillery.

Each paratrooper would be given a parachute, a Mauser pistol with four magazines, a grenade (minus the fuse), a flashlight (the specification mentions "a German example",) an individual first aid kit and enough food for a day. This consisted of 400g of water, 300g of wafers, 200g of *Zolotoy yarlyk* chocolate, and cans of tinned meat (400g). All the combatants and commanders, apart from the drivers of the vehicles, motorcyclists, and artillerymen also took one disc magazine with them for a DP machine gun. This was what they would jump out of the aircraft with.

Heavy weapons (including a large number of light machine guns) as well as transport, ammunition, demolition equipment, an entrenchment tool, communication systems, and a further day's provisions would be dropped separately by parachute or where possible, using a landing delivery once the paratroopers had landed and occupied their defensive positions. Everything apart from the vehicles would be stowed in bags and boxes with removable tags that would make it easier to find what was required. After these cargoes had been received and unpacked the detachment would commence their movements behind enemy lines.

The majority of the combatants were to move around on bicycles. The detachment was issued with 96 of them. The detachments would have a 'orderly officer' who in the event of an engagement with the enemy would collect these bicycles and collapse them so that they did not get in the way of the paratroopers.

The intention was to include five three-axle vehicles in the detachment's line up (at that time the Red Army had imported Ford *Timkens,* but no attempt had been made to transport these by air). Three vehicles would be allocated to the artillery. The detachment was equipped with 76mm recoilless guns or the same number of 20mm automatic *Oerlikon* Swiss guns. Alternatively, the latter could be 30mm German RM6 *Rheinmetall*) guns, which were also automatic. This weaponry was capable of opening fire both from vehicle bodies and from the ground for which they were fitted with tripods. These vehicles were fitted with two light machine guns each, that were adapted for firing at both ground and air targets. The ammunition for both amounted to 16 disc magazines. A crew of six were to service the artillery trucks.

The fourth vehicle was considered a 'cargo' one and could carry ammunition and a variety of equipment. In the event that only the DRPs were used the standard was for 160 shells. There were also two light machine guns

Paratroopers slide down the starboard wing of a TB-3 to perform a parachute jump, 1933.

in this vehicle and a driver and a further three soldiers would travel in it. The fifth vehicle was a communication's vehicle. It was fitted with a radio set and would actually carry Popham's flags as well, flare guns with flares, and portable device for sending messages to an aircraft using a grapnel. Part of the entrenching tool was actually carried in this vehicle.

The use of bicycles was considered temporary, and in the future the intention was for them to be replaced with a further two trucks.

Motorcycles and sidecars would carry out reconnaissance and protection of the detachment. With this aim in mind American Harley-Davidson motorcycles were selected and were acquired for the RKKA.

Since specially developed equipment was all but absent the series equipment was selected, taking into account its possibility for the further adaptation for transportation by air. In total in the intention was that the detachment would have 150 men, 18 machine guns, six light guns, five cars, eight motorbikes, and 36 bicycles. The proposal to include T-27 tankettes in the line-up was rejected.

By way of a decree issued by the RVS dated 11 December 1932, the formation of new airborne units began – these were the special airborne battalions. They were larger in terms of the number of personnel than the detachments and possessed a greater array of weapons and equipment. Their equipment though was again series production one and was not specially developed for airborne forces. They differed from the usual rifle battalions in that they were fewer in number, and also in their selection process and the fact that they were better equipped with automatic weapons. "The vast majority" of the commanders had to be members of the All Union Communist Party of Bolsheviks.

The battalion aside from the airborne companies consisted of a headquarters, a sapper platoon (made up of camouflaged and demolition sections) a signals platoon (including a messenger pigeon section) an Air Defence System platoon (with a single anti-aircraft machine gun), a machine-gun platoon, and an artillery battery with 76mm field guns and recoilless guns. In the future there were plans to turn this battery into a division. The battalion had a tank section as well that was equipped with three T-27 tankettes, and an aviation detachment (this had nine aircraft – reconnaissance and liaison machines), as well as a chemical and logistic section. The total compliment was 289 men.

In order to transport the battalion with all its equipment, a squadron of heavy TB-3 bombers was required as

Parachutists climb out of a TB-3 aircraft via the machine gun turrets.

Parachutists jump clear of a TB-3 aircraft.

well as two squadrons of TB-1s (these would consist of 12 aircraft each).

The special purpose battalions became part of the VVS and up to July 1933 they were subordinate to certain air brigades. The first of these appeared in the Leningrad (Krasnogvardeysk), Moscow (Lyubertsy) Belorussian (Bobruysk) and Ukrainian (Kharkov) military districts. The basis of these detachments were the different non-standard airborne detachments. A non-standard platoon consisting of 30 men was initially deployed to Kharkov for example. Sometime later there were eight such battalions, including two in the Far East and one in the Transbaikal region. The 1st Battalion was deployed to Bezymyanka (in the Far East); this was considered a separate detachment and was not subordinate to any of the air brigades. The 2nd served in Khabarovsk (under the 26th Heavy Bomber Brigade), the 3rd was in Spassk (under the 209th Light Bomber Brigade), the 4th was on Domno airfield (near the Ingoda station in the Transbaikal region, under the 101st Mixed Brigade), the 7th Battalion in Bobruysk (under the 453rd Mixed Brigade), and the 8th was in Kharkov (under the 452nd

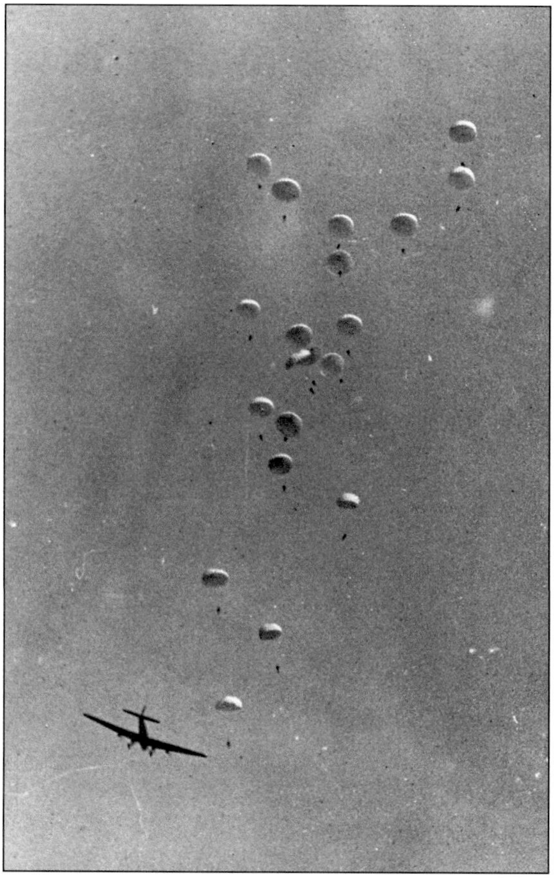

Dropping paratroopers from a TB-3 heavy bomber.

I.S. Bezugliy, Commander of the Battalion of the 3rd Special Purpose Brigade, became Commander of the 201st Airborne Brigade in October 1938. This photo was taken when Bezugliy was Commander of the 9th Airborne Corps at the rank of Lieutenant General.

Mixed Brigade). The numbering of the battalions was changed several times, together with the locations of their deployments. For example, the 3rd was considered a Kharkov battalion to start with but in 1935 was transferred to Kiev. The 2nd Battalion was formed in Bryansk but in summer 1934 it was sent to Khabarovsk, coming under the OKDVA VVS.

They were all orientated towards the enemy's actual potential, and the requirement from Moscow was that between five to ten percent of the personnel needed to have knowledge of a foreign language of the region where these given units were to operate. It was suggested that among the Red Army troops and junior commanders would be a large percentage of extended service soldiers and they were to be lured into the special purpose detachments by the increased salary. A proposal even emerged to pay them double compared to the standard regiments, but the leadership did not back this.

Each battalion was had an aviation detachment attached to it for training, including U-2, R-5 and TB-1 aircraft. To begin with the intention was for each battalion to have two aviation detachments attached to it, a heavy detachment (made up of four TB-1s and TB-3s) and a light detachment (12 R-5s and nine U-2s). Subsequently a single ANT-9 was added to the list but then this was deleted. In some of the documents 12 gliders were also added (evidently with a view to the G-31); but in reality, the pre-war period engineless aircraft did not join front line units.

An enormous amount of time was spent training the future paratroopers. First and foremost, the personnel had to be well trained in how to jump using a parachute. This could be done only one way – by jumping as much as possible. This decision was taken to stimulate this in a material sense. On 15 May 1933, the People's Commissar K.E. Voroshilov issued an order concerning a cash incentive for jumps made by parachute. For the first jump it

Paratrooper after landing.

Paratroopers embarking a TB-3 aircraft. Note their clothing indicating that they are not professional paratroopers.

Paratroopers from the 3rd Special Purpose Air Brigade standing next to a TB-1 heavy bomber before training jumps.

was 25 roubles, and 50 roubles for the fifth, and 100 for the tenth. Fifty roubles each was paid for a jump that was made by night or onto water. A moral incentive was also proposed in that special badges were introduced for parachutists, and commendation tags were issued for various achievements.

In the airborne detachments it was in fact quite easy to make the jumps, since the majority of the weaponry and equipment was to be dropped in cargo bags. Now the thinking was that a paratrooper should land fully armed; furthermore, he should know how to start the fighting whilst still in the air. The combatants began to jump armed with carbines, rifles and even hand grenades. They began to be taught how to fire from under a parachute canopy and how to throw grenades. For any jumps they completed with a pistol or a gas mask they would receive 25 roubles. The same amount was added again for firing in the air or throwing a hand grenade, and if the soldier had hit the target (this was usually in a firing range), they would receive 50 roubles.

The money was not paid in vain: a jump with a machine gun or a gas mask was both more complicated and more dangerous than a normal jump. General I.I. Lisov, who was to become famous subsequently and who was the Deputy Commander of the airborne forces was almost killed in 1934 when he was the commander of a machine-gun platoon. On his first jump from a TB-3 the barrel of his cumbersome DP machine gun caught the wing and he fell into an uncontrollable dive. He was enveloped by his own parachute as it opened up, but the paratrooper did not lose his composure. He cut the material with a knife and through the hole he opened the reserve chute. The reserve chute opened at relatively low level and the impact was very substantial. Lisov however got away with just bruises but the barrel of the gun was bent.

The jumps were undertaken from the same types of aircraft that it was planned would be used for real airborne assaults: The R-5, JuG-1, TB-1, and TB-3, and less frequently the ANT-9 (these aircraft were few in number).

A line-up of paratroopers next to a TB-3 aircraft.

Summer camps of the 3rd Special Purpose Air Brigade in Babolovo (Leningrad region).

A day off at the 3rd Special Purpose Brigade, their guests have arrived from Leningrad and from Detskoye Selo (now Pushkin).

Immediately after the arrival of examples of cargo bags and boxes in the battalions (the first batch arrived at the OKDVA in May 1933) the personnel began to be trained in packing and unpacking various cargoes.

The relatively small numbers of paratroopers were to be compensated by knowledge and skills. They would have a great deal to learn. Any one of the combatants had to know how to fire a revolver, a pistol, a rifle, as well as sub and heavy machine guns, and how to throw grenades. Furthermore, they would have to be familiar with not only indigenous but also foreign weaponry. For example, paratroopers of the OKDVA were shown how to use Japanese rifles, and machine guns and how to fire out of them; they were also taught how to use grenades belonging to a potential enemy. The programme also envisaged artillery unit training. After having captured an enemy gun a paratrooper would be able to load, aim, and fire it.

They were taught combat tactics for deploying small groups of forces against large forces, as well as how to lay an ambush, and to overcome barriers. Plans for sabotage attacks were worked out on an airfield, railway yard, warehouse and oil storage facility. As far as industrial sites were concerned two variants were examined. To capture them and take them out of action or to capture them and defend them until back up forces arrived and prevent the destruction of a power station for example. Skills in street fighting in a built-up area were added to this list, whilst avoiding any collateral damage "as being politically damaging".

They were also taught (as a minimum) how to ride a motorbike, a wheeled and tracked tractor, and somewhere or other they were taught how to drive a steam locomotive. Lectures were conducted on the design of auto-tractor equipment. It was mandatory that everyone be taught the basics of radio: how to send messages using a telephone and a telegraph. The latter entailed training in how to work telegraph keys. The airborne troopers were shown how to lay their own telegraph cable, how to connect to another cable, and how to listen in to a conversation or send a false message. The same was done in relation to the telegraph.

The most basic medical training was also compulsory – use of an individual first aid kit, group medical kits, and how to administer first aid to casualties for dislocations, fractures, and how to fight contagious but not life-threatening illnesses and sanitary measures when 'foraging for food'. One of the combatants could bandage up the other one and tie a tourniquet or make a splint.

The trainees were taught how to camouflage themselves against the terrain, and how to use special cloaks, nets, or just whatever is to hand like tree branches etc. Each of the districts had their own specifics: these centred around the regions in which they would be operational, in the mountains, in the *taiga*, or in the *steppe*.

The combatants and commanders gave lectures on the geography of neighbouring countries, and their customs, and the preferences of their peoples, their population, the structures of foreign armies, their armament, statutes and regulations. The study of foreign languages was a requirement, at least to a minimum level. Ideally

Training paratroopers in how to embark a TB-3 aircraft.

the proportion of combatants who knew the languages of neighbouring countries should have been, according to a variety of documents, from 10 to 20 percent.

Training courses were given in railway equipment, and trainees were shown the design of the track, railway points, a turntable in a depot, as well as semaphores. In some centers, training areas were set up with models of stations. This was needed so that the paratroopers would know how to take out a railway station. With this in mind they were taught how to use a special tool. For example, they would be trained in how to take up railway track. They would discuss how small components could be lost in such a way that it would be impossible to put things back as they were. Particular attention was paid during training to single track sections, which when they were taken out, would deprive the enemy of the possibility of drawing up ammunition, provisions, and reinforcements. Depending on the environment this disruption could be achieved in different ways, taking something out for a few hours, or for a few days, or 'permanently'.

In general, a great deal of attention was paid to sabotage training. One of the main points of the programme was the demolition aspect, from the use of dynamite sticks with bickford cord to specially developed high explosives for destroying bridges and secret radio-operated BEMI mines. The combatants studied different types of explosives and explosive substances, both indigenous and foreign. They were also taught how to use whatever was to hand – shells, mines, or aerial bombs. They had to know however not only what they could use to blow something up, but what they were going to blow up and how. They had to know how to blow up a bridge using the minimal number of explosives? What were they going to take out of action and blow up at a waterworks and how? How were they to take out a telegraph pole in an explosion so that they would not have to cut it down? How would they jam a turntable, leaving all the steam locomotives stranded in an enemy railway depot? How could they take a vehicle out of action quickly, or a steam locomotive, or an aircraft, if they did not have any explosives? The commanders themselves were not up to speed with much of this, everything was new, and some of what was required they invented themselves, and some of it they would borrow from the practices of other branches of the

Свидетельство №

Удостоверяется, что ....

совершил в добровольном порядке 1 парашютных прыжков,

покинув самолет .... на высоте 600 метров.

За выполнение прыжков выдан нагрудный значек № ....

Основание: приказ ВВС РККА № 28 от 7/III 1932 г.

Инспектор парашютного дела
ВВС РККА

м. п.

..... мая 1933 г.

A certificate and badge which were issued to paratroopers after the first parachute jump. It was considered very prestigious at that time to own one of these badges.

Paratroopers put on their parachutes before the training jumps, Detskoye Selo, 1934.

A T-27 tankette platoon from the 3rd Special Purpose Brigade moves across an airfield to a location where they are to be suspended underneath bomber aircraft.

armed forces.

Such an extensive training programme for personnel in the special purpose battalions demonstrated starkly that the battalions considered themselves an elite force of some kind among the armed forces as a whole. The paratroopers became soldiers who were able to fight using any weapon and in any conditions despite the numerical advantage held by the enemy. A more expansive course would probably only be found in the German *SS* training in the pre-war period. In the *SS* troops were trained in the rudiments of how to fly a light aircraft and a glider, and even how to perform simple surgical operations.

The VVS special purpose battalions represented the first, elite level of the Soviet airborne forces, and the best trained and the best equipped. On a second level the intention was to augment that with non-standard battalions, which would form part of standard rifle divisions. Furthermore, the total number of troops in the division did not change. According to the plan it was initially envisaged that 25 such battalions would be formed: in the Moscow Military District there would be three, in the Leningrad Military District there would be two, and in the Ukrainian Military District five, in the Belorussian five, in the North Caucasian there would be one, in the Volga Military District there would be two, in the Central Asian, one, and the Special Far East Red-Banner Army there would be six.

Soldiers and combatants were drafted into these detachments who in the opinion of a medical commission were fit to make parachute jumps. They underwent training in a month long programme and made two to three jumps each. If the commanders in the special purpose battalions were to be rewarded the same way as the rank and file Red Army soldiers, then in the rifle regiments the commanders were given less money for the same number of jumps. They were only taught how to board into aircraft, as well as how to behave in flight and of course how to make the jumps. As a rule, the missions the commanders were given where possible were simplified. For example, they were only allowed to jump out of TB-3 bombers fitted with M-17 engines from one wing, which was the one on which a hand rail was fitted to the fuselage. In the special purpose battalions the jumps were made from either side.

These detachments were on the UVVS register but they were not subordinate to it. The clothing, kit and equipment in the non-standard battalions were issued in accordance with the standards for rifle units. There was no special treatment. If in the VVS special purpose battalions, parachutes were considered standard equipment and were kept in the battalion stores they were only supplied to army battalions for training jumps. It was thought

After a training chemical air raid, the military chemical weapons specialists decontaminate the tankettes and armoured cars using backpack spraying equipment.

that VVS would be given parachutes to borrow for some time, but they would be supplied free of charge. After landing they were collected, stowed and left on a nearby airfield.

The non-standard battalions were treated as a reserve force that would, when necessary, be augmented by VVS special purpose battalions. They could be also be used in large-scale airborne operation usually in the second echelon, after letting the professionals go in first.

Aside from the VVS special purpose battalions, there was also a special airborne troop formation – the Special Purpose Air Brigade. On 11 December 1932 the Revolutionary Military Committee of the USSR took a decision to turn 'Detachment No. 3' into a brigade. In January of the following year, by way of a decree issued by the People's Commissar for Military and Naval Affairs, the 3rd Special Purpose Brigade was formed. This brigade was deployed just outside Leningrad in Detskoye Selo (now Pushkin). This was very much a self-styled brigade that united first one and then two heavy bomber squadrons (the 24th, and 25th, both of which operated the TB-1), the 26th (which was previously the 218th Squadron) that operated R-5 reconnaissance aircraft, an artillery division (armed with recoilless guns) and two, and later three airborne battalions, of those one of them was motorised battalion.

The brigade began to be formed on the basis of 3rd Air Brigade which preceded it, which was the same brigade that participated in all the previous airborne landing exercises. The first commander of the brigade was M.V. Boytsov who had previously commanded 'Detachment No. 3'. In May of 1933 the USSR's first parachute tower was constructed to train soldiers at Detskoye Selo, it was 25m in height.

In September 1933 soldiers from the 3rd Brigade participated in exercises on the range at Krasniye Strugi that were led personally by M.V. Tukhachevskiy. The one specific feature of these exercises was that in place of the assault an artillery raid was initially planned. Thus providing a demonstration of the possibilities of suppressing enemy resistance in order to reduce the losses among parachutists. Two platoons conducted the assault (30 men in total) who were fully armed. During the course of the exercises they worked together with tanks and the infantry who had marched alongside them.

By the end of 1933, the VVS had eight independent airborne battalions and one brigade, with a total compliment of around 8,000 men.

Training jump from a parachute tower.

Paratroopers watching the descent of their comrades, 1934. Note the parachutist's badges on their chests.

The brigade was to have 14 light 'Ford A' cars, 47 'Ford AA' trucks and two AMO-F15s, and two medical vehicles, 16 D-12 armoured cars, three STS tractors, nine motorcycles and sidecars, and 15 without sidecars. The brigade commander Boytsov it was true, had requested more: some 24 D-8 cars, and six D-12s, and a further six automatic RM6 guns to the recoilless guns that the brigade already had.

It was true that the redeployment of equipment by air became possible only in the summer of 1934 by virtue of the 24th Squadron and its TB-3s. On 26 July the Deputy Chief of Staff of the RKKA VVS V.K. Lavrov ordered the brigade be sent the two cargo frames designed to be carried under a TB-3 that Grokhovskiy had, together with an experimental attachment for a three-axle vehicle as well as beams for employing the separation method, as well as "all the remaining equipment for carrying heavy cargoes under a TB-1". This same document envisaged that all twelve of the TB-3s would be fitted with special attachments, with which the 24th Squadron was to be equipped.

Interestingly, the majority of the commanders of this brigade who replaced each other were not pilots but combined arms commanders. Boytsov left the Brigade in January 1934. Following on from him the 3rd Brigade was commanded by V.S. Kokhanskiy (until February 1936), then G.A. Vorozheykin (until September 1936) and then A.S. Zaytsev (until late 1937), P.E. Veshchev (until June 1938), and finally I.S. Bezugliy. Moreover, Bezugliy formally commanded another brigade, the 201st that was created on the basis of the 3rd. From 1935 onwards, the unit began to be known as the 3rd S.M. Kirov Special Purpose Airborne Brigade.

Its equipment was gradually modernised. T-27 tankettes were added to the fleet of military hardware and apart from the recoilless guns the brigade also received the standard 76mm field guns.

In the future, the plan was to form another such brigade, and then merge them both into a special purpose division. These plans however were realised but in a slightly different way.

28

Mass Parachute Activity as a Means of Rolling Out the Airborne Troops

In the first period of the introduction of parachutes into Soviet aviation, only VVS personnel were trained to use them. For aircrew training jumps became mandatory, and the ground forces would only carry them out if they wanted to. Parachute training in these units was carried out by instructors, who were themselves trained in Krasnogvardeysk. In 1931 just 621 jumps were made in the country as a whole. Then it was the turn of the combatants and the commanders of the first airborne units. When in 1932 work began on the formation of non-standard parachute battalions, training in making parachute jumps became accessible for ground forces personnel. Activity in this regard was welcomed and supported on any way possible. As already mentioned above from May 1933 all the military paratroopers began to receive financial rewards and honorary badges. Everyone would jump, from rank and file infantrymen, students at the military technical schools, and students at the academies. Even the legendary commander S.M. Budyonniy made a jump along with students from the Frunze Military Academy. In 1933 the *Air Fleet Herald* magazine already stated: "Parachute jumps will be assimilated fully not just from a production perspective but most importantly in respect of parachute training".

Mass parachute activity in the USSR, however, only took off after it had actually outgrown the confines of

A parachute training jump from a U-2 aircraft. The letters on the fuselage indicate that this aircraft belongs to the Osoaviakhim.

Line-up of parachutists on the Moscow Central Airfield before demonstration jumps, August 1934.

the armed forces. In January 1933, the Central Council of the *Osoaviakhim* took the decision to incorporate parachute activity into the sphere of its activities. From that moment on parachute jumps made by civilians who were not part of the military, which had been known prior to this point, but which formally were a completely partisan affair, came under a strict organisational framework.

From 12 March 1933, sportsmen who were part of *Osoaviakhim* completed demonstration parachute jumps for the first time at the aviation day celebrations in Tushino. Seven individuals took part in this, and furthermore the instructor Ya.D. Moshkovskiy performed a free-fall jump.

Over the course of three years *Osoaviakhim* created three parachute schools and manufactured 400 parachute towers. The Central Aeroclub was formed in Moscow and the Head was that same Moshkovskiy. Some 20,000 people made at least one jump by parachute from an aircraft, and 1,200,000 jumps were made from towers. Only at the Experimental Institute were 2,000 parachutists from among the personnel of the institute itself trained together with the workers from neighbouring factories even though Grokhovskiy had not ordered this himself. Individual and group jumps were practised and also high altitude and free fall jumps as well (in which the opening of the canopy was delayed). Soviet parachutists set a whole series of world records.

Parachute activity began to be seen as a practical military sport. Sporting titles began to be awarded for the various achievements. The first to master the sport of parachuting was L.G. Minov.

On 12 July 1935, parachutists in the Central Aeroclub in Tushino demonstrated their skills to the leaders of the country led by I.V. Stalin. Among others, five ladies jumped from a *Stal-3* passenger aircraft with bouquets of flowers in their hands. After they had landed four of them ran up to Stalin and presented him with flowers as well as the other leaders. The question concerning the whereabouts of the fifth girl gave rise to a story that her bouquet had been damaged on the way down and she was afraid to approach the leaders. Stalin said: "Let her come here anyway!" It turned out however that the girl had landed badly and dislocated her ankle. She was given medical help. This incident however did 'tarnish' somewhat the impression of the celebration.

Mass parachute activity did bear a distinct shade of military training, and no attempt was made to hide this. Furthermore, both men and women were trained. One interesting response was written by the wives of the commanders in one of the air brigades, which was addressed to Ya.I. Alksnis: "We set ourselves the task of ensuring that every woman who was medically fit (in the opinion of the medical committee) would complete a

Parachutists over Tushino airfield in Moscow.

Sports parachutist descending on his parachute.

A billboard calling for the youth to get involved in aviation.

Ya.D. Moshkovskiy, the Head of the Higher Parachute School in Tushino, 1933.

A competition on the precision of the parachute landing, Tushino, 1935.

jump from the parachute tower, and dozens of them became parachutists".

From 1937, *Osoaviakhim* was offering a course in educational and sport parachute training which incorporated a programme of training at different levels. This included training jumps with a rifle and with collapsible skis. These skis incidentally were one of Grokhovskiy's inventions. They were first tried in January 1936. Groups, made up of 11 sport parachutists, would jump out of U-2 airplanes. Ten pairs of skis were dropped down to them using a single cord. The trainees had to get to them, sinking in the snow. A.K. Popov jumped using these collapsible skis and was able to stand up in them immediately after landing. Parachutists would perform a cross-country ski run on a route from Aleksin–Tarusa–Serpukhov–Podolsk–Moscow. They would complete some of this route in gas masks! The collapsible skis passed this test successfully.

Engagement on a mass scale of the population in parachute activity provided the opportunity to define the suitability of individuals to making these jumps, providing them with the basic skills, which meant that the best could be selected from among them. Partially trained personnel began to join the airborne forces, which accelerated the process of bringing them up to the standard to join the formation.

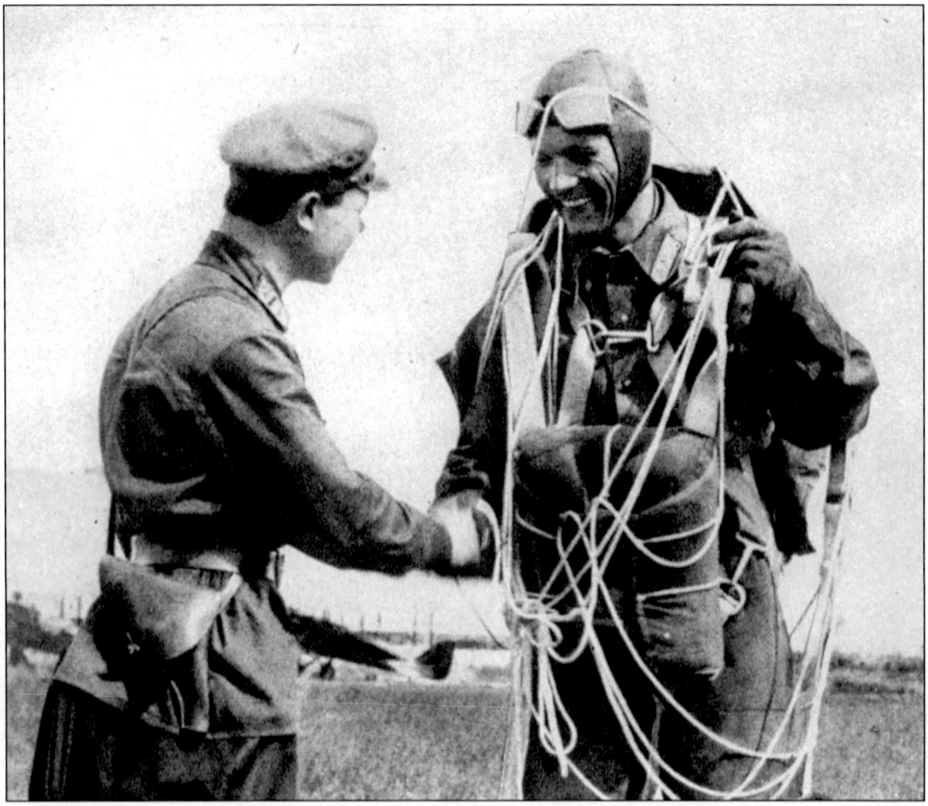

Parachutist instructor N.A. Yevdokimov accepts congratulations for setting a world altitude record in a free fall jump.

The woman parachutist after landing.

Mass parachutists' jumps at an aviation event, 1936. These parachutists jumped off a TB-3 bomber from which the photo was taken.

K.E. Voroshilov and I.V. Stalin with sports parachutists at an aviation event.

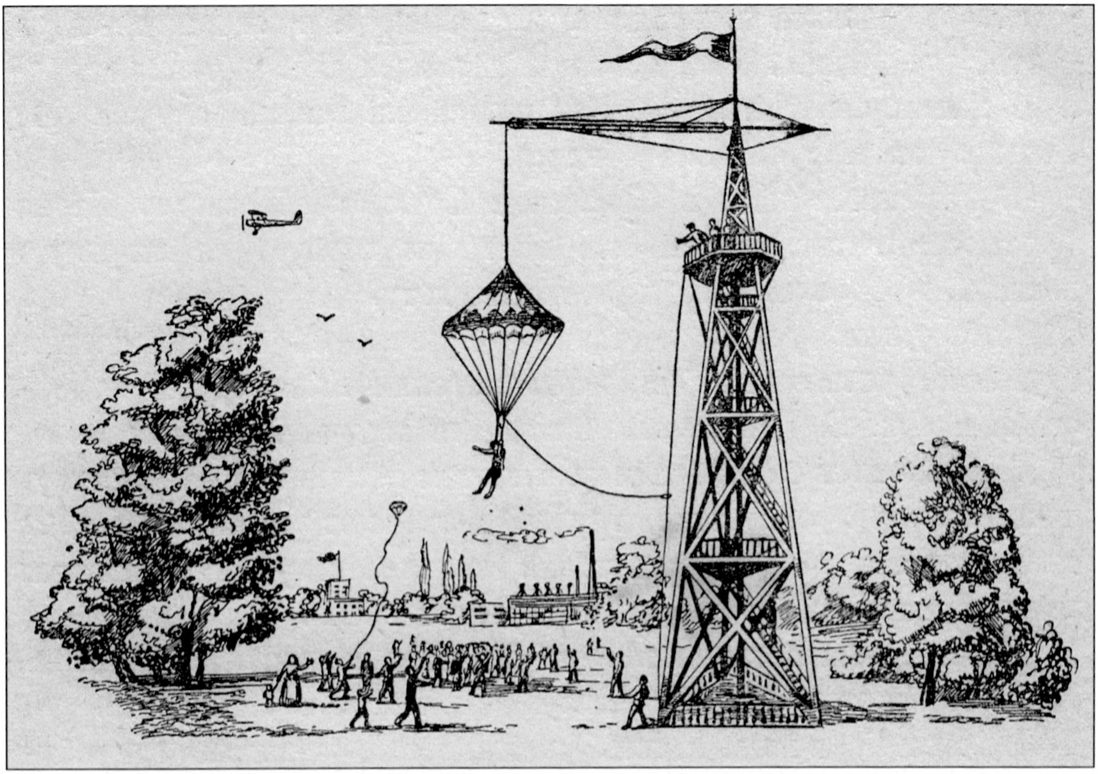

Parachute tower which was mounted as park amusement in Kharkov, 1935. The tower height was 65m.

'Parachutists' – a picture from *Voroshilovskiy Strelok* magazine, 1940.

A girl from Soviet Middle Asia after the first jump from the parachute tower, 1939.

29

War Plans that Never Took Place

The airborne forces had only just been formed and thoughts in the headquarters were already turning to how their potential was to be realised in future wars. Specifically, scenarios were written for assault troops in different theatres of war, scrupulously taking into consideration the number of troops that would be deployed, as well as machine guns and guns, shells and ammunition right down to loaves of bread and tins of canned meat. This was one plan that was developed in October 1932. At that time one of the main potential enemies of the USSR was Poland. It was to be the airborne troops who would capture the bridges over the Vistula River in the direction of the main attack.

Everything was to commence with the dropping of parachutists. Around 100 men with machine guns would land on the west bank, kill the guards holding the bridges and take up defensive positions on the approaches to the crossings and around the sites that were designated for the landing delivery. Then the aircraft would begin to land carrying the main contingent of soldiers and military hardware. In total some 300–350 infantry soldiers would participate in the operation, reinforced by a machine-gun company, as well as two or three platoons of light tanks, the same number of tankettes, a battalion artillery division, a battery of 76mm guns, and communications, Air Defence Systems and sapper detachments. In order to deliver all this some 100–150 TB-3s would be required or one tenth of this number of giant G-1s. The headquarters staff was not concerned by the fact that the former had only just began to enter service with the VVS, while the latter only existed as a blueprint. They had made an estimation of their plans for the future ... They would hold the bridge before the arrival of the rear guard in the shape of the mechanised and tank units of the Red Army, and then either join them or withdraw back behind their own lines.

Plans for conducting an airborne raid in this region were actually considered. This was designed to take out communications and signals, and to destroy trains, and installations behind the lines, as well as talking out enemy stores. The forces were more or less the same than in the previous example but some 50–60 'Fords' and three to four motorcycles had been added to the compliment of military hardware. Correspondingly around fifty additional TB-3s and five or six G-1s would be needed.

Larger scale operations were also planned, in which it was envisaged forces would participate that were capable of destroying an enemy infantry division. In order to land these troops on Polish territory, 45 G-1s would have to make two return flights. Many more aircraft smaller than the G-1s would be needed: the TB-3s would have to be drafted in from all around the country, from the western borders to the Far East.

There is still the question of an airborne sabotage raid in this same Polish territory. The military wanted to blow up an important bridge over the Neman River close to Grodno (this is now in Belarus). According to the plan 180 men would be needed for this, who would be armed with machine guns and demolition equipment and would be dropped by parachute. The departure points within the USSR could be Bryansk or Poltava (the aircraft would need to fly 680–720km) or Kiev or Orsha (400–450km). In the latter case they would carry less fuel but would gain in terms of the payload by approximately 10–15 percent. Different variants were considered for the transport, in terms of a hypothetical G-1 or a group of TB-3s. In the first instance just one aircraft would be needed that would be able to deploy all the paratroopers in the space of ten seconds and the detachment would land in a group with a separation of only 400–500m. Seven of the four engine TB-3s would be required but the deployment would unavoidably take time and the paratroopers would be more spread out. Once they had landed the paratroopers would take out the Polish guard and blow up the bridge.

Different variants for the destruction of a whole series of military enterprises between Warsaw and Krakow were considered. Furthermore, the intention was for the troops to act as raiding assault troops moving from one factory to another, as well as acting like separate small groups of saboteurs. One specific feature in this case was the need to deploy a large quantity of explosive materials. The possibility of obtaining some explosive materials locally as well as destroying a target without using dynamite or TNT was considered. For instance, a steam boiler could be blown up, by taking the safety valves out of action. All the landing sites for this assault were accessible from the same airfields that were considered for the assault near Grodno.

The plans for destroying Finnish coastal batteries on the Baltic Sea coast are interesting. This would start with an aircraft attack that was designed to force enemy soldiers to take cover. Then a parachute assault would land on top of them. Then one of two variants could be realised. In the first scenario the paratroopers were to keep the artillerymen in their shelters while ships pounded the silent batteries. The question of what would happen to the paratroopers during the barrage was conveniently ignored. In the second scenario demolition experts would arrive along with the paratroopers, destroying both the weaponry, and taking out their crews in their shelters. If one thinks about it clear parallels can be drawn with the organisation of a very successful German assault on Fort Eben-Emael in Belgium in May 1940.

In November 1933, at the OKDVA headquarters, a plan for an operation to capture the Chinese Eastern Railway and all the territory along it, as well as to the north of it, was developed. They were to operate in conjunction with mechanised infantry, tanks, armoured vehicles, and cavalry, which would advance across the crossings over the Greater Khingan range (as was achieved in August 1945).

The first wave of the assault was to drop the parachutists, and furthermore the intention was to use ventral pods and 'personnel cages' that would be carried by TB-1s. They were supported by teams that would arrive in the aviabuses. There were also plans to drop some of the armament and ammunition by parachute as well as the 76mm mountain guns, recoilless guns, motorcycles, 'Ford A' cars, and T-27 tankettes.

The first task for the paratroopers would be to capture the airfield. They would need to take enemy aircraft out of action on this airfield, after augmenting the VVS efforts to achieve air superiority. Apart from that there was a plan to deploy Soviet fighters and light bombers. These aircraft were to provide cover for the paratroopers from the air and support their operations. The fighters in addition would provide cover for the heavy bombers when they were outside of the range of fighters flying from inside Soviet territory. Lastly the captured airfields were the place where the troops were to land.

The second task would be to cut off the railway line from Tsitsicar–Khaylar cutting the enemy off from supply routes and depriving them of the capability to transport reinforcements and quickly manoeuvre their forces.

In the first echelon, the intention was to drop 6,000 men along with military hardware. A group of 1,500 paratroopers were to be dropped near to Khingan, who would take out the main junction stations on the Chinese Eastern Railway. The largest assault was planned for the station at Ikeshi where 3,500 combatants and commanders would be dropped. This group was tasked with penetrating behind enemy lines. The latter detachment made up of 1,000 paratroopers would land at Yalu station, in order to stop movement along the railway line.

The second echelon was to capture the approaches to Khingan, making it easier for the forces to advance away from the Soviet border. This echelon was deployed in one location, close to Zhalantun station and consisted of some 4,000 troops.

In order to achieve all this, the plan was to mobilise three heavy bomber brigades (around 150 aircraft) and four light bomber brigades (around 350 aircraft). An airborne corps was to be deployed that was made up of three brigades. This corps did not actually exist. The two special purpose battalions that did exist at this point in Khabarovsk and Primorskoye, it was proposed, would be made into dedicated brigades and a third new brigade would actually be formed. In order to hide that fact that they were airborne units the intention was to call them guard units, and they would serve as guards on the airfields.

All these plans seem like fantasy to us now in today's fashionable genre of 'revisionist history'. The headquarters staff wanted to deploy further units that did not exist, using non-existent hardware. There was a method to this however, in trying to develop ways in which the airborne troops could be deployed the theorists gradually got a feel for what they needed to train their soldiers and commanders to do, what materiel they still lacked, and so on.

30

Manoeuvres by the Belorussian, Ukrainian and Leningrad Military Districts, 1934

At the beginning of autumn 1934 in Belorussia, large-scale exercises took place in which paratroopers took part. According to the scenario there had been a 'heightening of tensions' with neighbouring countries, during which the 'red' forces had concentrated on the border and had crossed it. They were countered by the 'blue' forces who were carrying out a powerful aerial strike, followed by motorised and mechanised and tank units would be deployed jointly along with the airborne paratroopers.

For the latter a temporary airborne detachment was formed. The backbone of this airborne detachment was the 7th Special Purpose Battalion led by A.F. Levashov, which would be augmented by combatants and commanders from the detachments of non-standard rifle divisions. The latter underwent a month's training course, completing three parachute jumps each. In total 603 men were gathered together with 101 DP light machine guns, 300 rifles, 200 revolvers, and 300 grenades. The detachment received six 6PK radio sets. During the course of these exercises two airborne assaults took place. In the first instance the parachutists were given the task of cutting off the road from Pukhovichi to Minsk and capture a crossing across the Svisloch River near the village of Sitniki. This was designed to disrupt the organised withdrawal of a notional enemy's forces. Preliminarily aircraft would strike the

Paratroopers embarking an aircraft, 1934.

The commanders of the 28th Squadron brief the crews of the TB-3 bombers before the mission.

'red' cavalry. On the morning of 7 September, five TB-3s from the 9th Air Brigade led by Squadron Commander Utkin took off from Bobruysk. They were carrying 129 paratroopers from the 7th Special Purpose Battalion. The drop was made in the area around Skorbovka from an altitude of 400m on a single approach. The troops jumped out of the side of the fuselage of the aircraft and descended (this took approximately three minutes), as well as jumping from hatches in the upper turrets. The combatants had rifles and grenades with them while the commanders had revolvers. Ten of the machine-gunners jumped with their DPs, for which they were issued with two disc magazines each.

The landing was successful, and only one of the paratroopers was slightly injured. The machine-gunners who had jumped along with their weapons occupied their positions immediately. Five R-5 biplanes dropped parachute bags down to the paratroopers containing additional weapons (including 14 DP machine guns) and their ammunition. During the course of this operation the parachutists cooperated with tank battalions that were advancing from the 'front line'. The TB-3s dropped eight tonnes of fuel in PDBB-100 tanks for the BT-2 tank company.

The airborne forces that were larger in number were deployed two days later, on 9 September. They were issued with an order to cut off the railway line that supported the encirclement of the 'enemy'. The operation was planned for 8 September but due to bad weather it was postponed for 24hrs. Some 600 men embarked on 31 (another document puts this figure at 33) TB-3s from the 9th Air Brigade. The personnel of the 7th Special Purpose Battalion embarked on the aircraft with 30 men being accommodated in each one, while the soldiers and commanders from the non-standard battalions who had undergone some considerable training embarked with 25 men in each aircraft, while for the rest the figure was 20. It took 45mins for all the men to embark. The bomber crews demonstrated an excellent level of training: five minutes later all the aircraft had started their engines.

Paratroopers are dropped during exercises in Belorussia, September 1934. Three TB-1 bombers in a formation can be seen.

A landing delivery of the 3rd Special Purpose Brigade on Volosovo airfield, winter 1934. Note the vehicles suspended under one of the TB-3s.

In flight the four-engine giants were accompanied by six R-6 'cruisers' and two detachments of I-7 fighters (approximately 20 aircraft).

The parachutists were dropped close to the village of Lyaskovka, some 12–15km north-east of Minsk. Some of the crews of the TB-3s made a mistake and the assault troops were split into two groups that were dropped approximately two kilometres from one another. The use of inexperienced aircrew led to losses. The parachute did not open for one of the paratroopers, while another's strap became caught up in the canopy and he fell backwards onto a stump, both were killed. Two of the men broke their legs as they hit the ground and six sustained bruises and sprains. Red Army soldier Morozov's canopy opened very early and it caught on the stabiliser, but he survived.

Dozens of R-5s from the 5th Light Bomber Squadron dropped weaponry and ammunition down to the troops. Consequently, they received all of the 101 DP machine guns that the airborne troops had. The parachutists advanced to their given positions, after having 'crossed' the railway line.

At that same time similar exercises were underway in Ukraine. The theme was the same as in Belorussia. The 8th Special Purpose Battalion in this location however were acting for the 'reds'. The landing was made by 12 TB-3s. The scales of the actions by the paratroopers were smaller than in Belorussia but the assault was preceded by a chemical strike that was made by R-5s from the 206th Light Bomber Squadron. Correspondingly the combatants were issued with gas masks.

In the winter of 1934, the 3rd Special Purpose Brigade carried out an airborne assault on Volosovo airfield. Moreover, the combatants landed with their guns, heavy machine guns and recoilless guns as well as two vehicles, using attachments that had been provided by Grokhovskiy.

31

Air Mobile Approach

Following on immediately from the descent of paratroopers at Klochkovo farmstead, estimates began to be made at headquarters concerning how to employ such a promising innovation. Reviewing different assault plans, it was decided attacks would not be limited to the deployment of highly-trained special airborne detachments. It was proposed that second and third waves be incorporated into these plans. These would be deployed using a landed assault and would usually comprise of infantry troops. They could of course only carry with them what the aircraft were capable of carrying. The majority of the artillery, and the huge columns of vehicles naturally had to be left behind their own lines.

The proposal to form special units that could be loaded onto an aircraft with all their equipment was a further development of this concept.

At the end of 1930, a project came about that was designed to create a mechanised air mobile division, which would be a pre-emptive strike formation of sorts, capable of advancing forwards decisively after having crossed the front line. Each of its battalions included a platoon each that was made up of 14 men. This though was not the principal force since the whole division was structured this way to enable it to be deployed by air, that is to say in modern parlance to be air mobile. There were no plans to drop the rest of the unit's compliment by parachute, they were to be deployed in a landing delivery on landing sites surrounded by paratroopers. Furthermore, the standard envisaged that the detachments would be well equipped with ground-based transport on a mechanised infantry level. The division was to have two brigades in each of these that would be equipped with 114 different vehicles, and 72 motorcycles. Fire power was provided by a saturation of automatic weapons (principally DP light machine guns) or by artillery (both standard and recoilless guns). The strike capabilities of the division were expanded by incorporating T-27 tankette companies into its line-up, which comprised 18 vehicles.

At that time, however, the deployment of this division was an almost impossible task for the RKKA VVS. According to the calculations in order to carry just a single brigade with all of its equipment 168 TB-1s, or 132 TB-1s and 68 JuG-1s would be required. It was planned to have two of these brigades in a division. There were however just three-dozen of the three-engine Junkers aircraft in the country at the time and less than a hundred TB-1s.

Soviet aviation gradually grew and new aircraft entered service. From 1932, the four-engine TB-3 bombers entered the fleet, immediately expanding the capabilities for transporting troops by air.

The concept of a joint operation with airborne troops and standard infantry who would be transported in aircraft became fashionable once again. The 'parachute' advanced guard would capture the airfield on which the transport aircraft would land that would be carrying the Red Army troops. Furthermore, the transportation of a rifle battalion (with a strength of 350 men, with rifles and machine guns) 12 TB-3s would be required and for a mechanised battalion using pickups some 25–30 would be needed (for an equivalent number of troops).

This plan was later tested successfully during different exercises. Furthermore, these exercises were carried out by personnel from standard rifle regiments that used their standard armament. Anything that was deemed 'unnecessary' was just left behind. Special units designed for a rapid deployment by air were beginning to be formed.

The idea of using groups of paratrooper aviators, who were a group of self-styled 'reluctant paratroopers' never came to fruition either. In April 1933, the Head of the Airborne Service E.I. Tatarchenko suggested training all the crews as a group of saboteur paratroopers. Up until this point it was thought that once the pilots were behind enemy lines, they should try by all means to get back to the front line, cross it and once again return to their own lines. Naturally a pilot or navigator's training at that time did not cost as much as nowadays. Nevertheless, they were considered valuable specialists who were much more valuable than a rank and file infantry soldier. Tatarchenko decided that by going through special training the crews could inflict serious damage on the enemy by remaining on that side of the front line. In order to enhance the fire power of the group some of the aircraft weaponry it was proposed should be made easily removable and should be adapted so that it can be dropped by parachute (in the event that the aircraft was hit and could not land). Tatarchenko, however, did not succeed in convincing the UVVS of the merits of this. They knew very well the value of experienced aircrew. Apart from that modifying an aircraft armament was very expensive and complex.

32

Military Exercises that Stunned the World

From 12–17 September 1935 large-scale Red Army exercises took place just outside Kiev in which more than 65,000 men took part, as well as more than 1,000 tanks, around 600 aircraft, and 300 artillery guns. The 'blues' fought against the 'reds'. The former was led by I.N. Dubovoy (who had commanded the forces of the Kharkov Military District) and the latter was commanded by his Deputy S.A. Turovskiy. General management of the manoeuvres was in the hands of the Commander of the Kiev Military District I.E. Yakir.

The 'blues' attacked Kiev. With aviation support. they broke through the defences of the 'reds', pushing their tanks forward, followed by their cavalry. The cavalry themselves were attacked by ground attack aircraft from the 256th Air Brigade. The raid turned out to be very successful, but the advance of enemy forces towards the city continued.

On 14 September, the 'blues' landed their airborne troops behind the 'reds' lines. For this to happen back in the July–August a temporary air division was formed that was led by Kontsevich. This division comprised a separate parachute regiment (composite) under the Kiev Military District (commanded by P.E. Veshchev) and two standard rifle regiments, the 43rd from the 15th Division, and the 90th from the 30th Division.

In order to participate in manoeuvres, TB-3s from the 3rd Special Purpose Brigade made a six-hour flight from Detskoye Selo to Kirovograd. Due to bad weather, they flew at low level and took some of the tops of the fir trees with them in the undercarriage. On landing, several covers were found to have been damaged on the aircraft, but they were swiftly brought back to flying condition.

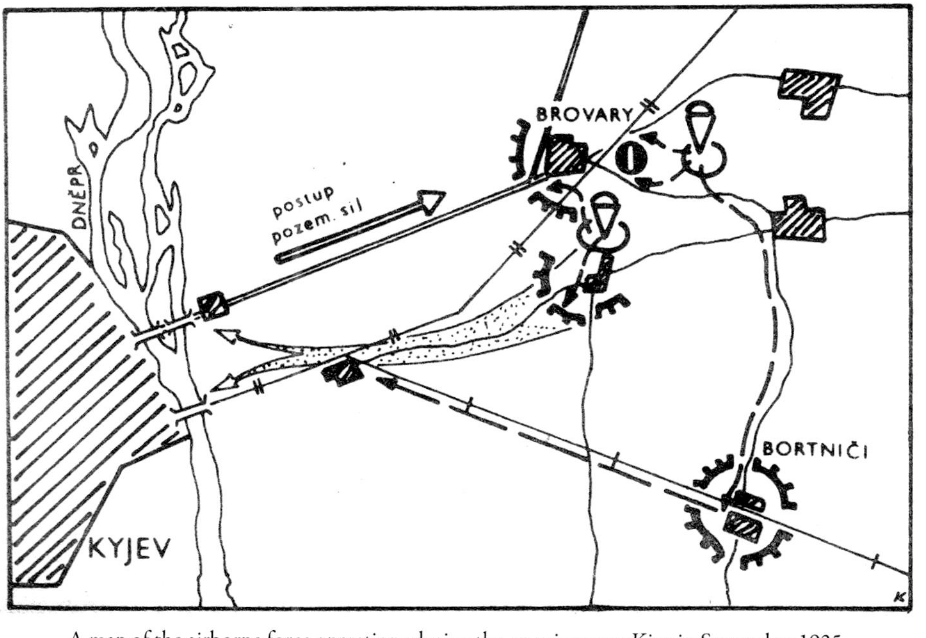

A map of the airborne force operations during the exercises near Kiev in September 1935.

Paratroopers climb aboard a TB-3 bomber.

The assault drop was organised on Brovary airfield where according to the scenario for the exercises some of the aircraft belonging to the 'reds' were based. It was located on the other (in relation to Kiev) bank of the river. To begin with, it was R-5 biplanes that hit this airfield from the 206th Air Brigade, then came the TB-3 bombers along with their paratroopers. Furthermore, aircraft from the 15th and 18th Heavy Bomber Brigades, as well as the 3rd Special Purpose Brigade took part, some 60 aircraft in total. They were escorted en route by 22 R-6 aircraft from the 35th Cruiser Squadron, which were later joined by I-5 fighters from the 34th and 35th Squadrons. Paratroopers from the Motorised and Mechanised Battalion of the 3rd Brigade and the composite regiment led by Indzer, in total 1,180 men. They were armed with carbines and light machine guns. The advanced guard jumped using the free fall method, in order to accelerate the jump and enhance the element of surprise. The paratroopers captured the airfield and took up defensive positions around it.

Then came the landing delivery. The aircraft landed in Brovary and offloaded 1,765 men from the 43rd and 90th Regiments, 29 heavy machine guns, two artillery batteries, one light tank and several other standard and armoured vehicles. The entire compliment of military hardware belonged to the 3rd Special Purpose Brigade and was delivered by these same aircraft, fitted with the corresponding attachments. The entire assault took one hour and fifty minutes.

The paratroopers were ordered to slow the advance of the reserves of the 'reds' and capture river crossings across the Dniepr. Two battalions of the 90th Regiment were, along with two battalions of the paratroopers to attack along the road from Chernigov to Kiev in the direction of one bridge. The whole of the 43rd Regiment, the battalion of paratroopers and the motorised and mechanised regiment advanced via Darnitsa to another bridge.

Could the 'reds' actually beat the 'blues'? The advance of the 'enemy' was halted, and powerful blows had been inflicted on the flanks of the 'reds', and the advancing troops had been 'routed'.

The exercises ended at this point, leaving everyone who had participated in them with a powerful impression. The whole of the Soviet military leadership observed these manoeuvres: The People's Commissar for Defence

A.O. Indzer, Commander of the Composite Parachute Regiment.

TB-3 aircraft with paratroopers on board flying to a drop zone, September 1935.

Paratroopers prepare to leave the aircraft.

K.E. Voroshilov, his Deputy M.N. Tukhachevskiy, the Chief of Staff A.E. Yegorov, the Head of the Political Directorate Ya.B. Gamarnik, and S.M. Budyonniy. Also present was P.I. Grokhovskiy who observed how his inventions were used. Military attaches who had been accredited in Moscow were also invited. Among them was the German Colonel K. Student, who was a graduate of the Lipetsk Flying School. He went on to become Commander of the airborne forces in Germany. Military delegations from Italy, France, and Czechoslovakia also observed the exercises.

They saw for themselves the wonderful achievements of contemporary military science and technology. Heavy bombers flew through the air in a tight formation. In essence nobody else in the world had that many four-engine heavy bombers at that time. Only France had a couple of squadrons, and Japan had five similar aircraft.

The armadas of Soviet tanks attacked the 'enemy' at high speed, jumping over the tank traps. This was also discussed in the USA at the time, along with the issue of whether they actually needed tanks at all. The Germans had only just begun to manufacture their *Panzerwaffe*. The English only had a few of these kinds of tanks, and France a little more, but not as many as the Red Army was able to put on display.

The airborne troops really were something that was not seen in the West. No other country in the world had any airborne troops at that time. It was after the Kiev exercises that France and Germany began to take the creation of airborne forces seriously. In Britain and the USA they first appeared In fact during the Second World War.

Overall, the show was a triumph. This really was a show! All the actions of the participants in the show were choreographed at an earlier stage: which route to use, where to stop, where to fire, with what and in which direction. The roads were repaired in advance and even the fields were levelled out that the tanks were to attack. Many of the units were composite units and the best military hardware was selected for them to use as well as the best trained personnel. All the orders, instructions, and maps were prepared in advance and were checked by those higher up the chain. Any deviations from the scenario were forbidden in the strictest sense. The commanders were not allowed to use their initiative at all. The intermediaries would slow the advance of those moving too fast and would order slower units to speed up.

The assault landed on a well-equipped, large and flat airfield in Brovary that was capable of accepting a large quantity of heavy aircraft. Three tier stands were placed alongside the airfield from where the high-ranking bosses would watch the proceedings together with foreign guests, worker's delegations, journalists, and cinematographers. A commentator provided a commentary of the proceedings using a network of megaphones. The only tank was offloaded in front of the stands. The course of the entire set of manoeuvres was recorded on film, and the movie *The Battle for Kiev* was put together from the long rolls of film that were recorded, and some of the images can be seen in *Aerograd* movie by Dovzhenko.

Dropping paratroopers from TB-3 aircraft.

The reason this approach was used is still a point of debate today. Either it was because of a typical Russian love of putting on a show, or it was a large-scale deception for potential allies and enemies along the lines of the famous Chinese General Sun Tszu principle: "If you can't do something pretend that you can". The allies were shown military might that had not been seen before, while enemies were alarmed and put on their guard.

My opinion is that it was a case of one and the other. Each of the commanders wanted to show themselves in the best light. If they were asked to act strictly in accordance with the scenario then they would cozy up to it. This happened at every level. Later on, when the 'enemies of the people' were being rooted out someone or other would even stand accused of 'whitewashing' the Kiev manoeuvres.

The exercises tried to create a specific impression on the part of foreign guests. It is no secret that the individuals from among the commanders of the RKKA who were sent to observe them were ordered to comment on the events using an approved language, to convey the characteristics of the military hardware (as a rule to play them up) and to completely pull the wool over the eyes of the foreigners.

In this respect, the commanders of the Red Army got their way. Reports of the Kiev exercises and reports written by the foreign attaches and in the western press were impressive. At the end of the day there were armadas of tanks and squadrons of heavy bombers present at the exercises! Maybe in the day to day sense their technical condition was not so good, and the actual crews were not so well trained and in the 'ivory towers' the losses would not be so significant, but nobody else anywhere in the world had anything like it.

Thus the significance of the Kiev manoeuvres and the world's first mass airborne assault cannot in any way be overstated.

In the shadow of this huge event there remained another airborne assault, one which had come about a little earlier in July 1935. During exercises by the Leningrad Military District the 3rd Special Purpose Brigade's detachment landed by parachute wearing chemical protection suits (at the time they were referred to as 'anti-mustard gas suits') and gas masks. Preparations for chemical warfare were taken seriously in the RKKA and these exercises became the next step in this direction.

Paratroopers land at Brovary airfield.

Paratroopers running to the assembly point after landing.

Offloading the equipment at Brovary airfield.

Offloading vehicles that have been delivered using a TB-3.

Paratroopers drive away on pickups from the landing site.

Offloading GAZ-A cars.

Two pickups of not-lightened design next to a TB-3 aircraft.

A TB-3 aircraft with suspended T-37A amphibious tank taxies around Brovary airfield.

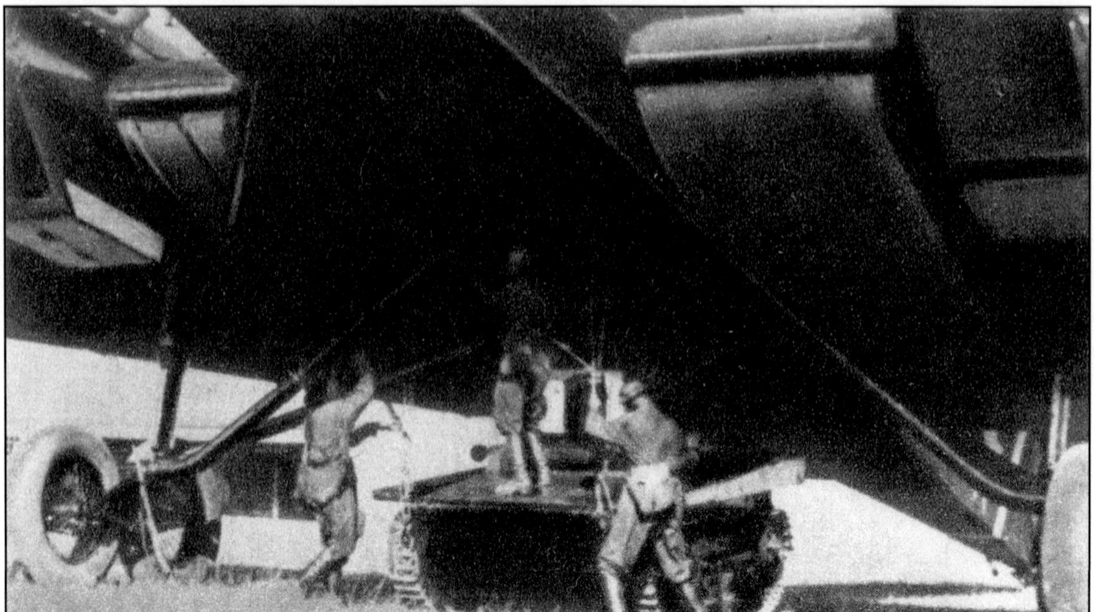

Paratroopers disconnect a T-37A amphibious tank from its attachment.

33

Reorganisation of the Airborne Forces

By the mid-1930s, the airborne forces had transformed into a realistic combat force. The Field statute dated 1936 stated: "The airborne parachute forces are an efficient means of disorganisation in the direction and operation of forces behind enemy lines. In conjunction with troops advancing from the front line, airborne parachute forces can have a decisive effect in a full-scale routing of the enemy in a given direction".

Back in November 1935, evidently under the influence of the successful manoeuvres near Kiev, I.S. Bezugliy proposed forming up to four new brigades from two, and the 3rd Brigade would be transformed into a corps (made up of two brigades). The strength of the brigade it was proposed would be set at 2,228 men. This was to form a parachute battalion and a motorised-bicycle battalion (this was how the bicycle forces were known back then) both made up of four companies. It was proposed that the motorised-bicycle battalion would include vehicles fitted with 37mm anti-tank guns. These detachments would be dropped by parachute. The Motorised and Mechanised Battalions were to be deployed in a landing delivery; both of these had two companies each. The first incorporated an armoured company made up of three T-37A tanks or D-8 armoured cars. The second consisted of a company of D-8 armoured cars, and two tank companies.

The Brigade was to have a fully-fledged reconnaissance squadron operating R-5 aircraft (made up of 31 machines) and squadrons of assault gliders (15 of them) attached to it.

To ensure the future growth of the combat capability of the airborne forces in September 1936 they were reorganised, but not in exactly the same way as Bezugliy had proposed. In the European part of the country in addition to the 3rd Special Purpose Brigade that was already in existence a further two were formed, in the Kiev and Belorussian Military Districts. The backbone of this were the VVS special purpose battalions and the non-standard battalions in the rifle divisions.

In Borovskiy (located in Belorussia) the 47th Special Purpose Brigade was formed and was led by Brigade Commander F.F. Karmalyuk, and in Borispol near Kiev the 13th Special Purpose Brigade was formed, which was commanded by Colonel A.O. Indzer.

The airborne brigades had a standard peacetime strength of 1,500 men. The brigades comprised a headquarters, a communications company, and three battalions with 381 men in each. Batteries of 45mm anti-tank guns (19 weapons) were envisaged as well as 82mm mortars (20 pieces). The line-up comprised ten light tanks and 17 vehicles, and the intention was to transport these by air. In total the brigade had 100 vehicles, 31 motorbikes, and two ChTZ tracked tractors. Not forgetting a musical platoon. In wartime the strength of the personnel in the brigade was to exceed 1,800 men, and around 20 light machine guns were attached to it, as well as another mortar battery (consisting of seven mortars).

According to other data, a brigade would be issued with 16 T-37A tanks and six D-8 armoured cars, 32 vehicles and six motorcycles, six bicycles and 18 mortars. The armoured hardware began to enter service with the new brigades from the end of 1936. A short time later a motorised and mechanised brigade was included in the line-up consisting of two companies with a total strength of 189 men.

A transport squadron was attached to each brigade (made up of 12 TB-3s) and a reconnaissance detachment (which operated ten R-5 aircraft). However, 30 TB-3s were required just to carry the artillery and the brigade's tanks.

Paratroopers in formation: some of them are armed with DP machine guns.

M.I. Denisenko, Commander of the 1st Airborne Regiment, later commanded the 202nd Airborne Brigade.

I.I. Zatevakhin, Commander of the 2nd Airborne Regiment, later commanded the 212th Airborne Brigade.

In the Far East, airborne regiments of the OKDVA were being formed. There were three units: the 1st (Khabarovsk) under the command of M.I. Denisenko, the 2nd (Zavitaya) Brigade led by I.I. Zatevakhina and the 5th (Spassk) Regiment led by N.E. Tarasov. As of 1935 the regiment had 1,070 Red Army soldiers serving in it, as well as 313 junior commanders, and 139 commanders. A heavy squadron (made up of 12 TB-1s) and a reconnaissance detachment made up of ten R-5 biplanes were also attached to the regiment.

Thus the formation of the 5th Airborne Regiment in June 1936 consisted of the 3rd Special Purpose Battalion, as well as the non-standard airborne regiments in the 21st and 26th Rifle Divisions and reinforcements that were sent from the central districts. The entire personnel underwent a strict selection process. The regiment was based in Spassk and was subordinate to the 51st Air Brigade. Based on the standard it was to consist of 67 vehicles, 1,172 'automatic guns', 120 machine guns, 20 PTRK anti-tank guns, and 14 mortars.

The 1st Regiment was deployed on the basis of the 2nd Special Purpose Battalion, which had been redeployed

Paratroopers embarking a TB-3 bomber.

from Bryansk to the Far East July 1934. According to one of the documents the first commander of the 1st Regiment was listed as one Latyshev (the initials were not shown), Denisenko replaced him in August 1937.

To begin with, the airborne troops relied upon a motorised and mechanised troop ration (that was augmented) but in 1936 they were transferred to the standard Red Army allowance. They were dressed in normal Red Army soldier's uniforms but in place of high boots they were given boots with flaps. In winter they wore warm felt boots. Judging by the photographs the boot top collars were rolled down, possibly, while the rubber was being inserted into them. The parachutists jumped wearing flying suits and helmets.

Training for parachutists continued in the rifle divisions. For example, some 1,322 men were trained in the Transcaucasus Military District in 1936. In the Moscow Military District in that same year three non-standard airborne regiments were formed: in Rostov, Gorokhovets, and Voronezh. The strength of each was set at 1,660 combatants and commanders.

In August 1936, during the course of exercises held by the Transcaucasus Military District, an attempt was made to land airborne forces in the mountains. According to the plan for these manoeuvres the 'blues' were defending a mountain pass. The paratroopers landed on a plateau near the village of Korbouli at an altitude of 900m and struck behind the defending force's lines. Foreign observers were invited to the exercises.

Again, the paratrooper unit was non-standard, it was made up of volunteers from different units. The parachutes were taken from the district's Air Force, *Osoaviakhim*, and GVF local subdivisions. The district did not actually have its own transport aircraft. They approached a TB-3 squadron but were turned down. They decided to make the jump using R-5s and U-2s. Cargo it was envisaged would be dropped to the paratroopers using an R-6 with four packs being dropped per aircraft. The strength of the airborne unit according to the scenario for the exercises exceeded that of the detachment that was to hand, the remainder was made up by dummies, four of which were carried under an R-5.

However, owing to a strong wind it was forbidden for any of the personnel to make the jump, and only an imitation of the assault actually took place. A group of R-5s approached just under the clouds, at an altitude of 200–250m and dropped the dummies by parachute. The assault, it was acknowledged, had been completed, as a result the 'blues' conceded the mountain pass and retreated.

During the exercises in July 1936, forces from the Moscow Military District in the area around Viyezd dropped some 2,000 parachutists. For this to happen three heavy bomber regiments were drafted in, the 4th, 11th, and 23rd, in total this amounted to 111 TB-3s. The TB-3RN bombers were used, which were in no way modified for paratroop operations. This led to the paratroopers becoming very scattered because they had less hatches to jump through than on the older aircraft fitted with M-17 engines. It would take the paratroopers around 40

Dropping the paratroopers during exercises of the Moscow Military District, 1936.

Dropping the paratroopers during exercises of the Belorussia Military District, 1936.

The People's Commissar for Defence K.E. Voroshilov congratulates Brigade Commander F.F. Karmalyuk, the Commander of the 47th Special Purpose Brigade, on the successful actions of his brigade during manoeuvres, 1936.

I.I. Gubarevich, Commander of the 204th Airborne Brigade.

A.F. Levashov, Commander of the 7th Special Purpose Battalion, later commanded the 214th Airborne Brigade (formerly the 47th Special Purpose Brigade).

seconds to actually get out of the bomber. The parachutists would jump without their weapons, which would then be dropped separately from different aircraft. This gave rise to an issue when some of the packages ended up not where they should have been, and occasionally the margin of error was five to seven kilometres.

The airborne paratroopers were landed in the area around Seym, in total 3,000 Red Army soldiers and commanders along with their military hardware (guns, GAZ-A vehicles, and T-27 tankettes). These were standard infantry troops who had not undergone any kind of special selection process or special training and this

A group photograph of the participants of military parachutists' muster in Voronezh, May 1936.

had a significant effect on their combat capability immediately after deployment. Firstly, the troops embarked on the aircraft in their standard kit, in greatcoats and *budyonovka* hats. They would freeze during the course of the flight at high altitude. Around a half of the soldiers became airsick and started to throw up. Overall, they did not land in a confident state of mind at allbut were tired and worn-out. In the heavy bomber brigades an unusual problem had arisen: who was going to clean up the aircraft that had become very dirty?

In the September of 1936, the airborne troops also took part in exercises to the east of Minsk, which were led by the Commander of the Belorussian Military District I.P. Uborevich. The People's Commissar K.E. Voroshilov, the Chief of Staff A.E. Yegorov, Marshal M.N. Tukhachevskiy and S.M. Budyonniy, and the Head of the VVS Ya.I. Alksnis as well as other high- ranking officials. The 'Westerners' under the leadership of I.R. Apanasenko were opposing the 'Easterners' led by E.I. Kovtyukh.

On 22 September, around 1,800 people were dropped by parachute. They had been drafted in from the 3rd and 47th Brigades and non-standard parachute battalions. Even a detachment of *Osoaviakhim* paratroopers was used. It was during these exercises that the disruptive camouflage was first tried. During the airborne manoeuvres the 84th Rifle Division were redeployed, transferring more than 5,000 people along with their armament and different types of equipment.

Exercises involving landing airborne paratroopers not only took place in the European part of the country. The 29th Heavy Bomber Air Brigade in the spring of 1936 in the area around Olovyannaya station in the Transbaikal region an entire regiment consisting of 940 men was landed using a combined daytime assault. The plan was such that parachutists would 'capture' a designated site, and then an operation would begin at that site: to start a bomber would land carrying personnel and their armament. In total 32 aircraft were used. For the paratroopers 72 heavy machine guns were landed, as well as four 76mm guns, fifteen 45mm guns and four recoilless guns. Four 'cruiser' R-6s escorted the TB-3s on their way to the landing site.

The exercises near Kharkov in the summer of 1937 were sufficiently prototypical. TB-1s from the 21st and 15th Air Brigades landed the paratroopers who then captured a small airfield. IP-1 ground-attack fighters provided air support for the paratroopers. R-5 biplanes would land on the 'captured' airfield, which were carrying machine guns and three 45mm anti-tank guns.

The airborne paratroop exercises conducted in the Leningrad Military District in the autumn of 1937 ended in a very unfortunate way. On 9 September an airborne assault was carried out from a TB-3 aircraft near the

Senior Lieutenant V.D. Kozulya, instructor on the parachute and airborne training. In July 1935 he set up a world record, jumping for an altitude of 7,445m without oxygen equipment.

TB-3 airplanes arriving to the airdrop zone. The paratroopers have climbed to the aircraft wings and are ready to jump (picture of 1937).

Massive airdrop from TB-3s, 1938.

Right after landing, the trumpeter signals for the group assembly, 1938.

Velikaya River (in the area around Pskov). A decision was taken to carry out this drop even though the wind was strong at more than six metres per second. The paratroopers who had landed were traipsed along the ground or landed on rocks. Four of the men were killed, and 44 injured. The exercises were brought to an immediate stop and a medical train was despatched to this location.

The 3rd Air Brigade still retained their special status in January 1937. The line-up for this brigade at that time consisted of the 22nd Heavy Bomber Squadron that operated TB-1s, and the 24th that operated the TB-3, as well as the 2nd Reconnaissance Squadron that operated the R-5. This was the last formation in which the TB-1 was used as a combat aircraft.

The purges of 1937–38 hit the commanders of the airborne troops hard. In 1937 A.O. Indzer, V.S. Kokhanskiy, F.F. Karmalyuka (who shortly before this had been awarded the Red Star) and N.E. Tarasov were arrested. The first three of these individuals were shot as 'enemies of the people', but Tarasov served two years in prison as he was under investigation, he was later released without charge. As a result of the new Commander of the 13th Brigade was I.I. Gubarevich, and A.F. Levashov was made Commander of the 47th Brigade.

In February 1938 a special ration was introduced for paratroopers with a large proportion of concentrates and conserves.

34

At Khasan Lake

At the end of July 1938, Japanese and Manchurian forces crossed the Soviet border near the Zaozernoye volcano not far from Khasan Lake in Primorye. They killed Soviet border guards at the volcano and began to dig in. Both sides began to deploy reinforcements to the border. Red Army units moved along the ground on sparse, bare earth roads or were deployed by sea towards Posyet Bay. On 6 August the Red Army went on the attack. For the most part SB bombers and fighters provided cover for the advancing tanks and infantry. By 10 August the forces had reached the border and stopped.

Airborne troops, moreover, were not deployed. Some of their special equipment needed to be utilised. The point being that a flood had started in the Primorye region that had cut the Soviet forces off from their logistics; they had to organise supply drops from the air. The aircraft brought biscuits, oil, croup and *makhorka* tobacco. These cargoes were delivered by R-5, TB-1, and TB-3 aircraft and were dropped both by parachute and without them. It emerged that the personnel in the VVS units did not know how to handle parachute bags properly; they had not learnt the tactics of how to drop them. The bags were dropped like bombs, and they forgot about how the parachutes would be carried in the wind. Owing to this a number of cargoes were irretrievably lost.

On 20 August 1938, TB-3RN aircraft from the 3rd Squadron, 10th Heavy Bomber Regiment took off to drop cargo by parachute in the area around Malaya Savelovka. The squadron navigator, Izbatulin, however got lost and led the group eight to ten kilometres over Manchurian territory. Close to Saldingou he regained his orientation and turned the aircraft back but on the return journey the bombers were fired upon from Japanese anti-aircraft artillery and machine guns. The aircraft flown by the Commander of the detachment Senior Lieutenant Mityanin was damaged and made an emergency landing in Soviet territory, near Sakharnaya Golova mountain. The rest of the aircraft dropped their cargoes safely down to the waiting Red Army troops.

35

The Second Reorganisation

In March 1938, the second widespread reorganisation of the Soviet airborne troops took place, which was on a larger scale than the first. To begin with, it was decided that they would change over to a uniform structure. The existing brigades, regiments and battalions were transformed into newly formed brigades. Each of them would incorporate two airborne battalions, and one motorised and mechanised battalion and artillery battery. The total strength in terms of personnel was 1,689 men.

Second, the airborne troop formations were withdrawn from their subordination to the VVS, although they did not become at that point an independent branch of the Armed Forces, as the armour troops had for example. Aviation was withdrawn from the line ups of the brigade and regiments. Now there were no longer any aircraft in the airborne units. This of course made the lives of the commanders much more difficult, since they were no

Paratroopers lined up in front of TB-3 aircraft.

V.A. Glazkov was the Commander of the 5th Airborne Regiment, this was later reformed into the 211th Airborne Brigade.

Paratroopers on the 1st May parade. Note the distinctive Russian-style faceted bayonets of their rifles.

longer able to mobilise aircraft directly for training exercises. Along with the aircraft the VVS took all of the special attachments for the military hardware as well as the parachute boxes.

In reality, this transformation commenced from the spring of 1938. It was proposed that six airborne brigades be formed: the 201st (based in Pushkin), the 202nd (based in Khabarovsk), and the 204th (based in Zhitomir), the 211th (based in Chernigovka in Primorye) the 212th (based in Kuybyshev in the Amur region), and the 214th (based in Mar'ina Gorka, in Belorussia).

The 201st Airborne Brigade was reformed from the 3rd Special Purpose Brigade and was led by I.S. Bezugliy. The basis for the 202nd Brigade in Khabarovsk was the 1st Air Assault Regiment that was led by M.Yu. Denisenko. The 204th Brigade in Borispol was the former 13th Brigade led by I.I. Gubarevich. The 221st Brigade was reformed from the 5th Regiment and V.A. Glazkov was made commander of this Brigade. The 212th began to be reformed from the 2nd Regiment in June 1938 under the leadership of I.I. Zatevakhin. The 214th was the 47th under A.F. Levashov and was based in Mar'ina Gorka.

The situation with respect to the three non-standard regiments in the Moscow Military District is not entirely clear. In 1939 they on paper were transformed into standard regiments and were given the designations as follows: the 1st based in Rostov, the 2nd in Gorokhovets, and the 3rd in Voronezh. After that the trail for these regiments goes cold. Whether they were subsumed into the existing brigades by way of augmentation, or they were used as training units is not clear.

According to disparate documents, it turns out that three brigades in the European part of the country were already at full strength and were fully armed in mid 1939. Two of the three brigades in the Far East remained regiments for some time, as they had been previously, but they were given new designations.

They were soon to go into battle, albeit without the airborne landings.

36

At Khalkin-Gol

The poorly delineated border between Mongolia and the puppet state of Manchukuo, which was controlled by the Japanese, was always sparking conflict. The Japanese strove to capture what it considered disputed population centres in Manchuria. According to the Soviet–Manchurian agreement Soviet forces were accommodated in Mongolia and they were amalgamated into a Special Corps (later the 57th Rifle Corps). This corps was a very powerful one and had its own aviation, which according to RKKA VVS documents was designated "The Air Forces of the 57th Corps" or simply "The Air Forces under comrade Feklenko" which was the Corps' Commander's surname.

For several years in a row there were periodical battles on the border that were fought either at regimental or brigade level, and furthermore both sides used armoured vehicles, tanks and aircraft. The Japanese and the Manchurians fought on one side and the Soviets and the Mongolians fought on another.

From May 1939, in the region around Khalkin Gol, combat activity broke out once again between the Soviet–Mongol and Japanese forces. This time the scale of this conflict was unusual. In fact, a small undeclared war broke out, which in Russia has become known as the 'battles for Khalkin-Gol' and in the West as 'the Nomonhan incident', since the operations were for the most part conducted on the Nomonhan plateau.

There were no railways in this area and the nearest station was hundreds of kilometres away in Soviet territory. All the supplies for the 57th Corps (which was subsequently transformed into the 1st Army Group led by G.K. Zhukov) as well as the Mongolian allies, had to be brought from the Transbaikal region using road transport as well as aviation.

A similar situation with respect to transport supported the decision to redeploy the 212th Airborne Brigade led by I.I. Zatevakhin to the front line since the greater part of its equipment could be transported by air. It was true that aircraft did not transport the entire brigade, just its advanced guard, which amounted to 400 men plus the obligatory cargoes that went with them. They were transferred by 'shuttle flights' between Tamsak–Bulak and Chita using TB-3s from the 19th Transport Squadron under Major Yegorov. All the rest was redeployed to the front using road transport.

The headquarters led by G.K. Zhukov did not envisage any airborne operations since the paratroopers were to be engaged simply as infantry. To begin with the 212th Brigade was in the 1st Army Group's reserve forces and was accommodated to the south west of the Khamar-Daban mountain range. When the Japanese succeeded in slowing down the advance on the Palets heights the paratroopers as well as the 9th Motorised and Mechanised Brigade were moved up from the reserve. They completed a rapid march to the north and attacked the enemy. The 9th Brigade encircled the Japanese positions to the north, and the 212th Brigade attacked them head on. As a result, the heights were captured by Soviet forces. During the course of the battle, the Brigade Commander Zatevakhin was injured. By the end of the combat activity the paratroopers had reached the line that formed the state border with Mongolia and took up defensive positions there.

Some 352 soldiers and the commanders of the 212th Brigade received orders and medals for the fighting at Khalkin-Gol.

37

Against Poland

On 17 September 1939, the Red Army crossed the border into Poland. The forces had been ordered to capture the western regions of Ukraine and Belorussia, which were given to the Poles after the end of the Soviet–Polish war of 1920. Three airborne brigades were drafted in for this operation: the 201st, 204th, and the 214th brigades. They would however move around as infantry, no airborne assaults were carried out. It immediately emerged that the Poles had not mounted any organised resistance. Only the border guards, police, and the garrisons at the fortifications tried to hold on to their positions. The pace of the advance by Soviet units and formations quickly surpassed expectations. The forward detachments advanced some distance from the supply depots. The air regiments that had redeployed to the captured airfields were stranded without fuel and ammunition. This was where the bags and fuel tanks that had been developed for the airborne troops came into their own.

Thus the aircraft of the 3rd Heavy Bomber Regiment had, in the space of four days from 20–24 September, dropped either by parachute or by means of a landing delivery, some 100 tonnes of fuel for the Dzerzhinskiy Mechanised Cavalry Group that had advanced on Grodno. The Headquarters of the Belorussian Front itself after it had been moved to Volkovysk relied upon provisions that were dropped by parachute for a period of 18 days. On the Ukrainian Front the 14th Heavy Bomber Regiment was engaged in these same drops.

During the course of the advance to an area behind the enemy's lines, several groups of reconnaissance paratroopers were deployed, who then joined up with Red Army units.

Operations in Poland came to an end in mid October 1939.

38

War with Finland

In November 1939 the Soviet-Finnish War began. The specific nature of this war against Finland, which Soviet aviation had not encountered previously, was the need to supply units and formations by air that were actually surrounded. The Finnish Army not only put up a stubborn defence. In Karelia they succeeded in cutting off the 44th and 54th Rifle Divisions. In order to supply them with cargo both transport aircraft from the GVF, and VVS bombers were used.

The first aircraft to begin dropping to the troops of the 54th Division that were surrounded were SB bombers from the 80th Mixed Air Regiment. These aircraft though were poorly suited to cargo transfers. An SB is not capable of carrying much in the way of cargo, no more than eight bags, since the bomb bay was small but any larger bags stored externally would have blown off at a speed of more than 250km/hr. Apart from that experience of dropping PDMM bags from an SB had demonstrated that the attachment eyelets would tear off once the aircraft reached speeds of between 200–220km/hr. Apart from that the pilots were afraid of carrying any cumbersome and shapeless cargoes externally. The speed of the SB was not so much an advantage but more of a hindrance. In conjunction with poor visibility from the cockpits this presented an obstacle to the sighting of signals laid out on the ground, particularly in forested areas.

Nevertheless, the command had a high opinion of the work of the high-speed bomber crews. After the cessation of hostilities, the Corps' Commander P.V. Rychagov, who commanded the 9th Army Air Force said of the supplies dropped by air for the 54th Rifle Division: "The division relied on the 80th Air Regiment for food for 45 days, and this regiment did actually save them ... from hunger and death". In actual fact though many other VVS and GVF units and formations participated in the operation to supply the division.

The heavy four-engine TB-3 bombers were used very successfully. They were slower but could carry much more cargo. This cargo was carried in the bomb bays and on the external attachments. Provisions, *makhorka*, cigarettes, matches, and vitamins were all carried in bags and the bags were packed inside a box that was designed for FAB-50 and FAB-100 bombs. Grenades were also carried. They were wrapped in rags and the bags were packed in hay or oakum. The cartridges were laid into bags in tin cans, boxes or buckets. Greatcoats, high boots, items of clothing, and padded woollen jackets were simply wrapped up in bundles. All this was packed into the bomb bay on make shift wooden bridges or suspended from external bomb racks. The cargo was dropped without a parachute from an altitude of 50–400m (depending on the environment around the drop zone). Rounds, charges, PPD submachine guns and the disc magazines, as well as radio sets, batteries, and telephony equipment, were dropped in PDMM parachute bags. If there were a shortage of specially designed cargo parachutes, these bags would be strapped to PN-2 or PN-4 combat chutes. Fuel was dropped using PDBB tanks or simply in barrels.

Only the TB-3s from the 2nd Squadron, 3rd Heavy Bomber Regiment (which comprised eight aircraft) completed 26 sorties to drop cargo, for the most part these were flown by night. For example, on 30 January 1940 the bombers dropped provisions in Ruskaset and Lovayardi.

A low-level pass by a TB-3 from the enemy's perspective was the most dangerous part of the mission. A single TB-3 was hit during the course of a drop of provisions and ammunition for the 54th Division and landed at the divisional command post. The crewmembers were unhurt. Another bomber that had been damaged over friendly territory was not able to reach the lake and landed in the forest. One of the pilots was killed and two were injured.

A take-off accident with a USB training bomber which was on a provisions drop mission, December 1939.

A further two TB-3s returned from their mission to drop their cargoes but with significant damage.

VVS reconnaissance detachments that operated R-5 and SSS aircraft were also drafted in to supply the besieged units. Thus aircraft from the 5th and 15th Artillery Correction Detachments were used to drop provisions in Lemetti in 1940.

The 201st, 204th and 214th Airborne Brigades were drafted in to the combat activities on the front line between February–March 1940. They again though acted solely as well-trained infantry. All the special equipment was left in the stores back in Pushkin. The 201st Brigade to begin with guarded the communications behind the 15th Army's lines. From 12 March the brigade participated in the fighting on the Uskalompia Peninsula and on Lunkolon-Sari. Some 51 men were decorated for their courage in the course of the Finnish campaign.

The 204th Brigade, which at that time numbered approximately 1,450 men, was initially part of the 15th Army but from 9–13 February was sent to Pitkyaranta (since the majority of the personnel were on skis) and immediately sent into the battle for the islands of Petya-Sari and Maksiman-Sari. The advance was poorly organised and there was no artillery support. Severe frosts set in, the semi-automatic rifles the soldiers had with them would not fire. The brigade incurred significant losses in terms of soldiers killed, wounded, or frost bitten.

The 214th Brigade was in reserve and did not advance up to the front line.

Only on the one occasion was there an attempt to deploy a full-scale airborne assault behind Finnish lines. The landing delivery was prepared at the 9th Army's base and it was SB bombers who were to carry out the task. The proposal envisaged 200 troops on skis landing on a frozen lake. Six men would be accommodated in each aircraft: three in the radio-operator/gunner's cockpit and three in the bomb bay, where special seats had been installed. The skis would be suspended from the external bomb racks using harnesses.

The regimental commander's aircraft was to land on the lake first. This aircraft was ordered to fly the flag displaying the letter 'T' and would then control the landings of the rest of the aircraft using flags and rockets. After they had disembarked the ski equipped troops were to take up a circular defensive position. Where necessary they could be supported by covering fire from the SBs. There were no plans to switch the bomber's engines off; after all the combatants had taken up their positions the aircraft were to depart. After that the troops were to embark on a speed march through the forest and attack the Finns from an unexpected direction.

The paratroopers embarked on the aircraft and the crews took their positions. The weather, however, intervened. One aircraft did try to take to the skies, but without success. After that the operation was first postponed, and then cancelled completely.

39

Baltic Region Assault

In June 1940, the Red Army crossed the border into Latvia, Lithuania, and Estonia. In the documents that date from that period this operation was dubbed "the liquidation of the problem with the Baltic States". Careful preparation went into this operation. Several variants of this operation were discussed at headquarters – from a large-scale pre-emptive strike using aircraft to a comparatively peaceful one, but with all the key positions being captured rapidly. The latter variant envisaged the deployment of airborne forces.

The 214th Airborne Troop Brigade was active in Lithuania and Latvia under the command of Colonel A.F. Levashov. The brigade was at full strength and well-armed. Amongst its armament were T-37 amphibious tanks, D-8 armoured cars, D-A armoured personnel carrier on a wheeled chassis, anti-tank and field guns, and anti-aircraft machine-gun batteries mounted on GAZ-AA vehicles, mortars, and light machine guns.

In the event that the Latvian, Estonian or Lithuanian armed forces would put up any resistance bombing, and ground attacks were planned of the military towns, airfields, ports and other command and control and communications targets. With this in mind the necessary ammunition was brought forward to the operational airfields in the border regions.

The deployment of paratroopers was entrusted to the VVS heavy bomber regiments that were equipped with TB-3s. According to the plan they to begin with were to deploy 935 paratroopers to Gaizhukiai station. They had to capture Kovno (now Kaunas). Once in place the paratroopers were due to meet a group of seven reconnaissance troops who had been deployed to an area five kilometres south of the station sometime previously. Following this encounter a landing delivery comprising 475 men was to land on the airfield and deliver vehicles and artillery.

The plans were later changed. On 16 June 1940 some 63 TB-3s from the 39th Heavy Bomber Brigade redeployed the first wave of paratroopers to Shavli (Siauliai) and this wave comprised 720 men. The aircraft flew from Palestina airfield. Each aircraft carried between 15–24 men plus two to three PDDM bags containing ammunition and an entrenching tool. The personnel were sat in the navigator's cockpit, and in the upper firing points, while the majority of the paratroopers, 16 in total, were placed inside the wings. The bombers were escorted en route by two squadrons of fighters from the 17th Fighter Air Regiment.

The first Soviet tanks enter Riga, June 1940. Paratroopers from the 214th Airborne Brigade rode into the city sitting on these tanks.

Captain Starchak was already on the airfield, after he had been deployed by parachute. The TB-3s landed in groups of nine, offloading their troops in the space of 10–12mins and took off again, making space for the next group of aircraft.

A landing of a second wave of paratroopers was planned, which included eighteen 45mm guns (one of which was mounted in a vehicle body), 36 mortars, and 160 machine guns but in the end this was not thought necessary.

By the evening of that day the paratroopers had reached the Latvian border on foot and met with tank crews from the 17th Tank Brigade. The soldiers moved forward from that point riding on the armour of the tanks (between five to seven people per vehicle). On the morning of 17 June, the tanks crossed the Latvian border and in the middle of the day they had reached Riga. The paratroopers took control of the port, the bridges, railway station, airfield, postal service, telegraph and the state bank.

During the course of the operation, TB-3 formations also provided an airborne transportation service to the territories of Latvia, Lithuania, and Estonia. Furthermore, 402 packs had to be dropped by parachute to supply the mechanised columns that were moving away up from the Soviet border.

40

Bessarabia Assault

That same month (June 1940), the Soviet government was demanding of Romania that she return the territory of Bessarabia and Northern Bukovina, which before the revolution had formed part of the Russian Empire. The demand was underpinned by the concentration of Soviet forces in the border regions. The Romanian Army was not on a par in terms of strength with its potential enemy in any way. It was clear that the Romanians would have to concede without a fight. The Soviet leadership however was concerned by the possibility of the Romanians inflicting damage on the territory that they were being told to return. It was proposed in addition that the Romanians try to withdraw equipment from the factories, together with the agricultural machinery and to drive the transportation equipment and livestock away from the region.

The speed march for Soviet forces into Bessarabia was to have been conducted decisively. The use of airborne troops was again envisaged. During the preparations for the assault in June 1940 the following heavy bomber regiments were redeployed as follows: 1st (from Minsk to Gogolev), 3rd (from Reblitsy to Borispol), the 7th (from Reblitsy to Boripsol and Odessa) and the 14th (from Palestina to Borispol). In total, they comprised 136 TB-3 aircraft.

To begin with, the Southern Front Command that had the 201st (led by Colonel I.S. Bezugliy) and the 204th (that was commanded by Major I.I. Gurevich) airborne brigades at its disposal was planning to organise a single

The plan for the operation in Bessarabia. The airborne troops landings are shown by parachute marks.

large-scale assault in the area around Targu Frumos, some 20km from Yass, crossing a large road junction to obstruct the evacuation of valuable materials. The assault was to be made using 120 TB-3s, and the proposal was for these aircraft to be escorted by fighters from five fighter regiments.

In reality, only two assaults were carried out as the situation demanded. On 29 June an assault took place 10km north of Bolgrad. By dawn two R-5s had taken off to reconnoitre the chosen site. They were followed by 99 TB-3s with 1,436 men on board. Some 97 aircraft flew to this location, two made emergency landings due to failures. The landing site was very small for four-engine TB-3s to land on, so the personnel were actually landed by parachute. A strong wind caused a number of unfortunate incidents on landing. One of the combatants was killed (his canopy became caught in the bomber's stabiliser) and another lost consciousness and later died in hospital, five paratroopers broke their legs.

By the following day, Bolgrad had been completely taken over by soldiers from the 204th Airborne Brigade. One battalion advanced towards Cahul and after a small exchange of fire with the Romanians near Reni they captured the town.

The second assault took place on 30 June. Some 44 TB-3s were to redeploy the 201st Brigade to Izmail. They were ordered to capture the town and to prevent any ships from leaving the port.

The assault was conceived as a landing delivery. Some 43 aircraft took off for the target, one of them lagged behind the rest and the pilots lost orientation. The landing site was short for TB-3s but the pilots decided to risk it. Twelve aircraft landed but three of them were damaged and tore up the landing strip. Then the personnel had to be dropped by parachute. Two hundred and forty men disembarked from the aircraft that had landed successfully, and pickup vehicles and cargoes were also offloaded. A further 509 paratroopers landed by parachute. There were no casualties among them, one of the soldiers broke their leg, and a further dozen were slightly injured. Two TB-3s turned back to base fully loaded: one of them was carrying radio equipment that could not be dropped, while the other was carrying a musical group who were not trained in making parachute jumps.

The 214th Brigade that had redeployed rapidly from Riga to Skomorokhy was also readied for this operation. This brigade however was left in reserve.

Everything went more or less smoothly. The commanders however understood very well that both in the Baltics and in Bessarabia the paratroopers had jumped in what were very favourable conditions, in the absence of any resistance from aviation or anti-aircraft artillery. The Commander of the Kiev Military District Air Force Major-General Nikolayenko wrote in a report on the operation in Bessarabia: "The airborne troops need to be re-equipped with Douglas aircraft since the TB-3 is not suitable for this role in view of its flight performance characteristics". This was clear and concise.

41

The 'Douglas' Era

The Douglas American company designers created (1933) the first prototype version of the DC-1 passenger aircraft. This went on to become the DC-2, which was manufactured from May 1934. In that same year the DC-2 passenger went into service in the United States. They quickly gained popularity in view of their excellent flight performance characteristics, reliability and fuel economy. The numbers of orders continued to grow for the firm. The aircraft were manufactured in both the civil, and military variants, with a reinforced floor and a wide loading hatch.

In the course of the subsequent modifications in December 1935 the even more spacious DST variant appeared, which was equipped, just like a railway wagon, with sleeping berths. Subsequently the DC-3 variant appeared that was fitted with standard passenger seats. It was this latter variant that was to become the most widespread passenger aircraft at the end of the 1930s and 1940s.

In the USSR, the DC-2 had been attracting the attention of the leadership from the very beginning and a single example was purchased via the *Amtorg* organisation as a specimen. By the spring of 1936 after opinions had been exchanged between the GUAP NKTP, the Chief Directorate of the Civil Air Fleet, and the UVVS the decision to assimilate production of the 'Douglas' in the USSR had more or less crystallised. The Chief Directorate of the VVS wanted to begin with to assimilate this aircraft without a licence simply by carefully studying the example that they had. The head of the UVVS Ya.I. Alksnis was of the opposite opinion and he proposed that the firm's expertise be acquired in order to expedite a solution to this issue. The opinion of the military was very important, since the 'Douglas' amongst other things was viewed as a potential military transport aircraft.

After a more modern DC-3 had appeared, the intentions of the military were focused on this aircraft. The search for a suitable enterprise that would be able to assimilate what was a relatively complex aircraft from a technical perspective had already begun. In his report to the People's Commissar for Defence K.E. Voroshilov the Deputy Chief of Staff of the VVS V.K. Lavrov proposed in March 1936 that production of the American aircraft at Factory No.18 in Voronezh, after production of the TB-3 had been withdrawn at this location. This position gained support initially amongst the leadership of the People's Commissariat for the Aviation Industry. It emerged later that there were plans for a special factory to be built in Kuybyshev (now Samara).

On 11 April 1936, an order was issued by the STO to acquire a licence for the DC-3. A commission went to America that was led by the Head of the TsAGI N.M. Kharlamov. The company agreed readily to provide drawings, templates, fixtures, and kits of components to assimilate the assembly, but only after asking for over half a million Dollars and this was even without factoring in the training for Soviet specialists and the translation of the drawings over to the metric system.

On 15 July 1936, an agreement was signed via the *Amtorg* corporation for the production of the DC-3 in the USSR. This had cost \$207,500 plus another \$130,000 for an example of the aircraft. Later this sum increased significantly because of the purchase of moulds, templates, components and assemblies. The agreement that was drawn up was to be for three years. Groups of specialists began to travel to the Douglas company factory to receive the technical documentation and to assimilate new technology. By 15 January 1937 the Americans were to have completed the translation of the drawings into the metric system and to have handed over to *Amtorg* two sets of drawings on tracing paper ten sets of blueprints.

A DC-3 aircraft, purchased in the United States, pictured at Khalkin-Gol during the loading of injured soldiers for transportation to Chita, summer 1939. Note the lightly mottled camouflage applied for these operations.

One of the DC-3 aircraft in service at the Air Force, spring 1940.

Prior to the arrival of the documentation in the Soviet Union, a single aircraft that had been purchased in America arrived. This was a DC-3-196 fitted with Wright SGR-1820-G2 engines. The company Exello had acted as an intermediary in the purchase of this aircraft. On 1 December the aircraft, which had been dismantled, was sent by sea to Europe. The aircraft was delivered to the Soviet Union at the beginning of 1937.

Subsequently, around two-dozen more Douglas aircraft were acquired in the USA. Although these aircraft were acquired for two non-existent airlines, around two thirds of them joined the VVS line up. The Soviet DC-3s were used actively at Khalkin-Gol for cargo and passenger transportation as well as for evacuating the wounded. The passenger Douglas aircraft however were not suited to airborne operations. The weak floor in the cabin prevented heavy cargoes from being transported, and the narrow door made it impossible to fit any outsized cargoes through it. In addition, the door opened outwards which made parachute jumps more difficult.

On 26 December 1936, an order was issued by the STO in accordance with which the assimilation of production for these aircraft was entrusted to Factory No.84 in Khimki. The Douglas company were obliged to deliver a single aircraft in dismantled form and one in the pre-assembly stage (which would amount to a components and assemblies kit), two casting kits (castings, forgings and so on), as well as commercially available components.

The preparations for the assimilation of the DC-3 at Khimki were led by the factory's Chief Designer A.A. Senkov and Chief Engineer B.P. Lisunov; they both spent time on business trips in the USA.

One of the first PS-84 aircraft assembled at the factory in Khimki, with a fixed ski undercarriage.

The second example of the PS-84K during tests at NII VVS, May 1940.

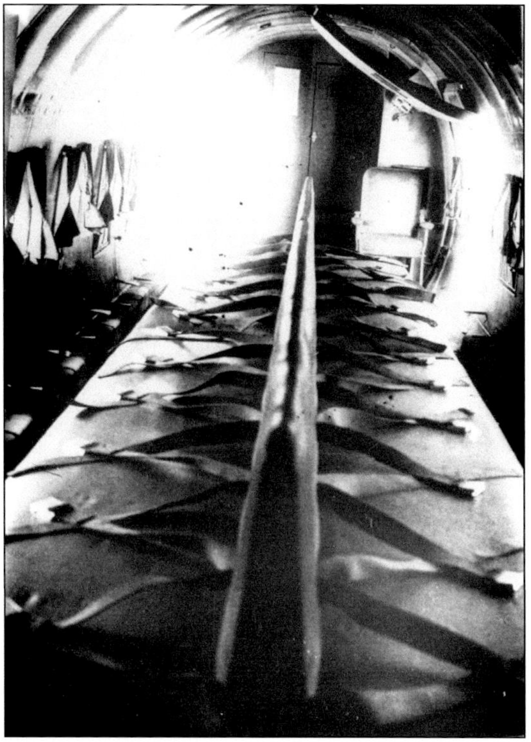

The transverse bench, on which the paratroopers sat.

One of the main features of the PS-84K was the large cargo door on the port side. This photo shows the door in open position (raised upwards).

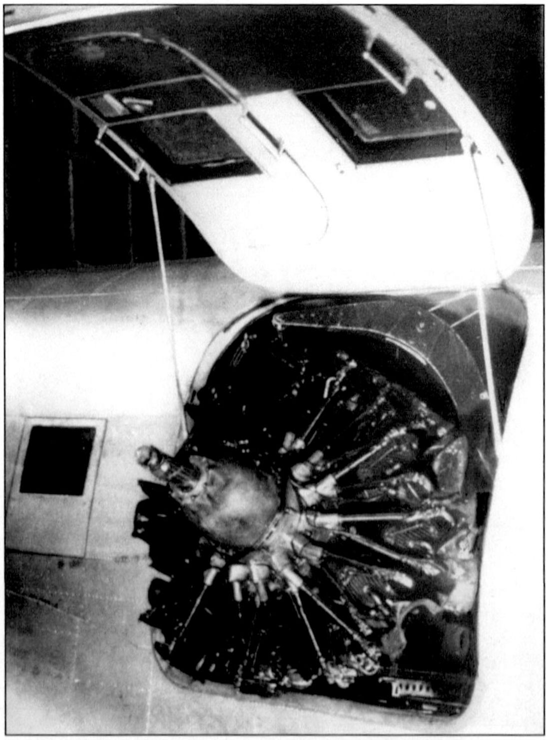

The cargo door opening enabled large-sized cargoes to be loaded; in this case it is an M-87A engine.

The aircraft that was designated the PS-84 in the USSR was to be manufactured in two variants, a civil passenger and a military transport version. The aircraft was fitted with Soviet M-62IR engines rated at 1,000hp on take-off. In terms of its dimensions, weight, and its mounting bracket this engine was closer to the American SGR-1820-G2 and this is no surprise, since it was the product of a modernisation of the earlier SR-1820-F3 engine produced by the same Wright company, and which was manufactured by Factory No.19 in Molotov (now Perm) under an American licence. The aircraft automatic propellers were also Soviet in origin, since they were VISh-21 type propellers. The propeller hub for this propeller was manufactured according to 'Hamilton Standard' drawings obtained in the USA. In comparison with the DC-3 the cockpit had been re-fitted to some degree as well as the passenger cabin, and the wheels were to be replaced with larger Soviet examples. The shock absorber legs were designed to take a higher load.

By 7 November 1938, a single 'Douglas' had been completed from American assemblies, with American engines and propellers. Owing to a significant number of imperfections the aircraft did not pass muster. By 1 January 1939 two almost complete fuselages had been manufactured in the workshop, and a third fuselage had been laid down. A single wing centre section was under assembly, as was one wing outer section, and two fins. The first aircraft was handed over to the NII GVF following a short period of factory testing to undergo state testing. This aircraft featured for some considerable time in the documentation simply as a 'Douglas', which was later designated a PS-84.

According to the plan for 1939, the handover of seven aircraft was envisaged, all of which entered service with the VVS as per the order. In reality only six were accepted. All these 'Douglas' aircraft had a significant number of imported components. The first four aircraft were almost completely manufactured from them. Later on, the PS-84s were fitted with Bendix wheels with American rubber, as well as Hamilton 3E50 propellers (these were interchangeable with VISh-21s), and Fairchild S-7 fixed loop radio compasses, as well as imported electrical equipment.

The VVS did not want to have standard passenger aircraft but specially manufactured machines. The

A 1927-model 76-mm regimental gun with a limber in the cargo cabin of a PS-84K.

specifications for them were developed by the NII VVS back in December 1937 and envisaged two variants: a transport and a medical variant. The first would carry 15 men plus 450kg of cargo, while the latter would carry 17–18 casualties lying on stretchers with two accompanying medics. The latter would be served by two weapon emplacements: an upper mechanised turret and a lower hatch assembly that was similar to that fitted to the SB bombers. The plan was to fit both of these firing points with a ShKAS machine gun with 500 rounds of ammunition. In April 1938, the specifications for the transport variant were detailed and made more specific. The total payload was raised from 1,680kg to 1,800kg, and an external attachment for PDBB-400 tanks was envisaged (for dropping fuel by parachute), the specifications also envisaged outsized cargoes being carried in the fuselage (artillery guns and aero engines), mechanised loading and movement of cargoes inside the cabin, a special cargo door (moreover one that opened internally or that slid to the side).

The first design for a military transport variant was presented by Senkov in June 1939. The order issued by the Committee for Defence, dated 29 July of that same year, specified that Factory No.84 would hand over a prototype example of this aircraft by December. In November one of the first production PS-84s was converted into a transport and airborne assault PS-84K and underwent factory testing, but on 4 January 1940 during a ferry flight to the NII VVS the aircraft was involved in an accident. A second example of the PS-84K was immediately manufactured at the factory. This time no testing was conducted at the factory, since state testing was done jointly with factory testing. This process began on 11 May. The test flights were flown by Captain Predeyn, and navigator Major Marin-Fyodorov.

The PS-84K differed from the production passenger aircraft in terms of the reinforced floor in the cabin, the wide hatch on the port side and the cover that opened upwards and the availability of a lifting hoist to make loading easier. Twenty-six paratroopers could be accommodated on benches along the aircraft axis, back to back, facing the sides of the aircraft. The Commander sat in a separate seat, and his seat was fitted with a connection for connecting the aircraft intercom system. If the aircraft were used to carry cargoes all the seats would be removed.

The PS-84K with a cargo bridge under the fuselage. In this case the cargo bridge is loaded with 100kg FAB-100 high-explosive bombs. This enabled the aircraft to be used as a night bomber where necessary.

The internal capacity of the fuselage enabled ten barrels of fuel to be accommodated inside, two 45mm anti-tank guns with limbers or one 76mm field gun (also fitted with a limber). Other cargoes could also be carried – oil, aero engines, or ammunition.

External transport of cargoes was also envisaged. A special bridge created in November 1939 by a group of designers led by A.I. Privalov at Factory No.468 was attached under the wing centre section. A variety of cargoes would be carried using the Der-19 and Der-31 bomb racks, such as PDMM parachute bags, PDBB tanks with a capacity ranging from 100 up to 400liters, and a universal pod (designed for 300kg of cargo each). The drop would be carried out with the help of ESBR-3 electrical bomb release mechanisms; there was also a reserve ASBR mechanical bomb release. The bridge was made to be detachable and a group of five workers could fit this in the space of seven minutes. The total payload for the PS-84K was 2,400kg or 400kg more than for a standard PS-84.

State testing of the PS-84K was satisfactory and it was recommended for service with the VVS. Furthermore, the shortcomings that had come to light needed to be eradicated: the position of the port door needed to be changed (this was the so-called 'gate' that had been built into the cargo hatch cover), the floor needed to be covered with rubber, and the seats for the paratroopers had to be made to fold back, and the armament had to be fitted (this was stipulated as "no less than two machine guns"), and seatbelts were envisaged for the paratroopers. The engines were left to simmer down on the ground, and the aircraft needed to be fitted with winter louvers, and the propeller cone had to be fitted onto the propeller hub at the same time (on the first PS-84s they were absent, as on the DC-3s).

On 31 May 1940, a PS-84K on the Central Airfield in Moscow completed a demonstration flight for the People's Commissar for Defence K.E. Voroshilov. The Marshal liked the aircraft.

In the course of combat testing from 17–18 June an assault was carried out from a PS-84K aircraft by paratroopers from the 201st Airborne Brigade on Reblitsy airfield just outside Leningrad. The combatants jumped out of the aircraft using both port and starboard doors: this took just 12–14 seconds. The assault took approximately one and a half minutes. The report concluded: "The airborne assault variant of the PS-84K aircraft is much better than the TB-3".

From the documentation that has survived it follows that there were plans to manufacture PS-84Ks specifically

PDMM-100 parachute cargo bags on a cargo bridge under a PS-84K aircraft.

The internal arrangements of a PS-84I medical aircraft.

for the VVS (and moreover they would be manufactured both with armament, and without) and having first looked into the possibility of converting standard passenger aircraft into this variant when necessary. The Head of the NII VVS A.I. Filin wrote in July 1940: "All the PS-84I aircraft are to be produced with all the necessary changes required for their conversion into military variants".

The second military modification of the Soviet 'Douglas' was the standard medical PS-84I. Factory No. 84 made partial use in this case of their experience with the modification of the three DC-3s that were used to transport casualties in Mongolia between August–September 1939. The bulkhead between the passenger cabin and the baggage compartment was removed which made the aircraft more spacious, and three rows of stretchers were set up in the aircraft expanded cabin. In total the aircraft was able to accept 18 casualties lying on stretchers and three casualties in a seating position, as well as one accompanying medic.

In reality, neither the PS-84K nor the PS-84I had entered series production prior to the outbreak of the war with Germany. A number of aircraft designers, however, would subsequently introduce many of the design elements of these modifications into wartime aircraft.

42

On the Eve of All Out War

In August 1940, the next exercises took place with the airborne troops. The 201st Airborne Brigade was drafted in for these exercises along with the reinforcing formations that were attached to them. The redeployment of the brigade, using TB-3 aircraft, was undertaken by the 3rd and 7th Regiments of the 29th Heavy Bomber Brigade. These notional attacks on the enemy were made by two squadrons of SBs from the 55th High-Speed Bomber Brigade as well as 12 I-15bis aircraft from the 149th Fighter Regiment.

The plan for the administration of the assault was already well developed. According to the scenario for the exercises the paratroopers captured Migalovo airfield and the landing delivery was received at this location. The first to arrive were the 27 TB-3 aircraft of the 3rd Heavy Bomber Regiment. Some 540 men jumped out of these aircraft by parachute – this amounted to a whole battalion. Some of them were injured on landing, and two were actually killed. Cargo bags were dropped by parachute from one of the bombers along with two motorcycles. A flight of R-5 aircraft then appeared also with cargo bags that they dropped by parachute.

The paratroopers took up a defensive position around the airfield and set to work preparing for the arrival of the bombers from the 7th Regiment. In total 32 TB-3 aircraft landed. They delivered a company of amphibious T-37 tanks comprising ten (other documents put this figure at nine) vehicles, a 76mm gun battery with 1927-model guns comprising four guns (two of these were loaded onto the aircraft minus the limbers), and a battery of 45mm anti-tank guns (comprising six guns). One each of these anti-tank guns was slung under an aircraft along with a GAZ-AA truck for good measure. In total some 13 of the 'one and a half tonne trucks' were carried, as well as one pickup (evidently this was based on an M-1 car) and two motorcycles. A mortar company with six mortars and a platoon of flame-thrower operators with 30 backpack flamethrowers also joined the ranks of the airborne troops.

Five years had passed since the exercises near Kiev but there had not been any significant changes. The assault was still achieved using what were already outdated TB-3s, and the equipment for the paratroopers remained just the same. It was true that more tanks and vehicles were being delivered. No other principal innovations however were observed in the course of these exercises.

Alongside this there was a very obvious need to move forward. In August 1940 the Head of the Operations Department of the VVS Headquarters Major-General Teplinskiy wrote a report on the need for a reorganisation of the airborne troops. He proposed returning them again to the VVS line up but in the form of a structure that would be reminiscent of the 3rd Special Purpose Brigade of the mid 1930s. The airborne division was to become the cornerstone that would be formed of two assault regiments, and one aviation regiment. The personnel would be carefully selected and would receive what would be, in comparison to the rifle divisions, comprehensive training. A paratrooper, aside from mastering how to jump by parachute, would need to know how to ride a bicycle, a motorbike, and how to drive a car. They would need to know how to fire a rifle, machine gun, and a mortar. In the future the paratroopers were to obtain special equipment and weapons.

The issue of training for the standard rifle divisions for deployment by air was raised once again. These formations could be used as a landing delivery force, building on the success that had been achieved using the elite paratrooper attack units. This however would require selection of personnel based on medical factors (this is reminiscent of the unsuccessful exercises of 1938) as well as a new approach to armament and equipment, ensuring their air mobility. Much of the equipment that had joined the rifle divisions at that time could not be

Paratroopers during a ceremonial review, 1940.

transported by air.

Teplinskiy was absolutely correct in identifying the main issue of that period – the lack of military transport aircraft. The VVS just did not have enough aircraft to be able to redeploy the existing airborne troop brigades. Even if the option of requisitioning aircraft from the GVF were taken into account the VVS would still not be able to ensure the transportation of both people and hardware. Apart from that the TB-3 bomber that was considered the principal means of delivering paratroopers had evidently become obsolete by this time and did not correspond to the amended specifications. On 1 July 1940 there were still around 340 of these aircraft in service with the VVS. There was however nothing to replace them.

As discussed above, attempts at fitting DB-3B and DB-3F long-range bombers with descent pods and cargo attachments were made, but in terms of lifting capability they both conceded to the TB-3. They were not able to transport vehicles, or tanks. The new TB-7 heavy bomber could not replace the old corrugated giant either. First, they were few in number, and secondly none of the attachments designed for this aircraft entered series production.

Opinion concerning the future of the TB-3 shifted constantly. In May 1940 the Principal Military Council of the Red Army ordered: "The TB-3 is to remain in service ... at least those examples that are airworthy and are to be used as transport aircraft". By July however, taking into account the shortage of equipment for the rapidly developing air force, these aircraft were ordered to be withdrawn from airborne and transport units and be converted back into bombers. The idea of writing off these old aircraft was rejected. On the contrary – a decision was taken to repair them to a fully combat capable condition.

However, this did nothing to stop further commentary on the fact of their obsolescence. On 21 November 1940 the Head of the VVS P.V. Rychagov in a letter to Politburo member A.A. Zhdanov pointed out: "The TB-3 aircraft that are in service at present do not meet the specifications of an airborne assault aircraft, and apart from that they are only available in limited numbers ... ".

In reality, in the European part of the country, the bombers that had been redeployed there were able to carry

Paratroopers on the 1st May parade, 1941. The first two rows are armed with PPD submachine guns, while the next two with DP light machine guns, from which the disc-shaped magazines have been removed.

an entire airborne brigade with all their vehicles, tanks, armoured cars, and artillery. The situation was slightly worse in the Far East since only a battalion could be transported using the aircraft available there.

In the report mentioned above, Teplinskiy proposed that a new transport aircraft be introduced into service as soon as possible, which furthermore would be suitable for operation as part of the GVF. This would enable a significant part of the expenses to be taken from the People's Commissariat for Defence, and for the necessary personnel to be trained, and it would also mean that valuable equipment was not standing idle.

The situation relating to air transport only grew gradually worse with the increasing imbalance between the strength of the airborne troops and the number of aircraft that were capable of transporting them. The point being that, in October 1940, the standard line up for the airborne brigades had increased significantly. Interestingly they were subdivided into parachute, gliding, and landing delivery groups. The RKKA VVS did not yet have any assault gliders in service, but military glider crews, taking into account the successful experiences of the German glider crews, were already envisaged.

On 23 April 1941, a joint order appeared that had been issued by the Central Committee of the All-Union Communist Party of Bolsheviks and the Sovnarkom (the Council of People's Commissars), which envisaged the further, and moreover vital, growth in the strength of the airborne troops. This document set out the formation of five corps made up of three brigades in each. The number of personnel in the brigade totalled 2,588 men. The brigade included the brigade headquarters, four parachute battalions, an artillery division, a reconnaissance and bicycle company, and a training school for junior commanders (in peacetime), as well as logistics services.

The airborne battalion comprised 498 soldiers, 78 sergeants (they were actually known as sergeants and not assistants of the platoon commanders as they had been previously), and 33 commanders. As standard the battalion would have 312 carbines, 101 PPD submachine guns, 30 DP light machine guns, nine anti-tank guns, and nine 50mm mortars.

A brigade would have six 45mm anti-tank guns, four 76mm field guns, six 82mm mortars, 30 flamethrower backpacks, nine amphibious T-38 tanks, 16 GAZ-AA trucks, and one light M-1 car. It was by no means easy to redeploy all this equipment. To redeploy the tanks nine TB-3s would be required, and six would be needed for the mortars, two for the flamethrower operators, and their armament, and 14 for the artillery.

The corps had to be formed by 1 June 1941. They were to consist both brigades already in existence as well as those that were newly formed. Two brigades were used in this case that had been transferred from the Far East in 1941: the 211th and the 212th Brigades. The 1st Airborne Corps was based in Zhitomir (Kiev Special Military District) and consisted of the 204th, 211th, and the new 1st Brigade. In the Kharkov district the 2nd Corps was formed from the 2nd (based in Nezhin), 3rd (based in Chernigov), and the 4th (based in Konotop) Brigades – all of these were new. The 3rd Corps was to have been based in Pervomaysk (in the Odessan Military District.

This corps was made up of the 5th, 6th, and 212th Brigades. The backbone of the 4th Corps in Pukhovichi (Belorussia) was to have been the 214th Brigade, which would be augmented by the new 7th, and 8th Brigades. The new 5th Corps that was made up of the 9th, 10th, and 201st Brigades was to be based in Daugavpils in the Baltic Region. In addition to the Corps the 202nd Brigade was retained in Khabarovsk that was subordinate to the Far Eastern Front.

The new brigades were made up of personnel from the standard rifle divisions. They were not able to undergo full parachute training prior to the start of the war with Germany. Thus in the 8th Airborne Brigade a quarter of the personnel had never jumped out of an aircraft at all with a parachute and approximately 65 percent had only recorded one or two jumps on their tally. The brigades were almost up to strength by the time the Germans invaded and yet there was a shortage of the lion's share of armament and military hardware in many of these units.

In order to deliver this entire armada behind enemy lines, thousands of transport aircraft would have been required. Neither the VVS, nor the GVF however had these aircraft available. On 4 June 1941 an order appeared for five regiments to be withdrawn from the Heavy Bomber Aviation line up that operated the TB-3 (this was approximately 200 aircraft) and to convert these aircraft to airborne assault variants. In addition to this a further two regiments were to be formed on that same day that would operate the TB-3 and the PS-84, and by 15 August another regiment would be formed, which made it three. Two regiments each were to be attached to each airborne corps, leaving one regiment for the 202nd Independent Brigade in the Far East. Two regiments were not even enough to transport the personnel in one brigade, let alone their equipment, but for training purposes this would suffice. This order was not completed in full before the outbreak of hostilities.

Prior to the start of the Great Patriotic War, the assault troops did at last become a branch of the Armed Forces. This was expressed in the fact that on 12 June 1941 the Airborne Troop's Directorate was formed. The Head of this Directorate was Major-General V.A. Glazunov, and the Chief of Staff was Colonel P. Ionov.

The pre-war history of the Soviet airborne troops all but ended at this point.

Conclusion

So, in the end, what did the pre-war period in the development of the Soviet airborne troops achieve? The Soviet Union has an unquestionable advantage in this respect. The first parachute assault took place in the USSR, along with the first instance of the transportation of a mechanised unit by air. The RKKA had no real rivals in this field for a period of five years. By that time the country had formed airborne units, which were provided with the necessary technical hardware. Around 400 TB-3 heavy bombers that were in the 'height of their service lives' were able to deliver them behind enemy lines. The manoeuvres in 1935 near Kiev demonstrated clearly everything the Red Army had learned over those years. Progress however slowed soon afterwards.

The airborne troops grew in strength, but had not been any cardinal changes in their equipment. The advent of special armament as well as the means to transport them, which had been anticipated at best remained at the prototype stage. The TB-3 was becoming gradually more obsolete and yet no replacement for this aircraft had been found.

In the end, by the outbreak of the war with Germany the USSR had an extensive airborne troop base, which the VVS was not able to transport. The only sufficiently successful large-scale assault was completed during the course of the counterattack near Moscow. Even after aircraft had been drafted in from the GVF aviation still had difficulty in delivering a significant number of troops to the battlefield. After the actual failure of the operation on the right bank of the Dniepr River the Soviet Army stopped using airborne troops during the course of the attacks on the Soviet-German Front. Airborne assaults during the course of the short campaign against Japan were few in number and were carried out without facing enemy resistance.

The airborne units in the majority of cases were deployed in the Great Patriotic War as infantry, who distinguished themselves only by virtue of their combat training and their ability to be deployed rapidly by air. By chance however in 1942 airborne corps began to be re-formed into rifle divisions.

It is appropriate to draw parallels with the airborne troops in Germany. They came into being much later than the Soviet assault troops but in many ways advanced further. The Germans were not drawn to gigantomania, creating airborne forces that were very well balanced with the capabilities of the transport aircraft (that the Germans had at that time). By the outbreak of the Second World War the *Luftwaffe*, which also comprised Germany's airborne troops, had supplied them with all the necessary equipment and armament. Specifically, they already had fully developed assault gliders. The three-engine Junkers Ju 52/3m aircraft were reliable and were known for their high degree of combat survivability. They were well suited to transporting cargoes, including artillery armament and motorcycles. Special aircraft were designed in Germany for transporting vehicles, tanks, and self-propelled guns. Many of their design solutions went on to become mandatory for all military transport aircraft: the high wing design, a low profile of multi-wheeled undercarriage bogies, and a loading ramp.

This ensured the Germans were successful in different countries in the initial period of the war. Successful assaults in Belgium, Greece, and an especially large-scale operation in Crete demonstrated the actual potential of the Reich's *Fallschirmjager*.

Great Britain and the USA set about creating their airborne forces back in the course of the Second World War. They also rapidly overtook their Soviet allies, who were marking time. Their designers created small, light tanks as well as armoured cars, and engineering hardware for their paratroopers, they could not be dropped by parachute, but they could be delivered in the fuselages of large assault gliders or in large transport aircraft. At that time the English conceded to them only in terms of scale, but not in terms of technical sophistication.

The English and the Americans completed a whole series of large-scale airborne operations: in Sicily, Normandy, and when they crossed the Rhine ... in the Pacific Theatre assault gliders were used in the Philippines and in the attack on Burma in 1945 and operated in conjunction with gliding and landing delivery troops supported by the supply of allied troops by air on a huge scale.

This was how the English and the Americans managed to overtake Soviet airborne troops in the post-war period.

Bibliography

Published Sources

Amiryants G.A., *Lyotchiki-ispytateli: Mikhail Nykhtikov so Tovarishchi* (Moscow: Kuchkovo Pole, 2008).

Anon., *Komandarm Krylatykh* (Riga: Liesma, 1973).

Bolotin, D.N., *Sovetskoye Strelkovoye Vooruzheniye* (Moscow: Voyenizdat, 1995).

Chutko, I.E., *Most Cherez Vremya* (Moscow: Politizdat, 1989).

Eyermann K-H., *Die Luftfahrt der UdSSR* (1917–77, Berlin, 1978).

Gribovskiy K.V., *Razvitiye Transportnogo Planerizma* (Moscow: Mashinostroenie, 1993).

Istoricheskiy Ocherk Razvitiya GK NII VVS (Monino: Editing & Publishing Department of the Headquarters of the State Red-Banner Red Army NII VVS, 1945).

Kaminskiy, M.N., *V nebe Chukotki* (Moscow: Molodaya Gvardiya, 1973).

Kaytanov, K.F., *Povest o Parashute* (Leningrad: Detskaya Literatura, 1981).

Kazakov, V.B., *Nebo Pomnit* (Moscow: Molodaya Gvardiya, 1988).

Kazakov, V.B., *Boevye Aerostsepki* (Moscow, DOSAAF Publishing House, 1988).

Lisov, I.I., *Sovetskiye Vozdushno-Desantniye Voiska* (Moscow, 1967).

Lushnikov, F.A. *Bratya Doroniny* (Moscow: DOSAAF Publishing House, 1977).

Shelest, I.I. *S Kryla na Krylo* (Moscow: Molodaya Gvardiya, 1977).

Shelest I.I. *Lechu za Mechtoy* (Moscow: Molodaya Gvardiya, 1973).

Journals

Avakollektsiya, Aviatsiya i Kosmonavtika, Vestnik Vozdushnogo Flota, Krylya Rodiny, Tekhnika i Vooruzheniye.

Archives

House of Aviation and Cosmonautics

Russian State Archive of Economics

Russian State Military Archive

Scientific-Memorial Museum of N.E. Zhukovsky